*Teaching
Elementary
Reading*

*PRINCIPLES
AND
STRATEGIES*

ROBERT KARLIN

QUEENS COLLEGE
OF THE CITY UNIVERSITY OF NEW YORK

Teaching Elementary Reading

PRINCIPLES AND STRATEGIES

HARCOURT BRACE JOVANOVICH, INC.

New York   Chicago   San Francisco   Atlanta

To Edith

ISBN: 0-15-588001-2

Library of Congress Catalog Card Number: 74-152582

PRINTED IN THE UNITED STATES OF AMERICA

COPYRIGHTS AND ACKNOWLEDGMENTS

For permission to use the selections reprinted in this book, the author is grateful to the
following publishers and copyright holders:

DODD, MEAD & COMPANY, INC. For material reprinted by permission of Dodd, Mead & Company, Inc. from *What Does a Peace Corps Volunteer Do?* by David Lavine and Ira Mandelbaum. Copyright © 1964 by David Lavine and Ira Mandelbaum.

EDUCATIONAL TESTING SERVICE. For an excerpt from "A Report of a Conference of Reading
Experts" in *Learning to Read,* 1962. Reprinted by permission of the Educational Testing Service.

FRANKLIN WATTS, INC. For an excerpt adapted from *The First Book of Vikings,* copyright ©
1962 by Louise Dickinson Rich, used by permission of the publisher, Franklin Watts, Inc.

HARCOURT BRACE JOVANOVICH, INC. For material adapted from *Reading Power: Skills Reader*
by Margaret Early, et al., copyright © 1970 by Harcourt Brace Jovanovich, Inc.; and for
material from the *Teacher's Edition for Sun Up and Reading Skills One* by Margaret
Early, et al. The Bookmark Reading Program. New York: Harcourt Brace Jovanovich,
Inc., 1970, 61–68.

HAROLD OBER ASSOCIATES, INC., and THE NEW YORK TIMES COMPANY. For an adaptation of "Are the Days of the Arctic's King Running Out? ("King of the Arctic") by Robert Murphy from *The New York Times Magazine*, March 28, 1965, copyright © 1965 by The New York Times Company.

HARPER & ROW, PUBLISHERS, INC. For an excerpt from *The Mind in the Making* by James Harvey Robinson, Harper & Row, Publishers, Inc., 1921.

HOLT, RINEHART AND WINSTON, INC. For excerpts adapted from a chart entitled "A Taxonomy of Literary Understandings and Skills," from *Children's Literature in the Elementary School*, Second Edition, by Charlotte S. Huck and Doris Young Kuhn. Copyright © 1961, 1968 by Holt, Rinehart and Winston, Inc. Reprinted by permission of Holt, Rinehart and Winston, Inc.

HOUGHTON MIFFLIN COMPANY. For an except from *Reading Instruction: Dimensions and Issues*, William K. Durr, ed., Houghton Mifflin Company, 1967.

INTERNATIONAL READING ASSOCIATION. For material from "Should Children Be Taught to Read Earlier?" by Morris Pincus and Frances Morgenstern, from *The Reading Teacher*, 18, 1964, p. 37; from "Vital Principles in Need of Application" by Constance M. McCullough, from *A Decade of Innovations: Approaches to Beginning Reading*, Vol. 12, Part 3, Proceedings of the 12th Annual Convention, 1968, p. 181; and from *Fusing Reading Skills and Content* by Robert Karlin, edited by Alan Robinson and Ellen Lamar Thomas. All reprinted with permission of the authors Morris Pincus, Constance M. McCullough, and Robert Karlin, respectively, and the International Reading Association.

J. B. LIPPINCOTT COMPANY. For an excerpt adapted from the book *Skin-Diving Adventures* by John J. Floherty and Mike McGrady. Reprinted by permission of J. B. Lippincott Company.

NATIONAL SOCIETY FOR THE STUDY OF EDUCATION. For excerpts from *The Changing American School* by Edgar Dale in The Sixty-fifth Yearbook of the NSSE, Part II, University of Chicago Press, 1966; from *Development in and Through Reading* by David H. Russell in The Sixtieth Yearbook of the NSSE, Part I, University of Chicago Press, 1961; from *Individualizing Instruction* by Fred T. Tyler and William A. Brownell in The Sixty-first Yearbook of the NSSE, Part I, University of Chicago Press, 1962; and from *The Teaching of Reading: A Second Report* edited by Guy G. Whipple in The Thirty-sixth Yearbook of the NSSE, Public School Publishing Company, 1937. All reprinted with permission of the National Society for the Study of Education.

RANDOM HOUSE, INC. For excerpts adapted from *John F. Kennedy and Pt-109* by Richard Tregaskis, copyright © 1962 by Richard Tregaskis; from *The Friendly Dolphins* by Patricia Lauber, copyright © 1963 by Patricia Lauber; from *Americans into Orbit* by Gene Gurney, copyright © 1962 by Gene Gurney; and from *Heroines of the Early West* by Nancy Wilson Ross, copyright © 1969 by Nancy Wilson Ross. Reprinted by permission of Random House, Inc.

THE JOHN DAY COMPANY, INC. For an excerpt from "Rivers Change the Earth." Copyright © 1961 by Irving and Ruth Adler. Adapted from *Rivers* by Irving and Ruth Adler, by permission of The John Day Company, Inc., publisher.

UNIVERSITY OF CHICAGO PRESS. For an excerpt from *Controversial Issues in Reading and Promising Solutions* by Francis S. Chase in Supplementary Educational Monographs, No. 91, University of Chicago Press, 1961. © 1961 by the University of Chicago. Published 1961. Composed and printed by the University of Chicago Press, Chicago, Illinois, U.S.A. Also gratefully acknowledged is an excerpt from *The Underachiever in Reading* by Constance M. McCullough in Supplementary Educational Monographs, No. 92, University of Chicago Press, 1962. © 1962 by the University of Chicago. Published 1962. Composed and printed by the University of Chicago Press, Chicago, Illinois, U.S.A.

HARBRACE PHOTOGRAPHS: facing-page 1, pages 38, 58, 72, 102, 140, 180, 198, 216, 227, 280, 312, 340.

COVER PHOTOGRAPH: Harbrace.

Preface

Old formulas are not wholly adequate to new problems. The general acceptance of this ancient truism has prompted leaders in the sciences, industry, government, and elsewhere to reexamine their programs and assumptions. This is at least equally true of educators generally and teachers of reading in particular. Large segments of our school populations, especially those from the inner cities and outlying rural areas, are not sufficiently literate to learn effectively or to become productive citizens in our changing society. Undoubtedly, many children come to school lacking the experiences and environment conducive to learning, but teachers also recognize that inadequate or weak programs are equally responsible for poor reading levels. Hence, they have sought and are still seeking ways of strengthening the programs and raising the levels of reading proficiency.

Teaching Elementary Reading: Principles and Strategies was written to give these teachers insights into the problems associated with reading and to demonstrate ways of improving the reading instruction that is given. Another objective is to provide schools with guidelines that will enable them to identify and correct weaknesses in present reading programs. New and established reading practices have been closely scrutinized during the past decade, and many have been questioned. This text synthesizes the most current ideas in reading instruction as an aid to prospective as well as beginning and experienced teachers in their effort to develop and improve the reading ability of all children.

One of the assumptions of *Teaching Elementary Reading: Principles and Strategies* is the need for teachers to understand the rationale underlying reading methodologies. For this reason, the first chapter, "Emerging Concepts in Teaching Reading," documents the most recent research findings that have a bearing on reading instruction. Furthermore, the chapter also summarizes the contributions of psychology, linguistics, and related disciplines from which sound reading practices might originate. Teachers can use this information as a basis for evaluating reading plans and programs.

I also believe that diagnostic teaching will produce better results than indiscriminate teaching. Children will achieve more in reading if teaching plans are based upon their known performances and directed toward specific learning tasks. This is why I have placed the chapter on evaluating reading growth near the beginning rather than at the end of the text.

I have striven throughout the text for balance between theoretical considerations and practical applications. Approaches to teaching have been worked out in detail. The prospective and beginning teacher will especially welcome the explanations that accompany the host of teaching strategies that bridge the gap between theory and practice. Moreover, current teaching practices have been evaluated, and those that, in my opinion, have merit are clearly indicated.

Teaching Elementary Reading: Principles and Strategies devotes as much attention to the middle grades as it does to the primary grades. The text is replete with references, examples, and models that apply to children who have mastered beginning reading skills and who are ready to move ahead to higher achievement levels. Chapter 6, "Reading for Meaning," Chapter 7, "Reading in the Content Fields," and Chapter 8, "Reading for Appreciation and Enjoyment," are devoted almost entirely to the improvement of the reading ability of children who have already achieved some independence. These chapters will enable the teacher to help pupils read narrative materials with greater understanding and appreciation and to study expository materials with increased effectiveness.

I wish to express my appreciation to Dr. Harvey Alpert and Dr. Gordon Eddy, who reviewed the manuscript and offered helpful suggestions for improving the text. I also wish to thank the editorial and production staff of my publisher for their assistance and encouragement in planning and completing this textbook.

ROBERT KARLIN

Contents

2

Diagnostic Teaching
of Reading *39*

3

Readiness
for Reading *73*

4

Developmental
Reading *103*

5

Teaching Word Recognition   *141*

6

Reading for Meaning   *181*

7

Reading in the Content Fields *217*

8

Reading for Appreciation and Enjoyment *281*

9

Meeting
Individual Differences 313

10

Overcoming
Reading Difficulties 339

1

Emerging Concepts in Teaching Reading

■ *Allen sets a 1970's Goal:*
Every Pupil Able to Read.[1]

In 1969, James E. Allen, Jr., then U.S. Commissioner of Education, set a national goal for the 1970s when he declared in a speech before the National Association of State Boards of Education that teaching children to read is the number one responsibility of schools and expressed the hope that no child would leave school by the end of the 1970s without adequate reading ability.

What prompted Commissioner Allen to initiate this "Right to Read" campaign and establish machinery to help insure its success? Undoubtedly, the fact that large numbers of children in every section of the nation fail to learn to read adequately must have been a major reason. There are no firm figures on the extent to which reading is a problem, but it is estimated that as many as one-third of our schoolchildren do not read well enough to meet the requirements of school and society. In some states and communities where data are available the proportion is even higher.

No one can deny that our schools have taught countless children to read well. But it is equally true that they have failed to reach large segments of the school population. Why children fail to learn to read well (most reach some level of achievement, however low) has been the subject of extensive research. Investigators have identified physical and perceptual, intellectual, emotional, language, and experiential factors as possible contributors to reading failures. But all these suggest weaknesses within children and tend to shift some responsibility away from the schools. There is an accumulating body of evidence which shows that the schools have not been doing as well as they might in teaching reading. Limited and fragmented

---

[1] *The New York Times*, Sept. 23, 1969.

1

instructional programs, unavailability and improper use of materials, and inadequately prepared teachers are some of the elements that have emerged from extensive surveys and specific studies.[2] Discussions with newly-appointed teachers reveal feelings of insecurity and uncertainty about teaching reading. Observations of classrooms taught by more seasoned teachers confirm what students of reading have been saying about the need for improving reading instruction in elementary schools.

It is hardly surprising that the International Reading Association (IRA) attracts a membership of over 35,000 and distributes its publications on reading to more than 50,000 individuals and schools. This professional organization's primary aim is to upgrade the teaching of reading through the activities of its affiliated local councils, its annual conventions and sectional meetings and through the dissemination of information on reading by its journals, proceedings, research bulletins, monographs, bibliographies, etc. That IRA is meeting a long-felt need is evident from responses to it by teachers, curriculum supervisors, and administrators. In recent years the National Council of Teachers of English (NCTE) has been devoting more time at its conventions and more space in its publications to the teaching of reading. Teachers everywhere are recognizing how important learning to read is and are seeking professional guidance and support in their efforts to help all their pupils achieve in reading.

In the federal government's plan to help every pupil learn to read are provisions for making the results of research on reading available to the states and offering technical assistance in improving their reading programs. Presumably this information and aid will filter down to local systems and individual schools and classrooms.

The major objective of our government's thrust on teaching reading is the same as this textbook's: to produce more and better readers. We know that inability to read is one of the major reasons why children drop out of school. Many school dropouts are not able to get or hold decent jobs, a condition that not only could perpetuate poverty but could also lead to loss of their self-respect. How can teachers help children enjoy more satisfying school experiences? What can they do to put the brakes on reading failure? *Improve instruction in reading.* It is to this task that each of us is dedicated.

Much has been said and written about the teaching of reading. Professional educators and others have contributed to an ever-growing body

---

[2] Mary C. Austin, *The Torch Lighters, Tomorrow's Teachers of Reading.* Cambridge: Harvard University Press, 1961; Mary C. Austin and Coleman Morrison, *The First R— The Harvard Report on Reading in Elementary Schools.* New York: The Macmillan Company, 1963; Betty Lou Broman, "Factors Associated With Teacher Knowledge of Reading Skills," *Dissertation Abstracts, 23* (December, 1962), 1966–67; George D. Spache and Mary E. Baggett, "What Do Teachers Know About Phonics and Syllabication?" *The Reading Teacher, 19* (November, 1965), pp. 96–99; Robert Emans, "Teacher Evaluations of Reading Skills and Individualized Reading," *Elementary English, 42* (March, 1965), pp. 258–60.

of literature. To sort out and sift this information are indeed formidable tasks. Each method of teaching reading has its advocates and its critics—critics who may or may not propose alternative methods. Large quantities of new materials regularly appear on the reading scene and each proclaims its superiority in fulfilling some mission. The teacher of reading is pulled and pushed in different directions by a myriad of suggestions and exhortations, some compatible and others conflicting. The reading teacher has ample choices, but which ones shall he entertain? Which shall he reject? About which shall he withhold judgment? And on what bases shall these decisions be made?

Teachers are able to place more confidence in some reading principles and practices than in others. These have emerged from the results of research in reading and learning as well as from applications of the science of language, or linguistics. Demonstrations and theory lend support to other promising plans and programs. Familiarity with some of the significant reading research and the contributions of allied disciplines will enable us to plan and offer superior reading instruction.

Implications of Reading Research

Annual summaries of published research in reading[3] contain as many as 300 entries. This total would grow were unpublished studies and those that were otherwise overlooked included. Over a ten-year span the number becomes quite large. Some of the research is supported by the United States Office of Education, private foundations, and universities. Other investigations are conducted by graduate students working toward master's and doctoral degrees and by school personnel.

The quality of these studies is uneven; many of their results have been rejected or questioned. On the other hand, there is research whose results can be viewed with greater confidence. And the results suggest trends that may be pursued until new data become available. Of course, there are many questions to which research offers no answers, and theoretical considerations and demonstrations must serve as rationales for practice until the answers can be confirmed.

For our purposes we will review the results of some less vulnerable studies in reading from which, in this writer's judgment, reading concepts emerge and from which implications for teaching may be drawn.

---

[3] One such annual summary is published in the winter issue of the *Reading Research Quarterly*.

Preschool and Kindergarten Reading

> ■ *THE AGE in which we live has been characterized as an age of great speed and power—The Space Age. . . . While great speed may characterize affairs in man's outer world, doubt, hesitancy, and indecision prevail in his inner world. Particularly with regard to child development, parents and teachers are in a state of perpetual concern about whether, with the best of intentions, they will look or talk or act in a potentially harmful way.*[4]

A nagging question that persists in the minds of teachers and parents alike is: "Can and should children be taught to read before they enter first grade?" There was a time not so long ago when one group of authorities would respond to each aspect of the question with an unequivocal "No!" Another group would say, "Yes, we know that young children can be taught to read, but should they be taught?" Now both groups are not as certain of their positions as they were in view of the fact that new information requires that they reevaluate them. The results of three longitudinal studies provide us with some reasonable guidelines that we might follow and implement.

The first of these investigations[5] studied children who learned to read before they entered the first grade. According to Durkin, parents reported that these children, many of whom were of average intelligence, frequently asked questions about the names on street signs and automobiles as well as the words in books that they and others read to them. Some of these children showed much interest in writing and the sounds of letters contained in words. Parents and in some cases older brothers and sisters provided help when the children requested it.

Some of the children learned to read, i.e., identified words in print and understood the ideas they represented, with casual incidental help; others were exposed to more formal treatments. Now that the data on these children are complete, one may conclude that they suffered no ill effects from early exposures to printed materials and that they generally maintained some advantage in reading over children who did not possess this ability upon entering school.

A second investigation[6] sought to determine whether a planned program

---

[4] Morris Pincus and Frances Morgenstern, "Should Children Be Taught to Read Earlier?" *The Reading Teacher, 18* (October, 1964), p. 37.

[5] Dolores Durkin, "A Study of Children Who Learned to Read Prior to First Grade," *California Journal of Educational Research, 10* (May, 1959), pp. 109–13. Follow-up studies by Durkin: "Children Who Learned to Read at Home," *Elementary School Journal, 62* (October, 1961), pp. 14–18; "A Fifth-Year Report on the Achievement of Early Readers," *Elementary School Journal, 65* (November, 1964), pp. 76–80.

[6] Joseph E. Brzeinski, "Beginning Reading in Denver." *The Reading Teacher, 18* (October, 1964), pp. 16–21.

of reading instruction in kindergarten could increase the numbers of children who learned necessary reading skills before entering first grade. A parallel study tested the hypothesis that parents could teach their children prereading skills. The kindergarten children, some 2000 of them, received instruction in how to use beginning consonant sounds with context clues to identify unknown words, i.e., to read what the word said, as part of their kindergarten experiences. An equal number followed the normal kindergarten program without the specialized reading instruction. The kindergarten children who engaged in beginning reading activities learned to identify letter forms and names and the sounds they represented. At the end of the first grade they scored significantly better on standardized reading tests than children who did not receive this regular reading practice in kindergarten. The investigator reported that the percentage of children who appeared to have visual, auditory, and adjustment difficulties was about the same for both groups.

In the parallel study, parents followed instructions in a specially-prepared guidebook and on TV programs and taught their preschool children to recognize letters and their sounds and to identify words. The results showed that children four and one-half years old and of normal intelligence could learn these skills at home with regular practice of at least thirty minutes a week for sixteen weeks. Another investigator, using the Denver materials and procedures, obtained similar results.[7]

A third investigation[8] sought answers to these questions: What happens to children who learn to read in kindergarten? Do their non-early-reading classmates catch up by the end of third grade? Kindergarten reading experiences were limited to 15 minutes a day and offered only during the second half of the year. Of 105 kindergarten children who were exposed to unstructured reading activities, 46 scored 1.3 or higher on a standardized reading test toward the end of the kindergarten year. These 46 children had a mean I.Q. of 115.5 compared to a mean I.Q. of 99 for the 59 other kindergartners who scored below 1.3. A third group of children with a mean I.Q. of 107, who did not have the same reading experiences in kindergarten, were used also for purposes of comparison. At the end of third grade the mean reading achievement scores for the three groups of children were 5.97, 4.32, and 4.57, respectively.[9] Subjective reactions by their teachers described the early readers as "book hungry." (Other children who scored below 1.3 initially or who were not exposed to early reading activities became more interested in books as they mastered reading skills.)

The investigator noted that rates of learning for different children and

---

[7] Anastasia McManua, "The Denver Prereading Project Conducted by WENH-TV," *The Reading Teacher, 18* (October, 1964), pp. 22–26.

[8] Marjorie H. Sutton, "Children Who Learned to Read in Kindergarten: A Longitudinal Study," *The Reading Teacher, 22* (April, 1969), pp. 595–608, 683.

[9] It appears that many children learned to read well in this reading program regardless of whether or not they had an early start. However, at the end of third grade the ranges of reading scores for the early readers, nonachieving early readers and nonexposed children were 3.4–9.1, 2.0–7.8, and 2.0–7.8, respectively.

for the same child varied. One child made his greatest gains in first grade while another did very well in first and second grades but hardly gained ground in the third year. Some children did better in the third grade than in the first or second.

What ideas might we extrapolate from the results of these studies? One is that some preschool and kindergarten children want to learn to read sooner than many of their age-peers. Another is that of those who wish to learn to read, not all will benefit to the same degree from exposure to a given series of activities. Both of these notions are consistent with the concepts of maturation and individual differences.

IDEAS FOR DISCUSSION

We are aware of the wastefulness and possible ill-effects of engaging children in certain activities before they possess the requisites for achievement. For example, it seems wise to postpone regular instruction in writing until children are ready for it. Does this mean that writing implements should be withheld from children until they are able to hold them easily? Or that all children become ready to learn to write at the same chronological age?

As others have pointed out, successful teaching does not depend merely upon the maturation of the learner. His motivation, the way in which the material to be learned is presented, and prior learnings will affect the results. These conditions seem to be satisfied where young children are successful in beginning reading. They want to learn; the way in which the material is handled is appropriate; and the children have the equipment to benefit from the presentation. If these conditions were not met, we could anticipate failure and frustration.

There doesn't seem to be much doubt about the fact that there are interested and able children under the age of six who can be taught to identify word forms and use simple word-identification techniques. The older notion that such teaching will impair their physical, intellectual, and emotional development is not supported by the new data. Furthermore, it appears that children who come to first grade with such skills have a reading advantage over those who do not possess them. What guidelines for school practice do these observations suggest?

1. Kindergarten programs ought to offer to those children who already possess some ability to read or who show real interest in learning to read appropriate reading activities in addition to their usual experiences. These reading activities should not make demands that children cannot satisfy.

2. It is clear that the school has the basic responsibility for teaching children to read. However, the school might determine how parents could be of assistance in engaging children in reading and related activities.

Envisioned in both of the above guidelines are reading programs that are appropriate for young children. Oral language activities and reading to children will be stressed. Lengthy and repetitive drills will be avoided. Attention will be given to individuals and small groups. Schedules will be flexible and offer children the opportunity to participate if they wish. Children will not be expected to meet predetermined standards. Herein lie the keys to enjoyable and successful early reading experiences.

Associated with preschool and kindergarten reading is the concept of readiness for beginning reading, which was referred to earlier. The significance of research findings on reading readiness will be discussed in Chapter 3.

Primary Reading

Although there never was any lack of interest in beginning reading in terms of research, the 1960s were markedly active years for research in reading generally and in primary reading particularly. From what sources did this activity arise? Perhaps it was part of a renewed drive for excellency spurred on by Russian achievements and *Sputnik*. Perhaps it was due, in part, to the sometimes acrimonious debates involving educators, parents, and others that were provoked by critics[10] who blamed reading failures on the way children were taught to read. In essence, they accused the schools of not teaching phonics or teaching it badly and proposed specific phonic programs as panaceas. In addition, there were leaders in the profession who were not satisfied with the status quo and sought to improve reading methodology generally.

The First Grade Studies

One big concerted effort to find out if there were really superior methods or approaches which teachers of beginning reading might use was sponsored by the U.S. Office of Education, and came to be known as *The First Grade Reading Studies*.[11] Twenty-seven independent studies which had similar basic objectives and followed comparable research designs were funded. Several investigations involved the use of different basal readers, phonic and linguistic programs, orthographic systems in individualized reading, and language experience—singly and in combination. Others sought to find out the effects of in-service training, reading readiness, organizational patterns, and teacher characteristics on pupil progress. The results at the end of first grade were mixed, although there were indications that insofar as word recognition was concerned, basal reading with strong word-attack programs produced results superior to those obtained from basal programs without similar word-attack emphasis. Inconsistent findings were common among similar studies; where significant differences were obtained these were often quite small. The coordinators (though not necessarily the individual investigators) concluded that combinations of approaches seem better than single ones and that pupil and teacher characteristics affect progress regardless of the program.

---

[10] Rudolf Flesch, *Why Johnny Can't Read and What You Can Do About It*. New York: Harper & Row, 1955; Sybil Terman and Charles Walcutt, *Reading: Chaos and Cure*. New York: McGraw-Hill, Inc., 1958.

[11] Guy Bond and Robert Dykstra, *Coordinating Center for First Grade Reading Instruction Programs* (Final Report, United States Department of Health, Education, and Welfare). Minneapolis: University of Minnesota, 1967; reports by participating investigators can be found in Russell G. Stauffer, ed., *The First Grade Reading Studies: Findings of Individual Investigations*. Newark, Del.: International Reading Association, 1967.

NUMBER OF STUDIES IN WHICH SIGNIFICANTLY SUPERIOR OR NO DIFFERENCES WERE FOUND†

Methods Compared	Number of Studies	Word Recognition			Paragraph Comprehension			Spelling		
		Experimental Method Superior	No Significant Difference	Basal Reader Superior	Experimental Method Superior	No Significant Difference	Basal Reader Superior	Experimental Method Superior	No Significant Difference	Basal Reader Superior
I.T.A. vs. Basal	5	4	1	0	1	4	0	1	1	3
Linguistic vs. Basal	4	1	3	0	0	2	2	1	2	1
Basal + Phonics* vs. Basal	3	3	0	0	3	0	0	3	0	0
Language Experience vs. Basal	3	2	1	0	1	1	1	1	2	0
Basal + Linguistic** Emphasis vs. Basal	3	3	0	0	2	1	0	2	1	0

*Basal Reader supplemented by Supplementary Phonics
**Lippincott Readers plus Visual Materials

† *Source: The First Grade Reading Studies: Findings of Individual Investigations,* edited by Russell G. Stauffer, 1968. Reprinted with permission of Guy L. Bond and the International Reading Association.

About half of the First Grade Studies were continued into the second grade.[12] The results were not unlike those at the end of first grade although some programs—modified alphabet, linguistic, and phonic—obtained results indicating superiority in word recognition and spelling. The available results of studies extended into the third grade do not seem to show great differences in the reading achievement of children in the several programs. [13, 14]

---

[12] Robert Dykstra, "Summary of the Second-Grade Phase of the Cooperative Research program in Primary Reading Instruction," *Reading Research Quarterly, 4* (Fall, 1968), pp. 49–70.

[13] J. Wesley Schneyer, "Reading Achievement of First Grade Children Taught by a Linguistic Approach and a Basal Reader Approach—Extended into Third Grade"; Albert Harris and Coleman Morrison, "The CRAFT Project: A Final Report"; Edward Fry, "Comparison of Beginning Reading with i.t.a. and t.o. after Three Years"; Robert Hayes and Richard Wuest, "A Three Year Look at i.t.a., Lippincott, Phonics and Word Power," *The Reading Teacher, 22* (January, 1969), pp. 315–19, 335–40, 357–62, 363–70.

[14] William Sheldon, Franga Stinson, and James Peebles, "Comparison of Three Methods of Teaching Reading: A Continuation Study in the Third Grade," *The Reading Teacher, 22* (March, 1969), pp. 539–46.

Like other research, the First Grade Studies suffered from weaknesses, which the coordinators and other evaluators have acknowledged. These weaknesses, among others, involve lack of comparability of some treatments even within those of the same trade names. In many cases it was not an approach that was being measured; instead it was one commercial program versus another. However, the results cannot be completely discounted. They might suggest trends which could be followed and studied. At the same time they need to be viewed in relation to the results of other existing studies and the degree to which they can be confirmed by carefully-designed research.

Chall Study: Early Phonics

Another large-scale study of beginning reading was conducted by Chall,[15] who surveyed more than fifty years of research. Although Chall was aware of the shortcomings of many of the studies she reviewed and decided that the results obtained and conclusions drawn from them were suspect, she nevertheless reached the conclusion that instructional programs which stressed early phonics helped average and below average children read better than similar children who were taught reading through programs with an early meanings emphasis. Chall pointed out that she could not conclude that one system for teaching phonics should be preferred to others or that any program with an early decoding emphasis would insure success in learning to read.

IDEAS FOR DISCUSSION

Chall's conclusions about early decoding emphasis have given rise once again to the either-or proposition in beginning reading. However, there seems to be agreement that children are likely to learn to read better if both decoding and meaning are stressed by teachers. The ability to decode words, while necessary to undertake the reading act, is not the ultimate goal of reading instruction. The ability to understand printed ideas is. Furthermore, exclusive emphasis on decoding —phonics—suggests a single approach to word attack. We know that all words cannot nor should be subject solely to phonic analysis.

Synthetic Versus Analytic Approach

The findings of another study that focused its attention on ten reading programs were reported in a different way. The five which were *synthetically* oriented, i.e., taught children letter-sound correspondences directly, produced significantly higher reading scores than the five which taught phonics *analytically* through words.[16] Henderson[17] obtained similar results for the

---

[15] Jeanne Chall, *Learning to Read: The Great Debate*. New York: McGraw-Hill, Inc., 1967.

[16] Emery Bliesmer and Betty Yarborough, "A Comparison of Ten Different Beginning Reading Programs in First Grade," *Phi Delta Kappa, 47* (June, 1965), pp. 500–04.

[17] Margaret Henderson, "A Six Year Experimental Study of Two Methods of Teaching Reading in Elementary School." Paper presented at the American Education Research Association Convention, Chicago, February, 1959.

first three grades, but Sparks and Fay[18] reported no significant differences in reading ability regardless of which program children followed in the primary grades.

Other investigations dealt with specific aspects of teaching reading in the primary grades: development of sight vocabulary, methods of teaching word analysis, vocabulary development, comprehension, factors affecting growth, organizational patterns. These will be considered as each topic is discussed.

Using Research Findings

We have noted flaws in the research on primary reading as well as inconclusive results. Plans to establish priorities in reading research and improve the quality of research are being studied by a committee of Phi Delta Kappa through a U.S. Office of Education research grant. In the meantime, we must use present knowledge to help develop sounder reading programs. We know that no single method or approach is best; that no one type of program is singularly superior to another; that no one packaged program contains all necessary elements; that teacher effectiveness can change the outcomes of any program regardless of its merits; that there are programs which are more suitable for some children than others. Perhaps we ought to consider the possibility of adapting our procedures so that the best elements of each practice known to have real potential become part of a total strategy for teaching reading. In the long run our own understanding of and ability to apply them will control the quality of instruction and its outcomes. These recommendations and observations may be inferred from the studies cited in this section and receive specific support from a study by Chall and Feldmann on how the teacher accounts for differences in reading achievement when reading methods are similar.[19]

Reading for the Middle Grades

Reading for the middle grades is in fact a continuation and extension of primary grade reading. In the primary grades children learn the basic skills of reading: how to attack words and comprehend written language. In addition they develop attitudes toward books and an appreciation of reading. Essentially they read in order to learn to read and to enjoy reading.

In the middle grades children continue to develop and strengthen their basic reading skills, but the focus of attention begins to shift from learning to read to reading to learn. New and difficult materials in the content fields contain concepts and ideas which teachers cannot always develop. Children must learn how to read and study in order to master them; therefore they

---

[18] Paul Sparks and Leo Fay, "An Evaluation of Two Methods of Teaching Reading," *Elementary School Journal, 77* (April, 1957), pp. 589–96.

[19] Jeanne Chall and Shirley Feldmann, "First Grade Reading: An Analysis of the Interaction of Professed Methods, Teacher Implementation and Child Backgrounds," *The Reading Teacher, 19* (May, 1966), pp. 569–75.

have to acquire additional insights about reading behaviors. Moreover, they extend their experiences in literature, reading more deeply and with greater appreciation. And they read more widely for enjoyment.

The research in middle-grades reading deals with both broad issues and specific problems. Most investigations are of the short-term variety and do not study children over extended periods. They also suffer from the same shortcomings as primary reading research. Nevertheless, some of their results provide us with insights into the directions reading instruction might take. They lend further support for adopting some practices and having reservations about others.

Basal and Individualized Reading

Are there general approaches to teaching reading in the middle grades that seem to produce better results than other systems? This is the same kind of question which dominated the primary reading research in the 1960s. Those who sought an answer to this question compared the results of programs which adopted basal readers and other teaching materials, individualized reading, interclass and intraclass grouping, and team learning.

One investigator compared children who were engaged in basal reading with those who had individualized reading. She reported no significant gains in reading achievement between groups. She did conclude that children in the individualized reading classes showed better attitudes toward reading than the other children.[20]

When a class using a basal reading series alone was compared to another using the same series in conjunction with packaged materials intended for individual use and a third following individualized reading, test scores favored the basal reading and materials groups in word meaning, but there were no significant differences among the three groups on paragraph meaning.[21] Inconclusive results were obtained in another investigation which compared the attitude toward reading and reading achievement of classes using a basal reading series alone and other classes using a combination of basal reading and self-selection. Achievement in both word and paragraph meaning was similar for both types of classes. The investigators reported that the children in self-selection classes read more books than the others.[22]

Individualized reading has been compared to ability grouping. In reality, programs which used basal readers and grouped children for instruction were studied against others that stressed self-selection of books for reading and individualized instruction. Reviews of research as well as separate

---

[20] Mary K. Huser, "Reading and More Reading." *Elementary English, 44* (April, 1967), pp. 378–82, 385.

[21] Billie J. Miller, "A Comparison of Three Types of Reading Programs—S.R.A., Individualized and Scott-Foresman," *Reading Research Quarterly, 1* (Winter, 1965), p. 62.

[22] Dorothy G. Talbert and C. B. Merritt, "The Relative Effectiveness of Two Approaches to the Teaching of Reading in Grade V," *The Reading Teacher, 19* (December, 1965), pp. 183–86.

investigations report inconclusive results. Vite[23] found that the results of four out of seven controlled studies favored individualized reading. Three definitely favored basal reading and grouping for instruction. Groff[24] surveyed the literature and reported that some results favored individualized reading and others grouping in reading. Greenman[25] and Sartain[26] reported differences in results that seemed to be influenced by the children's reading achievement. The better readers made the same or greater progress in individualized reading than did the slower readers.

The results of these and other studies on basal reading and individualized reading suggest that children can prosper under each; that some instructional programs using basal readers are superior to some individualized programs following the practice of self-selection of reading materials; that a combination of planned reading instruction provided by basal programs with opportunities for self-selection of books and individualized instruction is desirable.

Grouping Plans

The research findings on homogeneous grouping for reading instruction are inconclusive too. Carson and Thompson[27], Anastasiow[28], and Berkun[29] studied cross-grade grouping and self-contained classroom organization and reported no significant differences in results. Green and Riley[30] found that cross-grade grouping was more effective than traditional grouping, while Ramsey[31] reported that the former plan was effective for the upper third but not effective for the lower third of the class. In another study Balow[32] found that sectioning of pupils on the basis of grade placement scores did not obviate the need for differentiated instruction since total scores did not reflect susbstantial differences among individual children in rate, word meaning, and comprehension.

The formation of small pupil teams for learning and practice has been

23 Irene W. Vite, "Individualized Reading—The Scoreboard on Controlled Studies," *Education, 81* (January, 1961), pp. 285–90.

24 Patrick Groff, "Comparison of Individualized and Ability Grouping Approaches to Reading Achievement," *Elementary English, 40* (March, 1963), pp. 258–64, 276.

25 Ruth Greenman, "Individualized Reading in the Third and Fourth Grade," *Elementary English, 35* (April, 1959), pp. 234–37.

26 Harry Sartain, "The Roseville Experiment with Individualized Reading," *The Reading Teacher, 13* (April, 1960), pp. 277–81.

27 Roy Carson and Jack Thompson, "The Joplin Plan and Traditional Reading Groups," *Elementary School Journal, 65* (October, 1964), pp. 38–43.

28 N. J. Anastasiow, "A Comparison of Two Approaches in Upgrading Reading Instruction," *Elementary English, 65* (April, 1968), pp. 495–99.

29 M. M. Berkun, L. W. Swanson, and D. M. Sawyer, "An Experiment on Homogeneous Grouping for Reading in Elementary Classes," *Journal of Educational Research, 59* (May, 1966), pp. 413–14.

30 Donald Green and Hazel Riley, "Interclass Grouping for Reading Instruction in the Middle Grades," *Journal of Experimental Education, 31* (March, 1963), pp. 273–78.

31 Wallace Ramsey, "An Evaluation of a Joplin Plan of Grouping for Reading Instruction," *Journal of Educational Research, 55* (August, 1962), pp. 567–72.

32 Irving Balow, "Does Homogeneous Grouping Give Homogeneous Groups?" *Elementary School Journal, 63* (October, 1962), pp. 28–32.

recommended by Durrell on the basis of research by him and his graduate students.[33, 34] However, team study did not always produce higher achievement in all grades nor was it always superior to individual study. In the first year of a two-year investigation regular groups made significantly greater gains than did pupil teams in reading and study skills. The pupil teams made the greater gains during the second year.[35]

It is apparent that one grouping plan does not have a clear-cut advantage over other plans. There is a need to differentiate instruction which might be accomplished through grouping and individualization. We should remember that no organizational plan for teaching reading can guarantee success. The most important element is what the teacher brings to the plan —and this is what counts and makes the difference.

Content Fields

> ■ *The goal of all learning is to develop the independent learner—the individual who no longer needs the protective counsel and guidance of the school. . . . We may well expect, therefore, that instructional materials and methods will be used to decrease dependent learning and increase independent learning.*
>
> *Every individual must be prepared to meet new developmental tasks. He must be able to read, listen and view critically and thoughtfully. He must be able to use a library of books. . . . He must have methods of study and attitudes that will enable him to learn. . . .[36]*

Nothing is more important in the middle grades than teaching children to read and study informational materials. Prior to this time children mainly read story-type materials. Their language and ideas are fairly familiar. Now we expect them to read in science, social studies, mathematics, language, and other content. Many of the concepts in these fields are unfamiliar; the ways in which information is presented and treated are complex; yet we expect children to understand, retain, and use large segments of information. Children must learn how to satisfy these demands. We can help them learn.

[33] Donald Durrell, "Pupil Team Learning," *Instructor, 74* (February, 1965), p. 5.

[34] Donald Durrell and Helen Murphy, "Reading in the Intermediate Grades," *Journal of Education, 146* (December, 1963), pp. 36–53.

[35] Philip Lambert and Others, "A Comparison of Pupil Achievement in Team and Self-Contained Organizations," *Journal of Experimental Education, 33* (Spring, 1965), pp. 217–24.

[36] Edgar Dale, "Instructional Resources," in John L. Goodlad, ed., *The Changing American School* (Sixty-Fifth Yearbook of the National Society for the Study of Education, Part II). Chicago: University of Chicago Press, 1966, p. 108.

Are the basic reading skills that children learn in primary grades adequate for reading and studying in the content fields? Research offers some answers.

An early survey by Traxler and Townsend[37] of investigations on the relationship between general reading ability and ability to read in subject areas led them to recommend instruction in specialized skills pupils needed to read in content fields. Two related studies, one in social studies[38] and the other in science,[39] suggested that such skills as finding the central thought, drawing conclusions, and recognizing the author's purpose are relatively independent of general reading ability.

The abilities required to read for main ideas and to read to remember a series of ideas were the subjects of another investigation. The results indicated that good readers do both fairly well but that one could not be predicted from the other with real confidence.[40] McCullough[41] tested children on reading for main ideas and details, sequence, and inference and found relationships among ability to read for each of these purposes. However, she concluded that testing children for one type of reading did not preclude the necessity of testing them for other types of reading. Both of these studies lend support to the notion that there is a need for teaching specific reading skills.

The results of the above-mentioned studies seem to be confirmed by others whose sample populations were gifted pupils. The investigator of one of them reported a high relationship between general reading ability and ability to read in social studies but a low relationship between general reading ability and ability to read in science.[42] The second investigation involved children who were required to solve a social studies problem through reading. Each was asked to tell what he was thinking and doing and to explain why. More than half did not make use of the table of contents or index. While all the children had no difficulty in reading for details, most were unable to retain those which were needed to solve the problem.[43]

It seems clear that general reading ability is required for reading subject-

[37] Arthur Traxler and Agatha Townsend, *Another Five More Years of Research in Reading*, Bulletin No. 16, New York: Educational Records Bureau, 1946.

[38] Elona Sochor, "Literal and Critical Reading in Social Studies," *Journal of Experimental Education, 27* (September, 1958), pp. 49–56.

[39] Ethel Maney, "Literal and Critical Reading in Science," *Journal of Experimental Education, 27* (September, 1958), pp. 57–64.

[40] J. Harlan Shores, "Reading Science Materials for Two Distinct Purposes," *Elementary English* (December, 1960), pp. 461–68.

[41] Constance McCullough, "Responses of Elementary School Children to Common Types of Reading Comprehension Questions," *Journal of Educational Research, 51* (September, 1957), pp. 65–70.

[42] Edna Koehn, *The Relationship of the Basic Skill Development of Sixth Grade Gifted Children to Ninth Grade Achievement in the Content Fields.* Unpublished Doctoral Dissertation, University of Minnesota, 1960.

[43] H. Alan Robinson, "Reading Skills Employed in Solving Social Studies Problems," *The Reading Teacher, 18* (January, 1965), pp. 263–69.

matter materials. It is equally evident that specialized reading skills are needed too. Therefore, reading instruction for the middle grades should include provisions for further development of basic reading skills as well as for the introduction of additional ones needed to read and study different subjects.

Vocabulary and Comprehension

Vocabulary development appears to be a significant factor in reading for understanding. Word meaning is basic to comprehension and power in reading. There doesn't seem to be any question about the need for helping children expand their reading vocabularies. What forms might vocabulary programs take?

It appears that there are advantages in studying vocabulary drawn from the content fields with which children are involved. Growth in vocabulary as well as in understanding the subjects is possible when the two are related.[44] Teaching children prefixes and roots has not proved to be very productive when they are expected to apply this knowledge to new words.[45] Using words in meaningful ways does help vocabulary growth and concept development.[46]

The author reviewed the literature on vocabulary development and reached the following conclusion:

. . . While they do not demonstrate procedures guaranteed to be effective, [they do] suggest dependence upon no single method. Words with which students have immediate need to deal seem to be better candidates for study than words drawn from sources unrelated to present tasks. A combination of methods should produce better achievement . . . than any one method alone. Meaningful dictionary work; word study in context rather than in isolation; possible uses of context clues for specific word meanings; attention to multiple meanings and figurative language; study of the history and etymology of words relevant to current reading; application of new words in oral and written language. . . .[47]

Other ways to improve comprehension have been tested. Experiments with cloze exercises requiring pupils to supply words removed from selections and study the context to explain how the missing words are determined indicate that such activities might have favorable effects on

---

[44] L. G. Romano and N. P. Georgiady, "Vocabulary Learnings as Influenced by the Multi-Media Approach," *Illinois School Research, 2* (Fall, 1966), pp. 24–32; Louis Vanderlinde, "Does the Study of Quantitative Vocabulary Improve Problem Solving?" *Elementary School Journal, 65* (December, 1964), pp. 143–52.

[45] L. M. Otterman, "The Value of Teaching Prefixes and Root Words," *Journal of Educational Research, 57* (April, 1955), pp. 611–16.

[46] Mary Serra, "How to Develop Concepts and Their Verbal Representations," *Elementary School Journal, 53* (January, 1953), pp. 275–85; Marvin Nelson, *An Experimental Study of Three Methods of Vocabulary Instruction.* Unpublished Master's Thesis, Brigham Young University, 1961; Gerhard Eichholz and Richard Barbe, "An Experiment in Vocabulary Development," *Educational Research Bulletin, 40* (January, 1961), pp. 1–7, 28.

[47] Robert Karlin, "Combining Research Results with Good Practices in Reading," *The Reading Teacher, 21* (December, 1967), p. 221.

comprehension.[48] The use of motivating and guiding questions and establishment of purposes for reading appear to increase comprehension also.[49]

Speed and Flexibility

Most of the research on improving rate of reading has used older students as its subjects. A review of a few studies on increasing the reading rate of elementary pupils indicated that improvement could be obtained without the use of mechanical devices.[50] Conflicting results on the use of mechanical instruments to increase the rate of reading are reported in another summary.[51] There is evidence that rate of reading can be improved through purposeful practice, timed exercises, and some pacing devices. But increased reading rates are meaningless without reference to maintenance of levels of comprehension.

Flexibility is a more meaningful concept for teachers. To teach children to vary their reading rates as purposes for reading and types of materials change is much more useful than to merely concentrate on increasing reading rates. There is some evidence to show that children can vary their styles of reading.[52] Of course, they need instruction and practice in how to read different kinds of materials and how to read for different purposes. Furthermore, we assume that children who do receive instruction in varying the ways in which materials might be read do not have major difficulties in reading these materials. It doesn't make very much sense to deal with rate and flexibility if pupils lack fundamental ability in recognizing words and coping with the content of their materials.

IDEAS FOR DISCUSSION

Even if it were possible (and many do not believe it is) to substantiate claims made by commercial organizations and others that they can teach us to read 5000 words and more per minute—critics say that this is a form of skimming or scanning and that the maximum number of words of continuous text that can be read in one minute is about 900—would it be desirable to read at those rates? Would you want to read Camus that rapidly? Could you and still grasp the meaning and intent of his ideas? Rapid rates might be possible for reading some books without real losses but are they appropriate for others? We do skim some materials for

---

[48] J. Wesley Schneyer, "Use of Cloze Procedure for Improving Reading Comprehension," *The Reading Teacher, 19* (December, 1965), pp. 174–79; Richard Bloomer, "The Cloze Procedure as a Remedial Reading Exercise," *Journal of Developmental Reading, 10* (Spring, 1962), pp. 173–81.

[49] Helen Huus, "Reading Instruction at Later Levels," in Helen M. Robinson, ed., *Innovation and Change in Reading Instruction* (Sixty-Seventh Yearbook of the National Society for the Study of Education. Part II). Chicago: University of Chicago Press, 1968, pp. 132–34.

[50] Robert Karlin, "Machines and Reading: A Review of Research," *The Clearing House, 32* (February, 1958), pp. 349–52.

[51] Allen Berger, "Speed Reading: Is the Present Emphasis Desirable," in Nila B. Smith, ed., *Current Issues In Reading* (Proceedings of the Thirteenth Annual Convention, Vol. 13, Part 2). Newark, Del.: International Reading Association, 1969, pp. 45–70.

[52] *Ibid.*, p. 51.

general impressions and scan others for specific information. Are these the ways we would read Nabokov? Surely we would want to savor the flavor of his language. . . . Could we do it at more than pedestrian speed? These questions are equally applicable to young readers who would read materials appropriate to their maturity levels.

Reading Interests

Studies on children's reading consistently underscore differences in reading preferences based upon sex.[53] Intelligence, reading ability, and socio-economic levels do not seem to be factors in children's reading preferences. Perhaps the most comprehensive investigation of what children like to read about was conducted by Norvell.[54] His findings confirmed the results of earlier studies which identified sex differences in reading choices and the elements middle-grade boys and girls sought in reading materials. Boys preferred stories of adventure with action, courage and heroism, humor, real people, and animals; girls favored adventure without violent action, mystery, love, home and school life, pets, patriotism, and sentiment. More recent surveys do not add much new information about children's reading interests but they do question the methodologies followed to obtain the data.[55]

However valid or invalid the results of research on children's reading preferences might be, it is clear that we need to start where children are and provide materials that they prefer and can read. The content of newer basal materials reflects this attitude. Programs should have built-in opportunities for wide, independent reading and cater to diverse tastes and interests. The application of these principles might reverse a trend away from reading to an upsurge in reading.

Applications From Psychology

There have been a number of developments in the psychology of reading and learning which will be treated briefly here. From some of these we can draw possible implications for the teaching of reading.

Theories of Reading

Explanations of the reading process are quite different from descriptions of the reading act. The latter deals with surface activities and behaviors that are not difficult to describe. Thus the act of reading involves the

---

[53] Paul Witty and Others, "Studies of Children's Interest," *Elementary English, 37* (December, 1960), pp. 540–45.

[54] George Norvell, *What Boys and Girls Like to Read.* Morristown, N.J.: Silver Burdett Company, 1958.

[55] Sara F. Zimet, "Children's Interest and Story Preferences: A Critical Review of the Literature," *Elementary School Journal, 67* (December, 1966), pp. 122–30; Ethel M. King, "Critical Appraisal of Research on Children's Reading Interests, Preferences and Habits," *Canadian Education and Research Digest, 7* (December, 1967), pp. 312–26.

decoding of language symbols and understanding what meanings they convey. On the other hand, to know what succession of actions occurs to make the act of reading possible is quite a different matter.

Holmes[56] proposed the theory that different centers of the brain store information received in visual, auditory, and kinesthetic forms. These coded images are marshalled during reading through three levels of sub-abilities which interact with each other in hierarchical fashion. The product of these interactions, which serve to process incoming information with that already stored in the brain, produces power in reading. Holmes applied statistical treatments to data obtained from the results of over fifty tests administered to high school students to identify important subskills at each level. Word meaning in and out of context accounted for 32 per cent of the differences in reading power. Verbal analogies and listening comprehension accounted for another 32 per cent. Twenty-five per cent of the remaining differences were unaccounted for. Singer[57] followed the same model and obtained data for grades three through six. Word attack and word recognition abilities and visual verbal meanings accounted for most of the differences in power of reading. However, close to 30 per cent of the differences were not accounted for.

Although critics have raised serious questions about the research by Holmes and Singer, one of which is that the investigators dealt only with the reading act, their analyses, which identified relationships between certain subskills and reading, might provide a rationale for giving emphasis to particular sets of skills in reading programs.

According to Smith and Carrigan[58] reading is controlled through the synaptic transmission of impulses in the nervous system. This transmission is blocked if the body suffers from a chemical imbalance of acetylcholine and cholinesterase. This model essentially seeks to explain how words are recognized after subjects have been exposed to them, but it is based on a number of assumptions which have yet to be demonstrated.

Guilford[59] describes a model of the intellect which is characterized by a set of operations: cognition, memory, divergent thinking, convergent thinking, and evaluation. He suggests that content is dealt with on a unit, or larger, basis. Some of his constructs can be applied as we treat literal, inferential, and critical reading. Others have based their explanations of reading comprehension on aspects of this model.

---

[56] Jack A. Holmes, "Basic Assumptions Underlying the Substrata-Factor Theory," *Reading Research Quarterly, 1* (Fall, 1965), pp. 4–28.

[57] Harry Singer, *Substrata-Factor Reorganization Accompanying Development in Speed and Power of Reading at the Elementary School Level* (Office of Education Research Project No. 2011). Riverside: University of California, 1965.

[58] Donald E. P. Smith and Patricia Carrigan, *The Nature of Reading Disability.* New York: Harcourt Brace Jovanovich, Inc., 1959.

[59] J. P. Guilford, "Three Faces of Intellect," *American Psychologist, 14* (August, 1959), pp. 469–79; and "Frontiers in Thinking that Teachers Should Know About," *The Reading Teacher, 13* (February, 1960), pp. 176–82.

Concept Development and Cognition

How children learn to recognize and process information has been the subject of much speculation and some research. Perhaps no one has shed more light on the intellectual development of children than Piaget, whose findings have been used to support the concept of readiness in learning. Piaget describes four maturational stages of development:

1. *sensorimotor period* (birth to 2 years), in which objects are recognized through manipulation

2. *preoperational thought period* (2–4 years), in which classifications are based on one aspect; and *intuitive phase* (4–7 years), in which thought is in terms of relationships

3. *concrete operations period* (7–11 years), in which logical thinking occurs

4. *formal operations period* (11–15 years), when abstract thinking and conceptualization are strengthened.[60] These periods of intellectual development overlap, and all children do not reach them at the same time.

Piaget's theory is taken by some to mean that children pass through stages of intellectual development and there isn't much we can do to influence this movement. Piaget believes that some educational practices do not seem to affect a child's level of understanding but does not rule out efforts that may influence it. He recognizes that maturation does not occur in a vacuum.

Structure—the way in which ideas are related—is another construct associated with Piaget. Should we stress the structure of a subject or help children to discern the structure? Piaget believes that opportunities for discovering structures should be created. Children need to be active and explore for themselves.

Taba[61] was concerned with the development of cognition as described by Piaget and others and hypothesized that it was possible to train children in thinking processes. She found that through appropriate pacing and sequencing of discussions and questions children moved to higher thought levels.

Teachers can use what knowledge we have about cognition and its development and apply it to reading instruction. They move from concrete examples to abstract ideas in helping children to understand the concepts they meet in reading. They help children progress from literal reading to inferential reading to evaluative reading. They teach skills in hierarchical sequence. These are some applications that could have an impact upon the results of reading instruction.

---

[60] Kenneth Lovell, "The Philosophy of Jean Piaget," *New Society, 11* (August, 1966), pp. 222–26.

[61] Hilda Taba, "The Teaching of Thinking," *Elementary English, 42* (May, 1965), pp. 534–42.

Learning Climates

Are the same learning climates suitable for all learners? Wepman[62] and others offer data which suggest that some children have the innate capacity to process information better through one pathway than another. They hypothesize that these pathways—auditory, visual, and kinesthetic—may not develop at the same rates and that a child may have a predilection for one pathway or another. The use of the pathway furthers its development. Wepman would alter the learning climates to fit these predilections.

Teachers have followed the practice of telling children what they needed to learn. They looked upon themselves as sources of information and explainers of ideas. We have already referred to Piaget's insistence on active learning. He would change the traditional teacher's role to one of providing situations from which the child could do much of the learning for himself. Bruner[63] advocates a learning atmosphere that is similar, but he seems to place greater dependence on teaching the structure of subjects in order to help children understand better. He would provide generalizations that Piaget would wish children to discover. It is conceivable that however hard we tried to provide proper conditions for self-discovery some children would fail to see relationships. It might prove helpful to point them out. Suchman[64] justifies the discovery approach to learning on several grounds. It helps to clarify how knowledge is acquired; it is self-motivating and creates self-esteem; it serves to free the learner from total dependence upon others; it makes it possible for the child to set his own learning pace.

Skinner[65], a behavioral scientist, has applied his views about conditioning to human learning. He believes that desirable responses can be strengthened through immediate reinforcement and careful guidance. Although Skinner is not the father of programed instruction, his influence upon the development of materials that fulfill its requirements is great.

Ausubel[66] stresses the importance of starting where the learner is. He would eliminate all study that the learner cannot assimilate because of present cognitive development. He insists on the mastery of present materials before new ones are introduced; in fact, he points out

---

[62] Joseph M. Wepman, "The Modality Concept—Including a Statement of the Perceptual and Conceptual Levels of Learning," in Helen K. Smith, ed., *Perception and Reading* (Vol. 12, Part 4 of the Proceedings of the Twelfth Annual Convention). Newark, Del.: International Reading Association, 1968, pp. 1–6.

[63] Jerome S. Bruner, *The Process of Education.* Cambridge, Mass.: Harvard University Press, 1960.

[64] J. Richard Suchman, "Developing Children's Thinking Through Inquiry Training," in Albert J. Mazurkiewicz, ed., *New Perspectives in Reading Instruction,* 2nd ed. New York: Pitman Publishing Corporation, 1968, pp. 287–91.

[65] B. F. Skinner, *The Technology of Teaching.* New York: Appleton-Century-Crofts, 1968.

[66] David P. Ausubel, "A Teaching Strategy for Culturally Deprived Pupils: Cognitive and Motivational Considerations," *School Review, 81* (Winter, 1963), pp. 454–63.

the results of research which show that overlearning facilitates the transfer of prior learnings to new tasks. Meaningful learning can be promoted through the use of materials presented sequentially with provisions for feedback. Although Ausubel recognizes that extrinsic motivation serves to meet ego and prestige needs, he would stress intrinsic motivation for learning. He would not wait for this motivation to develop but would teach as effectively as possible with the expectation that satisfaction from learning could promote a desire to learn more.

There is a growing body of literature which deals with interaction analysis.[67] This analysis of the verbal behavior of teachers offers insights into their effects on learning. There is evidence to support the conclusion that learning is more likely to occur in the classroom in which the teacher accepts and clarifies the ideas of his pupils, where he praises the work they do and asks questions to help them make decisions and solve their problems. This pattern of behavior has been called integrative, pupil-centered, and democratic. Less learning seems to occur in classrooms in which the teacher lectures and criticizes children and dominates the classroom. Findings do not indicate that a teacher should maintain one type of behavior to the exclusion of all others.

What are some teaching applications that can be drawn from experimentation and study of learning climates?

1. Multisensory strategies to accommodate different learning styles can be adopted for teaching word recognition skills.

2. The inductive method of teaching is followed in presenting most reading skills. Teachers help pupils to generalize from data that reading materials contain.

3. Evaluation of pupils' reading strengths and weaknesses helps to determine what teachers stress. Instruction begins where the reader is.

4. Children learn to read from materials that are challenging but not frustrating.

5. Reading skills are taught in sequence and in a meaningful way.

6. The ways in which reading responses are made are as important as the responses themselves. Teachers stress the processes that children follow by encouraging them to discuss and explain what they did to make their responses.

---

[67] Arno A. A. Bellack, ed., *Theory and Research in Teaching.* New York: Bureau of Publications, Teachers College, Columbia University, 1963; Arno Bellack and Others, *The Language of the Classroom* (U. S. Office of Education Cooperative Research Project No. 1497). New York: Teachers College, Columbia University, 1963; Ned A. Flanders, *Teacher Influence, Pupil Attitudes and Achievement* (U. S. Office of Education Cooperative Research Project No. 397). Minneapolis: University of Minnesota, 1960; Donald Medley and Harold Mitzel, "Measuring Classroom Behavior by Systematic Observation," in N. L. Gage, ed., *Handbook of Research in Teaching.* Chicago: Rand McNally & Company, 1963, pp. 247–328.

Influences of Linguistics

> ■ *In applying linguistic knowledge to the teaching of reading, we must distinguish between linguistic knowledge and methods used by linguists in teaching language. It is a temptation to adopt both the knowledge and the methods; yet it must be said in all honesty that while linguistic knowledge is a product of rigorous scholarly endeavor, methods of teaching language range from ancient to modern, reflecting more of logic than of psychological soundness.*[68]

Linguistics is the science of language. Linguists are scientists who endeavor to explain the phonemic and grammatical structures of language. That linguists have had an impact on reading can be readily seen in terminology that is still with us, such as "linguistic" methods and "linguistic" readers.

There are different ways of looking at language. Briefly, *structural* linguists study oral language to identify its sounds, units of meaning carried by words and parts of words, and its syntax. They attempt to describe language from these utterances. *Generative,* or transformational, linguists seek to discover the knowledge one has in order to make such utterances or understand them. They wish to produce grammars that describe this unobservable knowledge of language. Of course, these linguists must study spoken language to deduce any hidden knowledge speakers and listeners might have.

Emphasis on Decoding

The so-called linguistic approaches to the teaching of reading have their origins in the efforts of some structural linguists and their followers to translate linguistic knowledge into teaching systems. Thus we have Bloomfield[69] and Fries[70], who prepared materials and recommended procedures for teaching reading. Both stress the importance of teaching children to learn the code through consistent sound-symbol representations. Actually, Bloomfield and Fries promoted systems of phonics which they believed were linguistically based and superior to those in use.

---

[68] Constance M. McCullough, "Vital Principles in Need of Application," in Elaine C. Vilscek, ed., *A Decade of Innovations: Approaches to Beginning Reading* (Vol. 12, Part 3, Proceedings of the Twelfth Annual Convention). Newark, Del.: International Reading Association, 1968, p. 181.

[69] Leonard Bloomfield and Clarence Barnhart, *Let's Read.* Detroit: Wayne State University Press, 1962.

[70] Charles C. Fries, *Linguistics and Reading.* New York: Holt, Rinehart and Winston, Inc., 1963.

Emphasis on Units of Meaning

Lefevre[71] deplores the emphasis that Bloomfield and Fries placed on words. He insists that it is the sentence and not the word that conveys meaning and that children have to be taught to relate stress and intonation of spoken words to written words. It should be noted that Fries and, less so, Bloomfield were not particularly concerned with meaning since they felt that beginning reading is basically a task of determining what words say. Lefevre's views seem to be more in harmony with some principles of basal and language experience programs.

Using Knowledge About Language

A number of questions about linguistics and teaching reading arise. What parallels exist between patterns of letters in spoken words and written words? What is linguistic about the constancy of phoneme-grapheme correspondences? Should meaning be ignored in teaching children to recognize words? The answers to these questions are by no means firm, but there are indications that what is "good" linguistically is not necessarily good reading practice. As Wardhaugh[72] has pointed out, linguistics can make a contribution, as other disciplines have, to the teaching of reading. However, it is the teacher and not the linguist who can determine ways to use knowledge about language. Insofar as word recognition is concerned, learning principles rather than linguistics support the notion of not isolating sounds from words and making efforts to minimize confusions due to phoneme-grapheme irregularities.[73] These same principles lend support to the idea that meaning aids recognition.

IDEAS FOR DISCUSSION

The notions that the child has great control over his language and that his language is as good as any other as long as he can communicate are generalizations which are gaining support. We know too that children who come to school speaking nonstandard English seem to have much more trouble in learning to read than those who speak standard English. Is this problem of learning to read standard English tied to inability to speak it? Some evidence indicates that it is.[74] What can we do about the problem? Try to change the speech of children so that it more closely resembles standard English? Use materials that are patterned after non-

---

[71] Carl A. Lefevre, *Linguistics and the Teaching of Reading*. New York: McGraw-Hill, Inc., 1964.

[72] Ronald Wardhaugh, *Reading: A Linguistic Perspective*. New York: Harcourt Brace Jovanovich, Inc., 1969.

[73] There is some evidence in favor of using irregular patterns to teach phoneme-grapheme relationships. See Harry Levin and John Watson, *A Basic Research Program on Reading* (U.S. Office of Education Cooperative Research Project No. 639). Ithaca: Cornell University, 1963.

[74] Ruth Strickland and Robert Ruddell conducted investigations which showed that the forms of children's speech differed from the structures of sentences in readers. Both reported an association between this difference and reading difficulty.

standard English? Ignore the problem and let the chips fall where they may? Goodman[75] believes that although no special materials have to be constructed, the child should be encouraged to read as he speaks. Thus, if the sentence were "I am going home," an acceptable reading of it might be "I (be) going home." However, the teacher would continue to speak naturally and serve as a language model for speakers of divergent dialects. Labov[76] would not correct the child whose pronunciations of words were different from standard pronunciations but would deal with errors that clearly resulted from lack of understanding.

Contribution of Psycholinguistics

An offshoot from psychology and linguistics is *psycholinguistics*, the study of the psychological aspects of language. How verbal learning occurs and what factors influence verbal learning are representative of some of the issues with which psycholinguistics deals. How meaning is derived from lexical and structural units is another major concern. The research on these and other questions having to do with thinking and language has not gone very far beyond the preliminary stages, although there are some who believe that significant contributions to increased understanding of the nature of language problems are being made. Some of this research involves the question of how meaning is derived from the context which contains structural and meaning clues. The cloze procedure of eliminating every nth word has been used in several studies.[77] An analysis of the context that helps readers determine what the missing words are may provide clues to the elements that influence the understanding of language.

Experiences with the cloze procedure show that it has possibilities for determining the difficulty of materials, of measuring levels of comprehension, analyzing and overcoming meaning difficulties, and suggesting ways to teach readers how to use the context in vocabulary development.

Current and Innovative Practices

Schools have been teaching reading for centuries. Evidences of early reading practices are still apparent in some classrooms. In fact, some practices have been resurrected from the past, modified by some changes and heralded as real innovations. We live in an era of change and schools are

[75] Kenneth S. Goodman, "Dialect Barriers to Reading Comprehension," *Elementary English, 42* (December, 1965), pp. 853–60.

[76] William Labov, "Some Sources of Reading Problems for Negro Speakers of Nonstandard English," in Joan Baratz and Roger Shuy, eds., *Teaching Black Children to Read.* Washington: Center for Applied Linguistics, 1969, pp. 29–67.

[77] Earl F. Rankin, Jr., "The Cloze Procedure—A Survey of Research," in Eric L. Thurston and Laurence E. Hafner, eds., *The Philosophical and Sociological Bases of Reading* (Fourteenth Yearbook of the National Reading Conference). Milwaukee: National Reading Conference, 1965, pp. 133–50; John R. Bormuth, "Factor Validity of Cloze Tests as Measures of Reading Comprehension Ability," *Reading Research Quarterly, 4* (Spring, 1969), pp. 358–65.

no less affected than other segments of society, although changes in school practices seem to come about slowly.

One senses attitudes that imply excellence in change and innovation and less than excellence in using conventional teaching methods. There is no doubt that some school changes are long overdue. Schools must be willing to explore changes, and many are. They should be ready to examine present and promising practices, holding on to those which are fruitful and trying others which seem to have merit. This mix might produce superior programs leading to improved instruction and learning.

In reviewing the research in elementary reading certain trends have already been noted: earlier instruction in beginning reading, varied instructional systems and materials, individualized and group plans, instruction in the content fields. The next section will cover specific types of programs and materials that are in current use. Some have characteristics which would place them in more than one category. Fuller descriptions of others will be reserved for later chapters as teaching methodologies are covered.

Basal Reading Programs

The familiar series which consist of paperbound and hardcovered books with teaching manuals and instructional aids (workbooks, word cards, ditto masters, etc.) are widely used. Some series are similar to those of the 1940s and 1950s, but changes in content, form, and instructional emphases are apparent in several basal reading programs. Some changes are quite drastic; others are less so and a matter of degree rather than kind.

Changes in Content

In the first and second year, books of a reading series formerly stressed home and family life characteristic of the white middle class. Imaginative stories and poetry were introduced, and as children progressed into more difficult materials they were exposed to a sprinkling of factual or informational selections.

Now, some beginning readers retain the familiar family circle, but their character has changed. In the *City Schools Reading Program*,[78] the middle-class family is black and participates in many of the same activities as its white counterparts. This series generally follows the typical format of traditional ones. Revisions of older reading series and newer ones picture characters of different racial backgrounds and develop selections about black people. Two other series for the primary grades, the *Bank Street Readers* and the *Multimedia Reading Program*[79] move their settings away from the suburbs into the big city. The family thread is not carried through

---

[78] *City Schools Reading Program.* Chicago: Follett Publishing Company, 1966.
[79] *Bank Street Readers.* New York: The Macmillan Company, 1966; *Multimedia Reading Program.* San Francisco: Chandler Publishing Company, 1966.

the selections as in others. The *Miami Linguistic Reader Series*,[80] intended for bilingual children, introduces animal characters that behave like people. Some of its stories are adaptations of fairy tales, and others might be considered realistic. Other reading series have combined the typical child-centered content with other features.

A few series have introduced more factual selections in their books. One, the *Bookmark Reading Program*,[81] has separate skills readers for grades four, five, and six which contain only informational selections and textbook materials in science, social studies, mathematics, and language. A separate set of literature books accompanies the skills readers. A second series, *Basic Reading Program*,[82] offers factual-type reading as one strand of a reading program and story-type and literature selections as another.

Changes in Form and Emphases

There are several reading series which stress sound-symbol correspondences based upon spelling patterns.[83] Some are intended for use only in the first few grades while others provide books through the sixth grade. There are variations to be found among them but most have these common characteristics: early concentration on learning the letter names of the alphabet with their corresponding sounds; emphasis upon learning the decoding system through the use of consistent spelling patterns in words. The latter is accomplished by introducing such words and sentences as:

> cat, Nat, fat
> Nat is a fat cat.
> Sit, Tiff, sit
> Zip and Pud jump in.

"Irregular" signal words such as *the* are introduced in some materials quite early, while other words with inconsistent spelling patterns follow after some relationships between sound and letter patterns have been established. Series that are intended for use beyond the primary grades contain the typical features of others.

A few reading series, though not classified as "linguistic," contain some of the consistent sound-letter patterns.[84] They do not sacrifice typical lan-

---

[80] *Miami Linguistic Reader Series*. Miami: Dade County Board of Public Instruction, 1966.

[81] *Bookmark Reading Program*. New York: Harcourt Brace Jovanovich, Inc., 1970.

[82] *Basic Reading Program*. New York: Harper & Row, Publishers, 1966.

[83] *Merrill Linguistic Readers, A Basic Program for the Primary Grades*. Columbus: Charles E. Merrill Books, Inc., 1966; *Let's Read*. Bronxville: Clarence L. Barnhart, Inc., 1966; *Palo Alto Reading Program*. New York: Harcourt Brace Jovanovich, Inc., 1966; *SRA Basic Reading Series*. Chicago: Science Research Associates, 1965; *Structural Reading Series*. New York: Random House, Inc., 1970; *Linguistic Readers*. Evanston: Harper & Row, Publishers, 1965; *Visual-Linguistic Reading Series*. St. Paul: Educational Service Press, 1966; *Miami Linguistic Reader Series, op. cit.*

[84] *Bookmark Reading Program*. New York: Harcourt Brace Jovanovich, Inc., 1970; *Reading 360*. Ginn and Company, 1969; *The Read Series*. American Book Company—D. Van Nostrand Company, Inc., 1969.

guage patterns in order to maintain consistency in sound-letter patterns.

In order to avoid inconsistencies in sound-letter relationships, one primary reading series substituted a 44-character lower-case alphabet known as i.t.a. (Initial Teaching Alphabet) for the regular 26 letters.[85] Although not completely phonemic, there is a great deal of consistency between the symbols and sounds they represent. This reading series stresses early phonics and writing opportunities.

Most current basal reading programs place a much heavier and earlier emphasis upon the decoding process—phonics being a major component—than previous ones. This is true of those that feature "linguistic" and

INITIAL TEACHING ALPHABET[86]

æ face	b bed	c cat	d dog	ee key
f feet	g leg	h hat	ie fly	j jug	k key
l letter	m man	n nest	œ over	p pen	ɼ girl
r red	s spoon	t tree	ue use	v voice	w window
y yes	z zebra	ʒ daisy	wh when	ch chair
th three	th the	ſh shop	ʒ television	ŋ ring
ɑ father	au ball	a cap	e egg	i milk	o box
u up	ω book	ω spoon	ou out	oi oil

[85] *Early-to-Read i.t.a. Program.* New York: i.t.a. Publications, 1966.

[86] *Source:* From the book *New Perspectives in Reading Instruction,* 2nd ed., by Albert Mazurkiewicz. Copyright © 1964, 1968 by Albert J. Mazurkiewicz. Reprinted by permission of Pitman Publishing Corporation.

unique orthographic forms as well as others that follow the older format. Many focus attention on sounds of letters and letter combinations as they appear in words while a few at the outset introduce individual letters and their corresponding sounds. There is a group of basal readers which introduce children to beginning reading through a synthetic phonics system.[87] Children study vowels and consonants together with their sounds and see how these letters are joined to form words.

Audiovisual Aids

There are on-going demonstrations which feature mechanical devices and other aids to teach reading. Some combine *auditory* with *visual* presentations.

Perhaps the most simple of these aids are tapes that contain stories and questions to which children listen and respond. Another form of this type of aid is a sheet with a text on one side and a sound track on the other. A special record player reproduces the sound, which may be a word-for-word reading of the text, that the child follows. The "voice" might indicate how the reader should respond to certain portions. A third variation is a card on which a word, phrase, or sentence is printed. The card contains a tape which "reads" the printed matter as it is passed through a special tape recorder.[88]

Teachers may use these simple aids to record their own messages and pupil tasks. They have obvious possibilities for providing individual and small group instruction for children whose reading is satisfactory and for those who required special help. If properly "programed," they can offer needed help at times when the teacher is unable to be physically present to direct a lesson.

More complex and expensive hardware is being used in demonstrations and projects to teach reading. One is the *"talking typewriter"* developed by Omar K. Moore of Yale University and the Responsive Environments Foundation. The machine can be programed in different ways to teach children the letters of the alphabet and to read words. When the pupil presses a letter key on the typewriter, the machine says the letter's name. A word might appear on a screen and the child is expected to type it out. In this case, all but the correct letters on the typewriter lock so that in order to copy the word he must press the proper keys in sequence. This equipment combines auditory and visual presentations to which the learner is expected to respond.

Computer-assisted instruction is a more recent development. A keyboard

---

[87] *Basic Reading*. Philadelphia: J. B. Lippincott Company, 1965; *Economy Reading Program*. Oklahoma City: The Economy Company, 1957; *Open Court Series*. La Salle, Ill.: The Open Court Publishing Company, 1963.

[88] A number of manufacturers produce different versions of similar devices. One coordinates sound and visual images that appear on a screen, and the student pushes a button to indicate his responses to instructions and questions.

is tied into a computer which feeds information to the student. The student reacts and the computer accepts or rejects the response and presents more information as required. A more elaborate system uses a television-type screen on which images in the form of pictures, words, or sentences appear. The pupil responds to oral instructions and uses a special pen with which to indicate his responses on the screen. The voice tells the pupil if he has made a correct or wrong response.

The aim of these sophisticated devices is to make individualized instruction possible and free the teacher for other tasks. Some of their more enthusiastic supporters claim that they can do what no teacher can to promote learning. It is apparent that some children respond favorably to this hardware and form of instruction. It is equally apparent that the "software" (i.e., books) produces whatever learning occurs, although children may be attracted to the machines and respond with greater motivation. This equipment has real possibilities for helping the teacher to individualize his instruction and offer special help to children who need it. But better ways to coordinate what the classroom teacher is doing and what the machines provide must be found. This requires flexible programing, for which little provision is now made. Existing systems do not require much teacher participation except where children fail to respond. The instruction is "canned," and there are no opportunities to modify it.

The present cost of purchasing or renting this equipment is high, and it is not likely many school districts will be able to afford any unless they obtain financial assistance from other sources. Federally funded programs, such as the one in New York City where the "talking typewriter" has been used with disadvantaged children, have made tryouts of some equipment possible. Reductions in cost and improvements in design may bring more of these newer products of technology into the schools.

Two *writing systems* which rely on visual clues have been tried in beginning reading. One is known as *Words in Color*[89] which uses a different color for each of forty-seven sounds. Drill charts and workbooks are used to teach children the sounds and combine them into words. A second (the DMS system) uses diacritical marks to indicate the values of certain letters and letter combinations.[90] Consonants and short vowels that are "regular" do not have any marks over them. A bar over a vowel represents the "long" vowel sound; letters combining to form unique sounds have a bar under them; silent letters are marked through with a diagonal line. These marks plus a few others make up the system.

There are other *alphabet systems*[91] which have their adherents. Each hopes to eliminate the problem of inconsistency in letter-sound relationships. Although many educators have doubts about the values of these

[89] *Words in Color.* Chicago: Learning Materials, Inc., 1962.

[90] Edward Fry, "A Diacritical Marking System to Aid Beginning Reading Instruction," *Elementary English, 51* (May, 1964), pp. 526–29, 537.

[91] Unifon, Simplified Spelling, etc.

Sample of Primer
Printed in ITA

"dœn't run awæ," ben sed too his cat.

"dœn't fiet," miek sed too his cat.

"wæt heer," sed ben and miek.

"wee will bee at scœol."

Sample of Primer
Printed with DMS

"Lȯȯk, Bill," sȧïd Lindȧ.

"Hēr¢ cȯm¢s̱ Ri¢ky.

Hē is̱ ȧll rea̸dy fȯr sc̸hȯȯl.

Lȯȯk up and sēe̸ funny Ri¢ky."

Sample of Primer
Printed in Unifon

⊥EN M⼲CT∃R H⼲PꝖ TRⱭD.   HI

P⼲KT UP BⱭBI HⱲB∃RT, HELD

H⼲M ⼲N H⼲Z B⼲G ORMZ AND CAИ

U LULUBⱭ.

[92] *Source: First Grade Reading Programs,* perspectives in Reading No. 5, 1965, by Edward
Fry. Reprinted with permission of Edward Fry and the International Reading Association.

writing systems, it seems that those which adhere most closely to the letters
of our regular alphabet are less likely to produce new learning problems
than those which depart radically from them.

Individualized Programs

Provisions for individualization are included in the teaching plans of
basal reading systems. Teachers have adopted different organizational patterns to facilitate their efforts to meet individual and group needs. Pro-
ducers of teaching machines promote their wares by pointing out how they
make individualized instruction possible. We all agree that individualization
is necessary but implement the concept in different ways.

Programmed Materials

There are materials for teaching beginning and upper-level reading
skills which are intended to be used by pupils virtually without teacher

assistance.[93] Of course, in the beginning stages of learning, young pupils need a great deal of teacher guidance before they can work through the materials independently. Programed materials are self-instructional and self-correcting. Small bits of information are given in sections or "frames" and pupils make responses such as supplying a missing word in a sentence or answering a question. Each frame contains material which is based upon the preceding frame; the frames break down the material into small, sequential steps, a procedure which can facilitate learning and reduce the number of errors a learner might make. Some programed materials are presented in book form while others are designed for use in a teaching machine.

Although the publishers of programed materials report real advantages over other plans, there isn't much carefully-controlled research on them. In one of the First Grade Studies sponsored by the U.S. Office of Education the investigator reported mixed results when the reading achievement of children using programed materials was compared with the achievement of those using typical basal materials.[94] In any comparisons it is difficult to determine what element or group of elements produces growth. In the case of programed materials, it might be the programing, the content, or some combination of both that produced the results.

The principles underlying programed instruction are consistent with general learning constructs. There is evidence that immediate reinforcement (knowledge about the correctness of responses) and hierarchy in learning (frames in graded sequence) can facilitate learning. But another ingredient must be added: the programer's understanding of the material to be learned. This factor might explain why some programed materials are weak and do not seem to be as useful as other materials in traditional formats.

Individualized and Language Experience Reading

Self-selection, self-pacing, and self-motivation are the principles on which individualized reading is based. In this program children select the books they read and meet individually with the teacher for discussion and instruction. Although the teacher might see groups of children, he spends more time working with individuals.

In a language experience program a child might dictate a story to the teacher which will be used as material for teaching reading to him and possibly others. As children learn to write, they might create their own stories with or without teacher assistance. There are advantages to using materials that originate in the learner himself.

The research previously cited shows that no single approach to teaching

---

93 *Programmed Reading*. New York: McGraw-Hill Inc., 1966; *Lift Off to Reading*. Chicago: Science Research Associates, Inc., 1966; *Reading: A Programed Primer*. New York: Grolier, Inc., 1962.

94 Robert Ruddell, "Reading Instruction in First Grade with Varying Emphases on the Regularity of Grapheme-Phoneme Correspondences and the Relation of Language Structure to Meaning," *The Reading Teacher, 19* (May, 1966), pp. 653–60.

reading is measurably better than another. However, there is support for exposing children to many kinds of programs. Individualized reading and language-experience reading offer advantages that other programs might not; aspects of each could be incorporated into total reading programs.

A Comprehensive Reading Curriculum

> ■ *Many teachers are concerned with the problems of teaching one grade or subject. . . . They tend to think of their work as being at one grade level, and, through many activities related to reading, they enrich a* horizontal *program. . . This enrichment is as it should be, for reading abilities are strengthened by . . . applying them in various fields. Reading can have both breadth and depth. But in addition . . . the teacher must be concerned with the past and the future, with the* vertical *aspects of a child's reading development, and with a sequential and interrelated pattern of reading procedures over a period of years.*[95]

A viable reading program is one which develops the basic skills children need in order to read, which teaches children how they can use reading as a tool for learning, which fosters an appreciation of and taste in literature, and which develops permanent interests in reading for enjoyment. These four characteristics become the objectives of our instructional program and at the same time serve as guidelines for evaluating the progress children make in reading. How we achieve these objectives is what reading instruction is all about.

Reading is not simple, nor is it a single skill. It is complex and consists of many different components. Children do not learn to read in one, two, or three years, just as they don't learn to master any other complex activity in a brief period of time. They learn some reading skills and develop some attitudes toward reading as they complete one stage of development and move into another. But it takes children a long time to achieve proficiency in reading. What they may be able to accomplish at one point in their reading development will not be good enough at another. This fact explains why some children can cope with early reading demands but not later ones. It also underscores the need for continuous and orderly reading experiences throughout the school years.

It has been a practice in the past to identify reading requirements of the first grade, second grade, third grade, and so on. This policy of fragmenting the reading curriculum fails to take into account the fact that children in

---

[95] David H. Russell, "Continuity in the Reading Program," in Nelson B. Henry, ed., *Development In and Through Reading* (Sixtieth Yearbook of the National Society for the Study of Education, Part I). Chicago: University of Chicago Press, 1961, p. 230.

the lower grades need to learn an array of reading skills. If they are to function satisfactorily in higher grades and at higher levels of reading, they must learn to use these skills in greater depth and with more confidence. Children in the fourth, fifth, and sixth grades use word-attack skills for long and difficult words. Some may require intensive instruction in word recognition to do this successfully. Children in these same grades read for literal and inferred meanings and react to ideas. Unless they have been brought up through the grades on a curriculum which provides for these reading experiences, children will have problems meeting the requirements of higher-level literal and inferential reading and teachers will have little upon which to build their instructional program. Children in the earliest grades should read for main ideas, to draw conclusions, and to react. They do these kinds of reading in later grades, too, but in more difficult materials and in greater depth. This is what we mean when we refer to sequential and developmental reading programs. In addition, children will require new reading skills at higher levels because there was no real need to learn them earlier and they lacked reading maturity to benefit greatly from them. But these also are not introduced randomly. They assume mastery of previous reading tasks and a readiness for learning new ones.

Skills Components

We say that children learn to read; what we really mean is that children master the skills and develop the attitudes they need in order to acquire the ability to read. Reading is not a unitary ability, for it consists of many different interrelated processes. Children with reading ability draw upon a body of skills which they use to understand and assimilate printed messages. All children do not necessarily use the same skills in reading identical materials. Their levels of achievement and the nature of the reading task determine which ones they apply. Some children are more efficient in using their skills than others. They develop proficiency in them through guided learning and meaningful practice.

We should regard any classification of reading skills merely as a way of identifying what children have to learn. The development of reading ability depends in great part upon how well the skills are mastered. Thus teachers make the mastery of specific reading skills one of their major objectives. Their other main objective is to foster positive attitudes toward reading.

The following *classification of reading skills* will provide an overview of them. Each category will be analyzed further in subsequent chapters which treat them in detail. We might classify these skills differently; but it is less important to remember their classification than to make provisions for their inclusion in the reading curriculum.

I. Word Recognition Skills
    A. Contextual Clues
    B. Phonic analysis

C. Structural analysis
D. Dictionary
E. Sight vocabulary
II. Word Meaning Skills
A. Contextual clues
B. Structural clues
C. Dictionary
D. Multiple meanings
E. Figurative language
III. Comprehension Skills
A. Literal meaning
B. Inferred meaning
C. Critical evaluation
D. Assimilation
IV. Study Skills
A. Location of information
B. Selection of information
C. Organization and retention of information
D. Graphic and typographical aids
E. Previewing
F. Flexibility
V. Appreciation Skills
A. Language of literature
B. Forms of literature

This skills outline does suggest that there is continuity and sequence in reading development. It is not always possible to determine exact sequences for there is interaction among skills. However, we can in a general way decide what it is we have to teach first before exposing children to other learning tasks. For example, it would hardly make sense to concentrate on inferred meanings if children had difficulty with literal meanings, or to try to teach children to use respellings in the dictionary if they had not learned letter-sound relationships. Knowledge of one depends upon understanding of another.

Note that one category is labeled Study Skills. This is not to suggest that the other reading skills are not needed for study. Of course, they are. But over and beyond word recognition, word meaning, and comprehension skills are other skills which are particularly relevant to the reading and study of informational-type materials associated with content areas. This is why the latter skills have been placed in a separate category.

Teachers become involved with appreciation when they teach children how to read literature. Children need all their word and comprehension skills for appreciation. In addition, they have to understand literary language and style, for it is these elements which help to convey meaning and mood. Reading for appreciation is one important aspect of a total reading program and exerts beneficial influences upon another—reading for enjoyment.

Reading for enjoyment is an important component of a total reading program as well as one expected outcome of teaching reading. Time within the school day is set aside for engaging in a variety of experiences which hopefully will lead to more recreational reading. It is apparent children cannot enjoy reading unless they have learned skills well enough to allow them to read easily. So we concentrate our efforts on building, refining, and extending reading skills in every grade, not merely to help children use reading as a tool for gathering information but as a means of fulfilling a basic need. Pleasurable moments can be enjoyed through reading. One of our tasks is to make them possible.

SUMMARY

1. There is a need to improve the quality of reading instruction in our elementary schools. Too many children fail to learn to read well enough to meet the ordinary demands of the elementary curriculum and enjoy reading as one leisure-type activity. Reading instruction may be improved by applying the knowledge that has been gained from research and demonstrations in reading, learning principles, and such allied disciplines as linguistics and psycholinguistics.
2. Some children enter kindergarten and first grade with varying degrees of reading ability. There does not seem to be any reason for withholding reading instruction from five- to six-year-olds who have already learned some reading skills or who show a real interest in learning to read. Instruction can be discontinued if children lose interest in formal reading activities.
3. The findings of the twenty-seven First Grade Studies did not reveal consistent, marked superiority of one reading system or program over another. There were indications, however, that basal reading with strong word-attack programs produced superior results in word recognition. Since many of the systems and programs tested appeared to have validity and produced more favorable results in some aspects of reading than others, combinations of approaches, e.g., basal reading and language experience, seem better suited to children than single approaches alone. Teacher competence and pupil characteristics appeared to be significant factors in determining the results. The results of other studies on beginning reading are also mixed, although they give support to the idea that teachers should take the best of each practice and include all in their instructional programs.
4. There are advantages to having children engage in basal reading and individualized reading. Individualized reading seems to foster favorable attitudes toward books while basal reading programs offer systematic skills instruction. Children can profit from individual and group instruction if their learning requirements are met. No organizational plan can insure reading success; a knowledgeable teacher uses different forms of organization as conditions warrant them to achieve his reading goals.
5. General reading ability is needed to read in the content fields. Specialized reading skills for some subjects are needed too. There-

fore, reading instruction in the middle grades should provide for further development of basic reading skills and introduction of others associated with reading subject materials.

6. Flexibility in reading is a more useful concept than reading speed. Children have to learn to vary their styles of reading in accordance with their purposes for reading and the nature of the materials.

7. The reading interests of children change as they become older and grow in reading. Differences in reading preferences at a given age seem to be influenced more by sex than intelligence or other factors. One way to encourage children to read widely is by providing them with a range of materials which appeal to their diverse tastes and interests.

8. The cognition studies of Piaget and others have some implications for the teaching of reading. Teachers should move from concrete examples to abstract ideas in helping children understand the concepts found in reading materials. They should develop sequences in structuring lessons designed to help children progress from literal reading to inferential and evaluative reading. They need to establish conditions which will permit children to discover relationships among ideas and to make generalizations, rather than tell children what these generalizations and relationships are.

9. There is evidence that some children can process information better through one modality than another. This suggests that teachers offer auditory, visual, and kinesthetic experiences in helping children learn to read. Other research in learning lends support to practices which stress readiness for engaging in reading activities through preparation for them and selection of materials of appropriate difficulty.

10. The science of linguistics reveals information about the phonemic and grammatical structures of language. Teachers might use this knowledge in helping children understand sound-letter relationships and recognize structural clues to meaning.

11. Innovations and changes in reading programs should be judged on their merits and not by their newness or unique character. The content of some basal readers has been modified to reflect social changes and the learning needs of children. Efforts to maintain consistency in sound-letter relationships have led to the introduction of modified alphabets, color-coded alphabets, and uniform spelling patterns. A much heavier emphasis on the decoding process is evident in beginning reading instruction. Some schools have introduced electronic devices which combine visual and auditory presentations of reading materials and skills instruction. Programed skills lessons designed for machine and book presentations are supplementing and in some cases replacing current instructional reading programs.

12. A comprehensive reading curriculum contains provisions for developing basic reading skills, teaching children how to use reading as a learning tool, fostering an appreciation of literature, and building permanent interests in reading. These objectives may be achieved

through appropriate learning experiences involving the development of reading skills, habits, and attitudes.

STUDY QUESTIONS AND EXERCISES

1. How might we account for the fact that in spite of the progress this country has made in social development, medicine, science, and technology, many of its children still fail to learn to read adequately?
2. What conclusions, though possibly tentative, might be drawn from the findings of research on preschool and kindergarten reading?
3. What were the results of the First Grade Study and other studies on primary reading? What do they imply for teachers of reading?
4. Why is it important to continue reading instruction into the middle grades?
5. "Explanations of the reading process are quite different from descriptions of the reading act." Explain this statement.
6. What influences have developments in language and learning had upon the teaching of reading?
7. Indicate how innovation and change have affected the methods and materials of teaching reading. What cautions do such innovations and changes suggest?
8. "The teacher must be concerned with the past and future, with the *vertical* aspects of a child's reading development. . . ." Explain how a reading curriculum founded upon this principle differs from one which stresses reading achievement grade by grade.

SUGGESTIONS FOR FURTHER READING

Students who wish more information about the status and nature of reading instruction throughout the nation should refer to M. Austin and C. Morrison, *The First R—The Harvard Report on Reading in Elementary Schools*. New York: The Macmillan Company, 1963.

Brief reports by the investigators of the twenty-seven First Grade Studies are compiled by R. Stauffer in *The First Grade Reading Studies*. Newark, Del.: International Reading Association, 1967.

For a comprehensive discussion of learning theory and its application to education see E. R. Hilgard, ed., *Theories of Learning and Instruction* (Sixty-Third Yearbook of the National Society for the Study of Education, Part I). Chicago: University of Chicago Press, 1964.

For a brief but fairly comprehensive discussion of linguistics and psycholinguistics and their application to reading see K. S. Goodman and J. T. Fleming, eds., *Psycholinguistics and the Teaching of Reading*. Newark, Del.: International Reading Association, 1969.

Two volumes published by the International Reading Association deal with trends and innovations in reading: N. B. Smith, ed., *Current Issues in Reading*, 1969 and E. C. Vilscek, ed., *A Decade of Innovations*, 1968; also see H. A. Robinson, ed., *Reading: Seventy-Five Years of Progress*, Proceedings of the Annual Conference on Reading. Chicago: University of Chicago Press, 1966.

2

Diagnostic Teaching of Reading

■ *The best materials and the wisest methods lose their effectiveness when we know too little about the reading of our pupils. . . .*[1]

There was a time, not too many decades ago, when reading was viewed mainly as the ability to recognize what words said. This is one reason why so much oral reading was stressed in schools. Perhaps even some of you were in classes where children took turns reading aloud not merely from readers but also from social studies and science textbooks. "Read with expression" was a reminder you may remember very well. Usually this oral reading was followed by some questions which the reader or others were expected to answer. These questions rarely challenged children's thinking; if anything, it was their ability to remember rather insignificant details that was tested.

This simplistic attitude toward reading left its imprint upon most programs. Reading activities in the primary grades consisted mainly of sounding out words and reading orally. Many children learned to do both quite well. There were other children who fared less well and who repeated one or more years experiencing much of the same teaching. Oral reading continued into the higher grades but here children were expected to read silently too. Almost all of the silent reading was of the "read these pages" variety followed by questions which children answered orally or in writing. The purpose of any discussion was to test rather than to illuminate. Children were expected to complete their reading assignments, and those who did not or could not received low grades. Two con-

---

[1] William K. Durr, ed., *Reading Instruction: Dimensions and Issues.* Boston: Houghton Mifflin Company, 1967, p. 311.

ditions were common: although children spent much time reading and answering questions in school and at home, they did not receive much help in *how* to do their reading; furthermore, all children were expected to read the same materials and complete the same assignments. Teachers made few allowances for differences in reading ability.

Testing under these learning conditions was at best only a means of grading children's performances. The results of weekly tests, which were so common in those days, gave teachers evidence of how well children learned and remembered the work and served as a basis for grading them. Successful performances were rewarded with high grades and failing efforts with low ones. Children took reading tests too, and the scores were duly recorded. The results were treated no differently from others—children were identified as superior readers or less able readers. Rarely did teachers see the test papers after they were marked; in fact, some schools had teachers score the tests of children in other classes and not their own. We can justify these procedures if we are satisfied that the tests yield reliable and valid results and our purpose is solely to assign grades.

We have defined the goals of reading programs in operational terms by identifying the areas on which teachers need to focus attention. The kind and amount of reading growth children achieve is proportional to the degree to which teachers manage to translate the objectives into learning tasks and guide children in mastering them. Teachers who operate within this framework will view the functions of testing much differently from those whose main concern is to grade pupils.

Let's examine the problems of a typical fourth-grade teacher who has thirty children in her new class. She has some understanding of what kinds of reading experiences these children have had in the first, second, and third grade. She also knows what new experiences she should offer the children to help them grow in reading, for her principal has provided her with a curriculum guide which spells out the reading objectives for the elementary program. "This is pretty simple," she thinks. "If I concentrate on these objectives—ability in word attack and word meaning, comprehension and appreciation, study skills, and on reading interests, I'll have it made."

But then she stops and realizes that it isn't all that simple. She wonders about the reading achievement of the children in the class. How well does each one read? How many of them are reading below, at, and above grade level? How far have they progressed in achieving each of the reading objectives? She knows that the answers to these questions will have a bearing on what kinds of reading instruction she must offer and what kinds of reading materials she will need.

To think about the children as this teacher has is to move away from a teacher-oriented program toward a learner-oriented program. The former operates on the assumption that there is a body of knowledge and skills that should be learned in a given grade. It assumes also that children must accommodate to its requirements. Failure to do so is the children's and not the teacher's problem. Each grade has its own set of books; to use any intended for another grade upsets the continuity of the program. So all children must do the best they can with the materials given them.

A reading program with a focus on the learner is based upon different assumptions. Learning to read is a continuous process, and it is as unrealistic to expect all children in an age group to reach the same level of reading achievement as it is for them to acquire identical proficiency in swimming or any other activity. Teachers take children from where they are and not from where they think they should be. Not all children are ready to learn from books intended for a given grade. They may be so difficult as to become frustrating and interfere with learning. Some pupils have progressed so far that these books are too simple and offer no challenge.

These, then, are some of the considerations that prompted our teacher to ask the questions she did. There was an additional insight which led her to doubt the wisdom of her original judgment. She realized that it was not enough to know that children were weak or strong in this or that aspect of reading. She had to direct her teaching toward specific rather than general requirements. "Shotgun" instruction might find its mark; she preferred to set her sights on some limited targets which needed attention. Successful outcomes would depend less on chance and more on her knowledge about children's reading.

IDEAS FOR DISCUSSION

Diagnostic teaching benefits children who are making satisfactory progress in reading. Teachers can anticipate superior results as they work with children who are experiencing difficulties in learning to read if there is a positive relationship between the problems and the remedies. Inherent in the concept of diagnostic teaching is the idea that evaluation is an on-going activity as long as instruction continues. The teacher formulates plans from the information he acquires about his pupils. But he knows as he teaches them he will receive new data. It is not unlikely he will have to modify his practices in order to satisfy the children's current learning needs. Occasionally he may have to revise them drastically.

This need for continuing evaluation raises questions about the initial effort to obtain information about the children's reading. How extensive should the analysis be? Should many different tests be administered to children before instruction begins? There are differences of opinion about these matters but it seems reasonable to suggest a middle course. Instead of spending many hours testing children's reading, teachers can take the time to find out where on the reading ladder children are and what some of their reading needs might be. Although this information is incomplete and possibly somewhat inaccurate, it can be used to plan early reading lessons. As teachers work with children, they will confirm and revise their initial judgments and note new behaviors that affect their reading plans. These practices are so much better than hit-or-miss, trial-and-error teaching.

Teachers can appraise children's reading by using standardized tests and informal measures. Each form of appraisal provides information that may be useful in assessing how well children are doing and planning activities for them.

Standardized Reading Tests

Many schools administer achievement tests to children periodically to find out how well they are doing. These tests might be given every year or every two or three years, depending upon the reasons schools have for testing children. There is a growing tendency toward more testing which is not limited to local populations. Presently underway is the National Assessment Project, in which school districts are participating on a voluntary basis. Insofar as younger students are concerned, the plan is to test nine- and thirteen-year-olds in different subjects and skills to find out how much and how well they are learning. Reading is one of the areas that will be measured. Although the directors of the project disclaim any intention of comparing the achievements of children, there is some uneasiness in educational circles about the ways in which test results might be interpreted.

Standardized reading tests yield objective data about reading performance. Ideally, they are designed in such a way that responses to test items are not subject to different interpretations. Authors of these tests sample large populations that are representative of children generally in order to determine the appropriateness of test items and establish reading norms. They seek to verify the validity and reliability of test results so that schools can be confident the tests measure what they are supposed to measure and that the results do not vary significantly if the same test is taken more than once. Equivalent forms are available for most standardized reading tests. To what extent the tests achieve their objectives will be discussed later.

Uses of Standardized Reading Tests

The results of more commonly used reading tests show in a general way how well children are reading. By examining pupils' grade placement

Grade Scores*	No. of Children
7.0–7.9	1
6.0–6.9	2
5.0–5.9	4
4.0–4.9	17
3.0–3.9	3
2.0–2.9	1
	N=28

* A grade score of 4.6 represents the average achievement made by the population used to standardize the test in the sixth month of the fourth grade. Raw scores are converted to grade scores by tables that accompany tests. A raw score of 30 may be equivalent to 4.6, a raw score of 34 to 4.9, and so on.

scores the teacher obtains a general impression of their reading achievement. He can group these scores to obtain some indications of the *range of reading achievement in his class.*

The distribution shown below approximates what the range of reading scores for a fourth grade class might be.

A cursory examination of this distribution shows that four children are reading "below" grade level, seventeen are at grade level, and seven are reading "above" grade level. It would not, however, be accurate to say that the seven above-average readers are reading as well as fifth, sixth, or seventh graders or that the four below-average readers are reading as well as second or third graders. The scores these children obtained are frequently extrapolations and are not based upon the reading performances of children in all the grades. But a teacher who has this information at the beginning of the school year knows that he must make provisions for individual differences.

Besides obtaining this general impression of his class's reading achievement the teacher can *compare these results with the performance of the general population.* He can determine how well his children are reading when compared to other children in the nation. If the majority of children in a class is reading less well than the average of the general population, he will try to find out why. Perhaps the school's reading program does not offer instruction in the areas covered by the test or is weak by any standards. The children in the sample population might be quite different from the children in his class. Whatever the explanation, the teacher will be alerted to a condition which requires study.

Knowledge of grade placement scores can help the teacher *group children for instruction.* A distribution such as the one above will enable him to place children of comparable achievement together. Teachers can form initial groups on the basis of these achievement levels and make necessary adjustments as they work with the pupils. The number of groups a teacher might form will vary with his ability to provide meaningful instruction for each.

Reading test scores may be used as *rough indicators of growth* for groups and individuals. If a reasonable interval of time has elapsed between the administration of two forms of the same test, growth in reading of the kind required of children can be noted by comparing the grade placement scores. If, for example, a group of children had an average grade placement score of 4.3 at the beginning of the school year and obtained a score of 5.6 on the second test at the end of the year, we can conclude that insofar as the test is concerned the pupils have grown in reading. It would not be completely accurate to subtract the first score from the second and say that 1.3 years of reading growth has occurred, although the practice is quite common. If we accept the test as a device that measures reading achievement, we can say that the children have improved in reading.

The results of standardized tests are expressed as grade scores. However, these scores do not reveal how children perform on specific reading tasks unless there are subscores for test components. Many reading tests designed for elementary children consist of two or more sections, such as word recognition, word meaning, comprehension, and so on. These tests yield separate grade placement scores for each section. A wise teacher will not merely be concerned with the total score but will want to know how it was obtained. Thus he can determine if the pupils are equally strong in all areas tested or if some pupils are stronger in one area than another. Two children may have the same grade score but obtain it in different ways:

	Child A	Child B
Word Recognition	2.5	4.5
Word Meaning	3.6	2.2
Comprehension	4.5	2.9
Total	3.5+	3.5+

This first analysis may indicate which children need more help in one or more areas. A more careful examination of the composition of the test items and the children's responses to them might provide the teacher with information about their specific reading requirements. Some reading tests which are presumably diagnostic identify the subskills so that teachers can categorize the children's responses. Most reading tests are not sufficiently refined to enable teachers to make this analysis easily. But more can be learned from the children's responses to test items than we have been aware of in the past. One way to do this is to sit down with children and go over the test items with them. Perhaps they can explain how they made their responses. It is possible that even correct responses were reached in inappropriate ways or that children guessed many of the answers. Teachers may be able to discern patterns of errors by comparing similar test items and responses. Standardized reading tests suffer from real weaknesses, but their impact would be lessened if teachers used them with more understanding.

Types of Standardized Reading Tests

There are different types of reading tests. One type is the survey test, which provides general information about reading ability and an estimate of reading level. Diagnostic tests are supposed to uncover with great accuracy specific reading strengths and weaknesses. Some diagnostic tests cover several aspects of reading while others are more specialized and limited to one or two. It is difficult to distinguish between some survey and diagnostic tests because they are similar in design.

Survey and diagnostic tests may measure either silent reading or oral reading. A test intended to be read silently cannot be used to check oral reading if grade norms are to be assigned. Survey-type oral reading tests consist of a series of selections. The oral reading of each selection is timed by the examiner and the reader orally answers questions based upon the selection. Scores may be computed for oral reading and comprehension. Silent reading tests, whether of the survey or diagnostic type, are generally timed also.

There are a few study skills tests intended for elementary pupils. These tests measure such skills as map reading, using an index, and understanding charts. Other tests measure speed of reading, but these are intended for high school and college students. Some reading tests intended for use at lower levels contain a section that does measure reading speed.

Lists of representative elementary reading and study skills tests, the grades for which they are intended, and abilities measured by them follow.

SURVEY READING TESTS

Burnett Reading Series: Survey Test. Scholastic Testing Service. Grades 1.5–2.4, 2.5–3.9, 4.0–6.9, 7.0–9.9, 10.0–12.9. Word identification, word meaning, comprehension.

California Reading Test. California Test Bureau. Grades 1–2, 2.5–4.5, 4–6, 7–9, 9–14. Vocabulary, comprehension.

Developmental Reading Tests. Lyons & Carnahan. Grades 1–2.5, 2.5–3, 4–6. Vocabulary, general comprehension, specific comprehension for grades 1–2.5 and 2.5–3; basic vocabulary, reading to retain information, to organize, to evaluate, to appreciate for 4–6.

Gates-MacGinitie Reading Tests. Teachers College Press, Columbia University. Grades 1, 2, 3, 2–3, 4–6, 7–9. Vocabulary and comprehension for grades 1, 2, 3, 2–3; speed and accuracy for 2–3; speed and accuracy, vocabulary, comprehension for 4–6.

Iowa Silent Reading Tests. Harcourt Brace Jovanovich, Inc. Grades 4–8, 9–14. Rate, comprehension, directed reading, word meaning, paragraph comprehension, sentence meaning, alphabetizing, index.

Metropolitan Achievement Tests: Reading. Harcourt Brace Jovanovich, Inc. Grades 2, 3–4, 5–6, 7–9. Word knowledge, word discrimination (grade 2), reading.

Sequential Tests of Educational Progress: Reading. Cooperative Test Division, Educational Testing Service. Grades 4–6, 7–9, 10–12, 13–14. Comprehension.

Silent Reading Comprehension: Iowa Every-Pupil Test of Basic Skills, Test A. Houghton Mifflin. Grades 3–5, 5–9. Comprehension, vocabulary.

S.R.A. Achievement Series: Reading. Science Research Associates. Grades 1–2, 2–4, 3–4, 4–9. Verbal-Pictorial association, language perception, comprehension, and vocabulary for grades 1–2; comprehension and vocabulary for grades 2–4, 3–4, 4–9.

Stanford Achievement Test: Reading Tests. Harcourt Brace Jovanovich, Inc. Grades 1.5–2.5, 2.5–4.0, 4–5.5, 5.5–6.9, 7–9. Word meaning, paragraph meaning, word study skills for grades 1.5–2.5, 2.5–4.0; word meaning, paragraph meaning for grades 4–5.5, 5.5–6.9.

DIAGNOSTIC READING TESTS

Botel Reading Inventory. Follett Publishing Co. Grades 1–12. Independent, instructional, expectancy, and frustration reading levels.

Diagnostic Reading Scales. California Test Bureau. Grades 1–8. Word recognition, instructional level (oral reading), independent level (silent reading), rate of silent reading, potential level (auditory comprehension), phonics.

Diagnostic Reading Tests. Committee on Diagnostic Reading Tests, Inc. Grades 1, 2, 3–4, 4–8, 7–13. Visual discrimination, auditory discrimination, vocabulary for grade 1; word recognition, comprehension for grades 2, 3–4, 4–8; word attack (oral) for grades 1–8.

Doren Diagnostic Reading Test of Word Recognition Skills. American Guidance Service, Inc., Grades 1–9. Letter recognition, beginning sounds, whole word recognition, words within words, speech consonants, ending sounds, blending, rhyming, vowels, sight words, discriminate guessing.

Durrell Analysis of Reading Difficulty. Harcourt Brace Jovanovich, Inc. Grades 1–6. Oral reading, silent reading, comprehension, listening, word recognition, phonics.

Gates-McKillop Reading Diagnostic Tests. Teachers College Press, Columbia University. Grades 2–6. Oral Reading, phonics, syllabication.

McCullough Word-Analysis Tests. Ginn and Co. Grades 4–6. Phonics, structural analysis.

Reading Versatility Test. Educational Developmental Laboratories. Grades 5–8, 6–10, 8–12, 12–16. Rate, comprehension, skimming, scanning.

Roswell-Chall Auditory Blending Test. Essay Press. Grades 1–4. Phonics, syllabication.

Stanford Diagnostic Reading Test. Harcourt Brace Jovanovich, Inc. Grades 2.5–4.5, 4.5–8.5. Comprehension, vocabulary, auditory discrimination, syllabication, phonics for grades 2.5–4.5; comprehension, vocabulary, syllabication, phonics, rate for grades 4.5–8.5.

Student Progress Individual Reading Evaluation. New Dimensions in Education. Grades 1–6. Word recognition, retention, comprehension.

ORAL READING TESTS

Gilmore Oral Reading Test. Harcourt Brace Jovanovich, Inc. Grades 1–8. Accuracy, comprehension, rate.

Gray Oral Reading Test. The Bobbs-Merrill Co., Inc. Grades 1–16. Accuracy, comprehension.

STUDY SKILLS TESTS

S.R.A. Achievement Series: Work-Study Skills. Science Research Associates. Grades 4–6, 6–9. References, charts.

Work-Study Skills: Iowa Every-Pupil Test of Basic Skills, Test B. Houghton Mifflin Co. Grades 3–5, 5–9. Map reading, use of references, index and dictionary, alphabetizing (grades 3–5), graphing (grades 5–9).

Many reading tests use similar techniques for assessing different reading skills. At the earliest levels of reading some tests attempt to measure a child's ability to recognize words by presenting a picture of an object or activity and expecting him to underline or draw a circle around one of four words which matches the picture. This same procedure with a slight variation may be followed in measuring comprehension. Here the child is asked to read a sentence or a paragraph which may require him to follow its instructions, answer questions, or respond to the statements. He is expected to mark the picture which indicates his response.

A.	did	egg
	dog	two
B.	bed	swim
	milk	fly

COMPREHENSION SAMPLES [3]

A. Where is the baby?

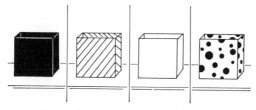

B. The white box is on the shelf.

[2] *Source:* Reprinted with the permission of the publisher from Gates-MacGinitie's Reading Tests (A Form 1) (New York: Teachers College Press), copyright © 1964.
[3] *Ibid.*

At higher levels several reading tests measure a child's knowledge of vocabulary and different aspects of comprehension. Vocabulary knowledge is tested by presenting a word alone or in context followed by four or five words. The child has to underline or circle one of the words which means the same or nearly the same as the first word. Here are a few examples of this type of test:

1. *animal*   a) house b) deer   c) money d) hat
2. *clothing*   a) chair b) paper c) suit   d) basket
3. *intelligence* a) large b) dark   c) happy d) clever

Comprehension is measured usually by presenting passages of one or more paragraphs and either asking a question or making an incomplete statement about the contents. Children are expected to respond to the question or complete the statement by selecting the correct answer from three or four choices that are provided them.

Part IV. Reading for Interpretation[4]

Directions: Read the paragraph. Then read the first statement under the paragraph. Draw a line under the word or phrase that best completes the statement. (If using a separate answer sheet, fill in the space which has the same letter as the answer you select.)

Jim and Jack had a quarter to buy supplies. Jim thought that a tablet was the best way to buy paper. Jack liked to buy paper for his notebook. Each boy bought two pencils and the paper he thought was best.

F. The best name for this story is _____.
a) School Starts   b) Pencils
c) Buying Supplies d) Jack

G. The boys had different opinions about

_____
a) money   b) paper
c) pencils   d) school

When your teacher tells you to begin, do the rest of the test as you did the sample. Do the paragraphs in order. Try to answer all of the questions that go with each paragraph before going on to the next paragraph.

4 *Source:* Reprinted with permission of the publisher from *New Developmental Reading Tests,* Intermediate Level, Bond, et al., copyright © 1968 by Lyons and Carnahan, Educational Division, Meredith Corporation.

Some reading tests which sample a number of different skills include a profile that the teacher completes for each child. This graphic representation permits the teacher to identify pupils' reading strengths and weaknesses quickly and make plans for dealing with them on an individual or group basis. A few reading tests provide an analysis of test items in table form. This analysis aids the teacher in classifying types of reading with which children are having difficulty. A teacher can obtain this information if the test doesn't provide it by studying each section and its parts and identifying the skills areas covered by them.

Problems in Using Standardized Reading Tests

If standardized reading tests are understood and their results properly interpreted, they can be of help in assisting teachers plan for reading instruction. But they have their limitations, and teachers should be aware of what they are.

Which standardized reading test should schools select? Is the test equally *appropriate* for all groups of children? These are questions which schools should seek answers for. A test is inappropriate if the sample population used to standardize the test is significantly different from the population for whom it is intended. There have been instances in which a group of children were known to be readers of average achievement but scored far above their reading ability on a test. Examiners discovered that the sample population as a group were poorer readers than might be expected; the

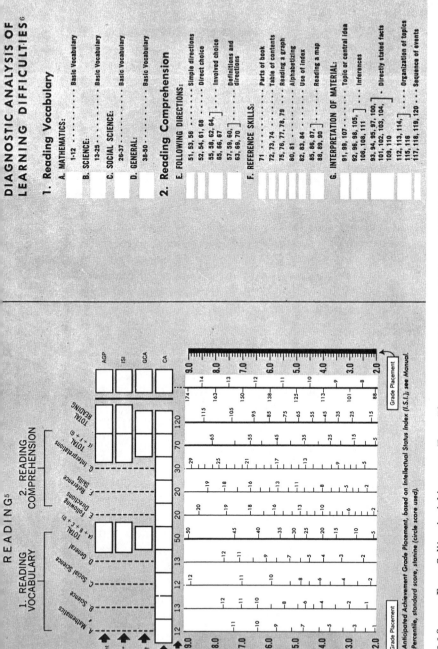

5-6 Source: From California Achievement Tests, Elementary Level, by Ernest Tiegs and Willis W. Clark. Copyright © 1963 by McGraw-Hill Inc. Used by permission of the publisher, CTB/McGraw-Hill, Monterey, California.

sample was not representative of the population as a whole. By comparison, the readers of average ability scored so much higher than the sample population that they obtained inflated grade scores. Test manuals should contain information about the way in which the sample population is selected and what its character is, i.e., from what geographical areas and socioeconomic groups it is drawn. Grade scores based on the performance of a unique group of children may not be appropriate for typical groups of children.

Another factor related to the selection of reading tests is their *content*. Does the reading test cover skills children have been taught? It wouldn't be realistic to expect most children to respond well to items that were unfamiliar to them. How many different skills do the test items sample? Children who participated in a comprehensive program would be penalized if the reading test was narrow in scope. Many of them are.

A related question involves the test's *reliability and validity*. How much confidence can we place in the stability of the results? Will successive testings yield similar scores? Many reading tests report high reliability coefficients, but those which provide no information about reliability should be questioned. Perhaps a more important issue involves validity: the extent to which a test measures what it says it measures. Does a vocabulary test measure word meaning? It may, but if children are expected to read the words themselves, then the ability to recognize words becomes a factor. If the teacher were to read the words, poorer readers might score much higher on this test. Does a test that limits its questions to literal meaning truly measure comprehension? Comprehension involves inferential meaning as well. Tests which sample but one kind of comprehension surely are not as valid as tests which measure several types.

Most reading tests require from thirty minutes to one hour to complete. Tests of such short *duration* cannot possibly sample many different skills nor can they include more than a few items covering any one skill. Thus, many reading tests at best must be viewed as gross instruments. Schools would have to administer several different tests in order to partially overcome this shortcoming. However, they would have to be selected with great care since there is overlap among them and the same skills might be covered in the same way.

It is doubtful that the results of standardized tests can be accepted with great confidence. There is a body of evidence which demonstrates that the scores place children at a level higher than their ability to read indicates.[7] Teachers should not assume that the grade score and basal reader levels are comparable. Some investigators found that the grade score represented the child's frustration level insofar as reading books was concerned. The

---

[7] Robert McCracken, "Standardized Reading Tests and Informal Reading Inventories," *Education, 82* (February, 1962), pp. 366–69; Edward Sipay, "A Comparison of Standardized Reading Scores and Functional Reading Levels," *The Reading Teacher, 17* (January, 1964), pp. 265–68; Joanne Williams, *A Comparison of Reading Test Scores and Reading Inventory Scores.* Unpublished Doctoral Dissertation, Southern Illinois University, 1963.

discrepancy between grade scores and what level books children can read profitably is usually even greater for those who are having difficulty with reading. Furthermore, grade scores at the lower and upper ends within a range of possible scores are not as valid as those which fall in the middle. These weaknesses are due to problems of test construction and statistical treatments. Tests which cover many grades suffer more from this weakness than those intended for one or two.

We should recognize that the *kinds of reading* that tests require are not the same as those children engage in. Tests do not demand the sustained reading children do in school or elsewhere. It is one thing to understand a single paragraph and another to react suitably to several pages of material. Children ordinarily do not read words in isolation nor do they have to read under timed conditions which do not allow for much flexibility. Reading tests offer approximations of how well groups of children read, and values they don't possess should not be ascribed to them.

Teachers may use standardized reading tests if they understand what their limitations are and are able to interpret their results. The tests permit us to speak with some objectivity about the reading achievement of groups of children as well as provide us with some reading goals that specialists believe should be part of the reading program.

Informal Reading Tests

Teachers know that they cannot rely completely on standardized instruments even though test publishers strive to make them as precise as possible. Their experiences in teaching reading confirm some of the doubts they have about the accuracy of test scores and the diagnostic quality of test items. Teachers are depending more and more on their own evaluations of children's reading. This does not mean they merely observe children read and in haphazard fashion decide what their reading instruction ought to be. Instead, they follow fairly well-established procedures to find out how well their pupils are reading and plan their programs accordingly.

Values of Informal Reading Tests

There is a major difference between informal reading tests and standardized reading tests. The latter base evaluations of children's reading on the performances of a sample population, while informal reading tests are concerned only with the reading performances of the children who are being evaluated. The term "informal" suggests nonstandardized procedures for constructing, administering, and scoring tests—although efforts have been made to regularize the processes. Not unlike standardized tests, informal tests are not "good" in and of themselves. Their quality and effectiveness will vary with one's understanding of how they may be used to assess children's reading.

Informal reading tests do not yield a grade placement score. They do help us to identify four reading achievement levels: *independent, instruc-*

tional, frustration and *expectancy*. These levels are related to the materials children read themselves rather than to the test performance of another group. When a child is reading at his *independent* level, his fluency and comprehension are high. There is little in the material that he cannot manage himself. The *instructional* level is the book level at which a child might be taught. His ability to read and understand the material at this level is not as high as at his independent level. If a child's reading drops significantly below what it is at the instructional level, the material is too difficult to be used for instruction, and we say he is reading at his *frustration* level. *Expectancy* levels are mainly established for children who are having real difficulties in reading. This would be the highest level at which a child could comprehend satisfactorily were he able to read the material for himself.

As a result of some experimentation and empirical evidence, there are criteria for identifying reading levels. These criteria are intended to serve as guides and are not to be taken as absolute standards that children must

INFORMAL READING ACHIEVEMENT STANDARDS*

Level	Word Recognition	Literal Comprehension	Inferential Comprehension	Vocabulary
Independent Level	99%–100%	90%–100%	90%	100%
Instructional Level	90%–95%	80%–90%	70%	90%
Frustration Level	Below 90%	Below 70%	Below 60%	Below 80%
Expectancy Level	———	Same as instructional level		

* There is no complete agreement on the percentages children should attain for each of the components at any of the levels. Some reading specialists, for example, expect children to achieve at least 95% in word rcognition for the instructional level. Others believe that children can profit from instruction through materials in which they can recognize fewer than 90% of the words.

meet in order to qualify at one level or another. A child might fall slightly below a standard and still be able to profit from instruction at that level. What should be avoided are significant departures from the criteria. To use a book with a child who does not know the meaning of many of its words would not be fruitful. The same would be true of a child who can't recognize most of the words readily.

A child would meet the criteria for any level if he approximately achieved the percentages for each reading category. Thus the highest level at which he could recognize from 99 to 100 per cent of the words, comprehend from 90 to 100 per cent of the literal meaning, make inferences with 90 per cent accuracy and know the meaning of 100 per cent of the words would be his *independent* level.

The highest level at which he could identify from 90 to 95 per cent of the words, comprehend 80 to 90 per cent of the literal meaning, make inferences with 70 per cent accuracy and know the meaning of 90 per cent of the words would be his *instructional* level.

If the child fell significantly below any of the instruction level standards in any category, he would have reached his *frustration* level.

The standards for *expectancy* level are the same as for instructional level except that no criteria for word recognition will have been met. The material is read to the child and he responds to the content in the same way as he did at other levels.

There is one other consideration that should be taken into account as children's reading is evaluated: the way in which they read orally and silently. A child may meet the criterion for word recognition but read very haltingly. He might require two or three times as many minutes to complete reading the selection as other children. The length of time he took would be one indication of how difficult the material was for him. Children in book levels that correspond to grades one, two, and three can be expected to read from 60 to 100 words per minute orally. The silent reading rate might be slightly higher at second and third book levels. Children at middle grade levels may be expected to read somewhat faster—from 100 to 150 words per minute orally and from 120–200 words silently. Children whose sight vocabularies and word-attack skills are not well developed will not be able to read as rapidly as these standards suggest. Their independent and instructional reading levels might be lower than ones determined solely on the criteria of accuracy in word recognition, literal and inferential reading, and vocabulary.

In addition to establishing reading levels, informal reading tests can be used to *assess different reading skills.* Oral reading, comprehension, word recognition, study skills—there really is no limit to the reading areas and specific components that can be sampled. Typical tests designed for classroom use will not be as extensive and precise as those that might be required for remedial or clinical evaluations. Teachers will determine how deeply they must probe in order to answer questions about the reading performances of their pupils.

Administration of Informal Reading Tests

The first task which teachers should undertake is the preparation of tests to *establish children's reading levels.* There is no reason why a group of teachers cannot prepare them cooperatively. Since the tests will be used at each grade level, a committee of teachers representing all grades can be formed for this purpose. The results might be duplicated and distributed to each teacher in the school.

Since most schools follow basal reading programs, tests are developed from their graded series of readers. Tests for other graded series in science or social studies might be prepared also if teachers wish to find out if children's reading levels were comparable for both kinds of books.

Step 1 Select *two* representative excerpts from the middle portion of *each* book in the series. One excerpt is for oral reading and the other is for silent reading. Each excerpt should contain approximately 100–200 words for primary levels and from 250–400 words for higher levels. Record

A Baby in the House [8] (255 words)

It was a cold, winter afternoon.
The snow that fell was mixed with
rain, and so Pat stayed in the house.
When a car came up the street,
Pat jumped up and looked out.
But it was not his father's car.

"He will come home before long,"
said the woman who sat with Pat.
"When he comes, he will tell you."

It was dark when Father came home.
He went to Pat and picked him up.
"Pat, old boy, I have a surprise
for you!" said Father.

"Is it a boy?" asked Pat.

"No, a girl!" said Father.
"We have a little baby girl.
Her name is Pam."

A girl! That was something for Pat
to think about.
He had wished and wished for a boy.
Just thinking about a baby girl
made him mad.

[8] *Source:* From *Together We Go* by Elizabeth K. Cooper, copyright © 1970 by Harcourt Brace Jovanovich, Inc. and reprinted with their permission. (Continued on next page.)

the exact number of words in each excerpt. An excerpt may be a portion of a selection, but be certain to terminate it at a natural point in the story.

Step 2 For each excerpt prepare five questions which measure literal understanding and five questions which test inferential reading. In addition, select five words in context to test word meaning. These words should represent more advanced vocabulary in the excerpt.

Reading specialists agree on the fundamental design of these informal tests but may differ in specifics. Some would reduce or increase the length of excerpts while others might recommend fewer or more questions.

Two excerpts drawn from different level books follow. One represents the first-reader level, the other the fifth-reader level.

LITERAL QUESTIONS:
1. For whom was Pat waiting?
2. Why wasn't he outside playing while his father was away?
3. How did Pat's friend know he was unhappy?

In four days, Pat's mother came home with the baby.
On that day, Pat and his friend played together in the snow.

"You look mad," said Pat's friend.

"I am mad," said Pat.
"Mom came home with the baby this morning.
Who needs a baby girl around?"

"Oh, a baby girl is not so bad!" said the friend.
"All I have is a dog."

"I wish I had a dog," said Pat.
"I'll trade the baby for your dog."

"You can't do that," said Pat's friend.
"But I'll tell you what.
You can live at my house so you won't have to stay around her."

"Good," Pat said as he began to run.
"I'll go home and get my things."

When Pat got home, his mother was in the kitchen.
She was mixing milk for the baby.
In the next room, the baby cried.

4. What did the friend think of Pat's idea to get rid of the baby?
5. What idea did the friend give Pat?

INFERENTIAL QUESTIONS:
1. How did Pat feel as he waited for his father to return home?
2. Why did the news about his new baby sister make Pat mad?
3. Where had Pat's mother and baby sister been?
4. How did Pat's friend feel about the new baby?
5. How do you think this story will end? Why?

VOCABULARY:
1. snow that fell
2. woman who sat with Pat
3. "Pat, old boy"
4. made him mad
5. I'll trade the baby

9 (409 words)

DISCOVERIES COME FIRST

The prehistoric man who first used a rock as a weapon didn't really invent anything; he made a discovery. He discovered that a stone held in the hand did more than protect his hand from injury; it also increased the power of his blow. A stone is harder and heavier than a hand. Therefore it could strike harder and more heavily.

Prehistoric man was strong—stronger than the man of today. He had to be strong in order to survive in his wild and dangerous world.

But some of his enemies—the saber-toothed tiger, the huge woolly rhinoceros, the great elephant-like creature called a mammoth—were even stronger. Any of them could kill a man with a single blow or tear him apart with fierce claws or tusks. Yet man had to compete with these enemies for food and had to protect himself from their attack.

Two important things gave man an advantage over his enemies. First, he stood upright, while his enemies walked on four feet. Thus man could use his hands—his "forefeet"—to protect himself and to perform many tasks.

Second, he had a better brain than his enemies had. He could think better than they could. It was his brain that discovered how a stone could be used instead of a fist.

A SHARP EDGE AND A SHARP POINT

His brain led him to two more very important discoveries.

He discovered that a sharp-edged stone could serve him as well as sharp claws served his enemies. With a sharp stone he could cut up the animals he killed for food. With a sharp stone he could even scrape the hide clean and use an animal skin as a protection from the cold. His simple sharp-edged stone was the beginning of the tool we call a knife.

He also discovered that he could use a stick in the same way his enemies used their tusks—to dig up roots that were good to eat. He learned that the best stick for digging was one that had a pointed end like a mammoth's tusk. Often he looked for a long time to find a stick that had a sharp point. And finally he learned how to point the tip of a stick with his sharp stone.

Now he had three important discoveries: a stone to strike with, a sharp-edged stone, and a pointed stick. He would eventually do a great many things with these simple objects.

9 *Source:* Text adapted from *The Real Book About Inventions* by Samuel Epstein and Beryl Williams, copyright 1951 by Franklin Watts, Inc. Reprinted by permission of Doubleday & Company, Inc. Illustration from *Reading to Learn*, by Margaret Early, et al., copyright © 1970 by Harcourt Brace Jovanovich, Inc. and reprinted with their permission.

LITERAL QUESTIONS:

1. For what purposes did prehistoric man use stones?

2. Whom did prehistoric man fear?

3. In what way was prehistoric man different from modern man?

4. For what purposes did prehistoric man kill animals?

5. How did he make his stick a better tool for digging?

INFERENTIAL QUESTIONS:

1. According to the author, what is the difference between a discovery and an invention?

2. Why does the author compare prehistoric man's sharp-edged stone to the claws of dangerous animals?

3. How did prehistoric man learn to use a stick to dig with?

4. What enabled prehistoric man to keep alive in his dangerous surroundings?

5. What might he do with a heavy stone and a stick?

VOCABULARY:

1. he had to be strong in order to survive
2. compete for food
3. a stone could serve him well
4. point the tip of a stick
5. he would eventually do a great many things

It would be desirable to administer these informal reading inventories individually, especially with younger children who may have difficulty writing. In any case, each child has to read one of the selections orally so that the teacher will be able to note how he reads and to record his errors. Then the teacher might ask the child to respond to the questions and vocabulary orally. Since the selections are not long, teachers should be able to complete one evaluation in about fifteen minutes or less.

More advanced children may do the silent reading in a group and write the answers to the questions. When children complete the reading, they note on their papers the length of time they took to read the selection. (The teacher may record the time in fifteen-second intervals on the chalkboard.)

It might be practical for the teacher to have children read orally and silently their first selections from a book which is one level below that of the grade. If children were in the third grade, the teacher could use a book intended for the second half of the second grade. She would know quickly whether the book which was designed for children who could read at third-grade level was satisfactory, too easy, or too difficult for each child. She might adjust her materials and teaching plans accordingly until she were able to administer another inventory. In the meantime, she would be acquiring more information about the children as she worked with them.

As each child reads orally, the teacher keeps notes on a copy of the text of how well the child does. She records any errors he makes: omission and insertion of words and word parts, substitution of words, repetition of words, unknown words. These errors may be indicated in the following way:

omissions = The school(s) will (be) closed
red
insertions = a ∧ wagon
(big)
substitutions = bright sun
repetitions = a tall man
unknown word = survive the cold

The teacher does not correct the child as he reads but tells him an unknown word if he asks for assistance or stops reading. She also notes if he hesitates over words, reads word-by-word, ignores punctuation, or reads in a monotone. Upon completion of the oral reading the child answers the questions and tells what the selected words mean. The teacher also records these responses if they are given orally.

Now the child can read silently the second excerpt from the same book.

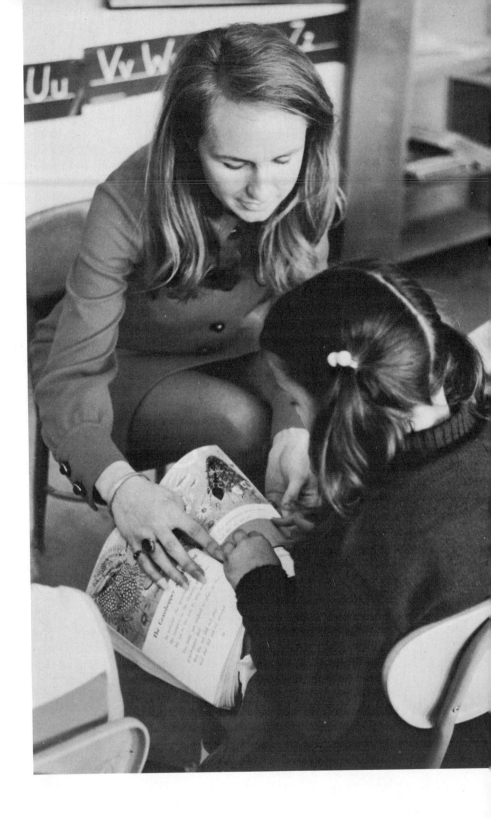

The teacher notes his behavior as he reads—whether he mouths words, points to words, moves his head, or gives other indications of having difficulty with the material—and records the time he took to complete reading the selection. He answers the questions and tells what the selected words mean as before.

Several children might read this excerpt at the same time; in that case the group would be kept small enough to allow the teacher to observe each child as he reads silently. As each one finishes reading the selection, he either meets with the teacher to answer the questions and explain the vocabulary or writes out his responses to them.

If children did very well on the oral and silent reading of the first inventory, the second inventory would be based upon the next higher level book. If they did less well, the teacher should select the inventory for a lower level. Thus perhaps over a period of a few weeks each child will have read and responded to selections from different level books. Now the teacher is ready to evaluate more accurately each child's reading performance and decide what some of his weaknesses are. She might chart the results to show how well the child did in each area covered:

	Word Recognition	Literal Comprehension	Inferential Comprehension	Vocabulary
2^2 oral (100)	99%	100%	80%	100%
silent (115)	——	100%	100%	100%
3^1 oral (95)	94%	80%	60%	80%
silent (110)	——	80%	80%	100%
3^2 oral (90)	90%	80%	60%	80%
silent (110)	——	60%	60%	80%
4 oral (80)	87%	80%	60%	60%
silent (100)	——	60%	40%	60%

The numbers in parentheses refer to the number of words per minute the child read. At the 2^2 level (second half of the second year) he made hardly any errors in word recognition—2 out of a total of 186 words, or 99 per cent accuracy. He answered the literal questions correctly but missed one of the inferential questions. He scored 100 per cent on vocabulary. In silent reading he didn't make any errors. At the 3^1 level (third year, first half) his percentage of accuracy in word recognition fell to 94 per cent and his ability to understand the selection was not as great as at the 2^2 level. His performance continued to drop in all areas as the material became more difficult.

This child met the requirements for the independent level at 2^2 (see chart). His ability to read orally for inferential meaning was slightly below the required level but he had no difficulty drawing inferences when he read silently. At the 3^1 level he made more errors in all areas but met the minimum criteria for instructional level. His performance at the 3^2 level did not satisfy all the criteria for instructional level; in the fourth grade material he fell below the standards of instructional level in all areas. The child's reading levels are:

independent level = second year, second half

instructional level = third year, first half

frustration level = fourth year[10]

An examination of oral reading errors would reveal the nature of some of his difficulties. Perhaps he leaves off specific word endings, recognizes the first part of words but guesses the rest, confuses certain vowel sounds, and so on. His answers to the questions might indicate that he has some trouble drawing conclusions or anticipating outcomes. Low performance in vocabulary could suggest a need for concentrating on how to use context clues and respond to multiple meanings of words. This analysis would provide a basis for initiating instruction and continuing the study of reading needs. Children with similar needs could be brought together for instruction.

The teacher-recorded inventory is the most accurate inventory and the most accurate method of estimating a child's instructional level. A less accurate but quick way to estimate a child's instructional level is to have him read words from a *vocabulary list* which samples vocabulary from a graded series of books. A separate list of words could be prepared from the vocabulary of each level represented in the series of readers, social studies, or science books. The primary word lists would contain about twenty words each and the higher-level lists thirty or more. If the child missed many more than 15–20 per cent of the words on any list, it would indicate the materials of that level might be too difficult for him. This procedure can be used to estimate at what level teachers should begin the informal reading inventory. A comparison of results from basal reader and content subject text lists could reveal differences in difficulty between the two. Teachers might discover that children have more trouble reading science textbooks than the selections in readers.

Another way to estimate the difficulty of material is to apply the *cloze procedure* to typical selections taken from a graded series. Two or three excerpts are drawn from each book level. Every nth word is eliminated from each excerpt and the reader is expected to supply the missing word or a synonym for it. If the child cannot supply from 70 to 80 per cent of the missing words in the excerpts for a given book level, this indicates that he fails to comprehend the material well enough to profit from instruction at this level. He would then "try on for size" the next lower-level materials.

---

10 A child with this record might be able to function with help at the 3^2 level. He would be likely to have much difficulty at the fourth-grade level.

CLOZE EXERCISE

Rivers Change the Earth[11]

Rivers are born high up in the mountains, from __(1)__ and melted snow.

HOW RIVERS ARE BORN

Much of __(2)__ rain that falls sinks into the earth. This is __(3)__ ground water. Some of this water flows out of __(4)__ ground again through openings in the rocks. When ground __(5)__ comes out again like this, it is called a __(6)__ . The spring water then flows downhill and joins other __(7)__ to make streams. The streams also get ground water __(8)__ goes into them right from the ground.

Some rain __(9)__ downhill right away. The rain water flows along gullies and __(10)__ into the streams. When there is a lot of __(11)__ , the streams become full. When there is no rain __(12)__ a long time, some streams dry up. Ground water __(13)__ other streams flowing even in dry weather.

If he had no trouble with a set of excerpts, he could try the next higher-level materials.

The cloze exercise above has every tenth word deleted. The excerpt is taken from a reader at fourth-grade level. This exercise may be administered to a group of children who will write the missing words in the blanks or on a separate sheet of paper.[12] A child would have to supply at least nine words correctly to achieve the minimum percentage of accuracy of comprehension ($9/13 = 70\%$). The average comprehension score is determined by totaling the number of correct responses for all the excerpts at a given level and dividing that number by the total number of words children must supply. If a child supplies 30 correct words out of a total of 50, his comprehension score equals 60 per cent.

Teachers may prepare individual and group tests to determine how well children do on *specific skills*. These tests should contain enough items so that each skill is adequately sampled. Care should be taken that the exercises require children to perform the intended skill. These tests may be prepared in the same way as the others—sets for each level book that are duplicated and available to all teachers.

Here are some sample test items to measure how well children perform in specific skills areas.

---

[11] *Goals in Reading*. The Bookmark Reading Program. New York: Harcourt Brace Jovanovich, Inc., 1970, pp. 168–69.

[12] The correct words are: 1) rain 2) the 3) called 4) the 5) water 6) spring 7) springs 8) that 9) flows 10) ditches 11) rain 12) for 13) keeps.

CONTEXT CLUES (Word Recognition): Supply the missing word in each sentence.
1. We keep our car in the _____. (garage)
2. How many pounds does the bushel of apples w_____? (weigh)

CONTEXT CLUES (Word Meaning): What does the underlined word in each sentence mean?
1. The weatherman predicted it would rain yesterday. He was wrong—it snowed instead.
2. Animals are born with instincts. For example, no one has to teach a cat to catch mice or certain kinds of birds to fly south in winter. Each animal knows what it must do.

PHONICS (Auditory discrimination): Listen to these two words. Do they have the same beginning sound?
1. window-wish
2. deaf-bed

PHONICS (Generalizations): Read these nonsense words. Which one sounds like a real word?
1. grig-cet
2. bete-hirm

SYLLABICATION (Visual discrimination): Look at these words. How many syllables does each word contain?
1. lack, roast, complex
2. illustrate, combinations, opinion

ROOT WORDS: Underline the root word in each of the following words.
1. action
2. subtopics

MAIN IDEAS: What is the topic of this passage?
Alaska is the fiftieth state in the union. It is larger than most of the other states but has fewer people. Some parts of Alaska are suitable for growing vegetables and raising cattle, but much of the land is wilderness. Alaska has good roads which connect major cities, but it is impossible to reach many places except by airplane. Exploration of its natural resources has led to the discovery of large oil fields, which are expected to produce millions of barrels of oil each year.
a. Alaska's people
b. What Alaska is like
c. Alaska's riches

UNIMPORTANT DETAILS: Read this paragraph and decide if it has any unimportant details. If so, list them.
Gravity from the moon and the sun causes tides. The moon is closer to the earth than the sun so that it pulls on the earth's surface with a much stronger force. The moon is about 240,000 miles from the earth. High tides occur every twelve hours and low tides halfway inbetween. On some coastlines boats are left stranded in the mud when the tide is low.

ORGANIZING INFORMATION: Rearrange these items so that each subtopic is placed under its proper heading.
proper diet, malaria, disease prevention, first aid, cleanliness, body diseases, measles, bacteria, vaccination, physical check-ups, tuberculosis.

ALPHABETIZING: In what order will the following topics appear in an index?
1. mining, dairying, lumbering, shipping
2. inventions, immigration, Indians, aviation

Each of the foregoing exercises is intended to measure a specific subskill. Exercises to test other subskills can be prepared in the same way. It may be necessary to include exercises in literal and inferential reading if verification of responses on the inventories that ascertain reading levels seems desirable or some aspects of comprehension were not covered adequately.

IDEAS FOR DISCUSSION

Professionals have raised questions about the practice of depending more on teacher-made tests than standardized tests to assess reading ability. They point out that the quality of individually-prepared tests is dependent solely on the ability teachers have to construct them and that as a result there will be great variability among them. Unlike the preparation of standardized instruments, test items are not tried out on large samples to determine if they are too difficult or too easy. No effort is made to verify the validity of the test content by having experts evaluate it or to measure the test's reliability by experimental or statistical means. There will be variability in scoring responses as a result of teachers' subjective judgments. The adequate construction of alternate forms requires specialized knowledge that most teachers don't possess; therefore, there is no objective way to measure growth. A group's reading progress cannot be compared with the achievement of others so that teachers lack a yardstick for determining how adequate their programs are. Finally, the time required to prepare tests might be better spent in planning lessons and preparing materials.

One cannot discount these arguments completely for they are based upon demonstrated experiences and observable practices. But the inference that standardized reading tests possess all the attributes which teacher-prepared tests lack is not supported by fact. All one need do to verify weaknesses of standardized tests is to examine critical reviews of them by reading specialists and educational psychologists. Many standardized tests fail to meet the same criteria demanded of informal instruments. The possibility that too much confidence will be placed in published tests and therefore that teacher attitudes will be adversely affected has prompted reading educators to urge caution in their selection and use.

Adequately prepared informal measures have one great advantage over commercial tests: they deal with the actual reading act in which a given group of children engages. While they admittedly are unsuitable for use in conducting controlled research, they do offer information about how well pupils can read the materials provided them. They do reveal reading information presently unavailable to teachers who depend upon standardized instruments.

Teachers and administrators working as a team can examine standardized reading tests to find out if they are suitable tools for measuring how well children are achieving the objectives of the reading program. Some tests will be preferred to others because as measures they are less gross and more adequate for the intended school population. There is no reason why teachers should have to prepare their own tests to measure certain aspects of reading achievement when perfectly acceptable ones are available. The problem arises when school people make unwarranted assumptions about their content and results. Better understanding of tests and test results should lead to more intelligent decisions about school-wide and classroom evaluations and their effects on the reading curriculum. Given present conditions, an adequate program of measurement and evaluation will include a proper mix of standardized and informal testing. The proportion of each will vary with the purposes to which they are put.

Measuring Reading Interest

One of the objectives of the reading program is the development and promotion of interest in reading. Reading growth occurs not only as the result of instruction but also through the act of reading. Children who have not developed favorable attitudes toward reading can learn to read satisfactorily but they are not as likely to benefit from reading to the same degree as others who find reading a satisfying experience. Voluntary reading is one leisure-type activity which reading programs seek to promote for reasons of personal development and pleasure.

Just as teachers inquire into pupils' habits and skills in order to offer them a meaningful reading program, so do they try to find out about the nature and extent of reading children do. They must rely on observations of children's reading behaviors and what children themselves reveal about their own reading.

Children-Selected Materials

Perhaps the most valid measure of children's reading interests are the materials they actually select and read in and out of school. If we assume there is an ample supply of reading materials, that they represent a wide variety of subjects, activities and themes, that children have the ability to read the materials, and that there is adequate time and opportunity for reading, what and how much they choose to read represents evidence of their reading interests. No statement of intent or preference is as convincing as their actual behavior.

Questionnaires and Interviews

Most investigations into the reading habits and preferences of children gather evidence through questionnaires and interviews. Teachers may use these same devices to assess the quantity and nature of their voluntary reading. Children may respond to such questions as:

1. Do you like to read (or listen to) stories about make-believe? Adventure? Animals? Sports?
2. What kinds of stories do you like to read or listen to?
3. What are some titles of books you read recently?
4. How many books did you borrow from the library and read last month? From friends?

5. What books do you own? Who selected these books? Have you read them all?
6. Which magazines do you like to look at and read? Do you read newspapers? Which sections?
7. How do you spend your free time?

Teachers may include comparable items about radio and television program preferences, films, indoor and outdoor games, hobbies—in short, any kinds of activities that might appeal to young people. Their preferences for one or another might suggest the kinds of reading they would do were conditions favorable. However, to believe that children who like to play baseball will want to read all books about baseball is a mistaken assumption that people often make. Some children might be interested in reading books that teach the skills of the game so that they may improve their own. Others may want to read about baseball heroes and their exploits. And there might be a group who are avid baseball players but who don't prefer to read about the game at all.

Talking with children about their reading activities may confirm some of their responses to more formal answer-seeking questions. The eagerness with which they discuss their reading might be a clue to what actually occurs. Questionnaires and interviews are appropriate devices for gaining initial information and making tentative judgments. Sounder decisions which affect the instructional program will be based upon what children do and not what they say they do.

Evaluation of Reading Programs

The emphasis in previous sections of this chapter is on the measurement and evaluation of progress children make toward achieving the objectives of a total reading curriculum: learning the skills of reading, learning how to use the skills in order to learn, learning the skills of appreciation, and developing favorable attitudes toward reading. The effectiveness of any reading program must be judged by how well children achieve these objectives. A teacher might prepare a *checklist* covering specific goals for each child in his class:

CHECKLIST OF READING OBJECTIVES

	GOOD	FAIR	INADEQUATE
Word Recognition			
Sight Vocabulary	√		
Context Clues		√	
Phonics			√
Structural Analysis	√		
Dictionary		√	

Comprehension

Vocabulary	√		
Literal Meaning		√	
Inferential Meaning			√
Critical Evaluation	√		

Study Skills

Location of Information	√		
Selection			
Organization		√	
Retention		√	
Graphic Aids		√	
Following Directions	√		
Flexibility			√

Then a composite checklist could be drawn for the entire group. If done for each major outcome of instruction, the emerging data will leave no doubts about what the program has accomplished and what objectives have not been realized.

Administrative and Instructional Practices

There is another aspect to evaluation of reading programs besides the determination of how well children are growing in reading: it is with what efficiency staffs implement the school's reading goals. Some practices, administrative and instructional, have been found to be more productive than others in promoting desired outcomes. Children do learn to adjust to different conditions even though these might possess less than desirable characteristics, but there are obvious advantages to having them participate in programs which have built-in features based upon sound and tried practices.

Survey Questions

The following questions may serve as a guide for assessing the program's effectiveness. The more positive the responses are to them, the greater is the likelihood that reading objectives will be achieved.

1. To what extent is there coordination of reading instruction throughout the school?
    a. Is reading taught at all grade levels?
    b. Is there an underlying philosophy on which all teaching rests?
    c. Are all teachers familiar with the total reading program and do they assume responsibility for it?
    d. Does an individual or a group assume responsibility for the program's coordination?
    e. Are efforts made to establish sequences in reading and learning? Are there provisions for filling gaps in the sequential development of reading ability?

2. How well are teachers and administrators informed about reading?
    a. Does the professional school library contain a representative collection of books and periodicals on reading? To what extent are they read?
    b. Are there on the staff individuals who by training and experience are capable of providing leadership in reading and whose responsibility it is to assume this leadership role?
    c. Does the staff have an opportunity to participate in reading study groups, workshops, and demonstrations?
    d. To what extent do staff members attend and participate in local, state, and national meetings on reading?
3. To what extent are there provisions for individual differences in reading?
    a. Do teachers provide individual and group assistance in reading?
    b. Are children grouped on the basis of instructional levels? On the basis of reading needs? Is there flexible grouping?
    c. Are different materials available for good, average, and poor readers?
    d. Are reading tasks modified to enable all children to achieve satisfaction in reading?
    e. To what extent are there special provisions for children who do not seem to profit from the regular instructional reading program?
4. How effectively is information about pupils' reading progress acquired and used?
    a. Are anecdotal records kept for all children?
    b. Are periodic and adequate health examinations that include vision and hearing tests routinely scheduled?
    c. Do teachers receive cumulative records for pupils before they work with them?
    d. Do pupil records contain up-to-date information about their physical, intellectual, social and emotional, and educational development? Can referrals be made to specialized personnel for new information?
    e. Are there provisions for teacher conferences to discuss the reading problems and needs of children?
    f. To what extent are parents involved in helping the school understand their children?
5. To what extent does the school librarian help to promote reading?
    a. Is the librarian familiar with the reading curriculum?
    b. Do the librarian and teacher cooperatively plan reading activities?
    c. Does the librarian assume some responsibility for teaching children to use the library effectively?
    d. Does the library contain an adequate supply of reading materials and other instructional aids?
    e. Does the librarian suggest and make available reading and other materials teachers might use in their instructional programs?

6. Are diversified reading practices followed?
    a. To what extent do teachers provide for oral and silent reading?
    b. Do children learn different ways to solve reading problems?
    c. Do children read story-type and informational selections for different purposes?
    d. How well do teachers utilize commercial materials to teach reading? How effectively can they prepare and use their own materials?
    e. Do teachers coordinate reading instruction with other learning activities?
    f. To what degree do teachers combine the best features of different reading approaches?
7. To what degree do teachers adopt generally accepted practices to promote reading growth?
    a. Do teachers avoid assigning busy work to pupils?
    b. Do teachers help to prepare pupils for difficult reading tasks?
    c. Are reading assignments made for specific purposes? Do teachers help pupils establish their own reading purposes?
    d. Do children have opportunities to learn about the reading process? Is less emphasis put upon correct responses than on appropriate ways in which they are obtained?
    e. Does silent reading generally precede oral reading? Is there an audience situation when oral reading occurs?
    f. Does the teacher try to pace his instruction in reading? Does he avoid covering more ground than children can assimilate? Does he provide practice in previously taught skills before introducing new ones?
    g. How often do children share enjoyable reading experiences? Do they have opportunities to make whatever contributions they can?
    h. How much information does each child have about his own reading? Is he aware of how well he is progressing? Does he know what his strengths are? Where he might improve?

Positive answers to these questions are indications that the reading curriculum is intended to fit children and not mold children to it. They suggest that reason and knowledge are the foundations on which the program rests. Reading curriculums are not fixed; they are subject to modification just as a teacher's evaluation of children's reading changes as he obtains new data. However, there is a basic design that is emerging from a wealth of experimentation and demonstration. How well teachers understand its structure will affect the ways in which they respond to the reading requirements of the children they instruct. They should be less likely to embrace reading practices which seem to be incompatible with the design if they become familiar with present knowledge. This should become a reading teacher's goal.

SUMMARY

1. The diagnostic teaching of reading is a continuous process. Diagnostic teaching focuses more on evaluation than measurement since its intent is to increase learning rather than grade children's performances.

2. The aim of diagnostic teaching of reading is to identify growth areas in which children are progressing satisfactorily as well as pinpoint others to which greater attention should be given. Teaching plans are based upon children's reading performances and directed toward specific learning tasks. Initial appraisal of children's reading precedes instruction and reveals where children are on the reading continuum. Further evaluation accompanies instruction and provides teachers with information they need to make their teaching relevant.

3. Standardized reading tests may be administered to ascertain how well a group of children are reading in comparison to other groups of children. Most standardized tests survey general reading ability by measuring vocabulary and comprehension skills.

4. The results of standardized reading tests may be used for grouping children initially, for identifying gross strengths and weaknesses, and for measuring general progress in reading over extended time periods. Some diagnostic reading tests provide specific information about performance in reading subskills and oral reading.

5. The administration of informal reading tests makes it possible for teachers to identify children's different reading levels much more accurately than standardized tests. Informal tests are based upon graded materials children actually are expected to read in school.

6. The *independent* level refers to the highest level at which a reader can function with ease. At this level his reading is quite fluent and he comprehends the material. The *instructional* level refers to the highest level at which instruction might be offered. Materials at this level might be somewhat difficult but with some help the reader should be able to function satisfactorily in them. A reader who is at the *frustration* level finds the reading material so difficult that he cannot learn what is being taught. The *expectancy* level is the highest level at which the reader comprehends material that is read to him.

7. Informal reading tests may be used to assess proficiency in word attack and word knowledge, comprehension, and study skills. The items on these tests should be graded in difficulty so that they serve as diagnostic tools and reveal in what aspects of a skills area the reader is strong or weak. Informal tests may be administered individually or in groups.

8. The nature of the materials children voluntarily select is a better indicator of what they prefer to read than their responses to interest inventories. How they spend their free time will reveal if they enjoy other activities more than reading.

9. The success of any reading program depends upon how well children

achieve its objectives. These objectives are stated in operational terms so that they can be evaluated. Teachers and administrators who are knowledgeable about reading and reading practices are likely to offer programs that foster growth and promote an interest in reading.

STUDY QUESTIONS AND EXERCISES

1. What is the difference between measuring and evaluating reading ability?
2. For what reasons is this chapter on measurement and evaluation placed at the beginning rather than at the end of this textbook?
3. List the differences between standardized and informal or teacher-made tests. What advantages do informal reading tests have over standardized reading tests?
4. How might the results of standardized reading tests be used more effectively to assess reading achievement and plan reading instruction?
5. Prepare informal oral and silent reading inventories based upon a graded series of readers for use in determining the instructional level and reading requirements of children with whom you are familiar or might work. Cover at least four different reading levels.
6. Compare the results of standardized and informal reading tests for a group of pupils. Are the results of one confirmed by the other? What type of information is it possible to obtain from the latter that most standardized reading tests fail to yield?
7. Compare the results of a cloze exercise with one which requires pupils to answer literal and interpretive questions. Select similar-type passages from the same source for each.
8. Below are some errors one pupil made in oral reading. What kind of help do these errors suggest this pupil might need?

Correct Word	How Read
hurts	hits
charge	change
flip	flap
cage	(no response)
bite	bit
burn	born
thin	than

9. Evaluate the effectiveness of one school's reading program with which you are familiar. Use the guidelines on pages 66–68 for this purpose and summarize your findings. What recommendations might you make to improve the program?

SUGGESTIONS FOR FURTHER READING

For a comprehensive study of reading measurement and evaluation see:

Mary C. Austin, Clifford L. Bush, and Mildred H. Huebner, *Reading Evaluation: Appraisal Techniques for School and Classroom.* New York: The Ronald Press Company, 1961.

Thomas C. Barrett, ed., *The Evaluation of Children's Reading Achievement* (Perspectives in Reading No. 8). Newark, Del.: International Reading Association, 1967.

Roger Farr, *Measurement and Evaluation of Reading.* New York: Harcourt Brace Jovanovich, Inc., 1970.

———. *Reading: What Can be Measured?* ERIC/CRIER Reading Review Series, International Reading Association Research Fund, 1969.

Ruth Strang, *Diagnostic Teaching of Reading*, 2nd ed. New York: McGraw-Hill, Inc., 1969.

The most complete descriptions of standardized reading tests plus critical evaluations will be found in Oscar K. Buros, ed., *Reading Tests and Reviews.* Highland Park, N.J.: The Gryphon Press, 1968.

Detailed instructions for the preparation, administration and scoring of informal tests will be found in: Marjorie S. Johnson and Roy A. Kress, *Informal Reading Inventories.* Reading Aids Series, Newark, Del.: International Reading Association, 1965; Ruth G. Viox, *Evaluating Reading and Study Skills in the Secondary Classroom.* Reading Aids Series, Newark, Del.: International Reading Association, 1968. (This latter publication contains information that can be applied to the elementary level.)

Sample inventories to establish reading levels are in Nila B. Smith, *Graded Selections For Informal Reading Diagnosis.* New York: New York University Press, 1959, 1963; and in Mary C. Austin, Clifford L. Bush and Mildred H. Huebner, *Reading Evaluation: Appraisal Techniques for School and Classroom.*

3

Readiness for Reading

■ *Few of us take the pains to study the origin of our cherished convictions; indeed, we have a natural repugnance to so doing. We like to continue to believe what we have been accustomed to accept as true, and the resentment aroused when doubt is cast upon any of our assumptions leads us to seek every manner of excuse for clinging to them. The result is that most of our so-called reasoning consists in finding arguments for going on believing what we already do.*

JAMES HARVEY ROBINSON

The sequential development of reading skills and habits extending from the lowest primary levels through the highest grades is one cornerstone of the developmental reading program. Within this concept of continuous growth is the idea that children learn a kind of reading at each successive level. The reader develops his reading skills and habits along a continuum, each step of his progress leading to a logical next step. At no time can all the steps be taken, for by the very nature of the reading act, to complete a step on the way to reading maturity is to make another step possible.

Learning to read is a continuous process during which one reading experience makes it possible for children to profit from subsequent experiences. Thus reading readiness is the concern of all teachers who wish to encourage growth in reading. While readiness for undertaking beginning reading is a concept which merits the attention educators have given it, the importance of readiness at each level of development should not be underestimated. Readiness might be treated as part of the evaluation process as teachers strive to determine how effective past teaching has been and whether children are prepared to proceed to a next stage and its difficulties.

Since stages of reading development do not fall into neat compartments or into a series of discrete steps, it is a mistake to view readiness as a problem that is resolved and then forgotten. From the viewpoint of the teacher who might be involved with first or sixth graders, readiness programs should be represented by an attitude of continuous searching to discover what children are ready for. The success of any learning experience will be affected by the children's ability to profit from it.

Beginning Reading Readiness

When should children begin to read? This has been the question educators have tried to answer over a long period of years. In fact, this very question was the subject of an investigation whose results probably influenced school programs as much as any other single piece of research.[1] Morphett and Washburne found that groups of children with average mental ages of six years, six months and seven years were more successful in first-grade reading than were groups whose mental ages were less than six years, six months, or 6-6. These results were taken to mean that since fewer children with higher mental ages failed in beginning reading, children should not undertake beginning reading until they have achieved a mental age of 6-6. There are schools which still subscribe to the idea of delaying reading instruction until this mental age is reached.

The notion of delaying formal reading instruction until children are ready for it has been reexamined in the light of new data that have been obtained long after the readiness concept was enunciated for the first time in the mid-1920s.[2] Although the National Committee on Reading, whose members included William S. Gray, Ernest Horn, and other outstanding educators, took the position that preschool and probably first-grade children should engage in activities that would help prepare them for reading, others interpreted the concept to mean that readiness could not be nurtured but had to develop in its own good time. Support for the latter position was found in the extensive and longitudinal studies of Olson[3] and Gesell,[4] who were among the leading proponents of the developmental point of view. Olson reasoned that learning to read is one aspect of total growth and that reading ability develops in a harmonious way with other aspects of growth—physical and intellectual. Therefore, there wasn't much

[1] Mabel Morphett and Carleton Washburne, "When Should Children Begin to Read?" *Elementary School Journal, 31* (March, 1931) , pp. 496–503.

[2] *Report of the National Committee on Reading.* Twenty-fourth Yearbook of the National Society for the Study of Education, Part I. Chicago: University of Chicago Press, 1925.

[3] Willard C. Olson, *Child Development.* Boston: D. C. Heath and Company, 1949.

[4] Arnold Gesell, *The First Five Years of Life.* New York: Harper & Row, Publishers, 1940; Arnold Gesell and Frances L. Ilg, *The Child From Five to Ten.* New York: Harper & Row, Publishers, 1946.

anyone could do to hurry along the growth pattern of one aspect of this development since it was closely tied to others. Gesell found that children at given age levels could be expected to perform certain tasks and that each child passed through successive stages of growth as a result of natural processes. Although there were some deviations from expected growth patterns, most children seemed to be ready for a given activity at about the same stage of development. To try to speed up performance levels by offering training was considered a waste of time and possibly even damaging to future performances.

Olson, Gesell and others believed that environmental factors were of lesser importance than constitutional ones in the development of children and that each child should be permitted to mature in his own way without outside interference. It was not an uncommon experience for parents to be told by teachers that their children would begin to read when they became ready or that the children were failing to learn because reading was introduced before they were ready for it. There is no doubt that some children really were not ready to profit from the kind of instruction teachers were offering them in first grade. There are children who seem to lack some requisites for successful reading experiences. Must we wait for children to become ready?

Proponents of the view that children need time to mature not only point to developmental stages in physical growth but also in cognition. They refer to what Piaget calls the *period of conservation*, approximately between the ages of four and seven, when young children seem unable to grasp the idea that a substance contains the same amount even though its shape changes. They can cope with this concept as maturation proceeds. This is taken as evidence that children should not be introduced to learning experiences directly associated with reading even though they may appear to need them for future success. Instead, they should enjoy the activities normally associated with the preschool and kindergarten years; and it is these experiences that will promote readiness for reading.

Other educators have wondered about the relationship between typical kindergarten experiences and those which are intended to promote development of prereading skills. They do not deny the importance of activities intended to develop the whole child but raise questions about the validity of sanctioning some and denying others. They do not understand, for example, why it is proper to provide young children with many and varied opportunities to develop oral language facility but wrong to help children focus attention on the ways in which words are similar or different as they hear them. Perhaps some excesses of the past have left their marks on the present-day thinking of those who would protect children from them.

IDEAS FOR DISCUSSION

Can proper training help children move from one stage of development to another? This is the old and persistent question of nature versus nurture. Insofar as intellectual development is concerned, there does not appear to be a pat answer.

Hilgard[5] described the work of Smedslund, who demonstrated that it was possible to help children move from one developmental stage to the next. Children between five and one-half and six and one-half years old learned to cope with the principle of conservation. They saw no reason to believe that the weight of a clay object changed when its shape changed. However, when the experimenter removed a piece of clay from one of two balls of clay without their seeing what he had done, these children had trouble explaining its loss of weight. Older children who had acquired the concept of conservation without the training had better explanations of the event. The latter results might be taken to show that training was of little consequence or that the training was not adequate enough to permit the children to apply their knowledge to a new condition.

This latter explanation would seem to be in agreement with the often-quoted statement by Bruner[6] that children are capable of dealing with any kind of information provided the material is presented in a way that is meaningful to them. Bruner was referring to the study of science and mathematics and not reading, but his concept could have implications for any learning activity. Certainly Bruner's ideas are not new but they do reinforce the requirement that educators not rely solely on data that confirm firmly-established beliefs but examine all information as it becomes available to them. Surely we cannot dismiss some of the successful efforts with culturally-disadvantaged children to reduce their deficits and raise their performance levels in school. Nor can the progress that many typical children make by engaging in relevant learning activities be ignored when they prosper more than those who have not had the benefit of these same preparatory activities.

Reading Readiness Factors

There is a significant amount of research on readiness for beginning reading. The results of over 130 studies completed before 1950 were summarized in one publication.[7] Seventy-five studies conducted by graduate students at one university between 1933 and 1963 were summarized by their sponsors.[8] Additional reports on reading readiness appear in other monographs and periodicals.[9]

Earlier investigations sought to determine relationships between physical, intellectual, social and emotional, and experiential readiness and success in beginning reading. Needless to say, the results of these studies were not consistent, but there was a measure of agreement among those who inter-

---

[5] Ernest R. Hilgard and Richard C Atkinson, *Introduction to Psychology*, 5th ed. New York: Harcourt Brace Jovanovich, Inc., 1971, pp. 64–65.

[6] Jerome S. Bruner, *The Process of Education*. Cambridge: Harvard University Press, 1960.

[7] Nila B. Smith, "Readiness for Reading," *Readiness for Reading and Related Language Arts* (A Research Bulletin of The National Conference on Research in English). Urbana: The National Council of Teachers of English, 1950, pp. 3–33.

[8] Donald D. Durrell and Helen A. Murphy, "Reading Readiness," *Research in Elementary Education, Reading: 1933–1963, Journal of Education, 146* (December, 1963), pp. 3–10.

[9] Doris V. Gunderson, *Research in Reading at the Primary Level* (U. S. Office of Education Bulletin No. 42). Washington: U. S. Government Printing Office, 1963, pp. 2–5, 33–42.

preted the findings as to what their implications for school practices might be. Among the conclusions were the following:

1. There appeared to be a small but significant relationship between physical development and success in beginning reading. Girls seemed to be more mature physically than boys, and had a smaller failure rate in first grade than boys.

2. Hearing and visual impairments might interfere with progress in learning to read. Poor health and general physical condition could be detrimental factors in beginning reading achievement.

3. Intelligence is a major factor in learning to read. However, the possession of high intelligence is no guarantee of reading success. Furthermore, the possession of no one mental age assures success in beginning reading.

4. Children who are emotionally and socially immature are less likely to respond satisfactorily to difficult learning tasks than those who have self-confidence and feel secure.

5. Children with rich language and experiential backgrounds seem to do much better than children with meager ones. Children who participate in activities that are associated with beginning reading seem better prepared for this learning task than children who have not engaged in them.

Many of these studies relied upon correlation procedures to establish relationships between readiness for beginning reading and the factors under consideration. While some relationships might have been found, none was large enough to warrant the judgment that any single factor accounted for differences in readiness levels. There was also the problem of causation. A mathematical association between conditions does not imply that one produces the other. It is entirely possible that unknown factors account for any relationship that is found to exist. Perhaps one of the significant outcomes of all this research was the idea that the readiness concept was complex and that there were no simple answers for helping young children get ready to participate in what is for many a difficult learning task.

Another reason why many readiness studies did not produce much useful information is the nature of the question they sought to answer: Is the child ready for beginning reading? To ask such a question is to infer that no matter how beginning reading is introduced the same abilities in identical amounts are required. Children could be weak in a given skill but they might very well be able to acquire reading ability without having to use the skill. It is conceivable that having once gained in reading, their ability to perform the skill will have grown. For example, the ability to discriminate between letters of similar appearance, such as *b* and *d*, is not crucial to reading if care is taken not to present the letters together, either in isolation or words. Adequate reinforcement so that one letter is learned well will serve to enhance the child's recognition of a difference when the other letter appears in his reading.

What is a child ready for in reading? is a more meaningful question than, Is he ready to undertake reading? The first question might also be phrased, What do children have to be able to do or know in order to respond properly to specific types of instruction? It is understandable why the great majority of early readiness findings, though important, did not yield high predictive measures. The conditions which were studied might have been related to reading readiness in a general way but were not tied directly to the actual learning tasks required of beginning readers. Maturational and other physical factors certainly are as important as any others in studying children and prescribing for their welfare, but the fact that certain undesirable conditions exist does not necessarily mean that children who are affected adversely cannot engage in activities that call for some physical involvement. Children who are immature in motor coordination might have trouble drawing lines from one word to another when they are asked to identify likenesses between them. This does not mean that they aren't able to see which words are alike or that they can't point them out in a different way. The same might be said about some weaknesses in hearing or vision. Children who do not hear or see perfectly might be at some disadvantage, but this is no reason to assume that they are unable to participate in learning activities. They may have to exert more effort to achieve. Naturally, any condition which could interfere with learning should be corrected insofar as it is possible to do so.

Although intelligence test scores seem to be among the best predictors of beginning reading success, they cannot be used to classify individual children as good or poor risks. Intelligence is a composite of many abilities that are influenced by personal and environmental conditions. The way in which intelligence is measured has some bearing upon the extent to which the results are related to reading. If a single ability were required for successful performances on both the intelligence test and in the reading activity, it could be said that the ability as measured by the I.Q. test is an index of how well one might perform in reading. There are abilities which children need for reading that intelligence tests do not measure; this is one reason why intelligence test scores are merely suggestive of how well children might do in beginning reading. Their predictive value is better for groups of children who score at the lower and upper ends of the distribution. Groups of children who score high can be expected to have less difficulty in learning to read than groups whose scores fall within the lowest ranges. But to use the I.Q. test score to predict how well any child in either group might do in reading would not be a viable procedure without knowing how well he did on each test item, the learning requirements of the reading program, and the relationships between them. In addition, other factors, such as the child's desire to learn and the classroom climate, could have an impact on any outcome.

Personality factors and their relation to beginning reading were studied by Blanchard and others.[10] Some children who experienced difficulties in learning to read manifested behaviors of anxiety and hostility and feelings of insecurity that were symptomatic of emotional disturbances. Although other children who were progressing satisfactorily exhibited these same behavior patterns, perhaps to a lesser degree, investigators assumed that learning problems were the products of personality dysfunction. Very few studies involved children before they experienced learning failures so that no one could be certain how the subjects behaved before they entered school.

Here too the same kind of question must be raised: Does emotional upset interfere with one's ability to perform certain tasks? If a child is unable to sit still for even short periods of time or concentrate on what is taking place, perhaps he isn't ready to participate in group situations which require some sustained attention, e.g., listening to and identifying words that end the same way. He might very well behave differently if the group were small or he were alone with the teacher. It might be that this particular task requires him to exert more effort than he is capable of at the moment and that his response to a less demanding one would be better. Emotionally disturbed children have become successful readers. It is possible that what and how they were taught had a significant bearing upon their achievement.

More recent research on reading readiness—studies conducted since 1950— has been less concerned with intelligence and personality and more with specific abilities associated with reading. In addition, there has been speculation about environmental conditions which seem to affect children's responses to school learning.

Visual Discrimination

What visual skills do children need in order to learn to recognize words? A number of investigators sought to find answers to this question but there is not complete agreement among them. There are indications, however, that some visual skills seem to be more directly related to reading achievement than others.

Barrett[11] reviewed the literature on visual discrimination that included studies on the recognition of letters and words, pictures, and geometric designs. He reported studies which found that the ability to discern likenesses and differences among words was of greater significance than the ability to discriminate among letters. He also noted the results of several

---

[10] Phyllis Blanchard, "Psychogenic Factors in Some Cases of Reading Disability," *American Journal of Orthopsychiatry*, 5 (October, 1935), pp. 361–74; W. H. Missildine, "Emotional Background of 30 Children with Reading Disabilities," *The Nervous Child*, 5 (July, 1946), pp. 263–72; Max Siegel, "The Personality Structures of Children with Reading Disabilities as Compared with Children Presenting Other Clinical Problems," *The Nervous Child*, 10 (1954), pp. 409–14.

[11] Thomas C. Barrett, "The Relationships Between Measures of Pre-Reading Visual Discrimination and First Grade Reading Achievement: A Review of the Literature," *Reading Research Quarterly*, 1 (Fall, 1965), pp. 51–76.

studies that placed high value on knowledge of letter names. Ability to perform on nonverbal discrimination tests also seemed to be tied to reading achievement.

On the basis of investigations conducted at Boston University, Durrell concluded without much equivocation that "familiarity with letter forms seems essential to the accurate perception needed to discriminate between words."[12] From the results of the First Grade Studies Bond and Dykstra[13] concluded that knowledge of letter names was the best predictor of beginning reading success.

As has been indicated previously, correlation studies do have value for deciding what elements might be relevant in learning but in no way do they make it possible to establish causal relationships between seemingly related variables. A third factor such as intelligence or background of experiences might account for both. One way to deal with this problem is to offer training in one element to see if differences in performance levels affect the performance levels of the other (e.g., teaching letter names to children who don't know them and determining if the new knowledge affects their ability to learn to read). It is not enough to prove that training in a given skill will lead to improvement in that skill unless it can be demonstrated with equal force that training effects alter performances on the criterion measure—in this instance increased ability in learning to recognize words. Results of experiments show that training in visual discrimination is capable of increasing recognition of letters, words, and forms.[14,15,16] Negative results would be difficult to explain unless the quality of the instruction was known to be poor or the subjects suffered from weaknesses that were known to interfere with learning. There have been programs in which children who received no special training in a skill surpassed the achievement of others who did.

In recent years there has been a great deal of interest in nonverbal visual discrimination skills because of their possible importance in recognizing words. The program which seems to have attracted as much attention as any is the one developed by Frostig.[17] The program contains

[12] Donald D. Durrell and Helen A. Murphy, "Reading Readiness," *Journal of Education, 146* (December, 1963), p. 5.

[13] Guy L. Bond and Robert Dykstra, *Coordinating Center for First Grade Reading Instruction Programs* (Final Report, U. S. Department of Health, Education, and Welfare, Project No. X001). Minneapolis: University of Minnesota, 1967.

[14] W. H. Wheelock and N. J. Silvaroli, "An Investigation of Visual Discrimination Training for Beginning Readers," *Journal of Typographical Research, 1* (September, 1967), pp. 50–57.

[15] Ethel M. King, "Effects of Different Kinds of Visual Discrimination Training on Learning to Read Words," *Journal of Educational Psychology, 55* (December, 1964), pp. 325–33.

[16] Merle B. Karnes and others, "An Evaluation of Two Pre-School Programs for Disadvantaged Children," *Exceptional Children, 34* (May, 1968), pp. 667–76.

[17] Marianne Frostig and David Horne, *The Frostig Program for the Development of Visual Perception.* Chicago: Follett Publishing Company, 1964.

exercises that are designed to strengthen eye-motor coordination, figure-ground perception, constancy of perception, perception of position in space, and perception of special relationships. Children focus their attention on figures and patterns with the expectation that this training will have transfer effects in learning to recognize words. Correlation studies show some relationship between the two. Is success in learning to recognize words dependent on visual discrimination of nonverbal forms?

Rosen[18] reported negative results of a perceptual training program based upon an adaptation of Frostig's program. Training did not produce improvement in reading scores. Cohen[19] offered experimental subjects perceptual training, following the Frostig program. These subjects made significant gains on visual perception tests over the control group but these gains were not reflected in reading growth. In another investigation, children who received perceptual training recommended by Frostig and others did not score significantly better in perceptual skills at the end of the kindergarten year than children who did not receive the training but did achieve significantly higher scores in word recognition at the end of the first grade.[20] It is questionable to ascribe differences in reading scores to perceptual training when there are no real differences in the perceptual performances of either group. Wingert[21] concluded on the basis of his study that activities designed to improve performances on the Frostig tests do not transfer to reading-related activities.

It seems that ability to discriminate among letter and word forms has a greater influence upon the ability to recognize words than the ability to see differences and similarities among nonverbal forms. If children are weak in recognizing letters, it would seem appropriate to provide training in letter forms; if they are weak in discriminating between words, then training with words ought to be provided. Experiences directly related to tasks children are expected to perform should be more productive than experiences which might have some tangential relation to the task.

Auditory Discrimination

Auditory perception involves acuity, understanding, discrimination, and retention.[22] It appears that each of these elements is relatively independent of the others, that high performance on one does not insure equal per-

[18] Carl Rosen, "An Experimental Study of Visual Perceptual Training and Reading Achievement in First Grade," *Perceptual and Motor Skills*, 22 (June, 1966), pp. 979–86.
[19] Ruth Cohen, "Remedial Training of First Grade Children with Visual Perceptual Retardation," *Educational Horizons*, 45 (1966–67), pp. 60–63.
[20] Marion Neal Faustman, "Some Effects of Perception Training in Kindergarten on First Grade Success in Reading," in Helen K. Smith, ed., *Perception and Reading* (Vol. 12, Part 4, Proceedings of the Twelfth Annual Convention). Newark, Del.: International Reading Association, 1968, pp. 99–101.
[21] Roger C. Wingert, "Evaluation of a Readiness Training Program," *The Reading Teacher*, 22 (January, 1969), pp. 325–28.
[22] Joseph M. Wepman, "Auditory Discrimination, Speech and Reading," *The Elementary School Journal*, 60 (March, 1960), pp. 325–33.

formance on another. Acuity involves keenness of hearing, and its relationship to reading is fairly established. Moderate hearing loss does not appear to interfere significantly with ability to learn to read.

Most of the investigations of auditory discrimination sought to determine if any relationship existed between ability to distinguish between spoken sounds and learning to read. Harrington[23] administered a series of tests involving recognition of initial and final consonants in words and rhyming words and reported superior performances by children who were significantly superior in word recognition. Durrell and Murphy[24] concluded on the basis of obtained correlation coefficients that success in beginning reading is tied closely to the ability to recognize separate sounds in spoken words. Dykstra[25] administered a series of auditory discrimination tests to first-grade children and found that performance on each was significantly related to reading achievement. He pointed out that this relationship was not sufficiently great to make possible predictions of how well individual children might perform in beginning reading. Girls performed better than boys on auditory discrimination tasks and also achieved better results in beginning reading. Morency[26] found a significant relationship between auditory discrimination abilities and third-year reading achievement. Flower[27] concluded that auditory skills are important in learning to read and that the results of their assessment to determine levels of achievement should be used in planning children's educational programs. Other studies lend support to the idea that auditory discrimination is related to word recognition.

None of the studies sought to find out if a change in auditory discrimination behaviors might produce changes in the way children responded to word recognition tasks.[28] But it has been demonstrated that auditory discrimination abilities will improve with training.[29] Perhaps by inference it becomes apparent that children who are weak in identifying phonemes in spoken words will have difficulty in using sound-letter correspondences

---

[23] Sister Mary James Harrington, *The Relationship of Certain Word Analysis Abilities to the Reading Achievements of Second Grade Children*. Unpublished Doctoral Dissertation, Boston University, 1953.

[24] Donald Durrell and Helen Murphy, "The Auditory Discrimination Factor in Reading Readiness and Reading Disability," *Education, 73* (May, 1953), pp. 556–60.

[25] Robert Dykstra, "Auditory Discrimination Abilities and Beginning Reading Achievement," *Reading Research Quarterly, 1* (Spring, 1966), pp. 5–34.

[26] Anne Morency, "Auditory Modality, Research and Practice," in Helen K. Smith, ed., *Perception and Reading* (Vol. 12, Part 4 of the Proceedings of the Twelfth Annual Convention). Newark, Del.: International Reading Association, 1968, pp. 17–21.

[27] Richard M. Flower, "The Evaluation of Auditory Abilities in the Appraisal of Children With Reading Problems," in Helen K. Smith, ed., *Perception and Reading, op. cit.*, pp. 21–24.

[28] Positive effects of auditory training on word recognition ability are reported by Donald Durrell and Helen Murphy in their summary of reading investigations conducted at Boston University. "Reading in Grade One," *Journal of Education, 146* (December, 1962), pp. 14–18.

[29] N. J. Silvaroli and W. H. Wheelock, "An Investigation of Auditory Discrimination Training for Beginning Readers," *The Reading Teacher, 20* (December, 1966), pp. 247–51.

to unlock unknown words. Many children who experience word recognition difficulties are able to associate individual sounds with corresponding letters, but they cannot make application of this knowledge if they have trouble distinguishing sounds within words. The problem will not be a severe one if the instructional program does not require children to depend solely upon these abilities. As has been noted earlier, some children might benefit more from initial presentations through visual modalities rather than through auditory channels. At the same time these children are learning to recognize words visually, they could receive training in auditory discrimination. As they grow in their ability to discriminate among sounds within words, both forms could be utilized in building sight vocabularies and teaching word recognition techniques.

Language Development

The findings of research on the relative importance of oral language development on beginning reading are far from clear-cut. Some of the research supports the observations of reading clinicians who know many young children with severe reading problems, but whose facility in using and understanding oral language is good. Oral language ability by itself does not seem to be a good discriminator of potential and actual reading achievement.[30,31] On the other hand, two investigators who conducted longitudinal studies of language usage found that superior language development and reading achievement were positively related.[32,33] Deutsch reported that socially disadvantaged children lack language facility necessary for school success. He felt that this inadequacy was one reason why so many of these children became reading failures.[34]

There doesn't seem to be much doubt that the language patterns of children from low socioeconomic groups vary significantly from those of children who come from higher income families. It is possible that for the former group oral language plays a greater role in causing difficulty in reading. Some feel that these children cannot cope with the language patterns found in readers, as well as in spoken language used in school, and as a result their reading achievement is adversely affected. "The more divergence there is between the dialect of the learner and the dialect of learning the more difficult will be the task of learning to read."[35] There is

[30] C. Martin, "Developmental Interrelationships Among Language Variables in Children of the First Grade," *Elementary English, 32* (March, 1955), pp. 167–71.

[31] Marguerite B. Bougere, *Selected Factors in Oral Language Related to Achievement in First Grade Reading.* Unpublished Doctoral Dissertation, University of Chicago, 1969.

[32] Ruth G. Strickland, *The Language of Elementary School Children: Its Relation to the Language of Reading Textbooks and the Quality of Reading of Selected Children* (Bulletin of the School of Education, No. 38). Indiana University, 1962.

[33] Walter D. Loban, *The Language of Elementary School Children.* Champaign, Ill.: The National Council of Teachers of English, 1963.

[34] Martin Deutsch et al., *The Disadvantaged Child: Studies of the School Environment and the Learning Process.* New York: Basic Books, Inc., 1967.

[35] Kenneth S. Goodman, "Dialect Barriers to Reading Comprehension," in Joan C. Baratz and Roger W. Shuy, eds., *Teaching Black Children to Read.* Washington: Center for Applied Linguistics, 1969, pp. 14–15.

no question that larger percentages of these children fail in beginning reading than children from higher socioeconomic levels.

It is entirely possible that oral language is an important element in reading for most children. How to measure fluency is a problem that has not been resolved. It seems clear that counting the number of words in sentences is not a useful way to assess language ability. Even if superior methods were designed, the answer to the basic question would not be fully found. A better answer could be expected if changes in oral language proficiency were produced through instruction and any influences on reading achievement noted.

Considering the present state of language knowledge, the results of limited research, and conclusions based upon empirical observations, it seems reasonable to conclude that provisions for the continuing development of oral language ought to be included in the school curriculum. It is not unlikely that oral language and reading are related and even possibly tied more closely together than one has been led to expect. Additional research might shed new light on this important question.

Evaluation of Readiness

Measuring readiness for beginning reading is no easy task. For one thing a constellation of factors seems to contribute to successful learning experiences. How much and in what combinations each operates to make learning possible is not yet established. Then, of course, there is the question of what is to be learned and how. Over thirty years ago Gates concluded that the instructional program really determines the degree to which children's efforts in beginning reading are successful. This observation seems to be as valid today as it was then.

In spite of the aforementioned problems, there are standardized readiness tests which their publishers claim teachers may use to help determine which children are and are not likely to make progress in beginning reading. Some teachers also use the tests for diagnostic purposes. How well readiness tests fulfill these purposes will be considered after an examination of representative testing measures.

Buros's *Reading Tests and Reviews* lists over twenty reading readiness tests that are in print. Many of them are similar in character; therefore, the most widely used tests will be included in this section.

Gates-MacGinitie Reading Tests: Readiness Skills. Grades kgn.–1, 1968, Teachers College Press, Columbia University. This test consists of eight subtests: listening comprehension; auditory discrimination; visual discrimination; following directions; letter recognition; visual-motor coordination; auditory blending; word recognition. Subtest scores are weighted on the basis of their predictive value in assessing readiness.

Harrison-Stroud Reading Readiness Profiles. Grades kgn.–1, 1956, Houghton Mifflin Company. The six subtests are: using symbols; making visual discrimination; using the context; making auditory discrimination; using context and auditory clues; letter naming.

Lee-Clark Readiness Test, 1962 Revision. Grades kgn.–1, California Test Bureau. The subtests are: letter symbols; concepts; word symbols.

Metropolitan Readiness Tests. Grade 1, 1966, Harcourt Brace Jovanovich, Inc. The seven subtests are: word meaning; listening; matching; alphabet; numbers; copying; draw a man (optional).

Murphy-Durrell Reading Readiness Analysis. Grade 1, 1965, Harcourt Brace Jovanovich, Inc. The subtests are: sound recognition; letter naming; learning words.

The authors of each of these readiness tests have included those subtests which they believe are appropriate for measuring the skills children need in order to achieve in beginning reading. All of the tests include sections on visual discrimination of letters and words and several tests for auditory discrimination. The Gates-MacGinitie and Harrison-Stroud Tests stress matching of letters and words rather than geometric forms; the Metropolitan Test uses both words and forms. Test items with similar names are not necessarily measured in the same way.

Tests of visual discrimination require children to select a letter from a series of letters which is the same as or different from the model letter. The same kinds of responses are required of words. Some of the exercises contain items that are grossly different from each other. They become progressively difficult as the letters and words look more alike.

f		t	h	l	f
g		g	y	g	g

run		rush	rat	run	sun
fall		fall	ball	fall	fall

Ability to discriminate among sounds might be measured by presenting an isolated sound and then asking children to listen for the same sound in words. Or children might listen to the initial sound in a group of words and pick out the word whose beginning sound is different. The ability to concentrate upon the task as well as remember the words could have positive or negative effects on the nature of children's responses.

Several readiness tests attempt to measure how well children understand language. The examiner either asks a question or makes a statement to which the children are asked to respond. Pictures are used to represent possible responses. Not only do children have to understand the language used by the examiner, but they must also be able to "read" the pictures and follow directions. Occasionally, children misread illustrations that are unclear or ambiguous. They might mean different things to different children, depending on the unique experiences the children have had. For whatever reason, some children might know the correct responses but not mark them properly. Only by reviewing the items with children would the teacher know how to account for the responses.

A careful reading of the manuals which accompany these readiness tests reveals that their results cannot be taken as firm indicators of readiness. In most cases, information about the reliability of the tests and test populations is incomplete. The predictive values of part and total scores are generally lacking. Even in cases where information is provided, it is clear that the tests suffer from shortcomings that are difficult to overcome. Their weaknesses are not very different from those of standardized reading tests.

Each test claims to contain valid items for measuring reading readiness. That they try to measure some of the skills which seem to be needed in reading is clear; how well they succeed is not as apparent. One investigator reported that a very small relationship existed among three measures of auditory discrimination taken from different test batteries.[36] Such results are understandable in view of the fact that tests do not sample the same items or in identical fashion. Users of readiness tests must evaluate how well the items discriminate among skills and whether they actually measure what they claim to measure.

How well do readiness tests predict future reading success? Do they sort out children who are likely to succeed and fail in beginning reading? Some readiness test manuals provide data on the relationship between their test scores and scores on reading tests in first grade. In most instances the correlations are so low that chance accounts for a good part of the variance. Independent investigators have been interested in their predictive value; they report correlations from below .30 to as high as about .75, with most between .40 and .60.[37] There are a number of explanations for these differences: the results from different readiness tests and criterion measures (reading tests) were studied, populations varied, reading instruction differed, and the statistics were not uniform. Failure to control for influences on the results, such as chronological age and intelligence, will inflate the correlations and lead to spurious conclusions.

Even where the coefficients of correlation are high, it is not possible to predict how well a given pupil will fare in reading. Chance and other factors play too important a role to make predictions feasible. Incidentally, intelligence test scores are about as useful for predicting progress as are readiness test scores. This would indicate that many intelligence tests measure the same things as readiness tests.

The results of reading readiness tests would be more meaningful if schools and teachers were to establish norms of their own. Thus if the children who did well in first-grade reading were to achieve within a range of readiness scores and these results were fairly consistent, the school would

---

[36] Robert Dykstra, "Auditory Discrimination Abilities and Beginning Reading Achievement," *Reading Research Quarterly*, 1 (Spring, 1966), pp. 5–34.

[37] Robert Karlin, "The Prediction of Reading Success and Reading Readiness Tests," *Elementary English*, 34 (May, 1957), pp. 320–22; Russell G. Stauffer and W. D. Hammond, *Effectiveness of a Language Arts and Basic Reader Approach to First Grade Reading Instruction* (U. S. Office of Education Cooperative Research Project No. 2679). Newark, Del.: University of Delaware, 1965; Roger E. Johnson, "The Validity of the Clymer-Barrett Prereading Battery," *The Reading Teacher*, 22 (April, 1969), pp. 609–14.

have a fair idea of what to expect from future populations who attended the school and experienced the same kind of reading program.

Of what use, then, are standardized readiness tests? They will yield information about performance on specified skills if the test items measure what they are supposed to measure. If there are indications that the skills were sampled adequately and that they are needed for reading achievement, teachers might use the results to identify children who required special help in overcoming specified weaknesses. If the readiness test meets the standards that have been set forth, teachers can view with greater confidence how well groups of children might perform in reading, especially for those pupils who do very well or very poorly on the readiness test. In any case, there seems to be little justification for assuming that nothing can be done for children who are weak in prereading skills. Nor is it realistic to wait for them to achieve. The surest way to find out how well children can perform is to teach them and see how they respond. There is too much evidence of self-fulfilling prophesies in situations where teachers believe children are incapable of learning. Furthermore, there is no hard line between prereading and reading skills, and instruction in reading could have a beneficial effect if the former is taken into account when teaching plans are made. As long as children do not need the skills in which they seem weak, reading can progress. General reading instruction combined with the passage of time might produce positive results even though specific attention has not been given to the weak skills areas.

The recognition that reading readiness tests are not good predictors of reading achievement led a group of investigators on a search for a battery of tests that would be more discriminating than single tests.[38] From over thirty tests these ten were selected: Pencil Use; Bender Visuo-Motor Gestalt Test; Wepman Auditory Discrimination Test; Number of Words Used in a Story; Categories; Horst Reversals Test; Gates Word Matching Test, Word Recognition I, II; Word Reproduction. Fifty-three children were tested and the Predictive Index identified fourteen of them as potential reading failures. Ten of the children did experience difficulty in learning to read while the Index failed to identify one reading failure. A judgment as to whether or not this or any other battery can do better than readiness tests must await the accumulation of additional data.

Another test that some experimenters have used to assess readiness is the Illinois Test of Psycholinguistics Abilities.[39] The subtests measure ability to understand spoken language, make verbal analogies, classify objects, manage concepts, and remember digit, picture, and geometric form sequences. It appears that some of the subtests are more closely related to prereading skills than others and that common factors could account for several abilities. How effectively the test identifies children with potential reading difficulties has yet to be determined.

---

[38] Katrina de Hirsch, Jeanette Jansky, and William Langford, *Predicting Reading Failure: A Preliminary Study*. New York: Harper & Row, Publishers, 1966.

[39] Samuel A. Kirk and James J. McCarthy, *Illinois Test of Psycholinguistics Abilities*. Urbana, Illinois: University Press, 1968.

ROSLYN PUBLIC SCHOOLS†
ROSLYN, NEW YORK

CONFERENCE MEMORANDUM

	MOST OF THE TIME	PART OF THE TIME	SELDOM	IMPROV-ING

I GENERAL PROGRESS

A. SOCIAL DEVELOPMENT
- WORKS AND PLAYS WELL WITH OTHERS
- SHOWS CONSIDERATION OF OTHERS
- IS READILY ACCEPTED BY THE GROUP
- PRACTICES GOOD MANNERS AND COMMON COURTESY
- SHOWS FRIENDLINESS TOWARD OTHERS
- ACCEPTS DECISIONS OF THE GROUP
- HAS CONSCIENTIOUS ATTITUDE TOWARD SCHOOL WORK
- IS AWARE OF GROUP RESPONSIBILITIES
- SHOWS LEADERSHIP ABILITY

B. EMOTIONAL GROWTH
- SHOWS SELF–CONFIDENCE
- PRACTICES SELF–CONTROL
- ADJUSTS TO CHANGE
- ACCEPTS CONSTRUCTIVE CRITICISM
- ACCEPTS RESPONSIBILITY FOR OWN ACTIONS
- RECOGNIZES OWN STRENGTHS AND WEAKNESSES

C. WORK HABITS
- LISTENS ATTENTIVELY
- FOLLOWS DIRECTIONS
- WORKS INDEPENDENTLY
- BEGINS WORK PROMPTLY
- MAKES CONSTRUCTIVE USE OF TIME
- COMPLETES WORK ON TIME
- WORKS NEATLY
- WORKS ACCURATELY
- TAKES PRIDE IN WORK
- WORKS TO BEST OF ABILITY
- CONCENTRATES ON JOB AT HAND
- SHOWS INITIATIVE
- IS RESPONSIBLE FOR CARE OF MATERIALS
- OBSERVES SAFETY RULES

	SATIS-FACTORY	UNSATIS-FACTORY	IMPROV-ING

F. PHYSICAL EDUCATION
- PREPARATION
- PARTICIPATION
- COORDINATION
- ATTITUDE

G. MUSIC
- PARTICIPATION
- ENJOYMENT

H. ART
- HANDLING OF MATERIALS
- EXPRESSION OF IDEAS
- ENJOYMENT

I. INDUSTRIAL ARTS
- HANDLING OF MATERIALS
- EXPRESSION OF IDEAS
- ENJOYMENT

IN VIEW OF _____ ABILITY, (HE) (SHE)

IN OUR BEST JUDGMENT
- IS DOING OUTSTANDING WORK
- IS DOING SATISFACTORY WORK
- COULD DO BETTER WORK
- NEEDS SPECIAL OUTSIDE HELP
- IS DOING UNSATISFACTORY WORK IN

IS WORKING UP TO CAPACITY ✱

MOST OF THE TIME	PART OF THE TIME	SELDOM

- RETENTION IS POSSIBLE

✱ CAPACITY AS DETERMINED BY MOTIVATION, PERFORMANCE, CONSISTENCY OF EFFORT, GENERAL APPRAISAL OF POTENTIAL.

TEACHER'S SIGNATURE _____ DATE

PARENT'S SIGNATURE _____ DATE

† *Source:* Conference memorandum from the Roslyn Public Schools. Reprinted with their permission.

Teacher Evaluation

There has been some interest in the possibility that teachers may be able to assess readiness for beginning reading as well as or better than readiness tests. Some teachers believe that they can predict with fair accuracy how well given children will do in reading on the basis of their observations of pupil behaviors and their teaching experience. Of course they know what kinds of instruction they will be offering. Then, too, there is the possibility that their attitudes toward children's chances to benefit from their teaching might be factors in influencing the outcomes.

The research on how teacher assessment of reading readiness compares with the results of readiness tests indicates that experienced teachers can do about as well as the tests.[40] What does this mean? Some teachers can make better predictions than others. Furthermore, not unlike the varied ways in which readiness tests measure different skills, teachers also apply different criteria in making their assessments. The degree to which the teachers' criteria are related to beginning reading achievement will have a bearing upon how effectively they can identify the children who are more or less likely to succeed.

Checklists that teachers might use to guide them in judging children do not vary widely. Ordinarily, these checklists are intended to supplement the information that readiness tests yield about specific skills performance. Typically they reflect what has been called the child development point of view, enunciated by such educators and behaviorists as Olson and Gesell.

GUIDE TO TEACHER JUDGMENT OF READINESS[41]

Physical Functioning
1. Has adequate vision
2. Has adequate hearing
3. Has adequate vitality and energy
4. Has good general health
5. Has adequate motor coordination
6. Shows consistent use of one hand and has not changed from left to right handedness

Mental Functioning
1. Shows ability to learn
2. Shows ability to follow directions
3. Shows ability to observe
4. Shows ability to remember
5. Shows ability to reason
6. Shows adequate attention span
7. Shows curiosity and interest
8. Shows interest in books and learning to read

---

[40] Elizabeth A. Zaruba, "Objective and Subjective Evaluation at Grade One," *The Reading Teacher,* 22 (October, 1968), pp. 50–54; Patricia S. Koppman and Margaret H. La Pray, "Teacher Ratings and Pupil Reading Readiness Scores," *The Reading Teacher,* 22 (April, 1969), pp. 603–08; Max S. Henig, "Predictive Value of a Reading-Readiness Test and of Teacher's Forecasts," *Elementary School Journal,* 50 (September, 1949), pp. 41–46.

[41] Adapted from the New York Reading Readiness Test, Form A.

Social Functioning
1. Gets along with other children
2. Can adapt to group activities
3. Responds well to group controls
4. Participates actively in group projects
5. Is satisfied with a reasonable amount of attention
6. Can perform usual classroom routines

Emotional Functioning
1. Is emotionally well-controlled for age
2. Is relatively free of nervous habits
3. Shows sufficient personal independence
4. Usually works with confidence
5. Usually seems happy
6. Shows relative freedom from hyperactivity

Language and Speech
1. Speaks clearly
2. Has English-speaking background
3. Has adequate vocabulary
4. Expresses his ideas adequately

Experience Background
1. Has had many opportunities to go places, see things, discuss
2. Has had many experiences with pictures, books, stories
3. Has had many experiences in expressional activities—painting, clay, dramatics, etc.
4. Has had kindergarten experience.

Although the usefulness of some checklist items might be questioned because of the results of more recent research and their apparent lack of relevancy to reading, many of them reflect the learning requirements of typical classroom settings and the expectations of teachers. Few would disagree that reading should be viewed in a larger context and that factors for which schools do not have primary responsibility can and do affect learning performance. What schools do or do not do can intensify conditions that might interfere with learning. Only when these conditions are identified can provisions for ameliorating them be made.

Readiness Activities

In not too many years past schools followed the general practice of delaying reading instruction in first grade to allow children to engage in readiness programs, usually offered through workbooks that accompanied their basal reading series. The length of time children needed to complete the workbook activities determined when they were introduced to book or other forms of reading. Most of the activities in the readiness materials involved the kinds of skills associated with some readiness tests: picture reading and picture and form matching. It is no wonder that some investigators did not find these materials very useful in promoting readiness for reading since the exercises in which the children engaged either were not needed by them or were not closely related to the skills of reading.[42]

Activities involving skills which have a more direct bearing upon reading and in which children show weaknesses give greater promise of fostering readiness than others which are farther removed from reading and offered indiscriminately. The simple fact is that many children come to school with the skills they need to engage in reading, and for them no delay in instruction is really necessary. Other less well-endowed children might engage in suitable readiness activities prior to and/or at the same time they are initiated into reading.

Although the results of research on reading readiness factors are far from conclusive, they do offer guides for determining what directions

43

.14

[42] Milton Ploghoft, "Do Reading Readiness Workbooks Promote Readiness?" *Elementary English, 36* (October, 1959), pp. 424–26; Margaret Silberberg, "Effect of Formal Reading Readiness Training in Kindergarten," *Minnesota Reading Quarterly, 11* (October, 1966), pp. 4–8.

[43] *Source:* **Teacher's Edition** *On Our Way To Read* **and Duplicating Masters. The Harper & Row Basic Reading Program. Copyright © 1966. Harper & Row, Publishers, Inc.**

readiness experiences might take. Some commercial materials still offer practice in listening to stories, interpreting pictures, developing concepts, and identifying forms in the belief that such activities contribute to readiness. More recent publications place more stress on auditory discrimination of sounds within words and visual discrimination of letters and words. For the exercise on auditory discrimination in the sample workbook page, the teacher asks the children to identify the animal in the first row of pictures. She then asks the children to listen to the beginning sound as she says the word *mouse*. She or the children identify the other pictures in the row. The children listen to the way the words *marbles, king* and *bicycle* begin. The children decide which of these three words begins with the same sound as *mouse*. The other rows of pictures are treated in the same way.

The exercise on visual discrimination requires the children to examine each row of letters and words (in upper and lower case) and decide which one is different from the others in the row. The pupils are asked to explain why they selected these letters and words. In this way attention might be

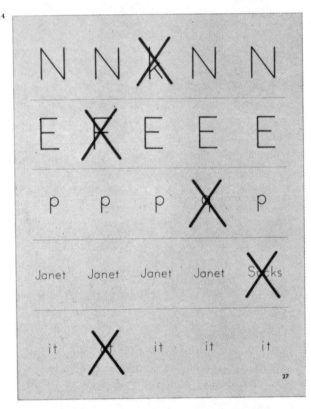

44 *Source:* Teacher's Edition *On Our Way To Read* and Duplicating Masters. The Harper & Row Basic Reading Program. Copyright © 1966. Harper & Row, Publishers, Inc.

directed to the parts of letters or words which make them different from others.

But exercises of this kind, by themselves, do not insure that children will gain adequate mastery of the skills involved in auditory and visual perception. Children who are weak in these areas will need further practice on both exercises and other types of activities. An effort should be made to present these activities according to their order of difficulty. Suggestions for developing auditory and visual discrimination skills follow.

AUDITORY DISCRIMINATION

SKILL	ACTIVITIES
Recognizing words that rhyme	Present paired words that rhyme: red-bed, boy-toy
	Present pictures of words which rhyme: pictures of a *fish* and *dish*
	Read simple nursery rhymes: Jack and Jill Went up the hill . . . .
	Read nursery rhymes which children complete: Hickory, dickory, dock The mouse ran up the ———.
	Present less familiar contexts with rhyming word to be supplied: Give the toys To the ———.
	Present word with rhyming word to be supplied: lap ———; burn ———
Recognizing words that have the same beginning sound	Have children whose first names begin with the same sound tell their names: Dick, Donald, Dorothy
	Present words that start alike: map-match, ate-ape
	Use pictures to represent words that begin the same way: pictures of a *boat* and *bone*
	Have children supply names of others that begin with the same sound: Tom, ———, ———
	Ask children to supply words that begin with the same sound:

sun, ——, ——
eat, ——, ——

Present paired words that do and do not begin the same way. Have children identify the paired words that don't start the same way:
lake-late; tap-happy;
over-open; end-in

Recognizing words that end the same way	Present words whose endings are grossly different: happy-big
	Present pictures of words that sound grossly different: pictures of a *fish, table, dog*
	Present words with final sounds that are obviously the same: lock-bike
	Have children supply words with the same ending sound: rush, ——; top, ——
	Present words with less obvious final sounds: read-had
	Present words with similar-sounding final sounds: wisk-wish; walked-hunted

VISUAL DISCRIMINATION

SKILL	ACTIVITIES
Distinguishing letters	Present letters that are grossly different: C C C T p p p u p
	Present letters that are somewhat similar: o c o o o N H H H H
	Present letters that are quite similar: F F E F F b d b b b
Distinguishing words	Present words that are grossly different: boy-carpet-boy
	Present words that are somewhat similar: swim-sits-sits
	Present words that are quite similar: what-that-what

Distinguishing phrases	Present phrases that are grossly different: in the snow-in the snow-at once
	Present phrases that are somewhat similar: to the store-in the sun-in the sun
	Present phrases that are similar: on my head-on my head-in my hair

Sometimes it is desirable to combine auditory and visual discrimination activities. For example, after children are able to recognize likenesses and similarities in the way words begin when they listen to them and can distinguish between letters when they see them, words might be presented visually while the teacher reads them. In this way children may begin to associate sound and symbol and to recognize the association when new words are presented.

Although the research is unclear as to how important a factor oral language is for beginning reading, it does seem wise to encourage children to use and respond to spoken language, since it is the basis of all forms of communication. Facility in the use of oral language can be developed through such activities as:

1. *Conversation:* greeting and speaking to each other, telling about one's activities, speaking on the telephone, listening to recorded conversations, experimenting and playing games with words.

2. *Discussion and reporting:* raising and answering questions, speaking on a topic, describing an event or personal experience, making announcements.

3. *Storytelling:* telling familiar stories, creating original stories, changing and predicting story endings, creating stories cooperatively.

4. *Dramatics:* acting out known stories and nursery rhymes, recreating familiar experiences, imitating others, using puppets.

Children will be reading selections for meaning. Most children who have a command of the spoken language will not have much difficulty following the ideas that are found in beginning readers or in the materials which they themselves may create. But children whose ability to use and understand language is not as fully developed might benefit from activities which channel their thinking in specific ways and develop the attitude that reading is a meaning-getting process. Preparation for literal reading, inferential and critical reading, and reading for main ideas and details may be provided through listening activities which focus children's attention upon these thinking skills.

The teacher could read stories and rhymes or children might listen to recordings of them. Questions based upon selected parts or entire narratives would help children listen for specific purposes:

Who are the main characters?
What is the story about?

Where is it taking place?
Which part (s) should be illustrated? Why?
Which parts aren't very important?
What happened to the main characters?
What would happen if ———?
Why is the story called ———?
Do the main characters behave like people you know?
How does the story make you feel?

In the discussion the teacher will ask the children how they arrived at their answers and will draw attention to reasons why one answer seems better than another or that more than one answer is correct. If questions arise about some responses, it may be necessary to reread or replay parts of the selection. It is this kind of directed thinking that children engage in when they read selections for themselves. The more relevant the experiences children have, the more likely they are to make the transition from understanding ideas gained through listening to getting meaning through reading.

IDEAS FOR DISCUSSION

There are indications that groups of children whose perceptual, cognitive, and affective skills approach the norm for their age-peers are ready to participate in beginning reading programs. Although no one can predict how well each child will do in the program he experiences, his chances for success are certainly better than those of another child who is less well endowed. Disadvantaged children are said to perform at much lower levels than children who are members of higher socioeconomic classes. Attempts to help these children overcome weaknesses in the perceptual, cognitive, and affective domains have met with varying degrees of success. But even if these children were to respond more favorably to training, some educators would raise another issue they believe has a direct bearing upon the success of efforts to teach them to read—that is, the nature of the reading materials they are using. Although beginning reading materials are not written in the way young children talk, they do follow the same structure that the average middle-class child uses in his speech. Herein, say students of language, is the problem that adversely affects speakers of nonstandard English.

Typical children have to learn the code in order to recognize what the symbols say and then relate what they read to the language they already know. Black ghetto children not only have to learn the code to know what the symbols say but they also must translate this unfamiliar language into the one they use. There is quite a bit of evidence that demonstrates a difference between the syntax used by these children and that of speakers of standard English. Other difficulties experienced by speakers of nonstandard English are related to the ways in which the pronunciation of words differs from that which they follow and are accustomed to hear.

Since efforts to get these groups of children ready for reading have not been very effective (if we judge these efforts by the number of reading failures), and remediation programs have not been too successful, some language students claim that the solution will be found in materials that represent the dialect spoken by the children. They propose that the language of these materials be changed to approximate the children's spoken language, just as the content has been changed to coincide more closely with familiar settings. Once children had learned to read in their own dialect, they could be taught to read standard English.

Is such a proposal feasible? Some do not think so. They point out that the materials would not be acceptable to the people who had to use them, just as radical changes in the content were rejected by them. Not all the children in the group might require these materials since some are able to speak standard English. There could be further interference in learning to speak standard English from the continuing usage of nonstandard English in speaking, reading, and writing.

Another alternative has been suggested. It is to use typical materials but not to discourage children from reading them in the vernacular. Thus it would be acceptable for the children to read aloud as they would normally speak, even if words or portions of them were omitted or seemingly mispronounced. A third alternative might be to postpone reading instruction until children have learned to speak standard English. There is some evidence that a delay of this kind could be desirable, but some children might never learn to read if instruction were postponed too long.

There do not seem to be ready and easy solutions to this difficult problem of language. Perhaps there are no panaceas. Nevertheless, the search for ways to provide more satisfactorily for large segments of the population must continue. It is not inconceivable that solutions will benefit other groups too.

Readiness at All Levels

Reference to the developmental nature of learning to read has been noted at the beginning of this chapter. Growth in reading is a gradual process, and each stage of development builds on earlier stages. The concept of readiness applies to these later stages as it does to the beginning ones. In fact, as children move up the reading ladder they probably encounter more problems with which they are not prepared to cope than at beginning reading levels.

Are pupils ready to read the materials teachers give them? More specifically, questions such as these suggest that the concept of readiness is one with which all teachers must be concerned, since they apply to any level:

1. Do the children have a sufficiently large sight vocabulary which will enable them to read with a minimum of hesitation and interruption?
2. How efficiently can they use decoding skills and context clues to identify difficult words and determine their meanings?
3. Are there large numbers of concepts which pupils will not understand and which the author doesn't explain?
4. Can pupils understand long sentences that contain complex structures?
5. How far removed are the pupils' experiences from those they will be reading about?

It seems clear that children might have a better chance of understanding what they read if they were prepared for some of the difficulties they would be meeting. If we assume that material is suitable for instruction, then there are a limited number of difficulties teachers have to be concerned about. *Before* children begin to read, teachers can help them relate what they know to the ideas they will be reading about. They can teach the words which they believe will be difficult for children to pronounce and understand. They can clarify strange and abstract ideas that the author fails to explain adequately. They can identify sentence elements that might be troublesome. And they can help pupils establish one or more purposes for reading so that aimless reading is avoided. These are practices which will help children respond to materials that might otherwise be quite difficult.

Are pupils ready to profit from instruction? The answer to this question depends upon what they have to know in order to advance. What do pupils have to know in order to use context clues for word meaning? What do they have to know to find an answer to a question through the index? Are pupils ready to learn how to summarize information if they are weak in separating important from lesser details? Can pupils learn to identify main ideas that are inferred without being able to find them when they are stated? The answers to these and similar questions imply the absence or presence of abilities on which future performances depend. Inherent in them is the idea of sequence which, if disregarded, can lead to unsuccessful learning experiences.

Teachers may avoid failures due to lack of readiness by finding out what pupils know about the skills they need to master. The purposes for which standardized and informal reading tests are administered have been explained in the previous chapter; insofar as readiness is concerned, knowledge of pupils' strengths and weaknesses plus an understanding of the sequential nature of skills development will increase the probability of offering meaningful instruction and reducing interference with learning. Lessons graded in complexity have built-in readiness guarantees that teachers cannot afford to ignore. Knowledge of where to begin in the sequence is the other ingredient of successful teaching.

The procedures for determining which level of books to use and how well pupils perform on specified subskills in word recognition, comprehension, and study skills have been explained in Chapter 2. Each of the skills areas will be studied in greater detail in subsequent chapters. All a teacher need do is refer to the subskills of the area he wishes to test and pattern brief test items after those given on pages 62–63. In this way he will be able to make some decisions about how well children perform and at what point on the skills continuum children need and are ready for instruction. Thus, if a teacher wished to find out how well children could use the index to locate information, he would prepare items that would test their ability to use alphabetization knowledge, determine entries (stated and inferred), interpret symbols, and find answers to questions. Within each of these subskills are different performance levels; the more careful their analysis, the more accurate will be the assessment of pupils' readiness to undertake advanced activities that assume previous learning.

SUMMARY

1. The concept of reading readiness is applicable to beginning and higher levels of reading. Inherent in the concept is the belief in the continuous growth of reading ability and the sequential development of reading skills.

2. The important question teachers should ask is not whether children are ready to undertake beginning reading but what children are ready to learn and how they should be taught. Children may be ready for one kind of instructional program but not for another.

3. More recent developments in child development indicate that readiness for any kind of learning is the product of maturational and environmental influences. It does not seem reasonable to expect the mere passage of time to bring all children to a satisfactory level of understanding and achievement. There is evidence to demonstrate the worthwhileness of training children to perform activities that they should and can learn.

4. A constellation of factors seems to account for beginning reading readiness. Intelligence, perceptual growth, emotional stability, language development, and experiential background contribute to readiness in unknown amounts. Visual and auditory discrimination of letter and word forms are abilities closely identified with beginning reading.

5. Reading readiness tests are unable to identify individual children who are likely to succeed or fail in beginning reading. The tests that measure subskills related to reading are fairly discriminating of groups of children who in performance are at the upper and lower levels. Too many factors are unaccounted for to make individual predictions possible.

6. Reading readiness tests are more valuable for the information they yield about individual performances on specified skills. Teachers' observations of children in prereading, reading, and other school activities can supplement the information obtained from tests. Checklists containing descriptions of classroom behaviors in various growth areas might be used in evaluating children's performances.

7. Activities which have a more direct bearing upon reading and for which children show a need are more productive than those only remotely related to reading. Activities involving visual and auditory discrimination of words and word parts are useful for developing sight vocabularies and learning phonic skills. These learning experiences should be graded in difficulty.

8. Oral language experiences involving children in conversation, discussion, and reporting, storytelling and creative dramatics will help develop language skills and possibly contribute to reading readiness.

9. Preparation for reading for meaning can be achieved through purposeful listening to stories and simple poetry. Discussions might revolve around answers to questions dealing with literal and in-

ferential meanings, main ideas and details, and evaluative thinking. The ways in which the children reason will receive more attention than the responses themselves.

10. Readiness for reading challenging materials can be promoted by relating children's experiences to ideas they will be reading about, by teaching difficult words, clarifying unknown concepts, and setting reading purposes. Graded lessons based upon known strengths and weaknesses will foster readiness for skills learning.

STUDY QUESTIONS AND EXERCISES

1. In what ways have new data on child development altered concepts of beginning reading readiness?

2. Why is it more fruitful to seek answers to the question, "What are children ready to learn?" than to ask, "Are children ready to learn?"

3. What factors seem to contribute to success in learning to read?

4. What is the teacher's role in promoting reading readiness?

5. How effectively do present tests evaluate reading readiness? What values do they possess?

6. Compile a list of activities that might be used to promote language development. Indicate the specific objective(s) for each activity.

7. Explain how the concept of reading readiness is applicable to all instructional levels. How might provisions for reading readiness reduce failures and promote achievement in reading?

SUGGESTIONS FOR FURTHER READING

For a succinct summary of the developmental viewpoint see Chapter III of Ernest R. Hilgard and Richard C. Atkinson, *Introduction To Psychology*, 5th ed. New York: Harcourt Brace Jovanovich, Inc., 1971; see also James L. Hymes, *Before the Child Reads*. New York: Harper & Row, Publishers, 1958, and Frances Ilg and Louise Ames, *School Readiness*. New York: Harper & Row, Publishers, 1965.

The history of the reading-readiness concept is traced in Chapter II of *Innovation and Change in Reading Instruction* (Sixty-Seventh Yearbook of the National Society for the Study of Education, Part II). Chicago: University of Chicago Press, 1968.

For additional information about and analyses of reading readiness tests see Chapters III and IV of *The Evaluation of Children's Reading Achievement* (Pespectives in Reading No. 8, 1967), and Chapter II of *Tests of Reading Readiness and Achievement: A Review and Evaluation* (Reading Aids Series, 1969). Both are publications of the International Reading Association, Newark, Delaware.

Lists of activities for developing reading and general school readiness will be found in: Lawrence W. Carrillo, *Informed Reading-Readiness Experiences*. San

Francisco: Chandler Publishing Co., 1964; Pauline C. Drumm, "Activities for Developing Readiness for Word-Attack," in Albert J. Mazurkiewicz, ed., *New Perspectives in Reading Instruction,* 2nd ed. New York: Pitman Publishing Corporation, 1968, pp. 204–12; *Handbook of Language Arts* (Curriculum Bulletin No. 8). Board of Education of the City of New York, 1966.

4

Developmental Reading

■ *Have you ever rightly considered what the mere ability to read means? That it is the key which admits us to the whole world of thought and fancy and imagination? To the company of saint and sage, of the wisest and the wittiest at their wisest and wittiest moment? That it enables us to see with the keenest eyes, hear with the finest ears, and listen to the sweetest voices of all times?*

JAMES RUSSELL LOWELL

This chapter is entitled "Developmental Reading." What does developmental reading signify? *Continuous* and *continuity* are the key words which describe the nature of the program. Reading instruction is one aspect of the school curriculum for which provisions are made in every grade. In this sense it is continuous. The reading curriculum is built on the established assumption that learning to read is an accomplishment that cannot be achieved in one effort. Instead, children learn to read and reach varying degrees of competence gradually. The reading they do in the primary grades is not adequate for the reading tasks they have in the higher grades. Children learn to sharpen their present reading skills and develop new ones through continuous learning and practice.

The other characteristic of developmental reading is continuity. Not only is learning to read a continuous and gradual process but also a sequential process. The curriculum, through graded learning activities and materials, provides for the orderly development of reading ability. It recognizes that children move from one stage of reading development to another, that as children grow in reading they learn to use what they have to progress to the next higher stage. This progressive movement is possible only if children are taken from where they are and encouraged to move forward at a rate they can manage. This means that progress in learning will not be uniform but that some children will reach a reading objective sooner than others. It also means that teachers will not expect mastery of specified reading skills or the development of reading maturity at stated intervals. They will understand that to proceed to higher and more complex learning activities before pupils have acquired the necessary prerequisites is not the best practice. Teachers will not regard themselves as third-grade or fifth-grade reading teachers but as teachers of reading.

Getting Started in Reading

What is reading? Is it simply a decoding process or is it more than that? The answer could be considered one of definition. Those who view reading as a decoding process would argue that most children understand the language of beginning reading materials and for them reading is a matter of learning to recognize what the words say. Once they have converted the written language into spoken language, reading ends. Advocates of this viewpoint say that beginning reading should consist of instruction in "cracking the code." For traditionalists this means concentrating upon letter-sound relationships or phonics; for members of one group of linguists it means focusing on spelling patterns. Essentially, both groups stress the importance of teaching grapheme-phoneme correspondences but differ in the ways they treat and teach them.

Opponents of the "cracking the code" school take the position that reading involves thinking and that the ability to convert written language into spoken language is not evidence that anything more than verbalism is occurring. The use of language and the ability to think are not synonymous, just as the inability to express ideas is no indication that thinking is not occurring. From the very first reading experience children should understand that written words represent ideas and that the function of reading is to discover what these ideas are. Advocates of this position do not minimize the importance of learning to recognize words, for without this ability reading cannot proceed. They do believe that thinking and learning to recognize words should not be separated, but that one should accompany the other. Thus they would prefer to use materials initially that are meaningful to children and can stimulate thinking. They would reject the exclusive concentration on learning to decode individual letters or graphemes into sounds or phonemes (as in some phonic reading systems) or on decoding words through the use of consistent spelling patterns as in "linguistic" systems.

Which position—decoding or meaning in beginning reading—is the sounder one? Both seem to have merit. There is no question that there has been some reluctance on the part of some educators to recommend working with beginning readers on word-attack skills. They have been stressing the importance of introducing children to reading through the use of meaningful materials and development of sight vocabularies. Later, teachers give attention to phonics and other word-attack skills, which are introduced gradually. By the time pupils have completed the third grade they have been taught these varied skills and can use them to identify unknown and difficult words. The charge that meaning is sought in materials which offer few opportunities for thinking has not always been undeserved.

Children who master the decoding process early—and there is more to word recognition than merely learning to use their knowledge of letter-sound relationships to pronounce words—can be given more meaningful materials to read and can begin to read for pleasure sooner than children who lack independence in recognizing words. These are reasons enough to offer beginning readers a well-conceived word recognition program that allows them to progress as rapidly as they can toward the goal of building an adequate sight vocabulary. This is an objective of any word-skills program.

There does not seem to be any justification for teachers to divide themselves into opposing camps and take divergent positions on this important issue. At the same time that they introduce children to reading through meaningful materials and concentrate upon comprehension, they can help children develop the skills which they need in order to grow in and through reading. This development does not preclude the introduction of word recognition skills that involve the use of context, phonics, structural analysis, and other aids at a level from which pupils can benefit. Inherent in this position is the idea that the learning of these skills will not be isolated from a meaningful context but that the instruction will occur within the framework of the total reading environment.

While there is research evidence from the First Grade Studies, independent investigations, and summaries of investigations that children benefit from instruction which does emphasize early decoding activities (see Chapter 1), the results do not endorse one approach over another. Taken alone, this could be interpreted to mean that any form of instruction meets the learning styles of children. However, the fact that the research has failed to identify superior programs does not mean that they do not exist. There is no need to repeat the shortcomings of research in beginning reading. Moreover, the study of psychology, linguistics, and psycholinguistics has provided insights into learning and learning climates and the development and use of language as these relate to reading. Present knowledge supports teaching procedures that build on what pupils know and can use. Translated into teaching strategies this means that skills development in word attack will grow out of reading activities rather than be introduced in isolation. Reliance upon single "methods" will be avoided. Learning to recognize words will be a part of the larger context of learning to read. The learning of grapheme-phoneme correspondences will be tied to the ways in which they function in words and how idea-forming units affect correspondences. Children will be taught how to apply recognition skills in combination so that they can solve word problems efficiently.

Would it really make any difference if children were introduced to reading by teaching them to associate discrete spoken sounds with letters? Isn't this what language is all about? Doesn't the evidence show that children learn to read as well this way as any other?

Although children can make all of the sounds they need for speaking, since infancy they have not been isolating the sounds of speech but combining them in various patterns in order to communicate. To require them to make separate sounds is as unnatural as asking them to break into distinct movements an action they perform without hesitation and hardly any thought. Young children can and are being taught to associate these isolated sounds with letters but until they are formed into normally-spoken words these sounds do not represent the sounds of language.

Children, we are told, have different learning styles. Some seem to favor one modality over another while others, insofar as can be determined, do equally well with any modality. This might be one of the reasons why some pupils are very slow in learning to recognize words—one modality of presentation is followed to the near exclusion of others. Early sound-letter instruction focuses attention upon the auditory with less emphasis on the visual. What would happen to a group of children who experienced this modality but required more attention to the other, writing (kinesthetic) opportunities, or a combination of all three? It is not always possible to ascertain which one is more favorable for a given learner. The suggestion that new experiences be offered through different modalities is one which might for some children make learning less burdensome and therefore more enjoyable. It might reduce further the number of beginning reading failures. And it would not be detrimental to those who preferred the visual mode or to others who responded equally well no matter what form the presentation took.

Acceptance of these tenets would rule out a number of reading systems which start by either teaching children to recognize the letters of the alphabet, introducing individual letters with their corresponding sounds and then combining the letters to form words, or following some combination of both.[1] The fact that teachers forgo programs that stress "synthetic" phonics is no assurance that all children will learn to read well. There is ample evidence that many children do learn to read in these phonics-oriented programs. Neither condition is justification for rejecting or accepting either one, for there are other factors which can influence the results. It has been said that a good teacher can teach reading with any "method," but what distinguishes a poor teacher from a good teacher has as yet not

---

[1] Basal or supplementary programs which are representative of one or more "synthetic" phonic systems include: *Functional Phonetics Series*, Benefic Press; *Phonetic Keys to Reading*, The Economy Company; *Royal Road Readers*, Educators Publishing Service, Inc.; *Early to Read Series*, Initial Teaching Alphabet, Inc.; *Reading With Phonics*, J. B. Lippincott Company; *Structural Reading Series*, L. W. Singer Company, Inc.; *The Phonic Readers*, Wenkart; *Carden Method*, Mae Carden; *Phonovisual Method*, Phonovisual Products, Inc.; *Basic Reading Program*, J. B. Lippincott Company; *Words in Color*, Learning Materials, Inc.

been clarified fully. Until there is evidence that suggests support for beginning reading programs of the synthetic variety, it seems prudent to follow others which have a meaning and a strong, well-balanced word-skills orientation.

Beginning Reading Experiences

Many children enter first grade with the expectation that they are going to learn to read. They have enjoyed a variety of experiences that have made them aware of the fact that spoken language can be represented by written forms. Not including the children who are among the 1 or 2 per cent who can read primary-level materials when they enter first grade, in most first grades there will be several children who can identify familiar brand names they have seen advertised on television and in the supermarket, recognize road signs, and read their own and possibly some of their friends' names. From having looked on and asked what a word was as someone read to them they have learned to recognize the written forms for a few familiar words. They might also know, from having followed along as parents or teachers read to them, that one reads a line from left to right and proceeds from the end of one line to the beginning of the next line.

Other children might not have enjoyed similar experiences, although they may be just as eager to learn to read. For these as well as the other children an environment that stimulates a curiosity about and interest in reading will provide the setting and a reason for learning to read.

What can a teacher do to make the classroom a laboratory for beginning reading? Here are some suggestions:

1. Fill bookshelves with colorful picturebooks and storybooks. These are books which children can look at themselves or which will be read to them.

2. Place some books on a table to attract the children's attention. Some might be open to encourage handling and examination. Chairs should be placed nearby for anyone who wishes to look at the books.

3. Attach children's name tags, written in manuscript, to the front of each one's place at a table or desk. The same might be done to identify the children's storage bins and clothes hangers.

4. Attach signs, in manuscript, to objects or stations in the room:

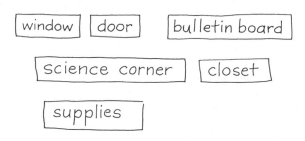

5. Mount attractive pictures and identify each with a label. These might include black-and-white and color photos of animals, school and neighborhood, children, well-known personalities, faraway places, etc.

6. Display children's artwork and writing with identification and subject tags.

7. Maintain a bulletin board for announcements, activities, weather conditions, birthdays, etc.

Today is [John's] birthday.

The weatherman says it will rain today and tomorrow.

Don't forget your lunch money!

Jobs for This Week
1. Check attendance.   Sally
2. Pass out supplies.   Chuck, Anne
3. Clean up after recess.   Sue, Tim, Andy

One of the purposes for having these captions, signs, and labels in the classroom is to help the children become word conscious. Another is to convey the idea that written words may be used like spoken ones. A third purpose is to provide opportunities for incidental learning of words commonly used by the children and teacher. The teacher might ask the children to find words around the room that start with the same letter. Someone might find two words that rhyme or that have similar parts, e.g., to*day* and birth*day*. All children will benefit from these learning experiences, particularly those who haven't had many experiences with written language. How children respond to these kinds of experiences provides a good indication of what they are likely to do when they are exposed to more formal reading activities.

What are the ways to teach young children how to begin reading? The synthetic approach—the study of separate sounds with their associated written forms, followed by the blending of known sounds into words—is not preferred for the reasons stated earlier. Two other systems, treated separately or blended into a favorable mix, come closer to meeting children's learning requirements; these are the language-experience approach to reading and the basal reading program. Each program is characterized by its own set of distinctive features, although variations in the ways they are developed are common. To avoid any confusion over terminology, basal reading as used in this textbook refers to instruction through the use of materials which are designed to develop reading skills and attitudes in a systematic, eclectic manner. Typical basal reading systems do not limit their treatments of reading to word recognition or phonics alone but cover the wide range of abilities and habits that mature readers display.

Language-Experience Reading

In the early 1960s Sylvia Ashton-Warner wrote a best seller, *Teacher*, in which she described how she taught the Maoris of New Zealand to read. The book made a profound impression upon the reading public, who wondered why teachers could not use the same techniques to teach their own pupils how to read. Miss Ashton-Warner explained how she taught Maori children to recognize familiar words. The words children used themselves became her materials for instruction. What many parents did not know was that children in schools in many different parts of the world are taught to begin reading in this way.

Not unlike Miss Ashton-Warner, this writer recalls how as a novice teacher he was at his wits' end trying to cope with a ten-year-old who could read no better than most children after three months of reading instruction. This boy came into the fifth grade with a long, well-documented record that revealed to everyone what a discipline problem he was. He lived up to his advance notices.

After several months of frustrating efforts to help the boy improve his reading as well as his attitudes toward school, the young teacher appealed to a colleague with whom he had attended some classes on teaching reading. He couldn't offer much help except to recall a reference the lecturer had made to a technique that had been found useful with some disabled readers. Although unaware of its rationale and procedures, the teacher asked the boy to make a few statements about George Washington, whose birthday was being celebrated the following day. He wrote down the comments on a sheet of paper. Then he asked the boy to read them. The boy did! This was the beginning of a slow but steady upward movement toward reading success for this child.

The language-experience approach to reading derives its name from its origins—children's language and activities. These become the sources out of which grow materials and methods for teaching reading. The rationale underlying language-experience reading is found in several principles of learning. Stated in simple terms they are:[2]

1. Learning takes place more readily if the child accepts as useful and important to him the activities in which he is expected to engage.

2. A child's learning is both richer and easier if he shares in selecting and setting the goals of learning, in planning ways to gain them, and in measuring his own progress toward them.

3. Learning is more efficient if it has satisfying emotional content—if feeling is supportive of thinking.

4. First-hand experience makes a deeper impression upon a person than vicarious experience.

---

[2] "Selecting and Evaluating Learning Experiences," *Guidance in the Classroom* (Yearbook of the Association for Supervision and Curriculum Development). Washington: National Education Association, 1955, pp. 52–62.

5. Learning is facilitated and reinforced when more than one sensory approach is used.

6. A child learns best when he is relieved of too great pressure to compete and when he feels reasonably confident that he can accomplish what is expected of him.

7. A child learns best when his efforts are appreciated by his teacher and his classmates.

8. Learning opportunities are richer for children when they are not restricted to the things which the teacher already knows.

Language-experience reading is not the only reading system which might fulfill these learning conditions. A good basal reading program likewise translates them into successful learning experiences. Moreover, whether language experience or basal reading is used, its creative implementation depends more upon teacher understanding and less on any of its inherent features. Its built-in characteristics do facilitate the teacher's task of providing meaningful instruction, but ultimately nothing becomes a substitute for the teacher's own skill in teaching reading.

Procedures in Language-Experience Reading

Language and experience—it is on these facets of growth that the program builds. Children use language to express their ideas, and they have something to say because they engage in activities in and out of school which leave an impression upon them. It is these impressions in their own language that language-experience reading captures.

The creation of language-experience materials can be a group or individual activity. Teachers will adopt both forms but initially they might find that children respond better when they are involved in a group activity. Also, teachers who haven't had much experience with the program might find that they can achieve superior results initially by not having to diversify their efforts among twenty or more individuals. Individualization will not be lost in the group activity.

STEP 1. *Stimulating discussion.* The first task is to get children to talk about what they know. This discussion might arise from an activity in which they have engaged or are participating in, from an event which they have seen or heard about, from plans that they are making, from ideas and activities they are interested in—in short, from whatever source has meaning for them. In response to a comment or question by the teacher, children could be stimulated to discuss such matters as:

what they learned about astronauts
how to find out what foods are nourishing
what stories they enjoy and why
how they like to spend their free time
what they should know about raising tropical fish
what they liked about the art exhibit

what they dream about

who their favorite TV characters are

how to make a magnet.

These topics are merely representative of a myriad of possibilities. Who the children are and where they live will influence the types of activities they might engage in and be interested in. Undoubtedly, there are experiences that are common to many children. The details might vary, but in essence they are similar. It hardly matters what the children talk about as long as they want to talk and have something to say. Reality and fancy are both fitting subjects for children to discuss, express opinions on, and speculate about. The teacher is a partner in the group and makes contributions as circumstances dictate. The teacher's role is largely that of a stimulator who encourages the free expression of ideas.

STEP 2. *Creating the story.*   Now that the children have had an opportunity to talk about the topic of immediate concern, they and the teacher are ready to compose a story about it. The following is an edited transcript of the way one class proceeded.

Teacher: Children, we've talked about our visit to the art show and how much we enjoyed looking at the pictures. Now let's write a story about our visit. Who can think of a good title for our story?

Hank: I think we should call our story "Funny Colored Pictures."

Teacher: Yes, we saw many unusual paintings at the exhibit.

Andrea: I have a better name: "The Art Show."

Phil: Let's call it "We Went to the Art Show."

Teacher: Does anyone else have a suggestion?

Paul: I like Hank's name.

Jack: Me, too.

Teacher: How many of you like Hank's title, "Funny Colored Pictures"? Most of you? Let's use that title. (The teacher said the name as she wrote the title on the chalkboard in manuscript.)

Teacher: How shall we begin our story?

Lila: Can it begin any way?

Teacher: Yes.

Harriet: Blue pictures, red pictures, zebra pictures.

Hank: What are zebra pictures?

Harriet: Black stripes and white stripes.

Chet: I like zebra pictures.

Teacher: Fine, let's write it that way. (Under the title she wrote, "Blue pictures, red pictures, zebra pictures," and read the line.)

Teacher: What else can we say about the pictures?

Hank: There were small pictures and big pictures.

Teacher: That's good. (She wrote and read the line.)

Margaret: The pictures were not real.

Teacher: What do you mean?

Margaret: They didn't look like real pictures. Just colors.

Teacher: We can write it that way. (She wrote, "The pictures were not real. Just colors," and read the lines.)

Phil: Many colored pictures.

Teacher: We'll write that too. (She wrote and read the line.) Now I'm going to read the whole story.

Funny Colored Pictures

Blue pictures, red pictures, zebra pictures.
There were small pictures and big pictures.
The pictures were not real.
Just colors.
Many colored pictures.

As the teacher read she swept her hand under each line in one continuous movement to indicate where she was in the story. The reading was in a natural voice with pauses where indicated.

Teacher: Who can read our story's name? (She moved her hand beneath the title.)

Andrea: I can. "Funny Colored Pictures."

Teacher: That's right, Andrea. Who can remember how we started the story? (She slowly swept her hand beneath the first line.)

Chet: I remember. "Zebra pictures."

Harriet: No. I think it says. . . .

Hank: I don't remember. . . .

Teacher: How were the pictures colored?

Chet: Blue pictures, red pictures, zebra pictures.

Teacher: Very good Chet. Harriet, will you try to read the same line?

Harriet: Blue pictures, red pictures, *zebra* pictures.

Hank: I know what it says next. "There were small pictures and big pictures."

Teacher: Who can remember what Margaret said about the pictures? (She moved her hand beneath the line.)

Lila: The • pictures • were • not • real. (Lila read very haltingly.)

Teacher: Lila, that's very good. Read the same line once more.

Lila: The pictures were not real.

Teacher: Excellent. What else did we say about the pictures? (She moved her hand beneath the next line.)

Margaret: Just colors. I said it.

Teacher: You certainly did. Paul, you read the same line.

Paul: Many colors.

Margaret: No. *Just* colors.

Paul: Just colors.

Teacher: Good. Now the last line. (With the same hand movement.)

Phil, Andrea: Many colored pictures.

Teacher: That's right. Jack, you try reading the last line.

Jack: . . .

Phil: Many colored pictures.

Jack: Many colored pictures.

The teacher then asked all the children to read the story in unison. Several hesitated at different parts and the teacher read along with the children when necessary.

Note that the teacher guided the writing of the story by interjecting questions and comments at appropriate times. She sought to write the story as the children dictated it—in their own language. Another teacher and another group of children are bound to produce a completely different story told in a unique way even though the experiences of the two groups might be quite similar. The teacher used manuscript so that the writing would resemble the way words look in books. Separate lines were used for each new idea to make it easier for the children to follow them. The spacing between letters and words clearly showed where one word ended and another began.

GROUP EXPERIENCE CHART[3]

splaSh doun!

the peepl hw bilt the rocket
ar fiksirg it soe that it can taek off
from Kennedy Spaes Senter. thae
loeded the rocket and started the
count doun. the rocket is blastirg off.
it is goeirg tw the mwn. a parashuet
is helpirg the rocket tw cum doun.
it splashd doun in the atlantic oeShun.
a boet brirgs the astronaut tw land.
it is a murgky. hee feels tierd becaus
it wos a lorg red.

Clean Air
Why do we need clean air ?
To breathe
To be healthy.
What makes the air dirty ?
Cars and trucks and busses.
SmokestacKs.

[3] In i.t.a.

INDIVIDUAL EXPERIENCE CHARTS

The Cool Rain

The cool rain feeds the plants. It cleans
the car. It snaps when it hits the ground.
It drips. It looks like tears on the window,
lightish blue, pink and silver.

Debbie

Once there was a child who had
a secret place.
    It was in some bushes,
    He would go there when he was mad
and when he was sad.
    And nobody knew where it was.
    And he liked it.

Sharon

My Father

    I like to read to my daddy. I like to go
to the store with him. I like to go out to eat
with him. He has a dimple when he smiles.
He has black hair. I love him.

Jennifer

There is one other point which might be worthwhile noting. All of the lines in the story the children dictated are not complete sentences. There is no reason why they should be, although many charts will consist of complete sentences. One of the strengths of experience reading is the advantage it takes of children's natural language. Moreover, children need to understand that writing serves different purposes and that its nature depends upon to what use it is being put. Thus a chart which tells what to do in a fire drill or how to perform an experiment is likely to consist of sentences, while one which expresses feelings might not. The writing should reflect what the theme is about and capture any flavor that might emerge from the children's speech.

The teacher involved as many children in the reading of the story as in the writing of it. She provided clues by helping the children recall different parts. (Who can remember how we started the story? How were the pictures colored? Who can remember what Margaret said about the pictures?) She encouraged the children to help each other read parts of the story. It should be obvious that the children were relying upon the context in order to read the words. Their familiarity with the setting enabled them to do as well as they did. The teacher rightly took advantage of their involvement with the content to have them reproduce the story. It is possible that a few children might have been able to identify some of the individual words, but the teacher was postponing this activity for another session.

The children who dictated the story about the art exhibit they visited had a good command of the language—an ability characteristic of many young children. The teacher recorded the story just as they told it. What if the group consisted of children who did not have such a command of the language or did not speak standard English? Should the teacher change the children's language and sentence structure to conform to acceptable standards or should she record exactly what the children say? Suppose the children had said, "The picture they not real." She might have written the statement as it should have been said or recorded the line just as they told it.

There is more than one view on this question. One is to write the story in the children's language, regardless of how divergent from standard English it might be. Children will read exactly what they say. A second is to translate the divergent speech into standard English and expect the children to read the corrected version as it stands. A third view is to write what they say in standard English but not require that they read it that way. They will read what they say. So, "The pictures were not real" could be read, "The picture they not real."

Those who hold the first view believe that after children learn to read their own dialect they can be taught to read another. Holders of the second viewpoint believe that the only way children who speak nonstandard English will be able to learn to use standard English is to use the latter at all times and under all conditions. Advocates of the third view do not believe it is practical to adopt the nonstandard written forms but that through example and gradual exposure the children will learn to speak and read standard English. However, there really isn't enough information about the outcomes of teaching plans which follow each of these positions to determine which has the greatest merit.

STEP 3. *Developing word skills.* The children's story is ready to be recorded by the teacher on oak tag. Oak tag is preferred to newsprint or other paper because it is much more durable and provides greater contrast between the manuscript writing and the background. The use of felt-tip pens enables the writer to make dark, bold strokes so that the words are large and sharp. At the same time that the large chart is prepared, many teachers make a ditto master using a primary typewriter so that each child has his own copy. The children might decorate the permanent chart with appropriate pictures, and each could do the same, if he wished, to his own copy.

Actually, the teacher will make two large charts. One will be a permanent record of the story; the other will be cut up for teaching word skills. It is not always necessary to have the second chart at later developmental stages since the children may know all the words which appear on it. However, in the early stages the children are learning to recognize words at sight and use beginning word skills; the second chart facilitates the teaching of them.

The teacher cuts up the lines of the story into separate strips so that they may be handled separately. These are placed along the ledge of

Funny Colored Pictures

Blue pictures, red pictures, zebra pictures.

There were small pictures and big pictures.

The pictures were not real.

Just colors.

Many colored pictures.

the chalkboard or on a stand so that everyone can see them. The first thing she plans to do is have the children match the cut-up strips with the lines in the story. She refers to the whole chart.

Teacher: Who will read the name of our story?

Phil: Funny Colored Pictures.

Teacher: That's right. Now, let's look at the strips of paper over here. Who can find the strip that says "Funny Colored Pictures"?

Harriet: I can. Here it is.

Teacher: Very good, Harriet. Now put the strip right under the name of our story. (The teacher may have to show the children how to do this.) Read the line again.

Harriet: Funny Colored Pictures.

Andrea: The words are the same.

Funny Colored Pictures

Funny Colored Pictures

The teacher asks different children to read the lines and match the strips with their counterparts in the story. This activity facilitates their discrimination abilities and develops recognition of some words. If a child were to select the wrong strip, the teacher would help him see that it is different from the line in the story by having him place it beneath the line and focus his attention on the dissimilarities.

The pictures were not real.

> Many colored pictures.

The teacher does not expect the children to learn all the words in the story. Some may recognize two or three while others will know many more. To facilitate recognition of individual words the teacher might write some on separate strips and compare each with the chart as she did with the cut-up lines. It would be wise to select initially words which don't look

| The | | Many | | pictures | | were | | colors |

too much alike. If the children have trouble recognizing a word, the teacher should refer to the story line in which the word appears.

As children read their stories, they can be alerted to use meaning clues to decide what an unknown word is. Many will be able to read the words because they do use the context. The teacher can ask the children to supply a word that makes sense for one they aren't sure of. She points out what the correct word is if they make a meaningful substitution. Once the children gained some phonic knowledge, they could use it together with the context to decide what a word is.

The teacher takes advantage of every opportunity to introduce word skills. The children will see that the only difference between some words in the story is the use of capital and lower-case letters:

Colored   Pictures

colored   pictures

She has the children look for words in the story that start with the same letter, listen to how these words begin and decide whether other words have the same beginning sound.

red   colors   There

real   colored   The

In this way she helps the children sharpen their visual and auditory discrimination skills and provides the first lessons of phonic analysis. Some children might be able to see the word "color" in *colors* and *colored* and look for known root words in other words. Recognizing root words is an important aspect of structural analysis.

If the first story did not contain words that enabled children to engage in all of these learning activities, others that followed would. A group might compose as many as eight or ten charts the first month; children progressing at a slower rate might develop fewer charts. In either case, there would be ample opportunities for teaching word skills.

Subsequent charts repeat some of the words of previous ones and provide reinforcement for their recognition. Children learn to recognize many words and to figure out what some others are. Thus, they build a stock of sight words as well as develop word-attack skills. Special lessons in word recognition extend their ability to use these skills efficiently and in different reading situations.

The children have copies of each story they have composed. These could be bound together in the form of books with illustrated covers. Classes might exchange copies for personal and group reading. The children might decide that some charts should not become part of their book. These could include ones which are not of particular interest to other groups, e. g., daily or weekly announcements.

Personal Language-Experience Reading

Individual language-experience reading may grow out of or accompany group reading. Children will be engaging in writing activities involving the words they are learning to read and others that they have some contact with. Even before they can do any independent writing children might dictate personal stories to the teacher, which she would record for each of them. The teacher could help each child learn some of his own words, as she did with the group. Children might prepare a file of personal words that they are working with; these could be used later in writing individual stories that each would read with the teacher. Some teachers have been able to use the tape recorder with some children. The children dictate their stories, which the teacher transcribes for them.

More mature children have or develop skills which enable them to do all or part of their story writing without a great deal of teacher guidance. These stories can be shared with other children just as the individual stories dictated to the teacher are read to the group by their authors. The teacher could use some personal stories for group reading and writing activities. In this way children would be exposed to a variety of learning experiences that contribute to growth in reading and possibly would be stimulated to express their own ideas in a unique way.

Language Experience and Other Reading

A child's first introduction to "formal" reading instruction might be through the language-experience approach. He might continue with this program until he is able to pick up one or more preprimers of a basal reading series and read them with ease. Some groups of children are introduced to the basal program in this way, and reading instruction through prepared materials and sequential lessons follows. There doesn't seem to be any reason why children cannot continue composing and writing experience stories that are used to reinforce and extend the skills, habits, and attitudes they are learning through the basal reading program. Experience reading is an activity that can be extended throughout the primary grades, not only to develop word-attack skills but also to increase comprehension abilities. Experience charts have a place in the higher grades too, although their primary purpose might not be to promote reading ability.

Children may move from language-experience reading into fictional and nonfictional books. Under these conditions teachers usually will continue with experience reading to develop additional skills that will allow children to read books of greater difficulty. Participation in an individualized reading program assumes the possession of reading ability; children cannot engage in such a program until they have enough independent reading skills to enable them to read books which are available.

Teachers can take advantage of the benefits that language-experience reading offers, whether it accompanies basal reading, is preliminary to it, or is used to start children on personalized reading. The more they understand what reading involves, the better able they will be to conduct such programs.

Basal Reading

How are basal reading programs different from other reading programs? The heart of basal reading programs is "a set of reading materials designed to develop important reading skills, to introduce the learner gradually to necessary aspects of reading, to cover all the important kinds of reading, and to provide for some over-all plan of development . . ."[4] Basal reading systems attempt to cover the complete range of reading skills and develop suitable reading habits and attitudes through sequential instruction via exposure to appropriate reading materials. These materials generally include readiness books, preprimers, primers and first readers, (all intended for use during the first year of reading instruction) and one or more books for each successive year through the sixth or eighth grade. Workbooks and supplementary reading books, filmstrips, ditto masters, and other teaching aids accompany the reading textbooks of several series. The publishers also provide a teaching manual that explains in great detail how all these materials plus others might be used to meet the reading needs of children at each grade level and stage of development.[5]

Although many basal reading systems offer these similar types of materials as the base of a comprehensive reading program, their content and manner of treating it vary from series to series. Thus, some first-year programs provide for stricter vocabulary control than others by introducing fewer different words and repeating them more. The sequence and pace for introducing word and comprehension skills are not uniform. Workbook exercises may precede or follow the reading of selections. There are series that have incorporated some features of the so-called linguistic materials by

---

[4] Virgil E. Herrick, "Basal Instructional Materials in Reading," in Nelson B. Henry, ed., *Development in and Through Reading* (Sixtieth Yearbook of the National Society for the Study of Education, Part I). Chicago: University of Chicago Press, 1961, p. 187.

[5] Among the publishers of basal reading programs are the following: Allyn and Bacon, Inc.; American Book Company; Ginn and Company; Harcourt Brace Jovanovich, Inc.; D. C. Heath and Company; Holt, Rinehart and Winston, Inc.; Houghton Mifflin Company; J. B. Lippincott Company; Lyons and Carnahan Company; The Macmillan Company; Row-Peterson Company; Scott, Foresman and Company.

reducing the amount of letter-sound variance. While some of the beginning reading materials focus on the family, others develop social studies and science themes. And, of course, the ways in which the manuals suggest how the selections should be treated and the skills taught vary from series to series.

For many, the teacher's manual is the most important component of the basal reading program, since it contains a step-by-step explanation of how teachers may use the materials to develop reading ability and what they might do to enrich the program's offerings. The inexperienced teacher of reading tends to rely upon the plan of instruction which the manual outlines and does not deviate greatly from it. Teachers with more knowledge and experience use the manuals with greater discretion, sorting, sifting, and evaluating the lesson plans, using the suggestions they consider appropriate for their children and modifying and supplementing them with instruction and activities of their own. The teaching plans reflect the point of view that learning to read is a continuous process and that the objectives of a reading program may best be achieved through a carefully organized and sequential development of learning experiences, without leaving to chance or teacher variation the fulfillment of the program's objectives. Ultimately, however, the individual teacher is expected to determine how best to make use of the plans, which are given to him in detail.

Beginning Instruction

Most basal reading programs offer some form of readiness activities before introducing their first preprimer. These include identification and visual discrimination of words, auditory discrimination of sounds within words, listening comprehension, and concept development. Ordinarily, the teaching manual points out that all children do not require intensive work in each of these areas and that some children might bypass all of them without suffering any loss. Teachers are encouraged to use the results obtained from standardized readiness tests and/or tests that accompany the basal program to determine what aspects of the readiness program groups of children should engage in.

Some prereading activities involve the association of letters with their corresponding sounds within words and the writing of these letters. These are taught through exercises provided in the teacher's manual and workbook with the view to helping the children use this knowledge in their first exposure to the preprimer. The letters taught are those which appear in the beginning of the new words so that the pupils may use this knowledge together with any context clues to help them recognize the few words in the first group of selections. The children are previously taught to use context clues to supply missing words in sentences given orally and to do the same when the beginning letter of the omitted word was given to them.

The selections in the first preprimers are limited in content for the obvious reason that most of the children have few word recognition skills and cannot cope with many different unknown words at one time. The first preprimers vary in the number of words they introduce but most do not contain more than twenty-five different words. The words are repeated in these books as well as in the other preprimers that follow the first. Some series use the rebus to introduce an occasional word; the use of this technique (in which words are represented by a symbol or picture) allows some freedom in extending the ideas contained in the preprimer selections. The criticisms that preprimers contain uninteresting and inane selections written in the stilted and unnatural language patterns of the oh-oh-oh, look-look-look variety and that children should read more exciting and better-structured stories are not completely warranted, although there is no doubt that some excesses might have been avoided. More recent basal series have changed their preprimer formats to meet some of these objections, but during the initial reading experiences children are not expected to learn many new words at one time, just as in language-experience reading a few words are selected from each story and learned by the children.

Basal reading systems follow a similar plan for teaching reading. This plan consists of several components whose treatments vary from series to series. These components are:

1. preparation for reading
2. directed reading
3. building and extending skills
4. enrichment

Preparation for reading consists of building some background for reading the selection, introducing new words, and establishing purposes for reading.

Directed reading consists of silent reading, discussion and questions about the reading, and oral rereading.

Building and extending skills involves practice in using previously-taught skills and activities that introduce new ones.

Enrichment involves activities that are related to the reading and includes other reading and writing and creative activities.

To give the reader a clear idea of how children might be introduced to their first experience in reading the preprimer, an adapted version of a plan from a basal reading series is presented here in some detail.[6] The text of the partial table of contents and story is presented also to help make the plan more meaningful. In an introductory note the authors remind the teacher that the initial consonants of most of the words which appear in the story have been taught previously.

---

[6] Adapted from the *Sun Up* and *Reading Skills One,* Teacher's Edition. The Bookmark Reading Program. New York: Harcourt Brace Jovanovich, Inc., 1970, pp. 61–68.

Sun Up

The sun was up.

Sandy was up.

Bing was up.

* *Source:* From *Sun-Up*, Student's Edition, by Margaret Early, et al., copyright © 1970 by Harcourt Brace Jovanovich, Inc. and reprinted with their permission.

Preparation for Reading   The children turn to a page in the workbook which has the picture of a cat with its name *Bing* beneath it. They are reminded that the name of the cat beneath the picture starts with a letter they know. "Listen for the first sound as I say the cat's name—Bing." The children compare the word on a card with the word in the story and say it. In the workbook they trace the word in a space below the cat's picture and then they read the cat's name. This same procedure is followed to introduce a dog whose name is *Sandy*.

The children are next introduced to *and*. They are referred to the picture of the cat and dog. "What do you see in this picture? The words under the picture tell about it. What word says *Bing*? *Sandy*? What word do you think comes between the names of the cat and the dog?" The teacher tells the word if the children don't know what it is. The teacher displays the word *and* on a card, the children read the word and then trace it in the workbook. The children practice reading *Bing, Sandy* and *and*.

The next step in preparation for reading involves the introduction of *the* and *was*. The children turn to the workbook page that has sentences made up of words and pictures. The children's attention is called to the first sentence which the teacher reads. "*The* (picture of sun) *was* (yellow-colored mass)." The children repeat the sentence, which the teacher might write on the chalkboard. Left-to-right progression is indicated. "*The* is the first word in the sentence." The teacher presents a card with *The* on it and shows that *the* is the same word. The children underscore it. "The other word is *was*. It begins with a *w*." She shows *was* on a card and the children find it in the sentence. The teacher calls the children's attention to the capital T. "The first word in a sentence begins with a capital. A dot which is called a period marks the end of the sentence." The children indicate where the period is and trace the words *The* and *was* in the workbook spaces. Then the children do a workbook exercise that uses the words *Bing, Sandy, The* and *was* in sentences. The sentences combine these words and pictures that represent words. Attention is called to the capital letters and periods in the sentences.

The last part of preparation for reading consists of teaching *sun* and *up*. The teacher asks questions about the picture in the workbook page to elicit from the children the idea that it represents a bright sunny day. She refers to the sentence below the picture—The *sun* was *up*—and teaches the underscored words in the manner described above. Then the children match sentences containing *Bing, Sandy, The, was* and *up* with their appropriate pictures. Exercises to reinforce the recognition of these words follow, e. g., a word that begins like *sun* is _____; Can you see _____ wind?

The teacher tells the children that they know all the words in the story. The children read the title of the book silently and then orally. Teacher and children discuss what this book is likely to be about from the title and cover illustrations. (The teacher clarifies the relationship of sun up to sunrise and sunset.) The teacher identifies the title pages and refers to the contents. "Who can point to the title of the first story?" The children indicate where and what it is. The teacher shows how to tell on what page the story begins and the children turn to that page. After a brief discussion of what the children do early in the morning the teacher says, "Let's read about the early morning and find out who is in the story."

Directed Reading   "Read the first page of the story to find out where the sun was." The children read silently and respond.

"Do you think anyone else was up? Read the next page to find out." After reading to answer the question, they read another page to find out who else was up. Discussion about the illustrations and how the children can tell the sun was up is suggested.

The children select from the word cards those they need to build sentences which the teacher reads, e.g., "The sun was up." The children read the whole story orally as they would speak naturally.

Building and Extending Skills   The teacher displays the word cards. "What word do you know that starts the same way as *Sandy.*" As the children suggest words, the teacher writes them on the chalkboard, underlining the first letter. Other words are treated in the same way.

The children read the following items printed on the chalkboard and decide which are sentences:

> The sun was up.
> Bing and Sandy.
> Sandy was up.
> Sun up.

The children play a word game. The teacher displays a word card, a pupil reads it, finds the same word in the exercise above, and then erases it.

Additional practice in reading sentences is provided in a workbook exercise. Children indicate if the picture correctly represents what each sentence says. Exercises in matching phrases and sentences are suggested for those who need extra practice in visual discrimination.

Enrichment   Two books that deal with starting a new day are suggested for the teacher to read to the children. A poem on the same theme is provided. "How does the poet feel about the sun coming up?" The title of a record, *When the Sun Shines,* is recommended for its rhythmic qualities. The last suggestion involves the writing of an experience story about what the children do when they arise in the morning.

IDEAS FOR DISCUSSION

The extent to which the teacher follows the lesson plan depends upon his own understanding of teaching reading and the children with whom he is working. Some children might not have to engage in every activity suggested in the plan while other children could profit from all of them, and even additional work which the teacher would devise. How rapidly the children cover the steps in the plan depends upon their levels of preparation and achievement. Some groups might be able to cover the whole lesson in two sessions; other groups might require more time. These judgments cannot be made by the series' authors, but must be left to the individual teacher, who decides how to adjust his teaching to the individual requirements of the children.

Note that many of the activities provided in the plan are not very different from those a teacher might adopt in the language-experience program. The same types of word recognition exercises could be offered in both approaches. Both programs prepare children for reading, give direction to reading, and offer direct instruction in reading. The major difference between the two programs is that in language-experience reading the materials originate with the children. Both programs might operate concurrently and reinforce the learnings children derive from each.

Continuing Reading Instruction

Reading programs that fulfill some requirements of beginning reading instruction may or may not meet the objectives of a comprehensive reading curriculum for the elementary school. Some beginning reading programs are not designed to accomplish much more than establish a foundation for subsequent instruction offered through other types of programs. This foundation is largely in the area of word recognition on which phonic, "linguistic," orthographic (spelling) and programed systems concentrate. Language-experience reading might continue in some form throughout the elementary grades—charts on which information and ideas are recorded can be useful at any level—but it is unlikely that teachers would satisfy children's major reading requirements by relying exclusively upon this method. Thus the tendency to depend more upon basal reading and other programs for offering continuing reading instruction is prevalent. The knowledge that no single program offers everything children should experience in reading has led to the suggestion that teachers adopt useful practices from whatever sources are available and combine them with their own to create a wide-ranging, goal-oriented reading program. This means that children will be exposed to many promising practices that are designed to promote growth in reading.

Individualized Reading

The idea that children cannot engage in individualized reading until they have acquired some independence in reading has already been suggested. By "some independence" is meant the acquisition of an adequate sight vocabulary and possession of word-attack skills that allow freedom to read available materials which children can understand. Thus any program that enables children to acquire these skills might be a forerunner of an individualized reading program. Some children could be introduced to individualized reading before the end of the first year's reading program while others might need more time to develop adequate reading maturity in order to engage successfully in the program. As a general practice schools tend to delay the introduction of individualized reading until the third or fourth grade, by which time most children will have mastered many basic reading skills. However, advocates of individualized reading would involve children in the program much sooner than this.

Individualized reading is based upon the principles of self-selection and self-pacing. Unlike the basal reading program, which provides the selections to teach children the skills of reading, children select from a variety of imaginative and factual reading materials the ones they wish to read. Their choices are limited only by the availability of materials, although teachers might in some cases where children always tend to select too difficult or too easy books guide them to more suitable ones. The principle of self-pacing implies freedom from conformity imposed by group participation.

Children progress at their own rate. They are not impelled to match anyone else's progress but proceed as rapidly or as slowly as their abilities dictate.

How does an individualized program work? Children are encouraged to select books that they might wish to read. A child might decide after sampling a portion of the book he chose that he doesn't wish to continue reading it. He is free to return the book and select another. Really free choices are impossible unless there is an adequate supply of materials of many different kinds and of varying difficulty. Estimates as high as fifteen to twenty books per child have been suggested. This would mean a minimum of from 300 to 500 books for the typical classroom. (Most classrooms in which individualized reading is the basic program have fewer books than this number. Basal readers are often part of the collection, which consists mainly of trade books.)

A major feature of individualized reading is the conference. This is the time when child and teacher meet on a one-to-one basis. These conferences may be scheduled at regular intervals and/or when children desire them. While all the children are reading the material of their choice, the teacher meets with one child to discuss what he has read and to deal with any problems he has encountered. The children understand that they are to keep a record of what they have been and are reading and note any questions they might have or difficulties they experienced.

During the conference period the teacher might seek to determine the extent to which the child understood what he read. Familiarity with the books would be necessary if the teacher were to ask questions that probed beneath surface meanings. He might ask the child to read some parts orally and/or silently if he thought some problems existed. If the child indicated some difficulties or the teacher realized what some were, the teacher would deal with those that he could in the allotted time and make a note of what he still had to work on during another conference with the child. If there were other children who required similar help, he could bring them together for a group lesson. Records of what children have read and what their reading needs are must be kept by the teacher.

What follows is an edited transcript of a conference one teacher had with a third grader. The book he had read was *The Big Green Book* by Robert Graves (The Crowell-Collier Press). This is a story about an unhappy orphan boy who lived with his aunt and uncle. One day Jack found a big green book which contained directions about how to cast magic spells . . .

T=Teacher   Ch=Child

Ch: Wow, I wish I could do what Jack did!

T: Who's Jack?

Ch: He's the boy in the story. He learned to do magic tricks and changed into an old man and played a trick on his aunt and uncle.

T: Why did he play a trick on his aunt and uncle?

Ch: He didn't like them.

T: Why do you say that?

Ch: It said in the story they didn't like him.

T: Turn to the part where it says that. Read it to me.

Ch: "Jack's father and mother were dead and the uncle and aunt were not very nice to him."

T: Does it say that Jack didn't like them?

Ch: No, but I wouldn't like anyone who wasn't nice to me.

T: Very good. Do you know what we call this kind of reading when you figure out ideas for yourself?

Ch: No.

T: Reading between the lines.

Ch: That's funny. Maybe Jack read between the lines too.

T: Why do you say that?

Ch: He read a book and found out about magic tricks.

T: Did the book tell how to do the tricks?

Ch: Yes.

T: Did Jack have to read between the lines to find out how to do the magic tricks?

Ch: No, the book told everything. Oh, I wrote a word I don't know. (The word is *disappear*.)

T: Let's find the word in the story. You say it's on page. . .

Ch: There are no pages. I mean the pages don't have numbers on them. I can find it. Here it is.

T: Can you figure it out from the sentences?

Ch: (He reads the page silently.) No.

T: Look at this word carefully. Do you remember we had it last week? (She writes the word *appears* below the word *disappear*.)

Ch: Oh, that's *appears*.

T: Good. Now look at. . .

Ch: The same word is in the other one without the *s*. Oh, now I know what it is: *disappear*. Jack made himself disappear.

T: Right. (She makes a note about the child's need to work on root words.) Were there any other words you didn't know?

Ch: There was another word. (He locates the word *ragged* in the story.) I don't know it.

T: Can you recognize a root word in it?

Ch: *rag*?

T: Good. We pronounce it in two syllables. Try it.

Ch: *ragged*?

T: How many syllables does the word have as you said it?

Ch: One.

T: We pronounce this word rág-ged. Now you say it. What do we mean when we say a *ragged old man*?

Ch: He was dressed in rags.

T: Right. ("I have to find other words that are pronounced like ragged.") What trick did Jack play on his aunt and uncle?

Ch: Jack changed himself into an old man and his aunt and uncle didn't know who he was. He played cards with them and won the house.

T: What happened then?

Ch: Oh, he gave it back to them. They never found out he was the old man. He changed himself back to a boy.

T: Did he do more tricks?

Ch: No.

T: Why not?

Ch: I don't know. . .

T: Turn to the end of the story and see if it tells you.

Ch: Oh, it says that he was scared to do more tricks. . .

T: What was one trick he was afraid to do? Look at Jack in the picture. What is he thinking about?

Ch: He's afraid that if he changes small animals into big ones they might do something bad. He only uses the magic in school to learn.

T: You said before that Jack's aunt and uncle weren't nice to him. How do you think they will treat him now?

Ch: Good.

T: Why?

Ch: Because the old man was good to them. He gave them back everything.

T: You could be right. What would *you* do if you could make magic tricks.

Ch: I'd make myself disappear.

T: Why?

Ch: Scare people!

Notice that the teacher did not dwell upon a lot of details in the story. She did ask questions which caused the child to reflect about what he had read. She made some references to the text itself and had the child justify some of the things he said by asking him to refer to the story. In addition, the teacher helped the child relate this fanciful tale to himself as well as speculate about future events.

The teacher provided on-the-spot instruction in inferential reading and word-attack. She reserved more intensive instruction in recognizing root words for another time. She also made a mental note to give a lesson on words that were pronounced the same way as *ragged*.

This child did not find the material too difficult. Another child reading the same story might require different kinds of help. Whatever the problem, the teacher stands ready to offer immediate help in the brief time she has and reserves for another time lessons that require more planning and time.

The length of the conference will vary with each child. Some will require less time than others although children look forward to meeting with the teacher and might feel shortchanged if not given their full share of time. But time limits must be placed on the conference if the length of the reading period is to be kept within reasonable limits. How long children can be expected to read by themselves is a question that each teacher must face. How often the teacher will meet with each child will be determined by the length of the conferences and the child's needs. Some teachers schedule reading conferences twice a day. If ten to fifteen minutes were allotted for the conference, the teacher could meet with four to five children an hour; with two sessions a day it would be possible to see each child once every three to five days.

If a few children read the same or similar books, the teacher might schedule a group conference during which their reactions could be sought or some unifying activity conducted. Some common writing and other creative activities might be planned as a result of having read these materials. This joint conference provides opportunities for children to share ideas and for the teacher to focus attention on important elements in which more than one child is interested.

IDEAS FOR DISCUSSION

It is apparent that to conduct a successful individualized reading program the teacher not only must be knowledgeable about reading but also be fairly creative. She must have a good understanding of the reading skills and know how to teach them. She must also know how to diagnose difficulties from the way children respond to questions and participate in the discussions. She must be alert to clues children provide about their reading and be ready to give immediate help when it is needed. And she should have a working knowledge of the materials children are reading so that she may be an active participant and be able to highlight ideas and use the materials to fuller advantage.

It cannot be denied that there are many teachers who are very capable and can assume all these responsibilities, and there are schools in which teachers are conducting good individualized reading programs. However, local and nation-wide surveys reveal that considerable segments of the teaching population do not know as much about teaching reading as they should. The responsibilities an individualized reading program would place upon them could become intolerable unless they were able to obtain on-going assistance and devote the time that would be needed to strengthen the reading program.

There are some other problems associated with individualized reading. There is evidence to support the position that it is better from the learner's standpoint to deal with skill-development in some sequential fashion—that is, to proceed from the simple to the difficult, from the known to the unknown, from lower to higher levels. Some groups of children might not be affected seriously by gross violations of sequential learning; but there are many others who fail to learn because of the interference produced by lack of organization. Unless teachers were quite knowledgeable about reading they wouldn't be able to provide on-the-spot assistance that meets the requirements of sequential instruction. Some educators have suggested that the program be reserved for better readers, but its supporters say that it is the poorer ones who need it more.

While some basal reading programs assume that children require extensive preparation for reading and leave little room for independent thinking and discovery, individualized reading takes the other extreme position that children do not need any preparation at all for reading. The latter view might gain support in those cases where children selected simple materials to read. It would be questioned where the material was more difficult and contained words that could not be identified, unknown concepts that were not explained well, and ideas to which children could bring few experiences. If children can choose what they read, they are bound to pick some books that present these problems. Readiness activities that deal with some of them do help make the reading more meaningful.

No matter what kind of reading program a teacher conducts, children should have access to many and different kinds of books. If the intent of individualized reading is to be met, the supply of books will be large in order to offer both narrative and factual types on varied themes and levels. It also will require replenishment; otherwise, the children will have few new choices to make. How many schools can provide such collections for each classroom is questionable.

A related problem involves the appropriateness of materials to teach specific reading skills: not all are equally suitable. Study skills instruction would not be very meaningful if conducted with story-type materials. If children did not select factual materials or they weren't available, no attention would be given to these skills unless the teacher offered reading instruction as children read their textbooks in science, social studies, and other subjects.

Can the best features of individualized reading be utilized in a well-conceived, comprehensive reading program? Few educators would maintain that any single type of program exemplifies the best that can be devised. It seems clear that the reading opportunities which individualized reading encourages should be part of any reading curriculum. The individual conference is another feature that teachers who follow other programs can and should adopt. It is even possible for teachers to conduct individualized reading classes and engage in more organized reading activities. Class schedules could be adjusted to accommodate both teaching styles.

Basal Instruction

Unlike individualized reading, basal reading programs provide the materials which children need to strengthen existing and develop higher-level reading skills. In addition, provisions for recreational reading, that is, reading of one's own choice, are built into most programs. Efforts are made to include in basal readers selections that have wide appeal for both boys and girls as well as other selections which meet individual requirements. Naturally, all basal reading programs do not give equal attention to the same types of reading and reading skills. Therefore, there are variations in the kinds of selections one finds in basal readers. At the upper reading levels the tendency to include more factual-type selections than has been the practice in the past is growing. In fact, a few basal reading programs offer separate books that are limited to story-type or informational reading. One series also includes actual pages drawn from different subject textbooks that children use so that they may apply the skills they learn to the kinds of materials they are expected to read.

In the section "Getting Started in Reading" there is a step-by-step lesson plan of the way in which one basal reading program introduces children to their first book reading experience. Now let us examine how this series uses its materials to reinforce and develop reading skills in the upper grades. The same basic structure is followed throughout each grade level. The lesson which follows is based upon a selection drawn from a sixth-level book[7] of factual-type and textbook materials. The components of the lesson—preparation for reading, reading and discussion, building and extending skills, and extending learnings—are characteristic of other basal systems, although the ways in which they are treated vary from one to another.

Each unit in this series focuses upon a major skill. Prior to reading any selections in the unit children receive instruction and practice in the skill. Then they are expected to apply this skill and others they have learned in their reading of the selection. Thus they read the selection not merely to acquire information but to learn how to use their skills in order to understand more.

The unit skill under consideration deals with patterns of organization, particularly comparison and contrast and cause and effect. An earlier unit covered topical organization and time order. One of the unit selections is *Insect Eaters of the Plant World*, for which the following is a lesson plan adapted from the teacher's manual.

Skills focus: noting organizational patterns; finding context clues to meaning.

Content understanding: Some plants satisfy their need for nitrogen by trapping and "eating" insects. Three of these are the Venus flytrap, the pitcher plant, and the sundew.

Key vocabulary: nitrogen, hinged, secreting, edible

Other words: thrive, bogland, lure, lobes, botanists, canopy, consciousness

---

This introductory material is intended to alert the teacher to what purposes she might put the reading of the selection and what word difficulties the children might encounter. The *key vocabulary* includes words which are particularly relevant to the selection and ones which the children should know; the other words are less important for understanding the selection.

---

[7] *Reading Power, Skills Reader.* The Bookmark Reading Program. New York: Harcourt Brace Jovanovich, Inc., 1970.

PREPARATION FOR READING

Developing Key Vocabulary and Concepts

The group discusses how animals and plants are suited to their environment (webbed feet of ducks, cactus need little water, etc.). Pupils are told that the selection is about plants that nature has provided for in an unusual way.

The pupils analyze the key words for pronunciation and meaning:

ni-tro-gen (first vowel sound is "long")
hinged (root word)
secreting (compare secrete with secret)
edible (suffix)

These words might be presented in sentences to clarify their meaning if unknown.

Setting Purposes

Children read the tagline which contains a brief note about the selection to establish their purposes for reading (to find out why and how some plants capture insects and "eat" them). They read the skills note, which points out that the author organizes the material topically and advises them to look for causes and effects. They then preview the headings in the selection and discuss what possible causes and effects they might look for.

READING AND DISCUSSION

Reading the Selection

The selection might be read silently without interruption. If necessary, the selection could be divided into two sections, the first ending before "Pitcher Plants." (The teacher circulates and provides help if individual pupils require it.)

Discussion

1. Noting organization. (topic and subtopics; purpose served by beginning paragraphs.)

2. Significant detail. (What is similar about the areas in which all three plants grow?)

3. Understanding description. (How each plant attracts and captures insects.)

4. Noting qualifying words. (*most* swampy areas, *perhaps* to help attract insects, it *usually* snaps shut.)

BUILDING AND EXTENDING SKILLS

Using Context Clues

Pupils refer to the selection to locate and explain clues to the meaning of *thrive, bogland, lure, lobes, botanists, canopy, consciousness.* (This activity serves as a reinforcement of previously-taught skills.)

Seeing Cause and Effect Relationships

1. Some plants in swampy areas don't get enough nitrogen from the ground. What is the effect of this?

2. The Venus flytrap does not close every time one of the trigger hairs is touched. Why is this?

3. What happens when the pitcher plant secretes a sweet-smelling substance?

4. What causes the insect which falls into the pitcher plant to stop struggling?

Pupils refer to the selection whenever necessary to find appropriate causes and/or effects.

Independent Skill Activities

Additional exercises for use in recognizing cause and effect relationships are provided on ditto masters for pupils who require them.

Further Reading: books on how plants and animals adapt to their environment.

Art: some pupils might wish to prepare drawings of the plants they read about.

Writing: short reports on unusual ways other plants and animals adapt to their environment.

This lesson plan is suggestive and not prescriptive. It merely indicates how a teacher could use the material to teach important skills that some groups of children might need. The teacher is advised to omit and modify any aspects he deems advisable and add to the lesson elements that he should stress with a particular group. For example, some groups might not require any introductory vocabulary work; other groups might benefit from instruction that deals with noting unimportant details, for which the lesson plan made little provision. Knowledgeable teachers do not have to rely on the plan; on the other hand, the plan shows how the specified skills might be treated meaningfully, and teachers could use it as a guide.

The fact that different basal programs do not feature the same kinds of reading materials and do not provide for the scope and sequence of skills in the same way means that their users cannot expect identical outcomes, all other conditions being equal. Basal reading programs must be evaluated in accordance with the objectives that a comprehensive program requires. Some basal programs are more likely to help children achieve the goals of reading than others, since the former contain built-in features that are designed to implement them. Teachers must know what the reading objectives are and determine how closely a program provides opportunities for achieving them.

Opportunities for promoting growth in reading do not exist solely within a basal program. The suggestion that language-experience reading and individualized reading might be combined with basal reading is one which could have real possibilities for aiding children to attain maturity in reading. The wise teacher selects supplementary learning materials with discrimination in order to reinforce or introduce reading skills which other programs may have treated lightly or hardly at all. He also does not limit his use of materials to those provided him but recognizes the values that other materials have for extending children's competence in reading. Thus the textbooks, newspapers, magazines, tradebooks, and reference sources which children read become potential media for teaching general and specialized reading skills and promoting favorable attitudes toward reading.

Reading and Other Language Arts

Throughout this presentation are examples of how listening, speaking, and writing activities are incorporated into developmental reading instruction. No single program has an exclusive franchise on fostering their development.

Opportunities for teaching and developing listening skills are constantly present in reading programs. In group language-experience reading children listen for important ideas and details and their sequential order as a story based upon a common experience unfolds. They decide whether what they hear tells the story as it should be, whether certain ideas and words convey the message they wish to impart. They are encouraged to be careful and discriminating listeners, sorting and sifting out that which they judge to be relevant from the unimportant. In personal language-experience reading they hear the stories that others have created, not only listening for the ideas they contain but also discovering the unique way each expresses them.

Listening skills are strengthened by purposeful activities. In both basal and individualized reading programs children have reasons to listen to what others read and say. The discussions which are part of basal reading lessons revolve around specific questions and issues to which members of the group respond. Children must listen carefully in order to participate in them and decide if the questions are resolved. Frequently children will refer to what they have read in order to support their responses; the others will listen to the excerpts as they read them. Then the listeners must decide if what they have heard supports the ideas that have been offered. In both basal and individualized reading the sharing of reading experiences requires children to apply their listening skills. Children tell about the books they read; perhaps they read selected portions for others to enjoy. The audience is listening for a purpose; to become acquainted with authors and books they haven't read and possibly decide if they wish to read some of them too.

The expression of ideas through speaking and writing is preliminary to and an outgrowth of reading experiences. There is no reason why children cannot express ideas that are their own and those of others if there is a need for doing so. Oral and written language skill development is fostered when children feel a need to talk or to write. At times the need is a practical one; at other times it is an outgrowth of emotional feelings. There are ample opportunities in basal reading for children to engage in both kinds. Children become committed to reading by having their interest and curiosity aroused through preparatory activities. They relate what they know to the content and purposes for which they might read. The emphasis at this stage is on oral language. After children have completed the reading, both oral and written language activities could follow, if they flowed naturally from the reading—spontaneous and planned dramatics, play and poetry reading, debating, interviewing, reporting, letter writing, creative prose and poetry writing. These same types of language activities would be integral parts of the total reading program were it to consist of one type or a combination of them.

Just as reading is one aspect of the language arts and requires special treatments, so do the other components. To expect the reading program to make total provisions for the language development of children is as unrealistic as demanding that reading be taught solely through speaking, writing, and listening. While these areas are related, each in its own right deserves and requires more than casual attention. Teachers must take advantage of the benefits that integration of language skills affords and at the same time recognize that each will be incompletely dealt with unless concentrated attention is given to promoting its full potentials.

SUMMARY

1. The two main characteristics of developmental reading are continuous instruction throughout the grades and continuity in instruction from grade to grade. There is no expectation that all children acquire equal mastery of reading skills or that they develop reading ability at the same rate. Inherent in developmental reading is the notion of sequence in skills development. Children progress from one level of mastery to another within the complex of a skills area and from one skills area to another.

2. Reading consists of perceiving written language and recognizing the meaning which the symbols convey. The meaning which each reader obtains from written language depends upon the nature of his experiences with the referents and the degree to which the written language represents his awareness of the spoken language. From this point of view reading is more than merely recognizing what the words say. Reading programs which stress the decoding act to the exclusion of other reading behaviors fail to underscore the real purpose for reading—to understand the written communications of others. The research has failed to establish the superiority of one reading program over another. The knowledge that has been gained about the learning styles of children and the nature of language development suggests that teachers adopt an eclectic attitude toward their instructional tasks and not rely upon any panacea to resolve all learning difficulties in reading.

3. Teachers may contribute to the curiosity children have about written language by surrounding them with signs which "speak" to them. Books attractively displayed and readily available promote an interest in reading and a desire for learning to read. A classroom which offers a stimulating atmosphere is one in which reading is likely to prosper.

4. The experiences and language of children serve as a basis for creating materials in language-experience reading programs. These materials provide another link in the concept that spoken language and written language are closely related and that spoken ideas can be captured in writing and converted back into oral language. They also become the means by which children are taught how to recognize what words say. Initially, children dictate their ideas and the teacher records

them; later they compose their own stories as their writing ability increases. These stories reflect either group or personal experiences. Language-experience reading is one suitable way of starting children on the road to reading maturity. Although it has a place in the reading curriculum at subsequent levels, few teachers will rely upon language-experience reading to offer the different kinds of exposures to materials children must have in order to develop the skills they must master to cope with all their reading requirements.

5. Basal reading offers a continuous, sequential program for reading development. These programs meet in varying degrees the objectives of a comprehensive reading curriculum, through sets of materials that are graded in difficulty and whose content ranges over narrative and factual selections. Instructional manuals inform teachers how they might use these materials to teach different reading skills and promote growth in reading. Basal reading programs ordinarily start with readiness and prereading activities and then launch children into an organized plan for beginning reading. Provisions to help children progress from one reading level to another are made by exposures to materials that become progressively difficult and instruction that is sequential in development. The format through which many basal reading programs foster reading growth provides for preparation for reading, directed reading, building and extending skills, and enrichment activities. Teachers are encouraged to differentiate instruction through modifications of and additions to the teaching plans. Some basal programs provide for direct transfer by including in their books subject materials drawn from sources children read and suggesting how teachers may help pupils apply their reading skills to them.

6. Once children have developed some independence in reading they may participate in individualized reading. Self-selection and self-pacing are the principles on which individualized reading rests. Children are encouraged to select the books they wish to read. At designated intervals each child meets with the teacher privately, and this conference period is devoted to discussion and teaching. Group activities may be scheduled for children who have common interests and similar learning needs. The demands which individualized reading makes on children and teachers have prompted expressions of concern about the program's conduct and outcomes.

7. No reading program has a monopoly on good features. There doesn't seem to be any reason why teachers cannot take the best of each and forge them into a meaningful whole. There are benefits to be derived from each program and children ought not be denied any solely because they are part of one and not another. The personal involvement fostered by language-experience reading, the orderly progression of comprehensive skills development characteristic of basal programs, and the individual character that is representative of individualized reading are ingredients which a total reading program should include.

STUDY QUESTIONS AND EXERCISES

1. Explain the meaning of the concept *developmental reading*.
2. Why is there little merit in taking an either-or approach in the meaning-decoding issue of beginning reading?
3. What is the rationale underlying the language-experience approach to reading?
4. Describe the steps a teacher follows in promoting language-experience reading. How might language experience, basal, and individualized reading systems complement each other?
5. What are the differences between most basal reading systems and other programs of reading instruction?
6. Of what does a typical basal reading lesson consist? What should a teacher keep in mind as she plans a reading lesson with basal materials?
7. Prepare a complete lesson from a basal reader. Indicate what the skills and content objectives of the lesson are. Outline the lesson in accordance with these objectives. Compare your lesson with the one offered in the teacher's guide.
8. Why do some educators favor individualized reading over other reading programs?
9. What are the essential elements of individualized reading? What specific requirements must be met if an individualized reading program is to be effective?
10. Why is it desirable to integrate the teaching of reading with the other language arts? In what ways might such integration be achieved?

SUGGESTIONS FOR FURTHER READING

For an overview of the developmental reading program and its relationship to other learning needs see David L. Shepherd, ed., *Reading and the Elementary School Curriculum*. Newark, Del.: International Reading Association, 1969; and Constance M. McCullough, "Balanced Reading Development," in Helen M. Robinson, ed., *Innovation and Change in Reading Instruction* (Sixty-Seventh Yearbook of the National Society for the Study of Education, Part II). Chicago: University of Chicago Press, 1968, pp. 320–56.

For a discussion of the pros and cons of basal reading see Nila B. Smith, ed., *Current Issues in Reading* (Vol. 13, Part II, of the Proceedings of the Thirteenth Annual Convention). Newark, Del.: International Reading Association, 1969, pp. 283–307.

The following sources contain detailed information about language-experience reading and how to conduct the program:

Dorris M. Lee and R. V. Allen, *Learning To Read Through Experience*, 2nd ed. New York: Appleton-Century-Crofts, 1963.

Vergil E. Herrick and Marcella Nerbovig, *Using Experience Charts with Children*. Columbus: Charles E. Merrill Books, Inc., 1964.

Russell G. Stauffer, "A Language Experience Approach," in James F. Kerfoot, ed., *First Grade Reading Programs.* Newark, Del.: International Reading Association, 1965, pp. 86–118.

Russell G. Stauffer, *The Language-Experience Approach to the Teaching of Reading.* New York: Harper & Row, Publishers, 1970.

Individualized reading is the subject of the following references:

Sam Duker, *Individualized Reading: An Annotated Bibliography.* Metuchen, N.J.: The Scarecrow Press, 1968.

Lyman C. Hunt, ed., *The Individualized Reading Program: A Guide for Classroom Teaching* (Volume 11, Part 3 of the Proceedings of the Eleventh Annual Convention. Newark, Del.: International Reading Association, 1967.

Jeanette Veatch, *Reading in the Elementary School.* New York: The Ronald Press Company, 1966.

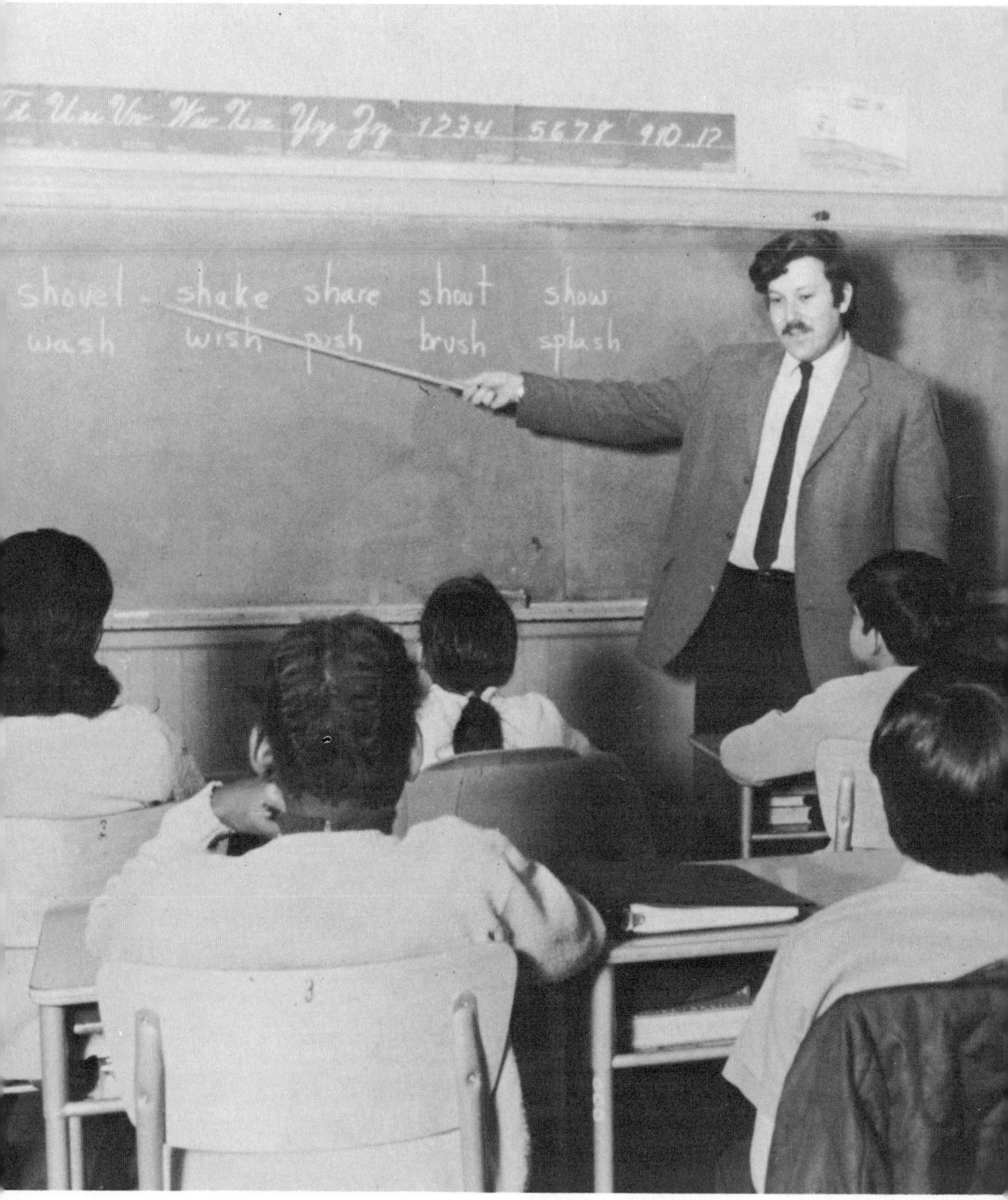
shovel shake share shout show
wash wish push brush splash

5

Teaching Word Recognition

■ *The mastery of the skills that lead to recognition and meaning of words may not be left to chance or haphazard practice. If this seems obvious, then it should be equally obvious that learning the word recognition skills should be carefully planned and expertly guided if it is to be effective. This means that the heart of the reading instruction program really is a competent, dedicated teacher who knows both the theory of reading instruction and the ways different children learn.*[1]

Word perception has been the subject of research, debate, study and speculation, and it is no small wonder that it continues to challenge the thoughtful efforts of reading educators, psychologists, linguists, and representatives of other disciplines to explain how it occurs. For it is the failure to recognize words quickly and easily that causes large numbers of elementary school children to be problem readers.

A major task that children face in reading is to master the process of converting written language symbols into oral language units. To engage in thoughtful reading they must learn to recognize a large stock of words that are commonly in their speaking and listening vocabularies. This is accomplished by frequent exposures to the words in a variety of meaningful contexts. Children who learn to recognize many words are free to think about the ideas they take from and bring to printed materials. In addition, they must be able to analyze efficiently the unfamiliar printed form of words which may be in their speaking vocabularies so that they can con-

---

[1]*Learning to Read*, A Report of a Conference of Reading Experts. Princeton, N. J.: Educational Testing Service, 1962, p. 9.

tinue to read with understanding and other words which, because they are totally new, have to be studied for their pronunciations and meanings. An ultimate objective of any reading program is to reduce to a minimum amount the number of words children have to stop to analyze. This number is not a constant but will vary from child to child and will be affected by the child's mastery of language and visual memory for written words. But, like the mature adult who does meet words he doesn't recognize immediately and has to study them, so children have to acquire the ability to deal with words they don't recognize. For in reading widely they will be faced with the problem time and again. The aim of the word skills program is to equip children to cope with any problems that arise and to become independent and resourceful readers.

The principles underlying a sound word-skills program are those which support the total reading curriculum. These have already been discussed in Chapter 1, but it is appropriate to review them here. Briefly stated they are:

1. Evaluation of pupils' strengths and weaknesses help to determine what skills will be taught and emphasized. Instruction begins where the pupils are.

2. Multisensory strategies to accommodate different learning styles are preferred to approaches that favor one modality. Adherence to this principle suggests a balanced attack on decoding words.

3. Reading skills are taught in sequence whenever a hierarchy can be discerned among them.

4. Children are not expected to learn rules in rote fashion. Meaning is stressed over memory and pupils generalize from observable data.

5. The ways in which reading responses are made are as important as the responses themselves.

There is no doubt that children have learned word skills by means that these principles do not support. There is no way of knowing how much better off they might have been were the conditions for learning the skills more in keeping with them. The fact that children do learn is no justification for the ways in which they have been taught. Experiences with slower learners and those who have not learned well seem to indicate a need for more favorable learning climates. There doesn't seem to be any reason, other than lack of expertise, for not making available to all children the best that present knowledge about teaching and learning offers. While no teaching procedure can guarantee outcomes, those which strive to meet the conditions which favor learning hold greater promise for success than others that are not based upon any schemes or are based on less-reasoned ones.

Instruction in word recognition involves the use of context clues, phonic and structural analysis, and the dictionary—individually and in combination—for determining what words say. The objectives of a word-skills program are twofold: to build a sight vocabulary and enable children to apply as many word skills as they need in order to identify unknown words efficiently. The more tools children have at their disposal to unlock words, the more likely they will be able to perform this task with confidence and precision. And the more steadily will their stock of words which they recognize without any deliberate study grow.

Sight Vocabulary

What is meant by the term *sight words?* These are words which readers learn to recognize without having to analyze them. As one reads the pages of this textbook, words appear in his field of vision and without any discernible effort on his part, he responds to the meaning they represent. On the other hand, a typical eight-year-old who attempted to read this book would recognize some words and not others. His reading would be marred by his inability to perceive words automatically because so many of them were not in his sight vocabulary.

Hopefully, most words which children encounter as they read for information and enjoyment will become part of their sight vocabularies. The more mature reader will recognize more words than the less-mature reader. The child's visual memory for words will affect the rate at which he acquires them.

Regular and Irregular Words

There is another way of thinking about sight words, particularly as teachers instruct children in reading. Sight words have been distinguished from other words on the basis of their utility and degree of "regularity." There are words which commonly appear in all kinds of materials, and the rapid recognition of these words facilitates the child's reading of them. At the early reading levels the sight words taught are such words as *in, it, up, make, on, them, will,* and so on. Other sight words are "irregular," in the sense that they do not conform to the ordinary way of pronouncing them and cannot be analyzed easily. Among the more common "irregular" words are *guess, could, thought, why, their, were,* etc. Words might have high utility and also be irregular, e.g., *were, who.* In teaching a sight word, the teacher presents the word as a "whole," with little or no attention to the word's make-up. Thus, children learn to recognize the whole word "at sight."

Configuration Clues

Efforts to discover how readers easily distinguish one word from another have not been completely fruitful. Allusions are made frequently to the configuration or shape of words that facilitate their recognition, but it is not entirely clear what elements constitute a word's shape. The recommendation that teachers outline a word to indicate its configuration and thereby facilitate the children's recognition of it is highly suspect. Many words have identical shapes if outlined in this manner. Moreover, there isn't any evidence which suggests that young or mature readers "see" words

in this fashion. Young readers will respond to the question, "What helped you to recognize this word?" by saying that "the first and last letters are tall" (as in *heard* and *brisk*) or that "some letters go below the line" (as in *gray* and *prayer*). Adult readers can give no answer to the same question for words they recognize easily.

There seem to be more identifiable characteristics in the upper portion of words than in the lower ones but this is no indication that readers rely

There seem to be more identifiable

There seem to be more identifiable

upon these distinguishing characteristics to recognize them. A related observation that consonant letters provide more clues for identifying words

| t – – ch – ng | r – – d – ng | – n | – l – m – nt – ry |
| – ea – – i – – | – ea – i – – | i – | e – e – e – – a – – |

than vowels does not lead to the conclusion that readers rely upon consonant and ignore vowel letters in word recognition.

Words that look alike are often confused. Immature readers confuse *them* and *there, where* and *when,* and *make* and *like.* These words are no problem for mature readers but occasionally they mistake one for another when they read hurriedly, e.g., *predict* for *predate* and *prohibit* for *promote.* These latter errors are corrected as soon as the reader realizes that the substitution doesn't make much sense in the context. Such corrections are not made when words in isolation are flashed on a screen at speeds of $\frac{1}{100}$ of a second.

Study of miscalled words and eye movement photography indicate that readers rely upon the beginning and final portions of words more than on medial parts for recognition. In contextual reading it appears that the initial parts of words are observed and the meaning the context conveys make it possible for the reader to supply the remaining parts to form the word. Short words are probably seen in their entirety but words of two or more syllables aren't unless they can be identified readily.

The practice of calling a child's attention to the way words begin and pointing out differences and similarities among them appears to be a more profitable way of focusing attention upon them than looking for esoteric features that probably don't matter. One of the best ways to avoid confusion over words that are similar in appearance is to concentrate upon having children learn one of the words well before dealing with the other.

Teaching Sight Words

Chapter 4, "Developmental Reading," explains in detail how young readers are taught to recognize words. Prior to formal reading instruction they engage in activities involving visual and auditory discrimination so that they learn to see similarities and differences among words and hear how words begin and end. In addition, they are exposed to written symbols which identify known objects and communicate familiar messages so that they begin to associate written symbols with their oral counterparts.

Language-experience reading features words which children use in their natural speech to express ideas. Familiarity with the ideas that they express together with repeated exposures to the words enable children to recognize them when they appear in familiar and new settings. The same may be said about the nature of basal reading materials. Much of the early content and all the words are within the experiential and language backgrounds of most children: and through oral, visual, and written responses they gradually learn to recognize more and more words which become part of their sight vocabularies. Thus in the normal course of learning to read children acquire sight words which make it possible for them to read some materials without any help or hesitation.

In both language-experience and basal programs children are introduced to words *in a meaningful context*. This, perhaps, is the key to successful recognition experiences; for the context is the major stimulus that triggers recall of words about which they are uncertain. Initially, most children have little else on which to rely. Later they combine meaning, phonic, and possibly structural clues—but not at the outset. Learning to recognize words in isolation is more difficult than learning them in context. Thus, when teachers review words or introduce new words, they present them in a meaningful context before children engage in activities that require them to deal with the words separately. Quick recognition exercises are good reinforcers *after* children have had opportunities to learn words in their natural settings.

Some children need more exposures to words than other children before they can recognize them readily. Then, too, there are words that confuse many immature readers; these are the words which look alike or contain some common elements. Practice exercises in reading and using these words can be a significant help to children whose visual memory for them is weak.

Exercises and Activities

Let us assume that some children regularly miscall these words: *again, many, should, went, want, money*. To deal with as many as six problem words at one time would be unwise. Furthermore, there are two pairs of words among them that look alike: *many-money, went-want*. The teacher might select two or three of the words for children to work on and save the rest for another time after the former have been learned.

STEP 1. The teacher presents each of the selected words in meaningful contexts. He is fairly certain the children can recognize all the words in each sentence except the ones on which they are working.

a. How much money have you saved?
b. Ten cents was all the money he had to spend.
c. People borrow money from banks to buy houses.
d. What do you want for your birthday?
e. I want a new bicycle for Christmas.
f. Tell me what animals you want to see at the zoo.

The teacher calls attention to the troublesome words by underlining them. He reads the first sentence, giving slightly more emphasis to the underlined word. Then a child reads the same sentence. The teacher reads the next sentence and another pupil does the same. This procedure is followed until all the sentences are read. Note that the teacher does not ask pupils to read any sentence before doing so himself. He wishes to avoid the possibility of having reinforced more incorrect responses. If the teacher were confident now that a child could read a sentence correctly, he might have each read in random order.

STEP 2. The teacher gives the children practice in recognizing the words out of context.

a. He points in random order to the underlined words in the sentences and children read them orally.

b. Children read the words orally, together with others which may have been troublesome in the past, as the teacher presents them in rapid succession.

c. A child calls a word and another child selects it from the group of words, reads it orally, and selects a new word to be read.

STEP 3. The teacher prepares a new set of sentences containing the words on which the pupils have worked. Children take turns reading them orally.

a. The team needs more money to buy new uniforms.
b. They want to go to the show on Saturday.
c. Do you have enough money for lunch and carfare?
d. Who wants to try his luck in picking a prize from the sack?

Children might require additional practice in reading these and other words. They enjoy playing word games and doing puzzles, and these troublesome words can be used in preparing them. There are commercial games which use words, but not much is gained from them unless the words are those that children need practice with. The children can help prepare the word games that are modeled after those they might know.

Words may be substituted for numbers on bingo cards. When children pick a word, they cover the corresponding word on the card only if they can read it correctly.

want	money	house
many		again
their	went	should

again	laugh	heard	money	have
where	great	were	thought	talk
talk	many		who	again
have	where	was	here	guess
thought	here	great	guess	who

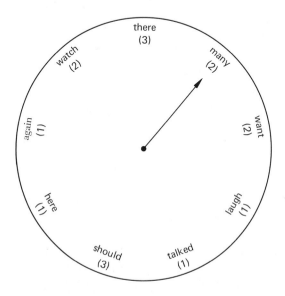

The ideas behind such card games as *Go Fish* and *Old Maid* can be utilized for word games. The words are placed on cards and the games are played as usual. Children select cards from the pack or each other and receive credit for matching words if they can read them. Games involving spinners can be adapted in the same way. The numbers in parentheses indicate how many moves on a board the child will make and the objective

again		where

should		should

is to get "home" first. Dominoes is another game that can be adapted easily to play with words. Children can even make their own word puzzles that others will try to solve. The words need not fit each other as they do in a regular crossword puzzle.

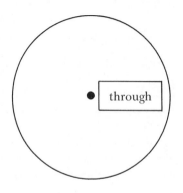

1 a	2 g	3 a	4 i	5 n
6 p	7 u	8 r	9 s	10 e
11 p	12	13 r	14	15 w
16 l	17 o	18 o	19 k	20 s
21 e	22	23 w	24	25

Across

1. more than once
6. pocketbook
16. rhymes with books

Down

1. fruit
2. you may invite a — — est for dinner.
3. bow and ———
4. He ——— six years old.
5. on radio and TV

Children who need more reinforcement might develop a file of words that are particularly troublesome for them. The word appears on one side of the card and a sentence containing the word on the other. Children can

FRONT SIDE

weighs

REVERSE SIDE

A ton of coal
weighs 2000
pounds.

review their own words; the sentence would help them if they can't recall the word. Or they can team up with another child to check each other's knowledge of the words.

A variation of this procedure is to have the children write these words in a notebook so that all that begin with the same letter or letter combination (such as *sh*) appear on the same page together with appropriate sentences. Children might refer to their lists for reading and for writing.

Word wheels are useful for rapid recognition practice. The words can be placed near the outside edge of a circular cut-out. Fastened to it is a slightly smaller circular cut-out with a window. As the outside circle is

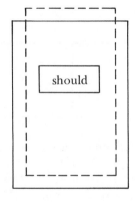

turned, a word will come into view through the window. Another simple device is a card with a slit and a window. Slips on which words have been typed or written are pulled up through the slit. Children can take turns working the devices and reading the words.

IDEAS FOR DISCUSSION

How effective are mechanical devices and commercial materials for teaching sight vocabulary? Only insofar as they meet the specific learning needs of children can they be considered effective. One mechanical device is a flashmeter, which projects images on a screen or wall. The timer can be set so that the image remains in view for varying periods of time, i.e., from about one-fifth of a second to intervals of shorter duration. Glass slides containing words, phrases, and sentences accompany the device, which is intended to widen eye-span. The instrument could be used to flash words that children are working with in order to strengthen their recognition of them. But to use the equipment and slides in the way the manufacturer proposes would hardly fulfill any real need. The same might be said for any other audio-visual device which provides a "canned" program that has little relationship to the reading children are doing.

There are many word games which can be purchased. It would be much simpler to use them as they are than to adapt them or merely adopt their ideas. Children might enjoy playing these games but the chances are they aren't very useful for helping them learn to recognize words that they meet in their daily reading. In many cases it would be fairly easy to substitute words for those in the games. Or a part of a game, such as a board that records moves, could be used with teacher-made materials to accommodate the words which children are studying.

To ignore materials that might help teachers in their work is foolish and wasteful. But to embrace them without review and to use them indiscriminately are equally unwise.

Context Clues

The context can be as much an aid in identifying words as any other mechanism. Context is associated with meaning, and it is this meaning plus visual elements that aid readers to recognize words easily. Anyone who reads with understanding anticipates which words are to follow, and this is as true of younger as it is of mature readers. Errors by both groups are not infrequent, and these occur when they fail to combine the meaning clues with others. Meaningful substitutions indicate that the reader is thinking about the content but failing to perceive the words as well as he should.

Teaching Context Clues

Not all children require instruction and practice in using context clues for word-identification purposes. Frequently all they need to do is develop the habit of using the context, and a reminder is sufficient to cause them to respond appropriately. Nevertheless, there are children who are not aware of the possibilities that context offers and who will benefit from planned exposures to context clues and their interpretation along with other aids they might use to identify unknown words.

Most of the materials younger children read do not contain ideas that are too difficult for them to comprehend. It is their inability to recognize words that interferes with their progress. In the ordered sequence of learning to use different skills to perceive words correctly, the use of context appears to be primary since it has its roots in children's familiarity with spoken language. And it is from spoken language that instruction can originate.

Teacher: Let's play a thinking game. I will read sentences to you but leave out some words. You decide what the missing words are.

Child₁: How can we tell what the missing words are?

Child₂: From the other words.

Teacher: Each word has to make sense. Listen to this sentence: I drink orange juice every _____. How can we end the sentence so that it will make sense?

Child₃: Day! I drink orange juice every day.

Child₂: Every morning!

Teacher: Both are correct. Would it be all right if we said: I drink orange juice every year?

Child₄: That doesn't sound right.

Teacher: Let's try another one: The street lights are turned on as soon as it becomes _____.

Child₁: Late.

Teacher: Why do you say late?

Child₁: That's when it gets dark.

Teacher: Then what word would be better than late? The street lights are turned on as soon as it becomes _____.

Child₁: Dark.

Teacher: Very good. Now listen to this next one. Wait until I finish before you decide which word is missing. The water was so _____ that we couldn't see the bottom of the lake. What word did I leave out?

Child₃: Dirty.

Child₂: Deep.

Child₅: Muddy.

Teacher: All of these words make sense, don't they?

It is easier for children to supply missing words at the end of the sentences than in the middle or at the beginning because they have had an opportunity to think about what has been said and can use all the meaning to complete it. That is why the teacher introduced context clues in a sentence with the final word missing. With the last example, children begin to realize that context clues might appear anywhere in the sentence. Later, the teacher could use two or more very short sentences (so that they will remember them) to convey the idea that context clues are found in sentences other than the one in which the unknown word appears:

Who is he? I never saw him _____. (*before*)

I like ice cream. It _____ good. (*tastes*)

When children have acquired the concept of what context clues are and how they might use them, it is appropriate to have them apply their knowledge to printed materials. Materials intended for beginning readers usually contain pictures that accompany the text, and these can be used along with meaning clues to help identify words. For example, there is a picture in a preprimer[2] that shows a rabbit sitting in a field and the sun is shining overhead. One of the lines on the page is:

The rabbit was in the sun.

If the reader were uncertain about the words *rabbit* and *sun,* he could refer to the picture for clues. If the child didn't recognize *was,* he might read the word as *sat, sits,* or *is.* This would be a meaningful substitution, and the essential idea is retained. However, the teacher would see to it that the sentence were read correctly because of the opportunity to wrongly associate the symbol with the word it represents. If the children were familiar with other words that begin with *w,* the teacher would call their attention to them, have them indicate what the word *was* has in common with the others, and then ask if the word in question could be *sat, sits* or *is.* Children's explanations of how they made up their minds are as important as the responses they give. Now that the three words are not possible, the meaning carried by the sentence doesn't leave much room for doubt as to what the word is.

Children should learn to recognize beginning consonant sounds early, if for no other reason than to combine this knowledge with context clues. Picture clues might be inadequate and the context alone could provide little help. But the ability to determine how a word begins together with some context clues could make the difference. Many more words which children use and know begin with consonant sounds than with vowel sounds, so that from a practical viewpoint (in addition to the fact that they can learn consonant sounds more readily) it makes sense to begin with consonants.

Examples of exercises that might be used to help children combine contextual clues and beginning sounds follow.

1. We had ice cream at Mary's birthday p (*arty*) .

_____

[2] *Sun Up.* The Bookmark Reading Program, New York: Harcourt Brace Jovanovich, Inc., 1970, pp. 16–17.

2. What did you eat for br *(eakfast)* this morning?

3. I like to drink milk with a str *(aw)* .

The same type of practice exercises in which beginning and final sounds are combined with context clues might be used:

1. Are you going to sleep in a cabin or t *(en)* t?

2. We like to dig in the sand when we go to the b *(ea)* ch.

As children learn to read more complex materials, opportunities to use context clues increase. However, phonic and structural clues play an increasingly important role as children use them with the context, for when somewhat meaningful substitutions are made for unknown words, preciseness in meaning is lost. Also, at these higher levels context clues serve another purpose; they are used to clarify the meaning of words which children may or may not be able to pronounce.

Teachers can present examples of words in context whose pronunciation is facilitated by meaning, phonic and/or structural clues and have the children explain how they might use the clues for pronunciation.

1. The prisoner was accused of forgery. 2. Several checks which did not belong to him were in his possession when he tried to cash one at the local bank. 3. The bank teller compared the signature on the check with one in the bank's files and realized that they were different. 4. The police were summoned and the man was arrested.

The second and fourth sentences contain meaning clues which might be sufficiently adequate for some children to pronounce the underlined word correctly. They will have been familiar with the word *forgery* from hearing it used orally and can associate it with the details of the paragraph. Children who have not had any oral experiences with the word will have to rely on other clues. In this case there is a discernible root word—*forge*—which they may identify. If they have heard the word *forgery* before, they will pronounce it correctly. If they haven't ever heard the word, an additional structural clue—syllabication—will aid them in pronouncing it.

Context clues have been classified according to type but they are more applicable to word meaning than to word perception. These will be discussed in Chapter 6.

Phonic Analysis

At the outset it should be clear that although the terms *phonics* and *phonetics* are often used interchangeably, they really refer to different concepts. Phonetics involves the study or science of speech sounds that one makes in speaking while phonics deals with the relationships between spoken sounds and written symbols. Children use phonics as one means of analyzing words. The knowledge that speech scientists provide is used by teachers to instruct children in phonic analysis.

Reading educators and teachers have been taken to task for their indiscriminate use of terms and the impreciseness of their language in describing grapheme-phoneme relationships.[3] Some linguists and other critics complain that teachers give children false impressions about a language with which they are already familiar. For example, they dispute the way in which teachers refer to "long" and "short" vowels and limit their number to five instead of fourteen vowel sounds. They object when teachers use the word "make" as in the case where "letters make sounds" or "the final e in bake makes the a long." They deplore the emphasis on the written form when the spoken form is paramount.

Some of these objections may have merit but they do not seem to help the teacher do his job more efficiently or effectively. Certainly teachers should be knowledgeable about the language they instruct children in and should utilize this knowledge in the best way they can. But a mere change in terminology will not improve teaching nor help children cope better with word problems. What reading teachers need more than anything else is an understanding of the craft and the principles on which it rests. This, combined with the applicable knowledge that other disciplines provide, offers the profession the reasonable expectation of greater success in teaching all children to read.

Phonic Principles

Occasionally teachers do give children incorrect information which interferes with learning. A common example is the failure by some teachers to distinguish between the vowel sound in "hat" and the schwa (or unstressed) sound in "sofa." The vowel sound of a in these words is not the same. (The schwa sounds like a short, soft u.) Teachers who say that both a's have the same sound confuse children who hear the difference. Knowledge of phonic content should reduce such confusion.

Phonic elements are classified as single consonants, consonant blends, consonant digraphs, vowels, vowel digraphs, and diphthongs. Consonants are classified as "voiced" and "voiceless," depending on whether or not the vocal cords vibrate when they are pronounced.[4] A *consonant blend* consists of a cluster of two or more consonants whose sounds are blended together in a word (e.g., *fl*ag, *dr*op, *sk*in). Even though the sounds are blended, each consonant retains its individual sound. In a *consonant digraph* two or more consonant letters are used to stand for one unique speech sound. For example, the *sh* in *sh*ort represents a single, unique sound and not a combination of the sound of s plus the sound of h.

---

[3] Ronald Wardhaugh, *Reading: A Linguistic Perspective.* New York: Harcourt Brace Jovanovich, Inc., 1969; Dorothy S. Seymour, "The Difference Between Linguistics and Phonics," *The Reading Teacher, 23* (November, 1969), pp. 99–111.
[4] The voiceless consonants are *p, f, h, k, s* (un), *t, th* (in), *sh, ch* and *wh.* The voice consonants are *b, d, g, j, l, m, n, r, v, w, ng, th* (is) *, z.*

Single Consonants			Consonant Blends		Consonant Digraphs	
ball			block	list	chip	character
come	city		bright	twin	laugh	ghost
dog	ruled	looked	drive	ask	photo	
few			flight	straight	show	
go	gem		free	spring	when	who
just			glad	screw	the	thin
run	lower		small	splash	ring	
see	wise	sure	skill			
top	bat		swim			

Vowels	Vowel Digraphs		Diphthongs
at later always,	meat	bread	few
art above law	see		oil
end be problem, her, chew	receive	weight	toy
tip kind, fir	bait		out
lock open above or	caught		shoulder
us use tune, fur	boat		buy
lady fly rhythm	toe		
	look	wood	
	through	touch	cough	soup

Most vowels are classified as "long" and "short,"[5] although some vowel sounds are neither. Vowel digraphs consist of two vowel letters which represent one vowel sound. A diphthong is a combination of two vowel sounds in one syllable. The first vowel is sounded and glides into the next vowel or semivowel sound. Examples of each type of vowel and consonant sound are given above.

Notice that several of the letters and letter combinations are used to represent more than one sound. This fact suggests the need for teachers to stress flexibility as they help children to make generalizations about letter-sound relationships. Rarely are there fixed "rules" that account for all pronunciations. Children should be encouraged to make responses that seem proper and if the results are unsatisfactory to try alternate possibilities. If the words are within their listening vocabularies, they will know whether or not their responses are correct; if words are totally unfamiliar, they will have to verify the results in a dictionary or glossary.

Phonic Generalizations

What phonic generalizations to teach has been the subject of several investigations.[6] Words found in basal readers and graded word lists have

---

[5] "Long" and "short" are arbitrary phonic terms to designate the vowel sounds in such words as lake and hit, respectively. In phonetics the length of a vowel sound refers to its duration in a word.

[6] Theodore Clymer, "The Utility of Phonic Generalizations in the Primary Grades," *The Reading Teacher, 16* (January, 1963), pp. 252–58; Mildred H. Bailey, "The Utility of Phonic Generalizations in Grades One Through Six," and Robert Emans, "The Use-

been analyzed to determine to what extent their pronunciations conformed to stated generalizations. The results varied with the sources and levels from which the words were drawn. Moreover, the criterion used to judge the usefulness of a generalization—the percentage of words whose pronunciation conformed—was not established in any scientific way. An added problem was the omission of certain generalizations in the analysis.

In spite of the aforementioned limitations there are some generalizations which will be of value to children who learn to apply them to new words. Most do not achieve 100 per cent utility; some even less than 50 per cent. What children need to understand when they learn the generalizations is that they are not foolproof and that it may be necessary to shift from one pronunciation to another. Children are more likely to recognize the inadequacy of a generalization they have used if words are in context rather than in isolation and if they are aware of structural clues. Teachers are advised to avoid introducing exceptions to generalizations until children have shown that they can apply them, but to acknowledge any exceptions which the children recognize. Although the generalizations which follow are stated without reservations, remember that some are subject to many exceptions, and others are less affected.

USEFUL PHONIC GENERALIZATIONS

1. When a vowel in a one-syllable word is followed by a consonant, its sound is short. (hat)
2. When a one-syllable word ends in e, the preceding vowel is long. (rate)
3. In the vowel digraphs oa, ea, ee, ai, and ay the first vowel letter has a long sound and the second letter is silent. (claim)
4. A vowel at the end of a word which contains no other vowels is long. (she)
5. A vowel followed by l or r is neither long nor short. Its sound is controlled, or influenced, by the l or r. (always, turn)
6. The i followed by gh is long and the gh silent. (light)
7. The i and o followed by nd and ld, respectively, are long. (kind, gold)
8. A y which is not preceded by a vowel has the long i sound. (type)
9. The letters c and g followed by e or i have the sound of the voiceless s and the soft g, respectively. (cent, city, gem, ginger)
10. The letters c and g followed by a or o have "hard" sounds. (cat, come, game, go)
11. The first letter in wr, kn, and gn is silent. (write, knew, gnaw)
12. In ay the first vowel is long and the second is silent. (day)

The purpose of listing these generalizations is to help teachers understand that there is some regularity in the English alphabet system and to aid them in developing lessons for children who fail to see relationships among words. Children may be led to formulate generalizations that apply to words which they can recognize. This procedure seems to be more productive than one which requires pupils to learn generalizations and then try to apply them.

fulness of Phonic Generalizations Above the Primary Grades," *The Reading Teacher,* 20 (February, 1967) , pp. 413–18, 419–25; Lou Burmeister, "Vowel Pairs," *The Reading Teacher,* 21 (May, 1968) , pp. 445–52.

Phonic analysis together with the use of context clues will enable children to identify many one-syllable words. But as children meet words of more than one syllable they will analyze them more efficiently if they recognize structural clues such as syllables, root words, prefixes and suffixes. The less they have to rely upon phonic analysis to identify multisyllabic words, the more readily they will be able to pronounce them.

Teaching Phonics

Phonic analysis involves the association of letters with the speech sounds they represent. There are two basic points of view regarding the way in which children should be taught to make and use these associations in analyzing words. One is called the *synthetic method* and the other the *analytic method*.

The Synthetic Method

The synthetic method is one in which children are taught the sounds of individual letters, and then they are shown how to combine these sounds to form words. Phonic systems which are based upon a synthetic approach do not necessarily follow identical procedures. Many do begin by teaching the vowel sounds first and then presenting some consonant sounds so that the vowels can be combined with the consonants to form words. Thus, the consonants *b* and *t* could be combined with vowels to form such words as *bat, bet, bit, but, tab, tub, at,* etc. Some systems require children to sound each letter separately, e.g., *b-a-t,* and "slide" the sounds together to say the word; others combine the initial consonant with the vowel, *ba,* and then add the *t*; a third group will have children sound the *b* and add the *at* to form the word. The use of pictures and key words is not uncommon in helping children to remember the sound-letter relationships (a picture of an egg to represent the short vowel sound of *e*).

Several objections have been raised against following a synthetic phonics program. Undue emphasis is placed upon phonics as a means of identifying words. Children do not have the opportunity to combine context and phonic clues when individual sounds are treated. Isolated sounds, particularly those represented by consonants, become distorted and are different from those heard in words. Isolated sounds are meaningless to children who must depend upon rote learning to master them. These arguments against synthetic phonics seem valid although the results of research do not clearly give analytic phonic programs an advantage over synthetic programs.

The Analytic Method

An analytic phonics program begins with words that children know when they hear or see them. Children are taught to hear sounds as they appear in words and to see how words are similar and different. There is no set formula for conducting an analytic-type program, but all do stress learning sounds within words. Some "linguistic" programs emphasize letter knowledge before presenting words containing a vowel sound in a spelling pattern: *cat, Nat, rat*. Children are expected to generalize the sound of *a* from such words. Another system that starts with vowel sounds takes known words but divides them by separating the initial consonant and vowel sound from the rest of the word: *leaf* becomes *lea-f* and *cake* becomes *ca-ke*. Children are asked to tell what sound they hear at the end of the first part of each word (ē and ā). Consonant sounds are taught in the same way. Pictures and guide words to help them remember the letter-sound associations are recommended.

The phonics program which will be described in this section is classified as analytic since it teaches children to make generalizations about sound-letter relationships that are found within words. It presupposes that through readiness programs children have had many experiences with spoken words, that they can hear that some words begin and end the same way and know rhyming words, and that they can see similarities and differences in words. Furthermore, it assumes recognition of *some* sight words that can be used to teach the phonic elements, although it is possible to follow the program without them. Learning to apply knowledge of phonic elements to new words is facilitated if the teacher uses words that children can read. Thus, the possibility that failure to remember words will interfere with learning is reduced. It might be better to stress auditory and visual discrimination of letters and sounds within words until children recognize enough words to allow them to take full advantage of the program. In this connection, teachers should note there is no set number of words a child should be reading as a prerequisite for participating in all phases of the program. All that is required is ability to recognize enough words so that what a pupil does is meaningful to him.

In the program described below, consonants are taught first, but there is no general agreement as to which phonic elements should be taught first. Consonant sounds seem to be easier for children to learn than vowel sounds. If children require instruction in both, it might be better to start with the consonants that trouble them and then proceed to the vowels. The knowledge of consonants plus the context could be sufficient to pronounce unknown words. It is not necessary to delay vowel treatments until all consonant sounds are learned. If children were learning to apply their knowledge of consonant sounds without great difficulty, it would appear they were ready to deal with vowel sounds too.

You will recall what was said earlier about the value of combining structural clues with phonic analysis in pronouncing multisyllabic words. The following program is intended mainly for dealing with words of one syllable; what children learn about phoneme-grapheme relationships they apply to words of more than one syllable.

Presenting a Single Consonant

A transcript of a lesson in beginning phonics follows.

Teacher: Last week we had trouble with some words that began with the letter *b*. One of the words was in this sentence: There was oil on the *beach*. Birds were covered with it. (The sentences are written on the chalkboard with the troublesome word underlined.) We'll read the sentences later. Look at these words as I read them to you. You know all of them. (The teacher reads the words on the chalkboard, emphasizing each beginning sound but not removing it from the word.) How are all these words alike?

> bee
> book
> Bill
> bird

Child₁: They all start with "b."

Child₂: They sound alike. The first letter sounds the same way.

Teacher: Very good. Will someone draw a line under the part that is alike in each word?

Child₃: I'll do it.

Teacher: We see and hear that *bee*, *book*, *Bill* and *bird* start the same way. I will read other words to you. Listen to the way they begin and decide if they start like the words on the chalkboard. (This group of words is in the children's listening vocabulary, but they do not have to be able to read them. The teacher pronounces the words naturally but does *not* write them on the chalkboard.)

> bend, back, bunny, bus, bark, beautiful,
> basket, dig, rich, best, buy, very, boat

Children: (As each word is read, they indicate whether or not these words begin as the others.)

Teacher: You name some words that begin the same way.

Children: Bank, borrow, bun, Barry, bicycle.

This first portion of the lesson stresses *auditory* and *visual discrimination*. Children see and listen to words which begin the same way. The second group of words was used to give the children more opportunities to hear words that begin with the letter "b" and check their ability to distinguish between such words and others. In order to avoid confusion, words which begin with consonant blends (*black, bright,* etc.) are not included in this oral list of words. If children have little difficulty with this phase of the lesson, they are ready for the next step.

Teacher: Here is a word you all can read. (She writes *went* on the chalkboard and asks a child to read it. She writes another word beneath it.)

> went
>
> bent

Look at the second word. How is it like *went*?

Child₃: It ends like went.

Child₄: They both have the same letters: *e, n, t.*

Teacher: What is different about these words?

Child₂: *Went* begins with a "w" and the other word begins with a "b."

Teacher: Everything is the same in both words except the way they begin. Look at them.

went

bent

The second word begins like *bee, book, Bill, bird.* (She refers to the list on the chalkboard.) Let's take away the "w" in *went* and write a "b" in its place. (She erases the "w" and writes a "b" in its place.) Remember how words that start with "b" sound. So now *went* is changed to _____ .

Child₁: *Bent!* Went, bent, they rhyme.

Teacher: Let's do another one. (She writes these two words on the chalkboard.)

day

bay

In what way are they alike? How are they different?

Child₅: (Points out similarity and difference.)

Teacher: Let's erase the "d" in *day* and write a "b" in its place. What is the word now?

Child₅: *Bay.*

Teacher: Here are a few more. Do the same to the word you know. (The known words are written first.)

day   ferry   fell

bay   berry   bell

Some children will understand immediately what to do and will be able to pronounce the new word. Others will have to work with the teacher on more words before they can make the substitution. This word-blending process starts with words that children can read. They learn to generalize from the known word how the letter "sounds" in the new word.

Teacher: Let's read our new words.

Children: (Read *bent, bay, berry, bell.* It may be necessary to call their attention to the known words if any have trouble reading them.)

Teacher: Read these sentences. Each sentence contains one of the new words.

1. Who bent the wire?
2. Please ring the bell now.
3. The boat is in the bay.
4. I like berry pie.

Children: (They read the sentences.)

Teacher: Now try reading the sentence that gave us trouble before.

Children: There was oil on the *beach.* Birds got stuck in it.

This last portion of the lesson requires the children to apply what they have learned. They read the new words in sentences because it is more natural to use phonics in context than in isolation. Children might not respond to the word *beach* in the same way. A few might associate *teach* with *beach* and make the consonant substitution. Others will have learned the sound of "b" and with the context will know what the word says.

Nowhere in the lesson has the sound of *b* been stressed apart from words. It is not advisable to do so for the reasons stated before. However, should some children have difficulty in separating the sound from others in words, it might help them to hear it alone but without the *uh* (buh) that distorts the true character of this sound as well as others.

Presenting Other Phonic Elements

Other phonic elements may be treated in the same way as the single consonant was. Troublesome elements will be taught as children become more confident, develop more skill, and recognize more words. They also will begin to generalize about the character of the elements and what they might expect as these occur in different words. Teachers can help children make these generalizations through lessons similar in nature to those that teach the phonic elements. A few sample lessons in outline form follow.

CONSONANT BLEND: *gr*

Auditory and Visual Discrimination

grow
green   Sight words known by children
great
gray

Auditory Discrimination

grass	glide	
grip	trap	Words in children's vocabulary
ground	dream	
creature	grease	

Word Blending

| sheet | plain | travel | will: | sight words |
| greet | grain | gravel | grill: | new words |

Contextual Application

1. Mary was picked to *(greet)* the visitor.

2. The road was covered with *(gravel)*.   Pupils supply missing word from the new words

3. Farmers store *(grain)* in big silos.

4. *(Grill)* the cheese sandwich.

SHORT VOWEL: *i*

Auditory and Visual Discrimination

it
tip   Sight words known by children
window
whistle

Auditory Discrimination

Indian	inch
wind	nest
lift	swirl
second	minute

Words in children's vocabulary

Word Blending

clap	most	rug	track:	sight words
clip	mist	rig	trick:	new words

Contextual Application

1. Put a paper clip on the bills that haven't been paid yet.
2. The sailors couldn't rig the boat because of the heavy winds, so they packed the sails away.   Pupils read sentences
3. We played a trick on my teacher, but she didn't seem to mind.
4. The mist over the water was very thick. This is why no boats left the harbor.

Phonic generalizations may be taught by presenting known words that have common qualities and having pupils make a general statement about them. For example, children who hear and see the same elements in the following words can be led to generalize that in one-syllable words followed by a consonant, vowels are usually short; or that in a one-syllable word that ends in *e* the preceding vowel is long.

hen	came
bit	hope
bus	mile
track	use
frog	Steve

In some instances teachers can show how a change in spelling patterns can affect the pronunciation of words:

rat	(short vowel sound)
rate	(long vowel sound)
gone	(hard sound of *g*)
gene	(soft sound of *g*)
fin	(short vowel sound)
find	(long vowel sound)

The objective of teaching phonics, by whatever system, should be to enable children to identify visual clues in words and to blend appropriate sounds to form words or syllables. The technique of substituting one sound for another avoids the need in the early learning stages of blending several separate sounds and reduces the new learning to but a single element, since everything in the known and unknown words is held constant except the phonic element on which the children are working. The substitution process facilitates the learning of letter-sound relationships and the blending of sounds *and is not intended to be used by children after they can scrutinize words and associate the proper sounds with single letters and letter combinations and blend them smoothly.*

To illustrate this point, consider what a child might do were he to meet a new word—*trap*—and try to pronounce it by applying his phonic knowledge. In order for him to take advantage of the substitution process, he would have to think of and visualize another word such as *clap* (if he were to focus his attention on the beginning of the word) or *track* (on the final part of the word) or *trip* (on the medial part). It is possible that on occasion children will respond to new words in one or more of these ways. But the requirement of having to supply one's own words to identify another will not be met easily. Children will be far better off if they have learned how to combine known sounds to pronounce unknown words. The substitution process is intended to accomplish this purpose and not become the means by which words are analyzed.

Phonic Materials

Teachers can use a variety of exercises to reinforce pupils' knowledge of letter-sound relationships and to give children additional practice in applying this knowledge to identify words. These exercises will be found in many workbooks that accompany basal readers and in other commercial materials intended to develop phonic skills.[7] The use of such exercises might prove helpful in a number of situations. For example, if some pupils needed help in recognizing the initial *s* sound in words, they would work on those pages that dealt with this phonic problem. If pupils were to require more practice than the material offered, it would be possible to use exercises from other materials that covered the same phonic element. Of course, there is nothing to prevent teachers from preparing their own exercises patterned after those found in commercial materials. Nor are teachers tied to using exercises similar to those appearing here if they can create superior ones.

The practice exercises in both basal reader workbooks and special phonic materials are quite similar in design. Many utilize pictures (both with and without texts) and require pupils to respond in written and/or spoken form. In the sample page that follows, pupils are required to underline the pictures whose words begin with the same sound as the word *sun*. Opportunities to associate the beginning sound of *s* with spoken and written words will have been provided before the exercise is introduced.

Sometimes children are unable to respond correctly to such an exercise because the word they use to identify a picture is different from the one intended by the author—e.g., *clothing* for *suit*. Teachers can overcome this problem by working closely with the pupils and discussing their responses

---

[7] Among phonic materials are the following: *Breaking the Sound Barrier* (Macmillan Company); *Building Reading Skills* (McCormick-Mathers Publishing Company); *Eye and Ear Fun* (Webster Division of McGraw-Hill Book Company); *New Phonic Skilltexts* (Charles E. Merrill Books, Inc.); *Phonics We Use* (Lyons and Carnahan, Inc.); *Phonics We Write and See* (Meredith Corporation); *Speech-to-Print Phonics* (Harcourt Brace Jovanovich, Inc.).

sun

► Recognizing initial sound /s/
● Underline pictures for words that begin with /s/. (See T.E. for oral introduction and complete directions.)

* *Source:* From *Reading Skills 1* by Margaret Early, et al., copyright © 1970 by Harcourt Brace Jovanovich, Inc. and reprinted with their permission.

with them. One way that teachers may improve upon an exercise containing a picture that might confuse children would be to offer a sentence orally to accompany the picture:

Mother took the blue _____ to the cleaners.

good · wet ·

wood · get ·

| gun | wing |
| goat | well |

▶ Relating sounds and letters to identify words.
● 1. Identify words, and write initial letters.   2. Underline the picture for the word, and write the initial letter.
(See T.E. for oral introduction and complete directions.)

* *Source:* From *Reading Skills 1* by Margaret Early, et al., copyright © 1970 by Harcourt Brace Jovanovich, Inc. and reprinted with their permission.

A related exercise is one in which words as well as pictures appear. In the next sample children combine auditory and visual discrimination skills by relating sounds and letters to identify words. From the pictures that represent rhyming words they must decide what the printed word is.

Other examples of exercises to strengthen phonic skills follow. The first one offers practice in combining context clues with initial consonant

* Underline the picture for the word that belongs in the sentence.

Penny put her new party dress on a h ___ .

Kim cut some flowers and put them in a v ___ .

Ted opened the w ___ when the room got too hot.

Ben put on his r ___ when he went out in the snow.

A little boy was playing with a y ___ in the schoolyard.

The woman needed some r ___ to put around the box.

Last summer the boys went for a ride in a h ___ .

▶ Inventory: Using context and initial consonant sounds

* *Source:* From *Reading Skills 5* by Margaret Early, et al., copyright © 1970 by Harcourt Brace Jovanovich, Inc. and reprinted with their permission.

sounds; the second covers short vowel sounds within words. Similar exercises for more advanced pupils will be found in graded phonic materials.

There is an ever-growing abundance of phonic materials, some of which can be used more profitably with children than others. Filmstrips, transparencies, tapes, and records add to the increasing supply upon which teachers may draw. How effective these printed, visual, and auditory mate-

*Say the word for the picture. Underline the letter that stands for the vowel sound. Then underline the words in the rows that have the same vowel sound as the word for the picture.

map	same	basket	candy
	glad	happen	land
	plane	shape	class
pin	sing	right	line
	sick	time	dish
	lips	trip	pick
mop	doll	joke	lost
	frog	vote	block
	home	rock	pond
jug	mud	bump	house
	just	trunk	stuck
	about	luck	build
well	yet	need	green
	see	penny	rest
	went	dress	spell

▶ Reviewing short vowel patterns

* Source: From Reading Skills 5 by Margaret Early, et al., copyright © 1970 by Harcourt Brace Jovanovich, Inc. and reprinted with their permission.

rials are in teaching children to use phonics functionally depends upon their nature and the ability of teachers to capitalize on their strengths. Such materials can add variety and interest to a phonics program, but few indeed can be depended upon to secure the results that can be obtained by skillful and knowledgeable teachers of reading.

Some children might benefit from cue word charts to which they can refer. These charts will contain sight words that illustrate different letter-sound relationships. Charts for younger children might have pictures that represent cue words in case they fail to recognize them.

Short Vowel Sounds	Vowels Followed by r, l, w	
apple	car	always
tell	her	awful
in	or	cow, low
on	sir	new
under	burn	

Structural Analysis

At the same time that children are learning to use phonics to analyze words, they are becoming aware of structural clues, which also aid them in pronouncing and understanding the meaning of words. These structural clues are confined largely to roots and inflectional endings (one type of suffix) in the early development of word-identification skills and later also involve syllabication and accent, prefixes and additional suffixes, and more complex roots.

The structure of words offers clues to meaning as well as to pronunciation. Children recognize that the word *boys* consists of two meaning-bearing units or morphemes: the root *boy* and *s*. The *s* tells them that there is more than one boy. The compound word *mailman* also consists of two morphemes—*mail* and *man*—which carry meaning. Similar conditions obtain for the other aspects of word structure.

Teaching Roots and Affixes

A root word is a base to which prefixes and suffixes can be added to form a new word. These are examples of roots: *starts, taller, going, heroic, lonely, submarine, action*. Root words may change their form when a suffix is added to them: *happiness (happy), riding (ride), division (divide), recognition (recognize)*.

Affixes are prefixes and suffixes that add new meanings to root words. Included among suffixes are the inflectional endings, which change the number, tense, or degree of root words.

number: school + *s* = *schools*
tense: start + *ed* = *started*
degree: high + *est* = *highest*

Children may be made aware of root words and affixes through oral activities which require them to focus attention upon these meaning-bearing units. The teacher can ask the children to complete sentences by using the same word and adding an ending to it.

I have a *pencil*.

John has two *(pencils)* .

We *play* games in the gym.

Yesterday we *(played)* games in the gym.

Do you know who *trains* animals?

Do you know the animal *(trainer)* ?

This book belongs to *Mary*.

This is *Mary's* book.

A rose is a *pretty* flower.

A rose is a *(prettier)* flower than a daisy.

Children should have little difficulty in supplying the correct forms if they speak standard English. Speakers of nonstandard English might respond with different oral forms but still know what meaning is intended: Yesterday we *play* games (instead of *played*).

Children learn to recognize root words and affixes in printed words by engaging in activities that involve auditory and visual discrimination of them.

Auditory and Visual Discrimination Activities

1. Present words containing known roots and have the pupils indicate what they are.

*sleep*ing   *wish*ed   *automobile*s   dis*believe*   *hope*less

2. Present sentences containing modified forms of known root words that children identify. Have them take note of the changes in written form and pronunciation.

The actor has a *pleasant* (*please*) voice.
The athlete *happily* (*happy*) accepted his award for winning the race.

3. Present sentences in which there are modified forms of root words that may not be recognized easily.

Some people have very *sensitive* (*sense*) noses.
Have you received your *invitation* (*invite*) to the party?

4. Present root words which children read. Then add a prefix or suffix and ask the children to read the new word.

taste + *s* = tastes	early + *est* = earliest
reason + *ing* = reasoning	herd + *er* = herder
chip + *ed* = chipped	usual + *ly* = usually
daughter + *'s* = daughter's	did + *n't* = didn't
decorate + *ion* = decoration	*re* + string = restring
argue + *ment* = argument	*non* + believe + *er* = nonbeliever
un + cover = uncover	*pre* + history + *cal* = prehistorical

5. The meaning of prefixes and suffixes can be conveyed through sentences containing root words.

The tennis star broke his new racket, and he had to have it *re*strung.
After three weeks in the hospital the player *re*joined his team.

Four is evenly divis*ible* by one, two, and four.
Some coats are revers*ible*; they can be worn on either side.

Teaching Compound Words

Compound words consist of two or more words. Children usually learn to recognize compound words as sight words in beginning reading. Some of the compound words that young readers become familiar with are *grandmother, mailman, grandfather, policeman*. These can become the basis for generalizing about the nature of compound words. Teachers may follow the same pattern for helping children to read compound words as they did when teaching phonic elements.

Auditory and Visual Discrimination

grandmother
mailman
grasshopper   known sight words
doghouse

The teacher reads these words as children look at them. The children identify and mark both words in each compound word.

Auditory Discrimination
The children identify the compound words which are included in a list of words the teacher reads: *teammate, football, seaweed, alleyway, beggar, toothpick, livestock, wooden, pocketbook*.

Word Building
The children build compound words from known words:

foot + *prints* = footprints
stop + *watch* = stopwatch
sky + *line* = skyline
sun + *rise* = sunrise
down + *stream* = downstream

The children should discuss how each of the words contributes to the meaning of the compound word. They should realize also that the words might not suggest the meaning of some compound words, as in *inside* and *however*.

Contextual Application

1. The waves washed away the _____ near the water's edge.

2. A _____ is better than an ordinary watch for timing races.

3. New York City is noted for its _____.

4. Roosters begin to crow at _____.

5. The canoe was washed _____ but it caught on a sandbar and was recovered.

The children select from the new compound words the one that belongs in each sentence and then reads the sentence.

Syllabication and Accent

It is more efficient to analyze words by recognizing their roots and affixes than by blending their phonic elements. However, many multisyllabic words do not contain these structural clues or children fail to recognize them. Thus children need other ways of breaking down unknown words of more than one syllable into manageable parts so that they can apply their phonic skills to them. A child is less likely to succeed in pronouncing a multisyllabic word if he analyzes it letter-by-letter and then tries to put it all together than if he divides the word into syllables first and then pronounces them. Many children who can divide words into syllables will know where the accent falls in a word because they recognize it as one they have heard before, particularly when the word is in context. It does not seem wise to burden children with many rules of syllabication or accent; if they analyze a word and it still seems totally unfamiliar, they can check its pronunciation in a dictionary or glossary.

Like phonic generalizations, those governing syllabication and accent cannot be expected to be foolproof. Each has its exceptions, but some rules have greater utility than others. Teachers should encourage pupils to modify their behaviors whenever it appears that their initial responses do not produce expected results. To illustrate this point, suppose a child reads the following sentence:

> The Jones family spent their vacation at a beach hotel.

He does not recognize the word *hotel* and divides it into syllables: hot-el. He tries to say the word but it doesn't sound like one he recognizes. He knows that the word contains two syllables and that the middle consonant might go with either vowel sound. So having failed to produce a recognizable word he tries the other possibility: ho-tel. He knows that the vowel sound in the first syllable could be long (as in *he*) and pronounces it this way. The rest of the word conforms to his expectations and he pronounces it easily.

Teachers might become familiar with the following generalizations and help their pupils to apply them in cases where other word-identification techniques are inappropriate or fail to help solve their word problems.

GENERALIZATIONS FOR SYLLABICATION

1. If two consonants follow the first vowel sound, the word is divided between the consonants (sum-mer, num-ber).

2. If one consonant follows the first vowel sound, the consonant might end the first syllable or start the second syllable (cov-er, ho-tel).

3. Prefixes and suffixes can be syllables (ab-duct, so-lu-tion).

4. If a word ends in *le*, the consonant which precedes these letters begins the last syllable (ta-ble).

5. The first syllable of two syllable words is often accented (win'-dow).

6. Roots in words that end with a suffix are often accented (green'-er, ring'-ing).

7. The last syllable of verbs that begin with a prefix is often accented (re-view').

8. The last syllable in a root word is accented when double consonants precede the suffix (up-set'-ting).

Teaching Syllabication

STEP 1.   A first step in teaching syllabication is to help children hear syllables in spoken words and to understand that a syllable is a word or part of a word that contains a vowel sound. Have the children listen for the vowel sounds in one-syllable words that appear on the chalkboard. Be certain they realize that some of these words contain more than one vowel letter but each has only one vowel sound.

run   go   her   maid   too   take

The children should mark the letters that stand for the vowel sound in each word.

Next, write such words as the following on the chalkboard and have the children listen for each vowel sound.

finish   window   pulleys   faucets

Ask the pupils to tell how many vowel sounds they hear in each word.

Now read words of three syllables and ask the children to listen for the vowel sounds and underline the letters that stand for them.

library   collection   regular   telephone

By this time some children will realize that words of one syllable contain one vowel sound, words of two syllables contain two vowel sounds and words of three syllables, three vowel sounds. Others can be guided to make the generalization that the number of vowel sounds determines how many syllables a word contains.

STEP 2.   All of the words that have been used for auditory and visual perception are known by the children. Now they should be able to look at words that they might not recognize and decide how many syllables each contains. They should underline the letters that stand for the vowel sounds.

flaw   terrain   veteran   utensil   elaborate

It should be obvious that children whose backgrounds in phonics are poor will not be able to examine words visually and decide how many syllables they contain. Nor will they be able to proceed to the next step on which this knowledge depends.

STEP 3.   In order to teach children how to divide words into syllables, write a number of them that represent a given syllabic generalization.

window   yellow   ignore   increase   connect

Ask the children to indicate how many syllables each of the words contains. Now draw a line to show where each word is divided into syllables.

win/dow   yel/low   ig/nore   in/side   con/nect

Have the children look at each word to see what kind of letter sound appears on either side of the line which divides the words into syllables (*consonant sound*). Now ask them to tell what kind of sound precedes the divided consonants (*vowel sound*). After the children realize that all these words have common characteristics and are divided into syllables according to their letter patterns, it is time to help them formulate the generalization governing these and similar words. (See generalization 1, page 171.) They should read sentences which contain words that they must divide into syllables in order to pronounce them. Similar treatments may be adopted for teaching them to cope with other kinds of words.

Teaching Accent

Pupils can be made aware of accent as they work with words of two or more syllables. Read such words as *father, window, color,* and *problem,* first placing the accent where it belongs and then saying the word with the accent on the wrong syllable: fa'ther-father'; win'dow-window'; col'or-color'; prob'lem-problem'. For each pair of words ask the children to indicate which one sounds strange to them. By using known words, e.g., *started, greener, ringing,* children can learn to generalize where accents fall in the same way they generalized about where to divide words into syllables. Later they can experience words of two or more syllables that have primary and secondary accents by listening for them and reading words that they pronounce by using the dictionary. They will also note that accents shift with the function and position of words in sentences.

1. We keep a daily *rec'ord* of the weather.
2. When will you *record'* the song?

The Dictionary

As children progress through the grades and read more widely, they encounter more and more words which they have never seen, used, or heard. Totally unfamiliar words are much more difficult for children to analyze because they can never be certain just how these words are pronounced. Even the most proficient readers will meet words which they cannot pronounce. Children should be encouraged to turn to the dictionary for the pronunciation of words they don't know after they have tried to figure them out but haven't succeeded or are uncertain about the results. The glossary in some books will serve a similar purpose. Of course, the dictionary is as useful a tool for ascertaining meaning as it is for pronunciation; in fact, mature readers are more likely to turn to the dictionary for word meaning. The use of the dictionary for this purpose will be treated in Chapter 6.

In order to use a dictionary efficiently children must learn to locate entry words. This involves knowledge of alphabetical order, the use of guide words and the ability to recognize root words. Many children can find words in a dictionary, but they require much time because they proceed in a haphazard fashion and fumble about. These problems may be overcome with instruction and practice in applying the skills to locate entry words in a dictionary.

In order to pronounce words children must have a working knowledge of phonic elements. Without it they will have great difficulty in associating the sounds represented by the symbols in the pronunciation key with the respelling of the entry word. They must be able to blend the sounds to form syllables and words and interpret accent marks correctly.

Here we have an excellent example of the readiness concept. Children will not master the dictionary unless they possess the prerequisites on which dictionary skill development rests. How well children use the dictionary to pronounce words will depend upon their knowledge of phonics and structural analysis. Teachers should not proceed with dictionary work unless children have some proficiency in these skills and know enough to benefit from exposures to new skills instruction.

Locating Words

By the time children have to refer to the dictionary they generally know the letters of the alphabet and may have had some experiences with alphabetical order. Perhaps they used a picture dictionary or kept a file of words which were alphabetized according to their first letter. In any case, children have to use alphabetical order to locate words, and teachers should not assume that they can use alphabetical order just because they say (or sing) the letters of the alphabet in sequence.

The following exercises will help develop knowledge of alphabetical sequence of letters and words.

1. Write these letters on the chalkboard and have the children supply the missing letters.

a) a_c; d_f; g_i; j_l; etc.

b) b,c_; e,f_; j,k_; r,s_; etc.

c) c___; f___; l___; o___; t___; etc.

d) ___c; ___h; ___k; ___p; ___s; etc.

2. Divide the alphabet into three parts: *a* through *g*, *h* through *p*, *q* through *z*. Write or say letters and have the children indicate in which part of the alphabet each is located.

3. Examine a dictionary with the children to help them establish the fact that words are listed in alphabetical order. Write such words as *soon, fall, to, dog,* and have the children turn to the section of the dictionary where each word should be listed.

4. Write pairs of words such as:

(a)	(b)	(c)	(d)	(e)
all	bat	hat	sun	free
ask	big	he	see	father

Ask the children to look at pair (a) and tell why *all* would appear before *ask* in the dictionary. Do the same for pairs (b) and (c). Have them examine pair (d) and tell why *sun* would follow *see*. Do the same with pair (e).

5. Follow a similar procedure for these groups of words:

(a)	(b)	(c)	(d)	(e)
ant	bridge	dam	novel	skeleton
any	brim	dare	notify	skipper

Help the children generalize that if the first two letters of words are the same, the third letter determines their position in the dictionary. If the first three letters are identical, then the fourth letter establishes the position of words (hai*l*, hai*r*).

6. Turn to a page in the dictionary that has guidewords which children can read.

minute   miser

Ask them to find *minute* on the page and tell where it is located. Do the same with *miser*. Select a second and third page and follow a similar procedure. Ask the pupils to make a generalization about the function of each guideword.

7. Have the pupils tell if a word will appear on a page by checking the guidewords. Ask them to indicate the reasons for their response.

chosen   chum
(chosen, chrome, confusion, chow, chubby, choir)

8. Locate words in the dictionary by (a) turning to the section in which the word is likely to appear, (b) using the guidewords to locate the proper page, and (c) using alphabetical order to find the word on the page. These words should include some with variants.

Special situations such as cases where entries consist of two or hyphenated words can be dealt with when the occasion arises.

Pronouncing Words

By this time children will have noticed that each entry in the dictionary is followed by some letters in parentheses. If they have failed to notice the respellings of words, have them locate known words in the dictionary and discuss why they may be respelled differently from their regular spellings. Review with them letters whose pronunciations change in words: *rough-shoulder*; *breath-leak*; *home-honest*; *chap-char*acter. Ask them to generalize from such words about the relationship between the spelling of words and their pronunciation.

Using the Pronunciation Key

STEP 1.   Refer to the pronunciation key at the bottom of a dictionary page. Point out that the letters in dark print are pronounced as they sound in the words which appear in the key. Ask the children to pronounce each word. Be sure the children understand why a special code

*a*dd, āce, câre, pälm; *e*nd, ēqual; *it*, īce; *o*dd, ōpen, ôrder; to͝ok, po͞ol; *u*p, bûrn; ∂ = a in *above*, e in *sicken*, i in *possible*, o in *melon*, u in *circus*; yo͞o = u in *fuse*; *oi*l; *pou*t; *ch*eck; ri*ng*; *th*in; *th*is; *zh* in vision.[8]

is used to show how words are pronounced. Discuss how the key distinguishes between short and long vowel sounds, other vowel sounds including the schwa (∂), and some consonant sounds. Point out that most of the consonant sounds are not included in the key since they are pronounced in the regular way and are often presented in words in the front of the dictionary.

STEP 2.   Select a word that the group knows (*chief*) and have them find it in the dictionary along with its respelling. Write them both.

chief   chēf

They know that *ch* go together because of their phonic knowledge. Have the pupils refer to the pronunciation key at the bottom of the page and find the word in which "ch" appears. Ask them to give other words that begin like the key word. Now have them locate the key word in which the

---

[8] *Source:* From *The Harcourt Brace School Dictionary,* copyright © 1968 by Harcourt Brace Jovanovich, Inc. and reprinted with their permission.

"ē" appears (equal). They will recognize the vowel sound as the familiar long *e*. Have the pupils check the pronunciation key to find out if the letter *f* appears. Since it doesn't, the children assume it is pronounced as usual. The last step is to blend all the sounds to form the word.

The children should follow this same procedure with other known words until they become familiar with the process of using the respellings and pronunciation key. Do not insist that they memorize which diacritical marks represent certain sounds, for there is no real need to do so. Teachers may refer to the special markings by their names: breve (∪), macron (—), circumflex (∧), dieresis (··). But they should not require children to use them. They can refer to them as a curved line, straight line, etc.

STEP 3. Select a one-syllable word with which the children are unfamiliar and have them find it in the dictionary with its respelling. Write them on the chalkboard.

butte   byo͞ot

Have them decide if the *b* is pronounced normally by checking the pronunciation key. Then have them look for the *y* which will be part of "yo͞o." Ask the pupils to indicate how the vowel sound will be pronounced. Now have them check the key to determine if the *t* is pronounced differently. Finally have the word pronounced. Select other one-syllable words and follow a similar pattern with them.

After pupils have worked with one-syllable words, introduce unfamiliar words of two or more syllables.

purvey (pər•vā′)   sanitize (san′ə•tīz)

rivet (riv′ it)   flotilla (flō•til′ ə)

Now they have to cope with the problem of pronouncing syllables and saying the words so that the accent falls where it should. Although pupils will need practice in pronouncing unknown words, they will not experience great difficulties in using the respellings and pronunciation key if they know the phonic elements and can blend the sounds to form syllables and words.

SUMMARY

1. The major objective of a word-recognition skills program is to teach chidren to perceive words quickly and easily. Instruction in word recognition consists of developing a sight vocabulary and teaching ways of analyzing unknown words through context, phonics, structural clues, and the dictionary. Mature readers depend less on word analysis than younger ones who are in the process of building a sight vocabulary, but the need for examining some words closely will always exist.

2. Children learn to recognize words as a result of repeated exposures to them. It is not entirely clear what mechanisms make it possible for them to distinguish one word from another even though they look alike. Children seem to recognize words by their general appearance and distingishing characteristics. They rely on the beginning and final portions of words to identify them, particularly when they read continuous text.

3. Rapid recognition of words may be developed by presenting them in a meaningful context, providing a variety of exposures out of context to afford quick perception, and reinforcing their recognition through wide and extensive reading. Children enjoy word games and teachers can use these as one means of providing additional practice for learning words. However, these games should be tailored to the children's learning requirements and not be introduced indiscriminately. Teachers might adapt and modify commercial materials so that children who use them gain direct rather than incidental benefits from them.

4. Contextual clues enable readers to anticipate and identify words. Invariably these clues together with the initial parts of words are sufficiently adequate to make recognition possible. This is one reason why it is so important to stress meaning in reading. Initial instruction might show through oral activities how the context provides clues to words. These lessons could be followed by similar ones with printed materials. Children can be shown how to combine phonic and structural clues with meaning clues to identify words.

5. Phonics deals with letter-sound relationships. These relationships may be established by studying them in words that are in their sight and listening vocabularies. Instruction in phonics should include such processes as auditory and visual discrimination, word blending, and contextual application. Some phonic generalizations have greater utility than others, and children may be helped to formulate them by studying the letter-sound relationships they have already learned. Phonic knowledge is combined with contextual and structural clues to attack unknown words.

6. Structural analysis involves the recognition of prefixes, suffixes, root words, syllables, and accent in analyzing words. It is more efficient to seek structural clues for identifying words than to rely upon phonics. However, the best use of structural analysis will combine context and phonics. Auditory and visual discrimination of structural components within familiar words should be a major strategy for teaching children to recognize and use them in identifying unknown words.

7. The dictionary is the ultimate tool for checking pronunciation of words. Children should be encouraged to use their independent word-attack skills on words they don't know before turning to the dictionary. A good background in phonics and structural analysis is required in order to use the dictionary for pronunciation purposes. Lessons on dictionary use should cover the location of entry words and application of the pronunciation code to the respelling of words.

STUDY QUESTIONS AND EXERCISES

1. What are the components of a sound instructional program in word recognition?
2. Select a few sight words to teach to a group of children. Prepare a lesson as outlined on pages 145–49 for teaching these words. Note which children had some difficulty in learning to recognize these words. Try to discover why some words were not learned as readily as others.
3. Prepare a word recognition lesson on using context with phonic and structural clues for the following words: *climb, mountainous, identify.*
4. Prepare a phonic lesson on the element *ai.* Include in the lesson provisions for auditory and visual discrimination, word blending and contextual application.
5. Why is knowledge of structural analysis generally more useful to older than younger pupils? How might the steps suggested for teaching phonic elements be adapted for teaching some aspects of structural analysis?
6. "The dictionary is the last resort for discovering the pronunciation of words." Explain this statement.

SUGGESTIONS FOR FURTHER READING

The single, most comprehensive treatment of word recognition will be found in William S. Gray, *On Their Own in Reading,* 2nd ed. Chicago: Scott, Foresman and Company, 1960.

Other books which cover different aspects of phonics and structural analysis include the following:

Anna D. Cordts, *Phonics for the Reading Teacher.* New York: Holt, Rinehart and Winston, Inc., 1965.

Dolores Durkin, *Phonics and the Teaching of Reading.* New York: Bureau of Publications, Teachers College, Columbia University, 1962.

Roma Gans, *Fact and Fiction about Phonics.* Indianapolis: The Bobbs-Merrill Co., Inc., 1964.

Arthur W. Heilman, *Phonics in Proper Perspective.* Columbus: Charles E. Merrill Books, Inc., 1964.

Suggestions for teaching word recognition will be found in most reading textbooks. Included among them are:

Emmett A. Betts, *Foundations of Reading Instruction.* New York: American Book Co., 1957.

Nila B. Smith, *Reading Instruction for Today's Children.* Englewood Cliffs, N. J.: Prentice-Hall, Inc., 1963.

Miles Tinker and Constance McCullough, *Teaching Elementary Reading.* New York: Appleton-Century-Crofts, 1968.

6
Reading for Meaning

■ *The conditions confronting us in the next decade call for the application of knowledge and wisdom rather than force. Therefore, I hold that the values which thoughtful men cherish are more endangered by illiteracy than by the atomic bomb and its offspring. The illiteracy which threatens civilization may be said to be of two kinds: simple illiteracy or the inability to receive and express ideas through reading and writing; and the higher illiteracy or the inability to relate the content of verbal communication to events which at each moment are shaping the future.*[1]

The reading act has been described in many ways: perceiving and understanding written symbols; reconstructing experiences behind the symbols; following the ideas and messages of others. In each of these descriptions there runs a common thread: that reading is a thinking and problem-solving process which involves not only the absorption of ideas but the creation of ideas. To describe reading in this way suggests that reading and thinking contain common elements and that they are mutually enhancing. As one renowned psychologist put it long ago in an oft-quoted study, "the mind is assailed . . . by every word in the paragraph. It must select, repress, soften, emphasize, correlate and organize. . . ."[2] To the extent that one engages in these thoughtful activities as he reads, reading really is thinking.

---

[1] Francis S. Chase, "Demands on the Reader in the Next Decade," *Controversial Issues in Reading and Promising Solutions* (Supplementary Educational Monographs, No. 91). Chicago: University of Chicago Press, 1961, p. 10.

[2] Edward L. Thorndike, "Reading as Reasoning: A Study of Mistakes in Paragraph Reading," *Journal of Educational Psychology, 8* (June, 1917), p. 329.

To teach children how to think is one of the aims of the elementary school curriculum. This does not mean that children do not know how to think when they enter school. There is ample evidence that they can and do use their thinking powers to the extent that their abilities allow and their environments stimulate. The school seeks to foster an inquiring attitude toward ideas and events and provide conditions which will help children increase their thinking abilities. These objectives may be served by numerous learning activities, one of the foremost of which is reading.

Lack of specificity is as apparent in saying that reading for meaning or comprehension is one strand of the reading curriculum as it is in claiming that schools teach reading. For unless reading comprehension is described in operational terms, it is not possible to plan instruction to increase comprehension nor determine how well children do comprehend what they read. Reading models and research on reading comprehension provide some clues as to what factors and processes might be operating and accounting for variations in reading performances. All seem to deal with simple cognition, convergent and divergent thinking, and evaluation. Cognition refers to the comprehension of information and ideas; convergent thinking refers to the process of seeing relationships through inductive reasoning (such as making generalizations); divergent thinking leads to implications and applications of information and ideas. Thus, cognition involves comprehension of vocabulary, concepts, and the relationships among words and ideas; convergent and divergent thinking leads to the production of reasonable and creative ideas; evaluation signals judgments of information that has been absorbed and created. Cognition could refer to *literal* reading, convergent and divergent thinking to *inferential* (or creative) reading, and evaluation to *critical* reading.

Literal, inferential, and critical reading are the three main strands of comprehension. Each serves as a basis for determining how well children read for meaning and what experiences teachers might offer to increase their comprehension abilities. Some writers allude to a fourth strand—the integration or fusion of one's ideas with those he has acquired. This application seems to be more a product of the three previous strands than it is a distinguishable component of comprehension. To what extent and how well readers integrate acquired ideas with those already possessed are highly personal outcomes of meaningful reading. Changes in attitudes and modifications of behavior are more the results of experiences than of direct teaching.

The division of comprehension into literal, inferential, and critical strands is intended to facilitate the teacher's task of implementing reading objectives, rather than to imply sharp separations among reading-thinking processes. The reader does not consciously seek out literal meanings first and then go on to higher-level ones; there is a blending and flowing together that often defies identification. But there is no doubt that the acquisition of literal meanings is fundamental and a precursor to other kinds of reading performances.

Literal Reading

Literal reading refers to the acquisition of *stated* ideas and information. The old and familiar "to tell it in your own words" is an effort to get at the surface meanings of written passages—what is *said* rather than what is *meant*. When a reader faces the opening line of Lincoln's Gettysburg Address—*Four score and seven years ago*—he is likely to convert this passage to *eighty-seven years ago*, if he knows the meaning of *score* in this context and then makes some rapid calculations. He does not have to go beyond what the writer said to grasp the meaning of the passage; he merely "translates" in terms of his experience. On the other hand, were the reader to speculate about Lincoln's choice of words, he could become involved with the author as a man. This would take him beyond what was said and literal reading into deeper meanings and higher-level comprehension.

As children move from simple into more complex materials they encounter difficulties which interfere with their ability to grasp literal meanings. Some of their problems arise from unfamiliarity with words and others from failure to follow the organization and realize the significance of ideas. Not all children experience the same difficulties but there are times when each one of them meets obstacles which limit his understanding. When such problems arise, children should know how to cope with them; moreover, some difficulties can be anticipated. Thus instruction in reading for meaning serves the dual purpose of reducing the extent of interference children meet when they read and helping them to remove new barriers to understanding.

Word Meaning

Studies by different investigators show that knowledge of word meaning is the most important single factor that accounts for variability in reading comprehension. All other conditions being equal, the child who meets few words he doesn't know will surpass the reading performance of one who fails to recognize the meaning of many words.

It is difficult to determine the size of elementary school children's meaning vocabularies, and estimates vary from a few to several thousand words. Of course, children recognize the meaning of many words they hear and read, words which they do not themselves use in speaking and writing. Personal as well as environmental conditions account for variations in the quantity of words children know when they come to school. The learning experiences they subsequently enjoy will have some effect upon the growth they realize in language development.

It is hardly possible to teach children all the words they need to know in order to read with understanding. Even if such an undertaking were feasible, there wouldn't be time for much of anything else. A much better strategy is to teach children to use their own and other resources to ascertain word meanings. These include awareness of contextual and morphemic clues, multiple meanings, figurative language, and dictionary usage.

Contextual Clues

Direct instruction in recognizing and interpreting contextual clues can be an effective method of helping children learn how to determine word meanings. This does not imply that all word meanings might be derived from contextual aids or that children will learn to use context equally well. What it does suggest is that children be taught to look for contextual clues and if they do exist to use them in the best way they can.

There are some cautions about the values of contextual clues of which everyone should be aware. They do not always allow the reader to uncover precise meanings of words and can leave him with vague impressions. Unless the clues are so clear-cut that they leave little room for misinterpretation, the experiences that the reader brings to them are an important determinant of how effectively he will be able to use them. Contextual aids might be so far removed in position from the unknown word that they would be difficult to associate with it. On the other hand, the expectation that clues are to be found usually in the same sentence as the troublesome word is hardly realistic, and children must be prepared to search for them elsewhere in the paragraph and possibly even in other paragraphs.

Examples of how contextual clues might leave a reader with an imprecise impression about a word's meaning and how important his background of experience could be are found in the following excerpt from a selection about Sacajawea, the Indian maiden who accompanied the Lewis and Clark expedition.

> Perhaps it was at Sacajawea's suggestion that Lewis and Clark staged a great entertainment for the Indians, with pipe-smoking, dancing and singing. The expedition had brought along a fiddler named Cruzatte. Cruzatte and his fiddle had often helped to cheer the men when they grew weary. . . .
>
> So Cruzatte got out his fiddle to entertain the Indians. He played old country tunes and all the men danced the Virginia Reel and the Irish Jig.[3]

If a child did not know the meanning of *fiddle,* he might use several contextual clues in deciding to what it refers: staged a great *entertainment*; *dancing and singing*; Cruzatte (the *fiddler*) and his fiddle . . . helped to *cheer* the men; got out his fiddle to *entertain*; *played* old country tunes. Few children would not know from all these clues that a *fiddle* is some sort of musical instrument. But what kind? There is nothing in the passage to help them decide. However, if they were familiar with the times when the incident occurred, they might know that the violin was commonly played at dances and make the proper association. Perhaps they might remember seeing country dances in films or on TV, or listening to recorded country music in which the violin predominated. In any case, to make the association between *fiddle* and *violin* they would have to rely on their own experiences. Without appropriate ones all they could know from the context was that a *fiddle* is a musical instrument.

---

[3] "Sacajawea," *Reading to Learn.* The Bookmark Reading Program, p. 82.

To effect the greatest utilization of contextual aids children should learn to recognize common types that they will encounter. Their recognition of these types will aid them to decide what a word means. These clues have been classified in the following ways: experience, definition, explanation, comparison and contrast. There are other classifications based upon typographical and structural forms whose elements overlap those found in one or more of the established categories.

EXPERIENCE   Children learn to interpret some contextual clues by using the knowledge they possess. This knowledge enables them to deal with words whose meanings they ordinarily might not know.

It was the last half of the ninth inning with the home team behind by one run. This was its last chance to tie or win the ballgame. As the first hitter approached the plate, the crowd began to *chant,* "We want a hit! We want a hit!"

Anyone who knows or watches baseball games has experienced situations such as the one described. Fans often repeat their cry of "We want a hit" in a rhythmic fashion when their team is behind. Children can recognize what *chant* means because they have participated in the event directly or as an observer.

DEFINITION   Not infrequently an author will follow a word with an actual definition, synonym, or illustration.

Irish folk tales are full of *leprechauns,* imaginary little characters who do mischievous things.

The Senate *ratified* or approved the treaty without a single negative vote.

Diamonds and rubies are *precious* stones.

Scavengers are animals which feed on the bodies of dead animals.

Dirigibles—large, inflated balloons which are driven by motors—have not been used as airships since several were destroyed by explosions in the 1930s.

Notice that definition clues appear in different forms. In the first example the clue follows the comma, which is a signal that there could be some information which might clarify the meaning of *leprechauns.* The word *or* in the second example serves as a signal to the reader that the writer might offer an alternate word for *ratified. Diamonds* and *rubies* are clues to the meaning of *precious* since both are examples of costly stones. In the fourth example the word *are* tells the reader he may expect information about *scavengers.* The last example uses another device, dashes, to signal the meaning of *dirigibles.*

EXPLANATION   These clues are akin to definition clues but appear in the form of explanations.

Some elections are decided by *majority* vote. This means that a candidate must receive more than half of all the votes cast in order to win. When more than two candidates run for the same office, one of them might receive more votes than the others but not a majority. We then say he has a *plurality.*

The meaning of *majority* and *plurality* is explained in the passage. In the first instance the words *This means* are the clues to what follows. The words *We then say* link *plurality* to the explanation of it.

COMPARISON AND CONTRAST   These word clues express similar or opposite meanings of other words and help the reader decide what they mean.

The city approved an *ordinance* which establishes a maximum speed of 35 miles per hour. It also passed a law which forbids all-night street parking.

The lack of fresh air in the meeting room made him feel *drowsy* but he became wide-awake as soon as he stepped out into the cold hall.

The contextual signal to the meaning of *ordinance* is the word *also*, which suggests that *law* and *ordinance* are closely related. There is also the parallel use of sentence structure—*The city approved* and *It also passed* —which offers another comparison-type contextual clue.

In the second example the word *but* signals a change in feelings from *drowsy* to *wide-awake*. The contrast between the two is evident. In this particular case the added experience clue (how one feels after being in a stuffy room and then breathing fresh air) should help the reader understand what *drowsy* means.

Examples of these and other types of contextual aids will be found in the materials children read. Relationships between these aids and the meaning of words can be established by presenting passages which contain different kinds of contextual clues and words whose meanings are known to them. Children may identify the clues and explain how they relate them to the known words. Another way to help children see relationships between contextual aids and word meanings is to give them several meanings for an unknown word and have them search for clues which provide support for one of the meanings. They should explain these clues and categorize them wherever possible. When children give evidence that they understand how contextual aids function in relation to other words, they may study unknown words and clues through exploration and discussion.

Some group of children will require repeated exposures to both known words and contextual clues which have been identified for them before they will be able to seek out and interpret the latter with some independence. In working with such children there are real advantages to limiting the type of contextual aid to one kind and providing many experiences with it before introducing another type.

IDEAS FOR DISCUSSION

We have seen how children might use context clues to help them understand the meanings of words they don't know. At the same time limitations affecting their use suggest the impracticality of total reliance upon them. All children are not equally able to interpret them; many clues are helpful only if children have had appropriate experiences which they can relate to the ideas they are reading about; some clues are not introduced by words that signal a relationship to unknown words; meanings acquired through contextual aids are not always precise and give children vague impressions with a false sense of security; and there are many passages which do not contain word clues.

Teachers and children should understand that the context does not always provide solutions to word-meaning problems but that it is one resource among others that might prove helpful. It can give the reader who is able to take full advantage of whatever clues do exist a greater degree of independence than he might have otherwise. To ignore contextual clues completely would be as unwise as not using whatever phonic and structural clues one can to identify words. But in both cases there will be occasions when none is very helpful and the reader must turn to another resource—the dictionary—for assistance and confirmation. The task of the teacher is as much one of developing proper attitudes toward behaviors as it is to improving reading performances. Too often children are unaware that they don't know and leave no room for possible alternate behaviors. The attitude that solutions to problems are tentative and require testing is one that will allow children to take advantage of whatever aids do exist. It also will lead them to seek firmer solutions when those they have reached appear tenuous and lacking real support. Such behavior is the mark of a mature reader.

Morphemic Clues

Clues to the meaning of words may exist within the words themselves. These clues are the morphemes which all words consist of. A morpheme is the smallest unit of language that carries meaning. The word *table* consists of one meaning unit or morpheme; *tables* is made up of two morphemes: *table* and the plural *s*, meaning more than one.

In addition to plurals, morphemes are represented by prefixes, suffixes, roots, and the parts of compound words. Children learn to identify each as they develop their word recognition skills; they then use the meaning these morphemes carry to help them understand what words mean as they read them in context.

Children can learn how to use the meanings that prefixes, suffixes, and roots convey if these are treated in more meaningful ways than they have in the past. The practice of presenting long lists of prefixes, suffixes, and roots with their meanings and requiring their memorization has been shown to be an unproductive method of teaching most children how to successfully determine the meaning of words not previously encountered. Instead, these morphemes are studied first through known words in context children are familiar with, and the knowledge they gain is later applied to unfamiliar words.

Sentences containing known words with the morpheme children need to learn can be drawn from materials they are reading or prepared for this purpose. Here is one example.

Mary was *unable* to attend the party because she had the sniffles and a fever.

Stories with sad endings make us feel *unhappy*.

The children will discuss what each of the underlined words mean and in what ways they are similar. They should realize that both words consist of a root and the same prefix. In order to fix the exact meaning of the prefix *un* the teacher might remove them from their roots and discuss why the words don't seem appropriate in their contexts. When the meaning of *un* has been established, other words in context might be presented and discussed in a similar way.

Fruit which has to be shipped long distances to market is usually *unripe* when picked. Otherwise, the fruit might spoil before it could be sold.

The apartment was *unoccupied* for only a week before it was rented and the family's furniture moved in.

By removing the *un* in each case children will realize that the root word doesn't make much sense in the context and that each requires a negative connotation which *un* carries. New words might be formed by adding the prefix to different roots and used in sentences to convey their new meanings.

un + observed = unobserved
The thief entered the house through the window
_____ by anyone.
(observed, unobserved)

un + natural = unnatural

When artificial flowers are placed next to real ones, they look *unnatural.*

Suffixes and roots in compound words may be treated in a similar fashion. Whatever procedures teachers follow to teach children to use morphemic clues in analyzing words, they should be meaningful and not stress rote learning. The use of words and context make it possible for children to develop understandings on their own and apply them to new settings in a thoughtful way.

Children who are taught to read thoughtfully are less likely to confuse a morpheme such as *un* with the beginning of words like *un*it and *un*iversal. Even if they were to do so they would realize their mistake as soon as they tested the word for meaning in the context. The same would be true in cases where there was a shift in meaning of a morpheme as in *re*wind (wind *again*) and *re*call (call *back*) or in some compound words whose morphemes fail to reveal their meaning (*figure*head, *cock*pit).

Multiple Meanings and the Dictionary

Some words are quite limited in their meaning while others take on additional meanings as context changes. For example, the word *ambassador* refers to a person who represents a country in a formal or informal way.

the United States *ambassador* to Brazil
a poor *ambassador* of American culture
a good-will *ambassador*

Its meaning is not changed in a significant way in these three contexts. On the other hand, such words as *bank* and *keep* do acquire unique meanings as they appear in different contexts. A few examples for each word will illustrate how shifts in the meaning occur within contexts.

> to *bank* one's savings
> a *bank* in the road
> to *bank* on his winning the contest
>
> *keep* the reward
> *keep* the audience waiting
> *keep* the food cold

Illustrations such as these should be discussed with children at all reading levels. Even at the preprimer and primer levels children will be reading words whose meanings change with the context.

> The sun is *up*.
> He looked *up*.

They certainly will be meeting these words through their language-experience reading. These are the best times to establish attitudes that cause children to react to words in a thoughtful and flexible way.

Specific opportunities to build new meanings for words can be outgrowths of discussions about the words whose meanings pupils are dealing with. Teachers might start with the sentence that contains a word for which there are multiple meanings and develop some others with the children.

> Welfare agencies distribute the food and clothing to the *poor*.
> *Poor* weather forced the cancellation of all flights.
> The old man was in *poor* health.

A useful exercise which will focus the children's attention on multiple meanings of words is to have them select from among several contexts those in which a word is used in a similar way.

It is practically impossible to consider word meanings out of contextual settings, and children should not be required to study them in isolation. They will encounter words which they recognize as being familiar but for which they cannot provide appropriate meanings. Thoughtful readers will realize that the meanings they know are inadequate, for they do not make sense in the given context. They will try to understand what these words mean from whatever contextual and morphemic clues exist and if they are unsuccessful, turn to the dictionary for their suitable meanings.

As an illustration of this point, consider the following sentence:

> The cat *inched* his way forward until he was within a few feet of the bird.

There are a few contextual and morphemic clues which some children could use to gain the sense of *inched*. From the word's position in the sentence they know that it is a verb. They recognize the morphemes *inch,* which they know is a small part of a foot and *ed,* which indicates the past tense. From their own experiences they recall how cats behave when going after birds. They put these clues together and decide that *inched* means to move "an inch at a time" or very slowly.

Other sentences do not contain the clues found in the previous one, and children will have to turn to the dictionary for help.

"*Mend* your ways now," the doctor advised his patient.

They find the following definitions for *mend*:

a. repair
b. remove defects
c. reform
d. make amends for

Now they must try out each meaning in the sentence before deciding which one is correct. It might be necessary to reword the meaning so that the substitution does not produce an awkward statement.

"Repair your ways. . . ."
"Remove the defects in your ways. . . ."
"Reform your ways. . . ."
"Make amends for your ways. . . ."

Discussion of each sentence with the dictionary meaning substituted for *mend* will help them decide which one makes the most sense in the present context. This procedure is the same children will have to follow when they encounter a totally unfamiliar word and have to rely upon the dictionary for help. Instruction in this process will establish an attitude in searching for meaning that all readers should develop.

Figurative Language

Helping children to distinguish between the literal and figurative meanings of words will not be difficult if in all their reading activities they have been encouraged to look for meaning. Without doubt most children will have used or heard figurative language and these familiar expressions could be used to establish the difference between literal meaning and figurative meaning

catch a cold	batter *on deck*
a *cool cat*	actions *speak* louder than words
a *tall* tale	raining *cats* and *dogs*
a *blanket* of snow	*stretch* your legs

A discussion of the literal and figurative meanings of words in such expressions as these will help the children understand any relationship which might exist between the words as used and their common meanings. Most children will be able to suggest other words that are used in special ways.

The purpose of dealing with figurative language is not to teach children what different expressions mean; there just would be too many to cover. Instead, children need to recognize them wherever they exist and realize that they must be viewed differently from other words. Most of the attention to figurative expressions should be reserved for times when children are reading materials that contain them. However teachers might select passages which contain figurative expressions and have children who need additional exposure identify and explain how they are used. As an added aid the figurative expression might be indicated along with suggested meanings.

By sign language they showed they wanted him to guide them across the desert to their own lines. He agreed. Or so they thought. A day and a half later *they wound up* behind the German lines, prisoners.[4]

What does the expression *they wound up* mean?
a. They went in circles.
b. They finally arrived.

Identify the figurative expressions in this passage and explain what they mean.

One evening he was alone in a desolate part of the desert called Rub Al Khali. He had been making a map of the area. As the sun went down behind the endless sand dunes, a dozen or so Arabs appeared out of nowhere.[5]

Sentence Meaning

In the beginning stages of reading most children do not seem to have much trouble understanding what ideas sentences convey, for sentence structure is quite simple and straightforward. The sentences are short and generally contain few modifiers. In addition, the ways in which the words are ordered are familiar.

Sentences do become more difficult to read as they grow longer and express a number of different ideas. At times these complex sentences confuse the reader with their syntactical structures. Some understanding of what sentences consist of and how they are constructed can help readers unravel the meaning of sentences which don't make a great deal of sense to them.

Sentence Parts

A sentence consists of simple subjects and predicates, either stated or implied, which carry the basic meaning. The rest of the sentence provides additional information about the simple subjects and predicates. Children should be taught to look for the parts which carry the basic meaning if they don't understand what the sentence tells them.

STEP 1. Select sentences which contain a single subject and predicate. Divide them as follows:

1. Horses/like sugar.
2. I/ate cereal for breakfast.
3. The dog/ran after the cat.
4. A cold rain/fell all day.

Explain that each of the sentences consists of two parts: the first part or subject tells *who* or *what* and the second part or predicate provides infor-

---

[4] "Communication Is More than Words," *Reading to Learn*. The Bookmark Reading Program, p. 123.

[5] "Communication Is More than Words," *Reading to Learn*, p. 123.

mation about the who or what. Provide other sentences and have the children indicate the subjects and predicates. Have them tell on what basis they identified each part of the sentence.

STEP 2. Refer to the subjects in sentences 1 and 2 to show that each consists of one word. Ask the children in what way the subjects in sentences 3 and 4 are different from 1 and 2. (They contain two and three words, respectively.) Discuss why the words *dog* and *rain* are more important than those which precede them. These are the simple subjects, like *Horses* and *I* in the first two sentences. Provide practice in selecting the simple subjects of other sentences.

Now refer to the predicates of each sentence and show which word indicates something about the simple subject:

Horses *like*   dog *ran*

I *ate*   rain *fell*

Have the children read the predicates but omit the verb in each case to help them realize that this word carries more information than the other words in the predicate. Discuss what the other words do in the predicate.

STEP 3. Write paired sentences such as the following to show that a sentence might contain more than one subject and/or predicate.

a. I ate cereal for breakfast.
   My mother and I ate lunch in a restaurant.

b. The dog ran after the cat.
   The dog was awakened by the noise and barked loudly.

c. A cold rain fell all day.
   A cold rain fell all day but people traveled great distances to see the football game.

Discuss with the children how the second sentence in each pair is different from the first. Have them identify the subject (s) and predicate (s) as well as each simple subject and predicate.

STEP 4. Introduce sentences in which other parts precede the subject or separate the subject from the predicate.

During the hot summer months we never turn off the air-conditioning system.

Captain Jones, *who lives next door,* flies jets to Europe twice a month.

Show how by moving or eliminating parts of a sentence the meaning becomes clearer.

We never turn off the air-conditioning system during the hot summer months.

Captain Jones flies jets to Europe twice a month.

Throughout each of these activities children should realize that all the parts of a sentence contribute to its meaning but that some parts carry the basic information. It is these parts which they should look for if they don't understand a sentence and after identifying them read the sentence again to acquire its total meaning.

Another way to approach difficult sentences is to analyze them for all the ideas they convey. Select complex sentences from children's materials and together with them list in separate sentences what information the sentences provide.

Since 1960, several African countries that were controlled by Europeans have gained their independence after a long struggle, but without bloodshed.

1. Countries have gained their independence.
2. They were African countries.
3. There were several of them.
4. They have gained their independence since 1960.
5. The countries had been under European control.
6. They struggled for their independence.
7. The struggle was a long one.
8. They gained independence without bloodshed.

The sentence contains eight related but separate ideas that the reader might not recognize unless he analyzed the parts. Such analysis requires careful attention by the reader to each group of words that carry meaning and to the relationships that exist among them. A rereading of the original sentence will now be more meaningful than it was initially.

Just as children are taught to use all their resources to determine the pronunciation and meaning of words, so must they learn how to cope with difficulties that stem from involved sentence structures. The procedures outlined above are useful tools in pupils' search for elusive meanings; facility in their application will lead to greater understanding should their use be required.

Pronoun Referents

Pronouns which stand for persons or things do not seem to be as difficult to associate with their referents as pronouns which represent ideas. Both, however, can create confusion, especially if they appear in complex sentences where the simple subjects and predicates are removed from them and where the pronouns represent words in other sentences.

Children should know what to do when they are confused about the referents of pronouns. They have to look for the words the pronouns stand for and substitute them in place of the pronouns. This substitution will reveal whether the pronoun and referent are properly matched; if they aren't, the restructured sentence won't make much sense within the framework of other sentences.

Trophy hunting by white men is no more popular with the Eskimos than the wasteful slaughter of the buffalo was with the American Indians. *It* seems to *them* a wasteful killing of an animal *that they* consider a resource. The polar bear is now disappearing so rapidly that *it* is included on a list of animals threatened with extinction.[6]

6 "King of the Arctic," *Reading Power*. The Bookmark Reading Program, p. 230.

Notice how far removed the pronoun *It* is from its referent. By asking himself, *What seems to them a wasteful killing?* the child should know that *It* refers to *trophy hunting.* The substitution of other words wouldn't make much sense in the context. The same holds true for the pronouns *them* and *they.* The child knows that both pronouns refer to people: *white men, Eskimos,* or *American Indians.* If he substitutes *white men* or *American Indians* for *them* by asking, *To whom does it seem?* and *Who consider?* the sentence will convey a meaning which doesn't coincide with the rest of the paragraph. Thus he will know that *them* and *they* probably refer to *Eskimos,* which he can confirm. The remaining pronouns are treated in the same way.

Each of these pronouns referred to a person or object. The same procedures can be followed where the pronoun refers to an idea.

"Well, there is one little catch," he said. "The lionfish belongs to the family of scorpion fish. His sharp dorsal fins can slice through your hand as though it were butter.

"But *that's* not the worst of *it,*" he continued. "Those spines are hollow and filled with poison. Just one drop of that poison is enough to kill a man.[7]

By asking, *What is not the worst of it?* the reader can discover that the word *that* refers to the whole idea contained in the sentence which precedes it: *His sharp dorsal fins can slice through your hand as though it were butter.* Once he knows what *that* means, he can deal with the pronoun *it* in the same sentence, which refers to *catch.*

There should be ample discussion about the referents so that children can learn to see the difference between pronouns which refer to ideas and others that mean persons or things. Some ideas are expressed through single sentences; others will consist of an entire paragraph or more. Raising such questions as "What did the writer mean when he said? . . ." and having children justify their responses will require them to think carefully about what they read and help to clarify their ideas.

Punctuation

An additional clue to meaning is the punctuation a writer uses. Young children learn that punctuation signals the end of a sentence, but not many realize that these marks carry some of the meaning which speech conveys. This point can be made clear by showing how punctuation will change the meaning of an identical sentence.

> Mary won a prize.
> Mary won a prize?
> Mary won a prize!

By reading each sentence orally to reflect the intended meaning, children can be led to realize how each of the punctuation marks changes the mean-

---

[7] "Bring 'Em Back Alive," *Reading Power.* The Bookmark Reading Program, p. 212.

ing of each sentence and not merely indicates its end. They should discuss what meaning a writer intends when he uses these different marks.

The comma is one of the most frequently used punctuation marks. It not only indicates a pause but carries meaning as well. See how the meaning that the comma conveys changes with each of the following examples:

a. I had orange juice, hot cereal, buttered toast, and milk for breakfast.
b. We climbed to the top of the mountain, rested, took pictures of the view, and then started back down.
c. My youngest brother, who is seven, is visiting our grandparents.
d. The water in the pipes froze, and the landlord had to call a plumber to thaw them out.
e. After the rain stopped falling, the children went outdoors to look for worms in the grass.

The commas in these samples represent different constructions that carry their own meaning. They can be clarified by asking questions which establish relationships about the content of a sentence:

a. How many different foods did the breakfast include? (*enumeration*)
b. What did we do after reaching the top of the hill? (*sequence*)

Questions such as these will help children understand what function the comma has in a sentence and how it signals meaning to them as they read.

The dash, colon, and semicolon can be studied similarly when children encounter them in the materials they read. They should be trained to ask themselves what message the punctuation mark conveys, and what kind of information they can anticipate. Questions such as these become tools that children use when the meaning of sentences is unclear because of the different ideas they contain.

Paragraph Organization

One measure of comprehension is the extent to which the reader sees relationships among ideas, i.e., how the ideas go together. His ability to understand is enhanced by his perception of the structure which ties a group of sentences together or the recognition that no firm structure exists. Children who learn to recognize patterns of organization will be able to think about ideas as the writer did. The closer the child follows the writer's thinking, the greater is his understanding of what he reads.

Paragraphs are organized in various ways—by time, enumeration, topic, comparison-contrast, cause-effect. In addition, some paragraphs serve special functions—they illustrate and summarize ideas and become a bridge from one idea to another. Other types might be identified, but these are the ones most commonly found in narrative and informational writing. Occasionally, writers combine one type of organization with another, e.g., topical with time order, to give form to their ideas.

A suitable way to help children follow organizational patterns is to cause them to think about the contents in the way the material is structured. This may be accomplished by framing questions which emphasize the relationships among the sentences. Illustrations of such questions follow the passages which represent different patterns of organization.

Time Order

When Abraham Lincoln *was a young man,* his family moved from Indiana to Illinois. The Lincoln family was poor and Abe had to find odd jobs in order to earn some money. But he found time in the evening hours to read whatever he could get his hands on. He *had had* very little schooling and practically taught himself to read. *As he grew older,* Abe became known as an ambitious person who was not afraid to work. He clerked in a store, he split rails, he did odd jobs. *At the same time* he managed to study law.

In 1834 Lincoln was elected to the Illinois legislature, and *later* received his lawyer's license. He was elected to the United States House of Representatives *in 1847* but *eight years later* lost the election for the Senate. *In 1860* Lincoln was elected President of the United States.

1. When did Lincoln's family move to Illinois?
2. What kinds of work did Lincoln do before he was elected to public office?
3. For how long had Lincoln been active in politics before he was elected President?

Paragraphs such as these contain words which signal time order—both definite and indefinite. Children should learn to recognize these clues as possible signals to idea organization. These words are indicated in the paragraphs. Note the words which signal the pattern in the next passage.

Enumeration

Animal intelligence is never easy to measure. And it is very hard to measure in an animal that lives in the water. Scientists cannot give a dolphin the same tests they give to chimps. They must study dolphins in *other ways*.

One way is to study the dolphin brain. It is a very large brain. This is *one sign* that dolphins may be highly intelligent.

Other signs are found in dolphin behavior. *For example,* teasing is a sign of intelligence. Teasing is action taken on purpose. The teaser expects something to happen because of his action. That is, he thinks ahead. Only the higher, more intelligent animals think ahead.

Dolphins can invent games. They can learn games from each other. And they learn quickly. . . .

Another sign is the ability to solve problems. And dolphins are good at solving problems.[8]

1. Why can't scientists study dolphins in the same way they study other animals?
2. How can the intelligence of dolphins be measured?

Topical Order

The earth is made of layers of rock, and vibrations are produced when these layers shift. The vibrations are called an earthquake. A slight movement of these layers of rock can produce vibrations strong enough to destroy buildings.

Earthquakes usually occur in certain parts of the world. California and Alaska

---

[8] "The Intelligent Dolphins," *Goals in Reading.* The Bookmark Reading Program, p. 18.

have been hard hit by them. The Pacific Ocean is where many earthquakes are born, and the vibrations have created huge waves which caused great damage to coastal cities of Japan.

1. What happens when the earth's layers move?
2. Why do people fear earthquakes?

Comparison-Contrast

European cities live in the *past* and the *present*. Almost every one has a section where people occupy brick and stone houses and shops that are hundreds of years old. Some of the streets are paved with cobblestones that date back to the fourteenth and fifteenth centuries. These streets are so narrow that there is room for just one car; when two meet one has to climb on the sidewalk to allow the other one to pass.

You don't have to walk very far from the "old city" to return to the twentieth century. Here the buildings are of steel and glass of the most modern design, and the wide boulevards are filled with automobiles and buses that carry their passengers to all parts of the city. Perhaps what makes European cities attractive is this combination of the *old* and the *new*.

1. In what ways are European cities different from ours?
2. Why do people refer to sections of European cities as the "old" and "new" quarters?

The children might make a table which shows the contrasting ideas paragraphs contain.

Old City	New City
buildings hundreds of years old	new buildings
stone and brick buildings	steel and glass buildings
narrow cobblestone streets	wide boulevards

Cause-Effect

Most of the top-ranked tennis players in this country come from the South or West Coast. The climate there makes it possible for them to practice and play outdoors most of the year. Tennis players who live in colder climates have to depend more on indoor courts which are few in number and expensive to play on. They do not have the same opportunities as other players to practice and develop their skills.

1. From what parts of the country do most of the best tennis players come from? Why?
2. What advantages do some tennis players have over others?

Cause-effect relationships can be stressed by having the child point out one where the other is given and explain his reasoning for linking the two.

Transitional Paragraphs

We do not know much about many prehistoric animals because nothing or little of their remains have been found. Scientists have to guess what these animals were like from the few clues they have been able to unearth. *However,* there are some prehistoric animals which the scientists know all about.

Transitional paragraphs are used to help the reader move from one idea to another. In the paragraph above, the word *however* ties two ideas together but suggests a change in the one that follows it. The reader is prepared for this change of ideas by the use of such words as *but, on the other hand, on the contrary*, etc. Children can compare these signal words with others that suggest more discussion on the same ideas: *also, moreover, in addition, then, first*.

Illustrative and Summary Paragraphs

Illustrative and summary paragraphs fulfill the functions their names suggest. The writer might use the initial paragraphs to state his ideas and follow them with one or more paragraphs that contain examples. Then he could restate the ideas in the form of a summary. Children can learn to view these paragraphs in terms of their functions by answering questions which require them to relate ideas and examples and find the statements which convey the same idea.

Interpretive Reading

To understand what a writer *means* is to know more than what he says. Literal reading deals with surface meanings—what information the writer provides—while interpretive reading involves implied meanings or reading "between and beyond the lines."

The previous section dealt with literal meaning, which is the first strand of reading comprehension. It is quite obvious that children will not be ready to think about the implied meanings of ideas if they fail to understand ideas that are stated. They must overcome obstacles—whether they are elements of vocabulary, sentences, or paragraphs—that get in their way of understanding them. This is the reason why teachers should not fail to offer instruction in how to cope with materials that children find difficult to read. This is a preparatory step for the next higher strand of reading comprehension.

As with literal reading teachers should know in operational terms what inferential reading encompasses so that they will be goal-oriented in planning instruction. To read inferentially is to draw conclusions, to make generalizations, to sense relationships, to predict outcomes, and to realize the author's purpose. These are not unrelated tasks for each one requires the reader to use whatever information and ideas are known in order to make appropriate inferences.

The ultimate objective of teaching children how to read for deeper meanings is to instill in them the attitude that reading requires them to do more than receive surface messages, that it is the reader's responsibility to think about what *other* ideas the messages might convey. This objective will be realized if provisions for inferential reading are included at every stage of reading development and if this type of reading receives the attention it merits.

Reading for Inferences

The way to teach children how to make inferences is to require them to think in specified ways. This can be accomplished through questions and discussions that focus their attention upon the ways in which they must think in order to solve the problem.

Drawing Conclusions

One of the most common types of inferential reading is drawing conclusions. Children can be taught to examine whatever information they have and to make some judgments from it. This process should be undertaken at the beginning reading levels and continued throughout the grades as they progress into difficult materials.

The following passage is from a first reader.[9] The simple ideas it contains can be used as a springboard for developing skill in drawing conclusions and the habit of reading inferentially.

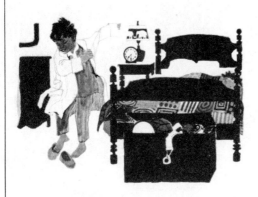

The Peter Rabbit Play[9]

Jeff jumped from his bed.
This was the day for the Peter Rabbit play at school.
And Jeff's teacher was going to let him play Peter Rabbit.

Jeff dressed very fast that morning.
He got something to eat.
Then he ran from his apartment.
Soon he was at school with all the other boys and girls.

"Boys and girls," said the teacher.
"You won't forget what to do in the play, will you?
Jeff, what are you in the play?"

---

[9] *Source:* From *Together We Go* by Elizabeth K. Cooper, copyright © 1970 by Harcourt Brace Jovanovich, Inc. and reprinted with their permission.

The teacher might first establish what facts the passage tells about Jeff and list them as the children indicate what they are.

- He jumped out of bed that day.
- He dressed and ate quickly.
- He ran out of the house.
- He was going to be Peter Rabbit in a school play.

Now the children are ready to examine the validity of some judgments the teacher offers them. He will ask if the information the passage contains allows them to say that:

a. Jeff did not always rush to get to school.
b. Jeff was a good actor.
c. Jeff was excited about playing Peter Rabbit.

The children should look for the information that might support the first judgment. A question such as *which information tells that this was a special day?* will help them decide that perhaps he did not rush on other days. (*Jeff jumped out of bed and dressed very fast* that *day.*) They should tell why they believe that the judgment is a proper one or not and read the parts which helped them decide. Children who disagree should also be encouraged to explain why.

The second and third judgments might be examined in the same way. The children should look for information that lends support for each one. In the second instance, they are led to realize that there isn't much information on which to base a judgment. However, should some suggest that Jeff was chosen to play Peter Rabbit because he *was* a good actor (the teacher wouldn't choose a poor one), this conclusion could stand or the children might agree to wait until more information was available.

The children should compare the last conclusion with the other two. They find a number of facts to support the judgment and therefore can be fairly certain about this one. This conclusion they are able to accept more readily than the others because they have more support for it. Not only do children have to learn that conclusions are based upon available information but that some conclusions are more easily reached than others.

A slightly different approach whereby the teacher offers a reasonable conclusion to a passage could be followed. The children would then have to find support for the conclusion.

In 1865 Jules Verne wrote a book entitled, *From the Earth to the Moon.* Three men and some animals took off from Florida for the moon in a spaceship. Over 100 years later men did blast off from Cape Kennedy in Florida and landed on the moon. The heroes in his book made a journey that few people believed would ever be taken. One of Verne's best-known books is *Twenty Thousand Leagues under the Sea*, which tells about adventures in a submarine. Another is *A Journey to the Center of the Earth*, that has been made into a film.

Conclusion: Jules Verne predicted scientific accomplishments long before other people thought them possible.

The discussion that ensues will help children see the relationship among the ideas in the passage and why such a conclusion is justified. They might restate the conclusion in their own way and suggest other conclusions which they could verify.

Making Generalizations

Another form of inferential reading is making generalizations. From a group of ideas or details the reader makes a general statement that covers them. Like conclusions, generalizations can be questioned if on the basis of available information they are too broad or if existing information is too incomplete to warrant a generalization.

In order to clarify to children what a generalization is, it might be necessary to use some examples of general statements which cover a set of known details or ideas and discuss them.

Dogs and cats have four legs. So do cows, pigs, sheep, goats, and horses. Wild animals such as lions, tigers, and elephants have four legs also.

Generalization: Many animals have four legs.

Deer *run* fast.   You should *rest* after meals.
The water is *running* in the tub.   The *rest* of us went home.

Pack your things now.   *Sign* your name here.
A *pack* of dogs chased the cat.   The *sign* said, "Park here."

Generalization: Some words can have more than one meaning.

The questions children have to answer are these: *Are there enough facts to make a generalization? Does the statement cover all the known facts? Does it cover facts that are not known?* Once children understand what a generalization is, they can learn to recognize valid ones and make their own. These same questions can be used to guide children's thinking about making generalizations when they read.

Before asking children to make generalizations on their own, it might be advisable to give them some point on which to focus so that they begin to think about the information in a generalized way.

What general statement can be made about our teeth?

A grownup who hasn't lost any of his teeth usually has thirty-two of them. The front teeth are wide and have sharp, thin edges for biting and cutting. The side teeth are shaped like a wedge and used for breaking up large pieces of food. The back teeth, the molars, have broad flat surfaces that can grind and tear pieces of food into small bits.

The three questions which were cited earlier can be used to test any generalization the children make about teeth. The answers to each of them should be supported by information found in the text. Children should discuss each generalization and decide which ones have merit.

Opportunities to ponder choices supplied by the teacher will help pupils think about what they read and to make appropriate generalizations which fit sets of ideas or information. They will learn also that it is not always possible to generalize from what is known because there are too many unknowns that have to be taken into account.

Countries which are located near the equator usually have tropical climates. Examples of such countries are Panama and Brazil, where hot, steaming jungles cover large areas of the land. But there are other countries that lie close to the equator where temperatures rarely rise high enough to make you feel comfortable. Parts of Ecuador, Peru, and Bolivia are located in mountains where the air is thin and cool. You won't complain of the heat there.[10]

Which generalization is appropriate?

All countries enjoy two kinds of climate—hot or cold.

The climate of some lands is affected more by their altitude than closeness to the equator.

Children should be aware of the fact that generalizations can be all too inclusive, and that qualifying words such as *some* and *many* are needed in order for some generalizations to be valid. Discussions about qualifying words and how they affect statements will help them realize the importance of examining information carefully before generalizing about it. A useful exercise is to take a statement and change it so that it more carefully reflects the state of affairs.

Years ago college and professional basketball was a game which depended mainly upon a passing and running attack. Players who could handle the ball well and were agile were sought by coaches. It didn't make any difference how tall they were, and many players well under six feet were stars.

Now, a player not only must be skillful but also must be tall. Many teams have players who can touch the rim of the basket while hardly jumping and some don't even have to do that to put the ball in. Present-day basketball players who are six-footers are considered short when compared to some who reach seven feet or better. Height on a basketball court is an advantage that is difficult to overcome, and good, tall players are preferred to good, shorter ones by the colleges and pros. Even many high schools have teams that average over six feet.

How are the last two generalizations different from the first?
1. College and professional basketball players are more than six feet tall.
2. Many college and professional basketball players are more than six feet tall.
3. Most college and professional basketball players are more than six feet tall.

---

10 *Reading Power.* The Bookmark Reading Program, p. 311.

Recognizing the Author's Purpose

Another aspect of "reading between the lines" is determining whether there are any personal messages that the author offers without stating them. On occasion, writers do express a viewpoint or attitude which the thinking reader will discern. Children will have a greater appreciation and understanding of what they read if they do follow the author's thinking.

Young readers can be taught to look for clues which help them decide how a writer feels about a subject or events and how he might want them to think about it. Questions will direct their attention to any viewpoints which they might discern in the content.

How does the writer feel about the cat in the story? How can you tell?

a. The writer doesn't like the cat.
b. The writer feels sorry for the cat.

Little Fog[11]

Fog was over the city.
The fog was over the streets.
It hid the tall buildings.

A hungry cat ran in the street.
He was cold and wet from the fog.
He had no bed to sleep in.
And he had no milk to drink.

The cat looked for things to eat.
He came to a big can.
He jumped into it and dug around.
But he did not see a thing to eat.
So the hungry cat went to sleep.

A truck came down the street.
A man got down from the truck.
He went to pick up the can.
As the man picked up the can,
the cat jumped.
But the cat did not run away.

---

[11] *Source:* From *Sun and Shadow* by Margaret Early, et al., copyright © 1970 by Harcourt Brace Jovanovich, Inc. and reprinted with their permission.

After discussing how they think the writer feels toward the cat, the children might consider how he would wish them to behave were they to see such a cat in the street. This is the type of discussion that will clarify how a reader decides if the author expresses a viewpoint and what it is. The children should refer to specific portions of a selection to justify their judgments about the author.

To show how some passages merely present information and others express the writer's feelings, have the children compare two passages and decide which one expresses a viewpoint.

A. The Volunteer is given an allowance for his living costs overseas. This amount is based on the wages paid in the country where he works, so that a Volunteer teaching in one country receives sixty dollars a month, while a road construction foreman in another country is paid a little more. In addition, our government banks seventy dollars a month for each Volunteer which he receives at the end of his service.[12]

B. A Volunteer in El Salvador has had his 4-H club growing a huge vegetable garden during the dry season. He has shown the boys how to protect the moisture in the ground, and the vegetables are sprouting, to everyone's delight. Before, the local farmers thought it was possible to grow food only during the rainy months. This same Volunteer bought an incubator and a hundred ducks with his own money. As the new duck eggs hatched, the Corpsman gave the ducklings to the townspeople. It makes a great deal of difference to these people, for they have never had enough food.[13]

1. Which parts show how the author feels toward the Volunteers?
2. In the writer's judgment, which of these apply?
   a. Volunteers are well-paid.
   b. Volunteers do important work.
   c. More people should become Volunteers.

Anticipating Outcomes

Children should develop the habit of thinking ahead and deciding what will happen next or what information the author will be covering. This kind of reading and thinking helps them to keep alert; in addition, it enables them to set their own purposes as they read. All too often it is the teacher who establishes reasons why children should read. Here we have a way for them to provide their own motivation, which should prove more satisfying and productive than that offered by someone else.

Children can be guided to anticipate what will happen in a story. For example, in the selection on page 206, the children might speculate about what the rabbit had in mind when he answered the fox.

---

[12] "Peace Corps Volunteers at Work," *Goals in Reading.* The Bookmark Reading Program, p. 219.
[13] *Ibid.,* pp. 219–20.

The Rabbit and the Fox[14]

A rabbit ran down the road in
the bright moonlight.
On the road he met a big bad fox.
The bad fox jumped at the rabbit.
The rabbit did not get away
from the fox.

The bad fox looked at the rabbit.
"I like rabbits when I am hungry,"
the fox said.
"I like to eat rabbits.
I will sit down and eat you now."

The rabbit said, "Eat me?
But then you can't see my jig!
It is very sad that you can't see
my funny little jig."

---

14 *Source:* From *Sun and Shadow* by Margaret Early, et. al., copyright © 1970 by Harcourt Brace Jovanovich, Inc. and reprinted with their permission.

Which do you think are possible? Why?

a. The rabbit really wanted to entertain the fox.

b. The rabbit wanted time to think how he might escape from the fox.

c. The rabbit was trying to get the fox's mind off eating him.

What other reasons might the rabbit have had for telling the fox about the jig?

The children will have to read the rest of the story in order to find out what the rabbit had in mind. Before doing so, they can decide how the rabbit might manage to avoid becoming a meal for the fox. This, then, becomes another purpose for finishing the story.

It is also possible to anticipate what is likely to follow when reading informational-type material. See how the next passage prepares the reader for what is to come and suggests purposes for reading ahead. The words which suggest what information may be anticipated are in italics and the purposes they suggest are noted in parentheses.

From the moment of launching, the men in the Control Center *had been greatly concerned* with the flight path of the Atlas. (Why? Of what importance is the flight path to the success of a space shot?) Any change from the planned direction would send the capsule into an orbit over areas where it could not be tracked and where it would be difficult to recover after landing. The capsule's speed *had to be just right, too.* (What would happen if the capsule's speed weren't just right?) If it didn't reach a speed close to 17,500 miles an hour at the proper point, it *wouldn't go into orbit at all* (What would be the result?) and would have to be brought down at once. *Too much speed* (What would happen if the capsule were moving too fast?) would result in an unplanned orbit that might expose the astronaut to dangerous radiation. *And* (here is another result) when the capsule came down, it might be out of reach of the recovery forces.[15]

Passages such as this one can be selected from various sources and used to teach pupils what kinds of words help them to anticipate information. The teacher could indicate first what questions might be raised from these clues and then have the children suggest questions for other clues. Later, the pupils could seek out clues on their own and discuss what questions they could raise about the content and what information they might expect to follow.

IDEAS FOR DISCUSSION

■ *The dynamics of teaching reading as a thinking process requires a teacher who believes that children can think and can be taught to read as scientific readers. The teacher's attitude and skill make the difference between a class in which there are freedom and spontaneity of thinking and discussion and one in which they are shut off.*[16]

■ *Unfortunately, the ability to comprehend printed material is not entirely subject to development. Teaching cannot accomplish everything. The . . . ability to reason with verbal concepts [is] probably a part of the child's native endowment. It is doubtful that even an optimum environment can do much to remedy inadequate brain development. Skill development is subject to the potentialities that already exist.*[17]

15 "John Glenn's Trip," *Goals in Reading.* The Bookmark Reading Program, p. 320.

16 Russell G. Stauffer, "Reading, Thinking and Concept Attainment," *Reading and Concept Attainment* (Highlights of the Pre-Convention Institutes). Newark, Del.: International Reading Association, 1968, p. 34.

17 Emerald V. Dechant, *Improving the Teaching of Reading.* Englewood Cliffs, N. J.: Prentice-Hall, Inc., 1964, p. 401.

It would appear that the ideas expressed in these two quotations are diametrically opposite. One assumes that [all] children have the capacity to think and thereby can learn to become thoughtful readers while the other states unequivocally that there are children who have intellectual deficits and that there isn't much anyone can do to improve their reading ability.

Few would maintain that all children are capable of attaining equally high achievement in reading. A far greater number would reject the notion that present levels of performance are solely the product of personal endowments and that environmental conditions have no effect upon behaviors. There are children in school whose performances mark them as mentally retarded or slow learners. Too many of them have been written off as being intellectually inferior and thus incapable of profiting from learning experiences that other children enjoy. Evidence shows that most children are capable of raising their performance levels under favorable learning conditions.

Perhaps one of the problems in the past has been the inability of some teachers to recognize the difference between *asking* children to read and *teaching* them how. Another was the low esteem in which they held pupils who performed less well than others. There are indications that pupils do fulfill teacher expectations, and when these are low their levels of performance are low.

No child should be sold short when it comes to teaching him how to read. Children will respond when they are encouraged and stimulated to do so. Teachers do have the responsibility of providing opportunities for growth. To do less is to abrogate one of the school's major roles—that of teaching children to think.

Critical Reading[18]

At times it is difficult to distinguish between interpretive and critical reading, e.g., determining the author's purpose. However, critical evaluation occurs after the reader has grasped the writer's ideas or gained the information he presented.

Critical thinking has been defined by Russell as "the process of examining . . . verbal materials in the light of related objective evidence, comparing . . . the statement with some norm or standard and concluding or acting upon the judgment then made."[19] According to this definition, we might view critical thinking and critical reading as practically one and the same or at the very least consider critical reading to be a form of critical thinking.

Many children have the ability to read critically. In fact, they have been thinking critically, though not always clearly, prior to their entrance into school. Slow and even mentally-retarded learners show that they are capable of making judgments and evaluations on levels that are meaningful to them. Thinking or reading critically is not so much a question of ability as it is a matter of attitude. Young people can learn to read narrative and expository materials with an inquiring attitude. They can do so only in

---

[18] The first part of this section is an adaptation of the introduction of an article written by the author, "Critical Reading Is Critical Thinking," and published in the September 1963 issue of *Education*.

[19] David Russell, *Children's Thinking*. Boston: Ginn and Co., 1956, p. 285.

a classroom climate that encourages creativity and participation and under enlightened leadership that nourishes their right to be wrong.

However, no one suggests that intellectual ability is not tied in any way to critical reading. Brighter children may be expected to respond more to ideas and in more varied ways than their lesser-endowed age-peers. But mere possession of high intelligence does not guarantee equally high performance in weighing ideas. The promotion and development of suitable attitudes toward them are responsibilities each teacher must assume.

A reader cannot evaluate statements completely unless he can compare them with known standards. His knowledge is a prime element in critical reading, as is his background and understanding. Meaningful experiences which lead to the formation of concepts constitute the yardstick against which he weighs statements and reaches decisions. It is less than realistic to expect prudent reactions from anyone whose background of experiences is unrelated to what he reads about.

Teaching Critical Reading

As with other aspects of reading for meaning the teacher must involve children in objective-oriented activities that are designed to foster the spirit of evaluative reading and refine the quality of their responses. Among the reactions that children can make at each instructional level are the following: judging accuracy, distinguishing between facts and opinions, recognizing persuasive statements.

Judging Accuracy

As children read narrative and expository materials, they can be taught to evaluate them. The kinds of questions teachers raise will cause the children to think about them in specified ways and encourage them to ask questions of their own.

In a second-grade class the children have finished reading a factual story about a boy who came from a very poor home and later became a renowned plant scientist. In the story are statements like these: *The boy had no teacher and so he had to learn things for himself; he learned how to make farm plants grow better; he learned to read and spell.* The teacher could have the children react to these statements by asking if it were possible to learn these things without a teacher. The children might decide that it is possible but not very likely. Perhaps the boy learned by asking questions and watching others at home. They agree that these statements probably are not completely accurate.

Other questions that raise doubts in their minds about the accuracy of the statements are related to authorship: When was this story written and how long ago did the boy live? How does the author know the boy had no teacher? In response to these questions the children discuss where the author might have obtained his information. Since the story was written very recently and the boy lived long ago, the children recognize the possibility that the facts might have become altered due to the passage of time and incompleteness of records.

To assess accuracy of information, questions such as these might be raised:

What is the source of information?
How recent is the information?
Is the information complete?
Who is the author? Is he an authority?

The children might not be able to find answers to each of these questions; in that event they withhold judgment until they can verify them. The recognition that they are not in a position to judge is as important as their readiness to accept or reject ideas on objective grounds.

At higher grade levels there are ample opportunities to raise questions about the accuracy of ideas and information children read about in literature, social studies, and science texts. Magazine and news articles are good sources for finding material whose accuracy could be questioned. Children should understand that to question is not to deny but that it is entirely proper to ask where a writer obtained his facts and ideas and if they can be certain about them.

A profitable activity is to check questionable information in other sources to see how it is treated elsewhere. One group of sixth-graders read a narrative account of what it would be like to journey to the moon. The writer described the blast-off and rapid ascent and then explained the weightlessness one would experience in the spacecraft. The children refused to believe the writer's statement that unless a man were strapped into his seat he would float about the cabin because he weighed nothing. Some sought information about the conditions of space flight in the encyclopedia; others studied science textbooks; one pupil read an account of space flight in the local newspaper. They compared notes and agreed that the part which described the man floating about was accurate, but they were unable to confirm or reject the statement about his total lack of weight. All agreed they would have to check further before making a final judgment.

Later, one boy reported his discussion with another teacher who had been a science major in college. The teacher had confirmed what the writer said about the absence of weight in orbital flight. Now the group was ready to accept the writer's statement, although they found it hard to believe.

Recognizing Facts and Opinions

It is important that children recognize when a writer is stating a fact and when he is giving an opinion. However, it is not always easy to distinguish between facts and opinions, particularly when opinions are not identified in any way and statements combine some of each.

Some facts are more definite than others. For example, it is a fact that Abraham Lincoln was the sixteenth President of the United States. There is hardly any reason to question this statement, for the record is clear. On the other hand, scientific experiments reveal the speed of light to be 186,000 miles per second. In this instance the record is not quite as clear.

Nevertheless, the reader tends to accept this fact as readily as the other even though he cannot confirm it in the same way.

There is another point that should be kept in mind when dealing with facts and opinions, i.e., an opinion is not necessarily "bad" or less useful than facts. Children should not be led to believe that opinions are valueless. In fact, they should be encouraged to express opinions with the realization that they are just that. Opinions that are based upon hard facts might be better than those for which there isn't much support. So it is as important to distinguish between the validity of opinions as it is to separate them from facts or what are believed to be facts.

Children can learn to analyze similar statements to determine how factual they are. They can compare one with another and discuss how they are different.

The present temperature is 70° F. This is the high for the day.
Today's highest temperature is expected to be 70° F.

This is the best restaurant in town.
This restaurant is the most expensive one in town.

Some statements contain qualifying words which make them easier to identify as opinions.

The President *believes* that . . .
Scientists who studied moon rocks *think* . . .
It *could* mean . . .
These pictures *seem* . . .
The exhibition will *probably* open . . .

However, children have a tendency to ignore such indicators. Passages should be studied for words which do indicate belief.

Other passages are not as clearly defined, and statements are made without equivocation. If the children do not recognize them as opinions, then the teacher must raise questions to help them understand why the statements might be rejected as factual. They could reach a judgment on the basis of the data provided by the writer and others or drawn from their own store of information.

The juju man often does his business at night; seen by the light of a flickering palm oil lamp mixing his magic charms and medicines to bring good or evil, it is easy to understand the power he still holds over the minds of many West Africans. True, more and more West Africans today are going to real doctors and nurses and to drugstores for medicine when they are sick, but it will be a long time before the juju man is a thing of the past.[20]

a. Is it easy to understand the power of the juju man? Why?
b. Are there indications that the West Africans will continue to prefer juju men to real doctors and nurses?

Children should be encouraged to evaluate opinions on the basis of available information. They can judge how reasonable an opinion is and accept or reject it on suitable grounds.

---

[20] "A New Way of Life for Africa," *Reading Power*. The Bookmark Reading Program, p. 289.

One of the secrets of the viking supremacy at sea, along with other things, may well have been the excellence of their food supply. Sailors in other parts of the world lived in dread of scurvy, a disease that could kill half a crew. This illness was unknown among the vikings. They ate properly at sea as well as ashore.[21]

The polar bear pretty much ruled his world, but times changed; explorers and whalers appeared in the king's domain, and traders followed them. Everyone who carried a rifle shot at the bears, whether he needed them or not, for they were big and exciting targets. Rifles came into use among the Eskimos. The bear's huge skin, which made such a fine trophy or luxurious rug, began to appear in the fur trade, and by the turn of the century about 150 of them a year were being sent out of Canada.[22]

1. Why does the author believe the vikings were able to control the seas? What proof does he offer in support of his opinion?

2. What proof does the writer give to support his statement that "everyone . . . shot at the bears, whether he needed them or not . . ."?

3. Are both opinions equally reasonable? Why?

Recognizing Persuasive Statements

Some passages clearly convey factual information while others attempt to influence the reader's thinking. The latter are characterized by the inclusion or exclusion of data and the use of words which tend to create desired impressions.

Notice how the following passage stresses a single point. Questions such as these can direct the reader's attention to it:

1. What does the writer say about smoking?
2. Does the writer present another side of the question?
3. What does the writer hope to accomplish?

Research by government and private organizations seems to show that cigarette smoking causes certain kinds of cancer. Cancers of the lungs and lips are much more common among smokers than nonsmokers. Some heart diseases have been traced to smoking too. "You lose one minute of your life for each cigarette you smoke."

Writers often use words which can influence the reader's thinking. Some words tend to produce positive feelings while others have negative connotations. Children can compare passages and discuss how the words are used in each to present facts or create feelings.

The sky was growing light with the dawn, and the little group of crewmen could see that they were deep in Japanese territory. To the northeast lay Kilombangara, a Japanese stronghold with more than 10,000 troops. Gizo, a small enemy-held island with a new military airfield, was to the west. It was so close they could see Japanese planes taking off and landing.[23]

---

21 "Sea Rovers of the North," *Reading Power.* The Bookmark Reading Program, p. 67.
22 "King of the Arctic," *Reading Power.* The Bookmark Reading Program, p. 230.
23 "Disaster Strikes PT–109," *Reading Power.* The Bookmark Reading Program, p. 327.

Again he had to resume the struggle to rejoin his crew, but this time he had no shoes. After crossing the reef, his feet and ankles were blood-raw with coral cuts. And in the dazzling morning sun beyond the reef, the swim across the bay to the home island was agonizing. It seemed to take forever. He finally reached the home island and crawled up on the beach exhausted.[24]

1. In what way is the second passage different from the first? Which is more factual?

2. What words does the writer use to create feelings? What feelings does he create with these particular words?

Even at the primer level the children can learn to recognize words which might influence their thinking by discussing how they feel when they read them. Such words as *cold, hungry, wet,* and *poor* elicit one set of feelings while *happy, play, bright* and other similar words produce another set. By relating the words to ideas in the story, they learn to associate the two and begin to realize why the writer chose certain kinds of words in one instance and different ones in another.

SUMMARY

1. Reading is a thinking and problem-solving process in which ideas are received and produced. Reading and thinking possess common roots, and to the extent that the reader processes information and ideas, reading and thinking are indistinguishable. To teach children how to read, then, is to teach them how to think.

2. Reading-thinking models involve cognition, convergent and divergent thinking, and evaluation. These components can be described in operational terms so that they may become teaching objectives for developing reading comprehension. Cognition which refers to the recognition of ideas is literal reading; convergent and divergent thinking which produces ideas is interpretive or inferential reading; evaluation which involves the assessment of ideas is critical reading. An instructional program for developing reading comprehension will consist of these three strands.

3. The ability to read for literal meaning, i.e., stated ideas, is influenced greatly by one's mastery of word meanings in context. Instruction in recognizing and using contextual and morphemic (structural) clues, adapting to shifts in word meaning, and understanding figurative language can increase pupils' understanding considerably. The purpose of vocabulary instruction is to provide children with self-help measures for dealing with unknown words and thereby help increase the size of their working vocabularies.

4. Complex sentence structures may interfere with literal comprehension. Instruction in identifying parts that carry basic meaning, recognizing pronoun referents which represent persons and things as well as ideas, and interpreting punctuation can reduce interference with sentence meaning.

[24] *Ibid.*, p. 334.

5. Literal comprehension is enhanced to the extent that the reader perceives the way in which ideas are related. Various forms of organizational patterns are used as vehicles for transmitting ideas: time order, enumeration, comparison-contrast, cause-effect. Paragraphs have the added function of illustrating, summarizing, and bridging ideas. Children should be taught to think about ideas in the form that they are structured, for to do so enables them to duplicate the way in which the writer was thinking, with the result that they understand more.

6. Inferential reading is a second strand of reading comprehension. In objective terms, to read inferentially or "between the lines" is to draw conclusions, make generalizations, sense relationships, predict outcomes, and recognize the author's purpose. These deeper meanings can be inferred only after surface meanings are fully understood. Instruction in inferential reading occurs at the earliest levels and continues as children mature in reading. In this way the attitude can be instilled that reading is a thought-getting activity that requires insight and thinking based upon what is known. Questions and discussion that focus children's attention on how to use known elements to produce new ideas are the means by which children can learn to read and interpret ideas.

7. Critical reading is the process of evaluating ideas or information. When the reader questions the accuracy of information, when he distinguishes between facts and opinions, and when he recognizes persuasive statements and then makes some judgments as a result of his examinations, he is reading critically. In a real sense, such a reader is *thinking* critically. As with interpretive reading, the teacher raises questions and directs discussions to cause children to think in specified ways so that they learn to ask questions of their own about the materials they read.

STUDY QUESTIONS AND EXERCISES

1. How is literal reading different from inferential reading?
2. What elements that are found in printed materials might interfere with a reader's ability to understand them? What can the teacher do to help pupils overcome such obstacles to comprehension?
3. For each of the following words prepare one or more sentences that utilizes a type of context clue for determining its meaning: *glow, temperature, ripples, beam.*
4. How might a lesson on the multiple meanings of words be combined with one on the use of the dictionary?
5. Locate paragraphs in a reader or other printed source which illustrate the different ways ideas may be organized. Prepare a series of questions which will help pupils ascertain how the ideas each contains are related.

6. Why is it important for teachers to emphasize interpretive reading? At what stage of reading development should interpretive reading be encouraged?
7. What types of printed materials might teachers use to promote critical reading? Select one excerpt from each type and indicate how it might be used for a critical reading lesson.

SUGGESTIONS FOR FURTHER READING

The International Reading Association has issued several publications on the reading-thinking process which provide a rationale for teaching comprehension skills and suggestions for developing them:

Paul C. Berg and John E. George, eds., *Reading and Concept Attainment,* Highlights of the 1967 Pre-Convention Institutes, 1968.

Mildred A. Dawson, ed., *Developing Comprehension, Including Critical Reading,* 1968.

William Eller and Judith G. Wolf, *Critical Reading: A Broader View,* An Annotated Bibliography, 1969.

Doris Lee, Alma Bingham, and Sue Woelful, *Critical Reading Develops Early,* Reading Aids Series, 1968.

Russell G. Stauffer, ed., *Reading and the Cognitive Processes,* Highlights of the 1966 Pre-Convention Institutes, 1967.

Russell G. Stauffer and Ronald Cramer, *Teaching Critical Reading at the Primary Level,* Reading Aids Series, 1968.

Other useful publications include the following:

Richard L. Henderson and Donald R. Green, *Reading for Meaning in the Elementary School.* Englewood Cliffs, N. J.: Prentice-Hall, Inc., 1969.

Marjorie S. Johnson and Roy A. Kress, eds., *Reading and Thinking* (Proceedings of the 1965 Annual Reading Institute). Philadelphia: Temple University, 1966.

A collection of over 150 articles is found in Martha L. King, Bernice D. Ellinger, and Willavene Wolf, eds., *Critical Reading.* Philadelphia: J. B. Lippincott Co., 1967.

Helen M. Robinson, ed., *Sequential Development of Reading Abilities* (Supplementary Educational Monographs, No. 90). Chicago: University of Chicago Press, 1960.

7

Reading in the Content Fields

■ *The teacher of every curricular field is recognized as a teacher of reading in the sense that he stimulates and directs the experiences of pupils and promotes increased efficiency in the various activities required. In the judgment of the Committee, the greatest opportunity for progress in teaching reading during the next decade lies in an intelligent attack on reading problems that arise in the content fields. Satisfactory results can be attained only as . . . teachers from the kindergarten to the university recognize clearly their responsibility for promoting the development of desirable reading attitudes and habits in the reading activities that they direct and greater intelligence and discrimination in the use of printed instructional materials.*[1]

Most reading instruction in the elementary schools consists of teaching children the skills they need to read imaginative or narrative materials. Whether children are participating in a basal, language-experience, or individualized reading program, the bulk of reading materials used for teaching reading is of a narrative, story-type character. Most of the reading children do in the primary grades is for the purpose of learning how to read, and the use of such materials is entirely appropriate. The emphasis of the reading program is upon learning and practicing reading skills and not really on the ideas that the materials contain, although in the process children do acquire some of them.

---

[1] Guy G. Whipple, ed., *The Teaching of Reading: A Second Report* (The Thirty-sixth Yearbook of the National Society for the Study of Education, Part I). Bloomington, Ill.: Public School Publishing Co., 1937, pp. 19–20.

In the intermediate grades reading instruction ordinarily consists of refining the skills children have learned in the primary grades so that they may use them with greater sophistication in reading more difficult materials. The emphasis is still upon learning to read. But what are the reading demands that teachers of intermediate grades make of pupils? Do they expect children to read only narrative materials with no deliberate content or do they require more than that? Children in grades four, five, and six do read social studies, science, mathematics, and language textbooks and reference materials for the purpose of gaining information from which they can build concepts and generalizations. They do have to remember and use important ideas and details, which is not the usual requirement when they read stories. Their purposes for reading informational materials are not the same as they are for reading narrative materials and therefore they have to read them differently. Reading instruction which is limited to helping children understand story-type and fictional writing fails to take into account the difficulties children may experience when they read other kinds of writing. It is not uncommon for teachers to find that many children seem able to read stories with adequate understanding but have real trouble when they read in the content fields.

There is no question that reading instruction in the intermediate grades should make definite provisions for refining and extending the skills children have learned in the primary grades. It should also include provisions for developing children's ability to read in the content fields, for it is in them that children are required to do most of their reading. This means that the program will help children learn how to solve the problems that reading content presents. It also means that children will be taught how to learn through reading.

Problems in Reading Content

All of the reading skills that children use in reading narrative materials are needed to read factual materials. To read the latter successfully they must be able to recognize words readily and know how to analyze unfamiliar ones. They must be able to read for literal and inferred meanings and evaluate information and ideas. What, then, is unique about reading in subject areas? Children have to learn to accommodate to a different style of writing, which is characterized by terseness, density of ideas, and inclusion of many unfamiliar and difficult concepts and vocabulary. In addition, they must learn to master another set of skills—reading-study skills—which enable them to read efficiently and solve problems associated with each subject area.

Compare these two excerpts from books intended for fourth graders. What differences are readily discernible?

These two excerpts are about the same length but this is where the similarity ends. The first excerpt deals with a situation that is as unfamiliar to children as the subject in the second but there is no comparison in their

Getting to Know the Big Cats[2]

by DAMOO DHOTRE *as told to Richard Taplinger*

It was six o'clock in the morning and just getting light. I ran into the tent containing the training cage. Mr. Chavan would be waiting there to give me my first lesson in training wild animals.

As I burst into the tent, my eyes traveled quickly to the cage to see which animals were to be my pupils. I stopped so fast I nearly fell down. My high spirits suddenly collapsed and I thought my uncle had arranged with Mr. Chavan to trick me. Mr. Chavan had not yet arrived, but there, in the center of the training cage, were two small lion cubs. They were hardly three months old and the size of big house cats. I was so disappointed I wanted to cry. Only my realization that animal trainers *don't* cry kept me from it.

difficulty. The second passage contains several technical words that are not easy to pronounce. The number of different concepts in the excerpt is far greater than in the first. The concepts come one after the other without more than a sentence or two separating them. Not only is the passage packed with these concepts, but they are foreign to many children and any explanation given of them is meager indeed. The style of writing follows a "no-nonsense" approach in which description and elaboration are reduced to a minimum. The reader is expected to understand these strange ideas and remember them besides. Surely no such requirements have to be met by readers of the first excerpt.

The nature of reading assignments in the content fields requires children to use their reading skills in a much more sophisticated way than they

Making Water Clean and Pure [3]

The water that comes from a faucet in a big city like New York or Los Angeles comes from many miles away. New York's water supply begins with rain that falls in mountains many miles away from the city. Some of the water in Los Angeles comes from mountains in other states. As rain falls, the streams and rivers over a large area of land collect the rain. The area in which the streams and rivers collect the rain and snow is called a **watershed**. Sometimes dams are built in a watershed, and the water is stored in **reservoirs**.

The water in a reservoir does not move much, so some of the particles of soil and rock in the water have a chance to settle to the bottom. Then the water goes to a purifying plant.

In the purifying plant, the water is placed in a settling tank. Substances are added to the water to make particles settle more quickly. Then the water is filtered through layers of sand. Now the water looks clean, but in it there may still be tiny invisible plants called **bacteria** that can make persons ill. So the water is sprayed into the air. Bacteria will be killed and the toxic gases will be removed by the air. Finally, a tiny amount of chlorine gas is added to the water to kill any bacteria left. The water is then fit to drink.

[3] *Source:* From *Concepts in Science, Orange,* Second Edition, by Paul F. Brandwein, et al., copyright © 1970, 1969, 1966, by Harcourt Brace Jovanovich, Inc. and reprinted with their permission. Photograph by Infilco and reprinted with their permission.

would in reading stories. They are bound to meet many more words whose meaning is essential for understanding and mastering information. This means that they really have to be able to use their independent word skills for pronouncing them and deciding what they mean in their special contexts. Although the sentences might not be any longer than those in stories, they are generally bare of description, and every part counts. The ability to see relationships among ideas is much more necessary when solving problems and remembering information than when merely following a story thread. So that while children use the same kinds of word recognition and comprehension skills to read different types of materials, they have to use them with greater finesse when the materials and reading requirements present real challenges.

Children study content to solve problems. They have to learn how to study so that they can solve them efficiently. This requires more than merely understanding what they read. They have to know how to establish purposes when none are given; they have to locate information from single and multiple sources; they must be able to select the information they need from the larger body of data; they have to organize the information so that they may use and remember it; they need to extract ideas from graphic materials that accompany written text, interrupting and continuing the reading and seeing how both complement each other; they must vary the ways in which they read (for all purposes and content do not require the same pacing); they must follow directions carefully when required to do so. All these activities are functions of reading and studying content.

IDEAS FOR DISCUSSION

A persistent issue that occasionally produces some disagreement revolves around the question as to whether or not one set of skills is needed to read efficiently in one subject area and another set is required for a different subject area. Efforts to differentiate reading requirements for several content areas have been made.[4] A careful examination of the literature reveals extensive overlap of reading skills listed for each of the content areas.

What seems to be unique about each subject field is its use of specialized vocabulary. There are words which take on special meanings as they are used in different content fields, e.g., *exponent* in mathematics and social studies, and other words which are generally reserved for a subject area, e.g., *molecules* in science. Then, too, there are differences in the types of graphic materials used in mathematics, social studies, and other subjects. Social studies books are likely to contain a variety of maps, which other books don't have, while science and mathematics books will have a profusion of diagrams and charts, which will be used with less frequency in other materials.

Some skills have greater relevancy for one subject area than another. For example, children who read science books often are told to conduct experiments, which means that they must follow directions carefully. When they read a mathematics problem, they are not given directions to follow; however, in developing a mathematical concept authors might enumerate a series of procedures which children carry out in sequence. They might occasionally read to follow directions in social studies.

It appears that most, if not all, of the skills which have been enumerated, i.e., word recognition, comprehension, critical evaluation, and all the reading-study skills, apply in varying degrees to each subject area but that some special requirements of a particular subject might require adjustments in the way in which a skill is applied to reading its materials. With instruction and maturity in reading development will come the ability to use reading skills in a flexible way. This is the justification for using a variety of materials to help solve the problems that children face when they read in the content fields.

---

4 John R. O'Connor, "Reading Skills in the Social Studies," *Social Education, 31* (February, 1967), pp. 104–07; George C. Mallinson, "Reading and the Teaching of Science," *School Science and Mathematics, 64* (February, 1964), pp. 148–53; *Improving Reading-Study Skills in Mathematics Classes.* Albany, New York: Bureau of Secondary Curriculum Development, State Education Department, 1968; Nila B. Smith, "Patterns of Writing in Different Subject Areas," *Journal of Reading, 8* (October-November, 1964), pp. 31–37; 97–102.

Integrating Reading and Content

At the elementary level the teacher ordinarily has the responsibility not only of teaching reading and other communication skills but also social studies, science, mathematics, and other subjects. Insofar as reading is concerned, he endeavors to help children improve their reading ability and use reading as a tool to solve problems associated with the curriculum in several subject areas. In addition to working with the children on the skills that apply to reading all materials, he teaches the children those skills that have particular relevance to reading in the content fields and assists them in coping with difficulties they are likely to meet and with which they need assistance. All this guidance has the objectives of teaching children how to learn and assume some responsibility for their own learning.

Guiding Content Reading

There is a much greater likelihood that children will encounter more difficulties in reading content than they will in reading stories, even if both are drawn from materials intended for the same instructional level. Therefore, it is desirable to offer instruction to all children in how to approach the reading task in content books and provide selective guidance in reading them.

Surveying Content Materials

Whether children are required to read and obtain information from single or multiple sources, it will help them to have a broad overview of the content of each of the books they will be using. Of particular value to them will be a knowledge of how the content is organized and what special features the books contain. Children should examine these books under the teacher's direction before they are required to read in them so that they will learn how to approach new materials they read independently and at the same time become ready to use the present materials efficiently to solve problems.

Most of the textbooks and many of the reference sources children use in and out of school possess common features, though they might not be identical. If children study the contents and make-up of the books they use, they aren't likely to meet any that are so different that they cannot deal with them in appropriate ways.

A first step in surveying a book is to find out what its contents are about. It will be useful to spend a little time having the children speculate about the book's contents from its title and cover. This is what each of us does as he peruses the library shelves in search of books which seem to fit a need. Unlike most books intended for adults, newer books designed for elementary school children use illustrations on the covers, and these often provide clues to what the books are about.

An example of such a book is *Four Lands, Four Peoples*,[5] with photographs on the cover of hieroglyphic carvings on stone, people and animals crossing a stream, a modern building, and a group of assembled adults. The teacher might guide a brief discussion about the book by raising such questions as:

1. Is this book likely to contain information about all countries of the world?
2. What kinds of information might this book contain?
3. What country or area does the picture of hieroglyphics suggest?
4. Which part of the world seems to be represented by the photograph of people and animals?
5. What does the large group of people seem to be doing? In what part of the world might this occur?
6. How can we check our guesses?

Now the children are ready to turn to the book's table of contents to verify their specifications. In addition, they have the opportunity to learn about the larger structure of the book and its special features.

Below are partial tables of content from two different books. They represent styles commonly followed by authors.

Contents[6]

---

[5] Ralph C. Preston et al., *Four Lands, Four Peoples*. Boston: D. C. Heath and Co., 1966.

[6] *Source: Four Lands, Four Peoples* by Ralph C. Preston, et al., copyright © 1966 by D. C. Heath and Company and reprinted with their permission.

[7] *Source:* From *Concepts in Science, Orange*, Second Edition, by Paul F. Brandwein, et al., copyright © 1970, 1969, 1966, by Harcourt Brace Jovanovich, Inc. and reprinted with their permission.

In addition to learning about what information the book covers, the children should examine the rest of the Contents to find out what special features the book contains, e.g., maps, glossary, index, etc.

At this point it is wise to turn to a few sections of the book in order to become familiar with its structure. By just looking at the Contents it is not possible to determine how the information is organized. In *Four Lands, Four Peoples* the subtopics under each unit refer to chapters, while in *Concepts in Science* (Orange) each unit *is* the chapter and the items listed under each unit are chapter topics.

Textbooks and reference sources use similar typographical features throughout a book. Children should compare the type and size of print used to set off the major topics and subtopics from the unit and/or chapter titles. They should examine several sections for internal consistency and discuss the relationship of one type of heading to another. Samples of the use of typography to set off unit, topic and subtopic titles follow.

UNIT ONE   THE BOUNCE OF SOUND [8]

1. Making a Sound
Sound and Movement
To and Fro

UNIT ONE   THE EARTH WE LIVE ON [9]
Looking at Our Planet
A Trip into Space
The Earth.
The Solar System.
Our Moving Earth.
Back to Earth.
A Closer Look at the Earth

Some books use typographical features for special purposes. For example, in *Concepts in Science* symbols (■ ● ▲ ◆) appear within the text and indicate to what graphic material a statement refers. By examining the text and illustrations children will be led to realize that the author uses these symbols to direct their attention to the illustrations. Teachers should study the books children will be using for unique features and teach how to interpret them.

This survey is intended for the purpose of becoming familiar with a book's contents and noting its organization and components. Another kind of survey is one in which the children obtain an overview of a unit or chapter before beginning to read it for general or specific purposes. This survey provides a "set" for reading, yields information about a topic and the way in which it is organized, offers opportunities for relating what one

---

[8] *Concepts in Science* (Orange).
[9] *Four Lands, Four Peoples.*

knows to the ideas and information which will be treated, and makes it possible to establish purposes for reading. All these benefits increase children's chances for comprehending what otherwise might be difficult to grasp. There is a long-term benefit that accrues to children who survey materials; they are engaging in self-help activities. In short, they are learning how to learn.

In order to teach children how to make a rapid survey of the contents of a chapter, teachers might proceed along these lines:

STEP 1.   Have the children read the chapter title and introduction or introductory paragraphs. By reflecting upon the information in this part of the chapter they may be able to gain a fair understanding of what the chapter will be about and what will be stressed in it. They should try to relate what they know to what they will expect to read about. The teacher can help them think about the material by raising questions that it suggests. This is what the children should do when they survey an introduction independently. A sample introduction with ideas and questions it could suggest follows.

UNIT THREE

THE TRAVELS OF
A DROP OF WATER [10]

There are some things you must have to stay alive. One of these precious things is water.

You cannot live without water. Plants cannot live without water. Animals cannot live without water.

The drops of water you see on these leaves fell from the sky. How did they get up in the sky? What made them fall? What happened to them after they fell?

We can begin the travels of a drop of water by putting a drop of water back up in the sky.

---

[10] *Source:* From *Concepts in Science, Orange,* Second Edition, by Paul F. Brandwein, et al., copyright © 1970, 1969, 1966, by Harcourt Brace Jovanovich, Inc. and reprinted with their permission. Photograph by E. R. Degginger, APSA. Japanese Maple.

Ideas and questions:
1. Living plants and animals need water to stay alive. Why?
2. Where does water come from? Rain brings water to the earth and fills lakes and rivers. What makes rain fall? Where does rainwater come from?
3. What happens to water when it dries up? Perhaps it is not lost.

The introductory material stimulates thinking about the subject and suggests questions about it which may serve as purposes for reading. Children should be encouraged to discuss what they know about the topic and formulate questions that are related to it with the expectation that the chapter will provide answers to some of them.

STEP 2.   Now the children are ready to look over chapter subheadings and graphic aids. By doing this they will gain a good idea of what they will be studying and whether their questions will be answered. A subheading such as "Water from the Air" will not only tell them that water exists in the air but that the information under it may answer the question about the origins of rainfall. "The Making of a Cloud," along with the diagram, will suggest a relationship between clouds and water. So this part of the survey will provide new information as well as raise new questions about the contents. (How is a cloud formed? Must there be clouds in order to have rain?) Each heading becomes a purpose for reading when it is stated as a question or provokes new ones.

STEP 3.   The final phase of the survey is to read a summary if one exists. Generally a summary will be brief and contain general statements that are considered important but will not include detailed explanations of them. The summary will confirm the children's expectations about what the chapter is all about and alert them to sections on which they have to concentrate when they begin to read the chapter. For example, the summary statement about water mentions water *molecules,* which the text and illustrations explain. It also lists the steps in the water cycle but doesn't elaborate. This information should serve as a guide to help the children decide what parts they must read carefully.

Taking children through the process step-by-step and helping them to understand the purposes and values of making surveys will, after repeated exposures, develop the habit of making surveys when they read independently This is an illustration of what the development of reading attitudes means. Instruction has as its objective more than merely building competency; without application the ability to perform isn't very meaningful.

Directed Reading
There are times when children will require careful guidance in reading content materials. This guidance will be helpful when the ideas that the books contain are complex and difficult for them to understand. Moreover, in classes where children work in groups on selected problems the teacher

may wish to make certain that the basic information on the topic is mastered before each group pursues its own interests.

The directed lesson for reading content can follow the outline which basal reading programs utilize for reading narrative materials. It might or might not include specific skill development and practice, depending upon the nature of the materials and the ability of the group to perform the required reading tasks. For reading some materials, teachers might find that they do not wish to include all the phases of the directed lesson because the children do not require them.

The directed reading lesson could consist of the following:

1. Preparation for Reading
   a. Relating experiences of children to purpose (s) for reading the content
   b. Introducing difficult words for pronunciation and/or meaning
   c. Clarifying difficult concepts
   d. Establishing purpose (s) for reading
2. Reading and Discussion
   a. Checking literal and inferential meaning
   b. Verifying information and ideas
3. Developing and Practicing Needed Skill (s)
4. Using and Extending Information and Ideas

In order to visualize how this format could be applied to reading content, a description for a directed reading lesson will be presented. It is based on a section of a chapter in a social studies book (intended for sixth-graders) which covers farming in the New England states.[11] The section includes information about surface features and climate.

---

[11] Ralph C. Preston and John Tottle, *In These United States*. Boston: D. C. Heath and Co., 1965, pp. 252–61.

1. Preparation for Reading

a. Relating children's experiences to purpose(s) for reading A brief period of time might be spent in discussing how the geographic features, location, and other conditions of the section in which the children live affect the way in which people in the area earn a living. Children who live in rural areas might consider reasons why certain crops are grown there and why others aren't. Children living in urban communities could sample industries represented by their parent's occupations and discuss explanations for the prevalence of some and the apparent lack of others. In either case, they would conclude that business activity is influenced by a variety of natural conditions over which people have little control.

b. Introducing difficult words In order to decide what words should be introduced in advance of the reading, teachers should determine if there are key words, i.e., words which are necessary for understanding important ideas, that the children probably will not be able to pronounce or be able to ascertain their meaning from the context. These words should be introduced and read. If the text fails to clarify the meaning of any key words, these should be introduced in a meaningful context. Occasionally, some words might appear in the preparatory discussion and it will not be necessary to do anything except to note them. Children should be reminded to apply their word skills (such as syllabication) to pronounce unfamiliar words.

Key words: *glacier, moraines, fertile, precipitation, poultry*

1. The soil in many parts of the U. S. is not *fertile*. Such soil lacks the materials crops need in order to grow well.

2. The weatherman predicted that some *precipitation* would fall this evening. He was wrong. There was no rain or snow.

c. Clarifying concepts The text may not treat some unfamiliar concepts at all. Others may not be explained well enough for children to understand them adequately. These should be identified and clarified through the use of pictorial aids from the book or other sources, discussion, and questions. Mere verbalization should be avoided.

Concepts: *mountain ridges; killing frost; hard land*

d. Establishing purpose(s) for reading The teacher and children can set the main purpose for reading by examining the major headings and deciding with what matters they deal. In this instance they suggest that the geography of the New England states has affected land usage and the people's lives. *How is the area affected by geographical factors?* can be the children's over-all purpose for reading the material.

2. Reading and Discussion

The children are ready to read silently. Some groups might read the entire section without interruption. Less able groups could read a portion of the section for a specific purpose, discuss it with the teacher, and then continue reading. For example, they might read to find out what the glacier did to much of New England's surface and discuss it before moving on to the next part. While the children read independently, the teacher circulates and provides on-the-spot assistance to anyone who requires it.

Upon completion of the reading the children discuss their responses to the problem—how geographical factors affected the New England states and its people. The teacher will guide the discussion and check their understanding of the content by asking questions that require both literal and inferential responses:

Why is manufacturing more important than farming in New England?
How did the glacier change New England's surface features?
Why don't present-day New England farmers consider the area a hard land?
What kinds of agriculture wouldn't be suitable for New England? Why?

Children will refer to the text whenever there is some question about their responses. They will read orally the parts which clarify or verify them while the others listen.

3. Developing and Practicing Skills

This part of the directed lesson, which isn't always necessary, uses the text to teach new reading skills or practice others. If the children are weak in a skill that will enable them to read this content with greater understanding, here is a real opportunity for them to work on it. The teacher will analyze the content to determine what reading skills are particularly applicable and concentrate on one or two. *Cause-effect* is apparent throughout most of the section. Children may find passages that show the *results* of glacial action and the *causes* of farm abandonment. Another pattern is *contrast*. They might prepare a chart which shows differences in agricultural activities before and after 1900.

Throughout the section are words whose meanings can be ascertained by *context clues*. These may be used to teach children how to interpret clues. Or children might identify clues that they used to determine the meaning of unfamiliar words.

4. Using and Extending Information and Ideas

The purpose of this part of the lesson is to apply and relate the information children have gained to other situations. Children might engage in a variety of activities that accomplish this purpose:

- read about present-day New England and its people.
- read fiction whose setting is rural New England.

- learn more about the influences of geographical features of lands and people.
- gather information about the area's economic growth and prosperity.
- prepare a chart or graph that compares population changes in New England with other parts of the country.

Teachers should be selective when deciding what sections of a book require such careful guidance. There would be times when a complete directed lesson such as the one described above was necessary for some groups of children. This would occur when the teacher anticipated that the children were bound to have real difficulties. There could be times when all but the purpose for reading would be eliminated from preparation for reading because the children are familiar with the words and concepts or they are capable of filling in any gaps as they read.

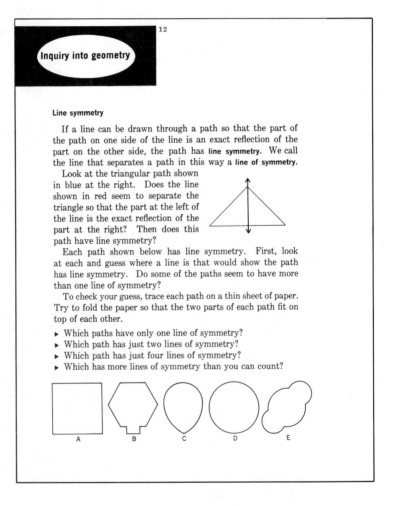

[12] *Source:* From *Elementary Mathematics 4,* Second Edition, by Joseph N. Payne, et al., copyright © 1968, 1966, by Harcourt Brace Jovanovich, Inc. and reprinted with their permission.

On occasion, teachers will want to deal with a small section of a page because of its difficult words, concepts, and/or sentence structures. Some help in advance of children's reading will go a long way toward avoiding problems in understanding strange and abstract ideas. The example of such a passage on page 230 is one on which teachers will want to work.

There are several words that children might not be able to pronounce: *inquiry, geometry, reflection, symmetry, triangular.* Then there are the *concepts* that these words represent. The text does explain *symmetry* but it isn't likely most children will understand it. Note the complexity of the first sentence; many children will be confused by it. The concept for which *path* stands is covered in an earlier section and unless really understood is another problem that needs to be overcome. If teachers did nothing more than help children with such difficulties *before* they were required to read, it would go a long way toward reducing failure to understand the content.

Study Guides

The directed lesson guides children in their reading so that they are better able to meet the demands which the content presents. One of its most important functions is to help children establish purposes for reading. Another is to help them with difficulties that could interfere with understanding. Both these objectives could receive additional support from reading guides that are designed to accompany selected portions of texts.

The *process guide* adds a new dimension to the directed reading lesson. Once purposes for reading have been established, the children are largely on their own before they discuss the content. The process guide in the hands of children provides each of them with a "teacher" who offers suggestions on how to read the material. It concerns itself with the ways in which children should apply the skills they have been taught so that they might read more efficiently and be able to cope with any difficulties that arise. It calls their attention to the skills they might need in order to resolve difficulties and makes them aware of any that might otherwise be ignored.

A PROCESS GUIDE

5. The Main Concept: The Use of Moving Molecules[13]

Long ago man could do only as much work as his muscles allowed; they were his source of "push and pull." He could lift and tug and haul. The energy from the food in his body was the only energy he could use. Later he learned to use animals to work for him. He began to modify and improve his environment by inventing new things.

Notice time order in the passage. To what does *they* refer?

Improve is a context clue for *modify.*

---

[13] Paul F. Brandwein et al., *Concepts in Science* (Brown), 2nd ed. Harcourt Brace Jovanovich, Inc., 1970, pp. 226–27.

Still later, he learned to use simple machines: the lever, the pulley, the wheel and axle, the inclined plane, the wedge, and the screw. With simple machines he could multiply force; but he could get no more work out of a simple machine than he put into it. He needed a source of energy. To add to his own energy man needed new sources of energy. So he learned to use the energy of wind and water and of fuels.

What does the colon signal?

But signals a new idea.

Man learned to use fuel as a source of energy to do work. In burning, the fuel combines with oxygen. The heat of the burning fuel is used to increase the motion of the molecules of water, for example. The result is that the water becomes expanding steam. Gasoline and kerosene, too, combine with oxygen to produce gases that expand suddenly. Expansion furnishes the force to do work.

What is the main idea of the paragraph?

Cause-effect.

Expand is the root.

The process guide can be duplicated on strips of paper and distributed to the children. It is not necessary to duplicate the text if the guiding comments and questions line up with the appropriate item to which they refer when the guide is placed alongside the text. The number and type of items the process guide contains depend upon the abilities of the children and the nature of the material. Even "good" readers need to be reminded to use their skills to solve problems and think in certain ways as they read. The guide serves both these purposes.

A *content guide* focuses the children's attention upon the information they read. This type of guide might be considered an adjunct to the main purpose for reading the material since it establishes minor purposes that the readers are asked to fulfill. Some children do require this kind of careful guidance, particularly if the reading is done at times when the teacher isn't available to work with them. Such a guide might stress responses on one or more levels of comprehension. A content guide could also be used to replace the discussion following the reading. In this case children would respond to the items in the guide after they read the content.

CONTENT GUIDE

Refer to the questions as you read. Answer each one orally before going on to the next one. The page and paragraph numbers covering each question are in parentheses.

1. What are bacteria and how are they classified? (pages 100–102, 3rd par.)
2. In what ways are bacteria like a fungus? (pages 104, 107)

3. What happens when decay bacteria grow on a dead tree? When harmful bacteria get into a body cut? (page 108)

4. How does nature protect us against harmful bacteria? (pages 110–114, 4th par.)

Now that you have read about bacteria, answer these questions.

1. Why do doctors recommend that you wash with plenty of soap and water?

2. How do you explain the fact that people become ill from harmful bacteria even though nature protects us against them?

Reading-Study Skills[14]

In order for students to acquire information through their own efforts, they must learn to provide self-direction. They must learn efficient ways of pursuing their objectives once they have established them. They must learn to be selective as they receive large quantities of information while separating ideas and retaining those which they need to complete their tasks. Pupils must learn to make decisions, test alternatives, reconstruct ideas. In addition to using the skills of word recognition, literal and inferential comprehension, and critical evaluation—skills that apply to all kinds of reading—pupils who engage in study activities must become efficient users of sets of skills that have special relevance for them. These sets are called study or reading-study skills.

An examination of the literature on study skills reveals a lack of agreement on what skills to include. Perhaps the recognition of a relationship between generalized reading skills and specialized study skills accounts for the global treatments which some writers have given them. Unquestionably, pupils who engage in independent study must understand and react to what they read. In addition, they have to locate, select, organize, and retain information; understand graphic representations; follow directions; and adjust reading modes. It is with these requirements that the study skills are involved.[15]

Behavioral descriptions of the study skills delineate what children have to do when they read content materials for the purpose of solving problems on their own. These tasks are translated into teaching-learning objectives: to *locate information and its sources* through tables of contents, indexes and appendixes, library-card catalogues and reader's guides, encyclopedias and almanacs; to *select information* by recognizing its significance, important ideas, and details; to *organize and remember information* through note taking, summarizing, and outlining; to *understand the significance of*

---

[14] The introduction of this section is an adaptation of a paper presented by the author at the Annual Convention of the International Reading Association in Kansas City and published in H. Alan Robinson and Ellen Lamar Thomas, eds., *Fusing Reading Skills and Content*. Newark, Del.: International Reading Association, 1969, pp. 184–90.

[15] Omitted from this list are the survey skills which have been covered in the previous section. These skills make it possible for the reader to learn about the contents and organization of materials and establish purposes for reading them.

graphic aids by reading and interpreting diagrams, charts, tables, maps, graphs, cartoons, and pictures; to *follow directions* by paying careful attention to sequence and details; to *develop reading flexibility* that is characterized by slow, careful reading and rereading, rapid reading, skimming and scanning.

Each of these requirements is not necessarily discrete; in fact, many are related and form a hierarchy. For example, *organization* depends upon *selection*, and selection upon *flexibility* and *location* of information. A failure in one adversely affects the performance in another. But the recognition of this interdependence does not mean that these sets of skills should be treated in global fashion. Not only do they have to be taught one at a time but also analyzed for their components.

Before considering how teachers might help pupils develop ability in using the study skills, it would be well to establish some guidelines on which teaching strategies could be based.

1. *Use the books and other materials pupils read to develop pupils' abilities in the study skills.* This procedure obviates any concern about transfer of learning that often fails to occur when they work with materials which have little relationship to the kinds they actually read. Remember that content materials are much more suitable for teaching the study skills than narrative-type materials.

2. *Concentrate on the skills that children need to solve current problems.* If they have to use the library to locate materials, this is the best time to teach how the card catalogue will help them find what they need. Undoubtedly, they will be using several different skills as they work on group and individual projects. These are the ones they have to learn and practice.

3. *Identify the children who are weak in the study skills and the skills on which they need to work.* It isn't likely every pupil requires the same concentration of effort in all areas. One of the best ways to determine what children's needs are is to observe them as they engage in study tasks. Perhaps the children themselves will be able to verbalize any weaknesses they have. The use of standardized and teacher-prepared study skills tests could confirm these observations and furnish additional information about how well children can perform.

4. *Select materials whose content children can manage.* If pupils have trouble understanding the vocabulary, sentence structure, or ideas of a selection, interference with learning will occur. Under such conditions they will be expending all their energies trying to overcome these difficulties and have little left for the immediate learning task. It is particularly desirable to avoid this interference when a skill is introduced or pupils are just beginning to master it. One way to reduce the possibility of failure is to use content that has been read for other purposes. Another is to analyze the content for difficulties and treat them before proceeding with the skill development.

5. *Develop a hierarchy of skills and teach them in sequence.* In order to develop some sequence, two basic questions should be studied: Upon what

skills areas does the mastery of another skills area depend? Of what smaller skills does a gross skill consist? An example of the first question would be the relationship that exists between selection of information and its organization. Children could not prepare outlines or summaries unless they were able to separate important ideas and related details. The second question is reflected in the separation of important ideas from lesser ones. A main idea may be stated clearly or hidden among other information; it may be a combination of ideas or inferred. Pupils who need help with main ideas should deal with those explicitly stated before having to cope with inferred ideas.

Location of Information

One of the more important skills that children who engage in independent learning activities need to master is how to use sources of information. The answers to problems which they are trying to solve will be found in materials that a well-equipped classroom will contain; in addition, they will be using the library as another resource. One of the first things children should be able to do is determine whether the books they have in their own classrooms will be of use to them as they search for information about a topic or seek the answer to a specific question. Then they have to know how to find other materials that are not readily available to them and which might contain what they are looking for. To pursue this organized search requires an understanding of what sources are available and what they might expect from each. It also means the application of some skills for which there has been no previous need and of others that have been used for different purposes. The ability to blend these skills and understandings in a favorable mix can mean the difference between efficient study and wasted efforts.

Book Parts

One of the first needs that children have is to become familiar with the way in which a *table of contents* can serve them. The table of contents will reveal the organization of a book—whether it is divided into units and/or chapters and how much space is devoted to each—and what kind of information it deals with. Children who understand these purposes will not waste time looking for information that the book isn't likely to have or seeking it in the wrong places.

The formats of tables of contents are not identical, and pupils should compare those that are in their books. Such examinations will show to what purposes these tables of contents can and cannot be put. Notice how these partial tables of contents, which appear on page 236, differ in their structure and makeup.

The first sample does not show any chapter titles but lists the topics the chapters cover. Children who seek information about a mathematical concept will have to examine such a table of contents much more carefully

Chapter 1 Names for numbers. Roman numerals. Our numeration system. Place value. Renaming numbers. Sets and subsets. Sets of numbers. Addition of whole numbers. Properties of addition. Using the addition facts. Subtraction of whole numbers. Relation between addition and subtraction. Using number sentences in problem solving. Greater than and less than. Addition and subtraction of tens. Estimating in addition and subtraction. Addition and subtraction of hundreds, tens, and ones. Renaming in addition and subtraction. Adding and subtracting mentally. Keeping up in mathematics. Self-help tests. Chapter test. **1**

Chapter 2 Decimal system to thousands. Place value. Approximations. Points, lines, and line segments. Planes and paths. Inquiry into geometry. Understanding units of length. Standard units. Estimating measures of length. Number pairs. Fractional numbers. Measuring to the nearest eighth inch. Keeping up in mathematics. Problem test. Chapter test. **32**

Contents [17]

[16] *Source:* From *Elementary Mathematics 4,* Second Edition, by Joseph Payne, et al., copyright © 1968, 1966, by Harcourt Brace Jovanovich, Inc. and reprinted with their permission.

[17] *Source: Four Lands, Four Peoples* by Ralph C. Preston, et al., copyright © 1966 by D. C. Heath and Company and reprinted with their permission.

[18] *Source:* From *Concepts in Science, Orange,* Second Edition, by Paul F. Brandwein, et al., copyright © 1970, 1969, 1966, by Harcourt Brace Jovanovich, Inc. and reprinted with their permission.

than another which contains chapter titles. In such a case they might find the index a more useful tool than the table of contents, particularly when more than a single topic is covered in a chapter and it is difficult to decide which chapter might contain the information sought.

The second table of contents reveals that each unit consists of several chapters (this can be determined from the numbering, which indicates that many pages are devoted to each topic and therefore they are not likely to be subtopics within a larger unit), whose themes are given in their titles. The contents of the book seem to be organized around definite topics so that pupils are in a position to decide whether or not such a book is likely to contain the information they require.

The third sample is different from the other two. Unlike the first, each unit (chapter) deals with a single topic whose subtopics are paged. The fact that only a few pages are devoted to each will indicate that they are not likely to be separate chapters. It also reveals information about the chapter which the second table of contents fails to do.

Children will benefit from exercises that require them to decide whether a given book has information they require and where in the book it can be found. They should explain what information in the table of contents helped them to make up their minds about the book's usefulness. Questions and problems such as those that follow, which are based upon the partial tables of contents on page 236, can be prepared for the tables of contents of textbooks and reference books to which they have access. The last two questions could apply to any table of contents.[19]

*1. What topic is stressed in the first part of Chapter 1? In the second part?
*2. Are fractions likely to be covered in the first chapter? In the second chapter?
*3. Which chapter discusses units of measurement?
*4. On what page does Chapter 2 begin?
**5. Which chapter contains information about present-day Egypt?
**6. Into how many chapters is Unit II divided?
***7. Into how many sections is the chapter on sound divided?
***8. On what pages does the author discuss the most important ideas about light?
9. How likely is it that this book will contain information about ——?
10. Does this book contain a glossary? Maps?

The *index* of a book will yield more specific information about the nature of its contents than will the table of contents. The table of contents serves the main purpose of providing a general understanding of the kind of information a book contains while the index relates specific topics to general ones. In many instances children will save time by checking the index to determine if the book deals with an area that concerns them. The index will pull together from different parts of a book references to a

---

[19] One asterisk (*) refers to the mathematics table of contents, two asterisks (**) to the social studies table of contents and three asterisks (***) to the science table of contents.

single topic that the table of contents will not indicate, as well as list entries which children would have no way of knowing about by merely studying the table of contents. Furthermore, the index is much more precise in giving page locations of definite information than the table of contents.

The ability to use an index efficiently depends upon the extent to which a number of subskills have been mastered. Included among them are the following:

1. Ability to determine what the entry words are.
2. Understanding and use of alphabetical order to locate entry words.
3. Ability to see relationships among topics and subtopics.
4. Ability to interpret symbols and style.

One of the better ways to teach children how to use an index to locate information is to take problems they have to solve and work through with them the steps that will lead to their solution. This procedure will point up the skills they need to develop in order to locate the information and provide opportunities for developing them.

How to locate entries in an index is one of the skills children must learn. Teachers first might select from a number of problems those which leave little doubt as to what the entry word could be. Examples of such questions and study areas are:

Who was Henry Ford?
What is flax?
Where are the Grand Banks?
How are glaciers formed?
Why is it difficult to forecast the weather?

In each case the children should ask themselves the following question: *What or whom do they want to find information about?* They shouldn't have much difficulty deciding that *Henry Ford, flax, Grand Banks, glaciers,* and *weather,* respectively, are the subjects that they wish to learn about.

At this point teachers might wish the children to examine an index which contains entries corresponding to the subjects they have decided are important. They should spend time examining the structure of the index before turning their attention to seeking entries. Through questions and discussion they can be led to make generalizations about the way in which the index is organized. Excerpts from two representative indexes and questions based upon them follow.

Questions and problems to guide the discussion about the structure of the index are:

1. In what order does the author list the entries in the index? Why? What other kinds of materials use the same system?

2. These are two entries in the index. What is different about the order of the words in each?

    accelerator, nuclear
    automobile engine

INDEX[20]

(Page numbers in **boldface** refer to illustrations.)

accelerator, nuclear, 298, 299
acid, 112
acquired immunity, 127
action, and reaction, 218, 220, 225
adaptation, 38, **38**, 39, 39
air, molecules of, 197, 198
air pressure, 212, 213, **213**, 214, **214**
aircraft carrier, nuclear, 310, 311
airplane, 212, 214, **214**, 215, **215**, 216, **216**
alchemist, medieval, 92, **92**
Algol, 374, **374**
alloys, 79, 80, 84, 93
Alpha Centauri, 385
alpha particles, 287, **287**, 297, **297**, 298
aluminum, 48, **48**, 49, 52, 53, **53**, 55, 93; uses of, 52–53
aluminum oxide, 49, 52, 53, 55
Antares, 373, 378
antenna: for radio, 271, **271**, 272; for satellites and waves from space, 277, **277**; for television, 274, **274**
antibiotics, 121, **121**, 126, 141
antibodies, 126, 127, **127**, 128, 141
antiseptics, 111, 114, 141; effect on bacteria, 115, **115**
Apollo spacecraft, 221, 222, **222**
applied science, 55; *see also* technology

Archimedes, 188
armature, 253, 254, **255**
association, 16, **16**, 17, **17**, 19, **19**
astronaut, 94, 218, 221, 222, 268, **268**, 272
atom(s), 54, 76, 82, 94, 232, 286, **286**, 288, **288**, 314; of carbon, 232, **232**, 289, **289**; of chlorine, 290, **290**, 320, **320**; of helium, 290, **290**, 368, 388; of iron, 289, **289**; of lithium, 288, **288**, 290, **290**; made of particles, 287, **287**, 288, 315–16; models of, 287, **287**, 288, 289, **289**, 293, **293**; new, made by bombardment of nuclei, 388, 390; of nitrogen, 289, **289**; nucleus of, *see* nucleus of atom; of oxygen, 289, **289**; of sodium, 320, **320**; structure of, 290, **290**, 291 (table), 292
"atomic gun," 297, 298, **298**, 388, 390
atomic number, 296, **296**
atomic pile, 302, **305**, 310, 390; *see also* nuclear reactor
atomic weight, 292; changes of, in fusion, 369
attraction, resulting from opposite charges, 232, 233, **233**, 234, **234**
automatic act, 21; *see also* habits
automobile engine, 208, **208**, 209, **209**

Index[21]

Page numbers that appear in italics indicate illustrations.

factories. *See* **manufacturing**
Fairbanks, Alaska, 465, 466
Fall Leaf, 416
Fall Line, map, 76; 78, 300
Fallen Timbers, Ohio, *142*
Faraday, Michael, *198*, 199
farms and farming
   in Central Lowland, *8*, 155–156; Middle Atlantic States, 295–298, 305; Mountain States, 405; New England, 258–259; Pacific States, 439–444; near Puget Sound, 450–452; Southern States, 77, 156, 314–328
   in coastal settlements, 76–77
   dry farming, 445–447
   exodus from, 226, 228
   improved methods, 230–231
   irrigation, 412–415, 440–442
   mechanization, 228–229
   as occupation, 35
   prerequisite to civilization, 49
   See also **dairying** and **fruit farming**
Federal court system, 130–131; diagram, 130

---

[20] *Source:* Adapted from *Concepts in Science, Brown*, Second Edition, by Paul F. Brandwein, et al., copyright © 1970, 1969, 1966, by Harcourt Brace Jovanovich, Inc. and reprinted with their permission.

[21] *Source: In These United States* by Ralph C. Preston and John Tottle, copyright © 1966 by D. C. Heath and Company and reprinted with their permission.

What is the natural way of saying *accelerator, nuclear*? Why is the order of these words reversed? How might *automobile engine* be listed in an index?

3. Notice how this entry is given.

   Faraday, Michael

Why is the person's last name given first?

4. Look at the entry *farms* and *farming*. To what is the first subentry under it, *in Central Lowland*, related? *Middle Atlantic States*? *Southern States*? In what order are these subentries listed? To what does *improved methods* refer? To what would you relate *as occupation* as you read this subentry?

5. How is this entry different from the others?

   factories. *See* manufacturing

Under what entry can you expect to find information about *factories*?

6. Compare these two entries:

   atomic pile, 302, *305*, 310, 390;
      see also nuclear reactor   factories. *See* manufacturing

Why are there page numbers after *atomic pile* but none after *factories*? Where would you look for more information about *atomic pile*?

7. On what page might you expect to find information about *acid*? Might you expect *acid* to be discussed on any other page?

8. Look at this entry:

"atomic gun," 297, 298, *298*, 388, 390

On how many different pages might you expect to find information about the "atomic gun"? Which page will contain an illustration of an "atomic gun"?

9. Which pages of this entry discuss the topic? What will appear on the other page?

Fall Line, map 76; 78, 300

10. Compare the way in which the page numbers are given in these two entries:

Fairbanks, Alaska, 465, 466

Federal Court system, 130–31; diagram, 130

Why does a comma separate pages 465 and 466 while a dash separates pages 130 and 131?

For children to whom the index is unfamiliar, its structure would not be studied in its entirety during one lesson. One or two aspects might be covered in a session with ample opportunities to explore each in depth. Other groups of children might not need to spend much time on some aspects of the index, but will need to spend more time on others. Once they become familiar with the organization of the index they will be using, they can use their own problems to seek information through it.

Knowledge of alphabetical order and the ability to locate items that are listed alphabetically are basic to using the index efficiently. Children who lack the ability to locate entries easily should engage in learning activities patterned after those that have been outlined in Chapter 5 on the use of the dictionary (pages 173–76).

It is while working on their own problems that children will learn to use the index properly. It was suggested earlier that teachers could introduce the index at the time pupils have to use it. Once they are somewhat familiar with its organization they can apply their understanding to finding information about the specific topics on which they are working. This means that they will determine what entry to look for, locate it in the index, turn to the page or pages given after it and read the page(s) to find the information they seek. (The section on flexibility, pages 268–76, will discuss how they might scan a page to locate specific information quickly.)

How to determine what entry to look for in an index was covered on page 238. Remember that in each case the problems used to decide what the entry word was were stated simply and contained but one possible topic:

Who was *Henry Ford?*
What is *flax?*
How are *glaciers* formed?

There will be times when pupils will be uncertain about what the entry word might be because the problem contains more than one possibility.

For example:

Of what importance is the *Columbia River* to the *Northwest?*
In what parts of the *United States* is *coal mined?*
What is the difference between the structure of an *atom* of *carbon* and an *atom* of *nitrogen?*

In each of these cases there is more than one answer to the question *What or who is the problem about?* It will be helpful to the children to explore problems such as these by discussing each one, deciding what the possible entry words might be, and then seeking them in the index. They should determine if each of the possible entries appears in the index. Even if all were listed, it would be necessary to examine the page numbers following each entry to make certain that they are the same. Otherwise, the pupils might miss some information which appears on a page with another entry.

A related difficulty is one in which a problem yields a possible entry which is not listed in the index. Pupils should discuss alternate possibilities and examine the index to determine if these are listed.

What is an *assembly line?*
For what purposes is *copper* used?

It might be advisable to suggest some possible entries under which the desired information might appear and discuss how each is related to the topic.

assembly line: factories, manufacturing, industries
copper: mining, natural resources, minerals

Later, pupils might offer their own alternate entries and test them to see under which entry, if any, the information is given.

Other Sources of Information

The *encyclopedia* is a reference source that children use frequently to obtain information about topics they study. The same skills required for locating information through an index are needed for the encyclopedia. Topics are treated in alphabetical order, and pupils must follow the same patterns of thought in selecting entries in the volumes.

Encyclopedias do provide indexes but it usually isn't necessary to refer to them in order to locate the volume and page numbers that are needed. Children should examine the index to see if its format varies from those with which they are familiar. If any features are different, these can be studied in the same ways that they learned about the organization of other indexes. Some indexes in encyclopedias use typographical features, such as all capital letters and upper- and lower-case letters and even color, to distinguish major topics from their subtopics. These should present no real difficulties to children if they are helped to generalize about the ways in which special features are utilized.

In order to help children learn how to use the encyclopedia, have them select a problem they wish to solve. Suppose they wish to find out about the *origin and nature of the Nobel awards*. Have them decide under what entry the information about these awards might be found. (Should pupils have had few opportunities to formulate entries, lessons such as those offered on the index would be required.) They agree to look for *Nobel awards* or *Nobel prizes* or *Nobel* and speculate about the possibility that *Nobel* is a person's name and that the awards might be associated in some way with the person.

Now have them refer to the set of encyclopedias to determine how many volumes there are and what information appears on the spine of each. They observe that some volumes are identified by the letter *A, C,* and *D,* while other volumes carry such designations as *E–G, L–N,* and *V–Z.* Discuss why some volumes cover one letter while others deal with two or more. Ask them to examine the entries in the volumes which have a single letter on the spine to determine what they have in common. Copy some entries from different parts of the volumes to make clear that they all begin with that same letter which appears on the volume from which they are drawn. Have the children note that the entries in any one volume are listed in alphabetical order. Follow this procedure for volumes that contain entries that begin with different letters.

If they understand how the set of encyclopedias is organized, they are ready to look for their topic—*Nobel awards* or *Nobel prizes* or *Nobel*. Ask them to select the volume that might contain the reference. As with dictionaries, they note that at the top of the pages in the encyclopedia are guide words that indicate the first and last topics on one or two pages. They use these guide words to help them locate the topic, which in this instance is *Nobel, Alfred*. They must read the information about Alfred Nobel to find out what the Nobel awards are. If pupils are unfamiliar with the way in which the guide words should be used, exercises similar to those on finding words in the dictionary (Chapter 5, pages 173–75) could clarify their functions and provide the needed practice.

The *library-card catalogue* is an information source with which children ought to become familiar. Children who know how to use an index will possess the skills required for locating materials through the library-card catalogue. What they need to understand is how the catalogue is organized and what information it provides.

Opportunities to examine the card files and discuss their contents will make it possible for pupils to generalize about them. They will see that cards are placed in alphabetical order by author, subject, and title and that the subject and title cards contain the same basic information as the author card. Answers to questions such as those which follow will help clarify the type of information the cards offer.

1. What is the difference between a subject card and author card? When will a subject card be more useful than an author or title card?
2. Why is the title of a book on a title card placed at the top of the card?

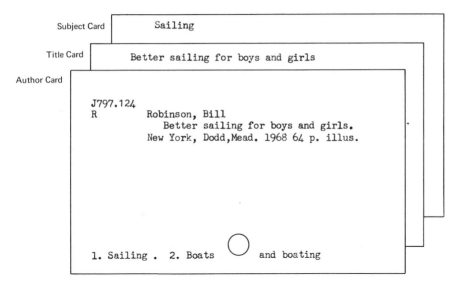

Subject Card — Sailing

Title Card — Better sailing for boys and girls

Author Card —

J797.124
R   Robinson, Bill
               Better sailing for boys and girls.
           New York, Dodd,Mead. 1968 64 p. illus.

1. Sailing .   2. Boats   and boating

3. To what do the letters and numbers in the upper-left corner of the card refer? What purpose do they serve?
4. Who is the author of the book?
5. What company published the book? Where is the company located? In what year was the book published?
6. How many pages does the book contain and is it illustrated?
7. What kinds of information does the book contain?

Instruction in the use of the library-card catalogue will not be too productive unless the children really have reasons for referring to it. It doesn't make much sense to spend the time that might be required to become familiar with this or other tools unless they serve a purpose whose benefits are obvious. Too many children have failed to learn how to use them properly because they had no reason or opportunity to do so. The circumstances under which real learning occurs are those that lead to the fulfillment of real needs.

Pupils might seek information that is more current than that found in books. In this event they could turn to the *Reader's Guide to Periodical Literature.* There is an abridged edition available which is less cumbersome to handle than the large, hard-bound volume. This monthly edition indexes articles that have been published in forty-four periodicals.

Once again, pupils will draw upon the skills they already possess and apply them to a new setting. Examination of the *Reader's Guide* will make clear to them that the entries are organized in ways similar to those found in indexes and that they have to use their entry and alphabet skills to locate suitable references. What they will have to become familiar with are the format and entry shorthand that are typical of the *Guide.* Discussion and questions based upon actual entries will help pupils understand the purposes to which this resource can be put and how to extract information from it.

AIR pollution [22]
> Another pollution culprit: singlet oxygen.
> E. Gross. il Sci N 96:538-40 D 6 '69
>> *See also*
> Automobile engines—Exhaust
> Plants, Effect of air pollution on

Control
> Green light for the smogless car. J. Lear. il
> Sat R 52:81-6 D 6 '69
AIR transport association of America
> Looking for a traffic cop in the sky. il Bsns
> W p76-7+ N 29 '69
AIR travel
>> *See also*
> Private flying

[22] *Source: Abridged Readers' Guide to Periodical Literature* (February, 1970), Volume 35, Number 6. Permission for reprinting granted by The H. W. Wilson Company.

There is no need for children to memorize what the abbreviations stand for since they can refer to two pages in the front of the *Guide,* one of which shows abbreviations for titles of periodicals and the second other abbreviations that are used. With usage they will remember some of them.

Here are some questions based upon the excerpt drawn from the *Reader's Guide* that will help clarify its use and meaning. Teachers might utilize similar questions with other portions of the *Guide* and build discussions around them.

1. In what ways is the *Guide* similar to an index? How is it different?
2. What are the three main topics which are listed? How can you tell these are the main topics?
3. What subtopic is given under "Air pollution"? Do the other main topics have subtopics?
4. What is the title of the article about air pollution? Who wrote it? Does it contain illustrations?
5. In which magazine does the article appear? What does the volume number signify? On what pages does the article appear? What is the magazine's publication date?
6. Under what other entries will there be articles about air pollution?
7. What is the title of an article about the *control* of air pollution? Who is the author?
8. Under what entry will there be an article about air travel?

Children should be encouraged to copy the complete references so that they have all the information they require to locate the articles. If they use the monthly edition of the *Guide,* it is likely that articles on a given topic will appear in different issues which they might have to consult. Pupils should use the magazines for which they have obtained references; otherwise, they participate in exercises that lack relevance and purpose.

Selection of Information

Once pupils have located the book and the chapter or pages on which information about their problems appears, their next task is to read and identify those portions which yield solutions to them. If they are seeking information about general topics such as the life of a famous person, scientific discoveries of the twentieth century, or how a camera works, they are faced with the responsibility of deciding what ideas and facts they ought to concentrate on. This means that children have to decide what ideas and facts are important. Thus they must read for main ideas and separate these from details. In addition, they have to decide whether to include certain details and omit others.

When they seek answers to questions that are narrow in scope, e.g., *What state leads in oil production?* or *Why did the colonists revolt against England?* pupils must focus their attention on sections that provide them with the information they desire. This type of reading task places fewer demands on them than one that gives them no specific direction. But teachers may not assume that it isn't necessary to guide children's reading merely because they don't have to make independent decisions about what kind of information to look for.

Recognizing Topics

The authors of content materials generally organize information so that paragraphs deal with few different subjects. This is not always true nor does it mean that all paragraphs must be limited in scope. However, once children have learned to recognize what paragraphs are about, those which do not focus on any one subject are readily identified. After they know what the subject of a paragraph is, they can look for main ideas and details.

Teachers might initiate instruction in identifying topics by selecting paragraphs from the children's books that deal with but one subject. This means that all the sentences in the paragraph are about one topic. Children are asked to read the paragraph and decide what it is about. By examining each of the sentences the group can determine if they tell about the same subject. For example:

Nonfiction books are grouped according to subject. Each nonfiction book is given a number, known as the book's *call number*. Each group of 100 numbers is assigned to books on the same general subject—for example: 100–199, Philosophy; 200–299, Religion; 300–399, Social Sciences. To locate a nonfiction book, you must get its call number from a card in the *card catalog*.[23]

In order to guide the thinking of the children, it might be advisable to suggest possible topics and then decide which one fits the paragraph. Each suggestion should be studied by asking if the sentences discuss that same topic.

The guide words printed in heavy black type at the top of each dictionary page are a great help in locating entry words quickly. If the word you are looking for comes between the two guide words in alphabetical order, the word is an entry on that page. For instance, does the word *whistle* come alphabetically between the guide words *whip* and *white*? Then is *whistle* an entry on that page?[24]

---

[23] *Language for Daily Use 6* (Harbrace edition—revised) by Dawson et al. New York: Harcourt Brace Jovanovich, Inc., 1968, p. 108.

[24] *Language for Daily Use 6* (Harbrace ed.), p. 67.

This paragraph is mainly about:
   a. alphabetical order of words
   b. the usefulness of guide words
   c. how to locate entry words

After children learn to identify topics of single paragraphs with and without teacher guidance, they should study multiple paragraphs which deal with the same subject. The same tests that apply to single paragraphs are applied to multiple paragraphs. In some cases the topic of two or more paragraphs is the same but what the author tells about the topic in each paragraph varies.

Some encyclopedias cover a very wide range of subjects and contain information on almost any topic of importance that you can think of. Others specialize in certain subjects, such as biography or science. Some encyclopedias are prepared especially for young students. They are easy to read and contain helpful pictures and study aids.

Even the best encyclopedia cannot give complete information about all subjects because of lack of space. Most of them, therefore, list at the end of many articles the names of books, magazines, or government pamphlets on the subject, or refer to other articles in the encyclopedia itself.[25]

These paragraphs are mainly about:
   a. what subjects encyclopedias discuss
   b. who uses encyclopedias
   c. what kinds of information encyclopedias contain

It might be necessary in working with some groups of children to examine the paragraphs closely in order to decide which of the suggested topics apply. This may be done by having the pupils read each sentence to determine if it deals with a specified topic. If all or most of the sentences tell about the topic, they can be certain that this is the topic of the paragraph. Paragraphs for which possible topics are not given may be studied in the same way. Pupils decide what the topic is by noting which subject is emphasized throughout the passage and verifying it in the same way as before. When pupils are able to identify topics of single and multiple paragraphs, they are ready to read for main ideas and details.

Recognizing Main Ideas

It is advisable to have children first work with passages whose main ideas are clearly stated before they study others that are less evident. An illustration of an introductory lesson on main ideas follows.

Teacher: We have learned how to find what a paragraph is about. In order to understand the information paragraphs contain we look for their topics. But a paragraph often gives information that tells about the topic. What the paragraph says about the topic is its main idea.

Here is a paragraph which we studied last week to find its topic. Read it again and decide what it is.

---

25 *Language for Daily Use 6* (Harbrace ed.), p. 105.

The guide words printed in heavy black type at the top of each dictionary page are a great help in locating entry words quickly. If the word you are looking for comes between the two guide words in alphabetical order, the word is an entry on that page. For instance, does the word *whistle* come alphabetically between the guide words *whip* and *white*? Then is *whistle* an entry on that page?[26]

Child₁: The paragraph tells about guide words. That's the topic.

Teacher: How can you tell the topic is *guide words*?

Child₁: All the sentences are about guide words.

Teacher: Now that we know what the topic is, let's look in the paragraph to see what it says about the topic, *guide words*. Read the first sentence. What does it say about *guide words*?

Child₂: They are a great help in locating entry words.

Teacher: Is that the main idea? Does the next sentence tell more about how guide words are a help in locating entry words?

Child₃: It tells about the guide words and entry words.

Teacher: Yes, it gives more information about how helpful guide words are in locating entry words quickly. Do the other sentences tell us more about using guide words to find entry words?

Child₄: Yes, they give an example about a word that comes between guide words.

Teacher: All the sentences emphasize one idea. What is it?

Child₂: Guide words help you locate entry words quickly.

Teacher: Which sentence has this main idea?

Child₁: The first sentence.

The children should analyze several paragraphs such as this one before going on to others whose main idea is not at the very beginning of the paragraph. Although the main idea is often the first sentence, it can appear anywhere in the paragraph. Where possible main ideas are suggested, they can serve as guides for analyzing the paragraphs in the way the teacher and children did in the sample lesson.

Ancient man worked the metals he found and invented *some* alloys. The scientist, with a knowledge of a concept, has a better way to make discoveries than by trial and error alone. Knowledge of a concept helps a scientist or an engineer to plan his investigations and his inventions. A good example is man's invention of new fibers, that is, new threadlike materials. From these new fibers, new kinds of cloth have been woven. In the search for new fibers the trials and errors of ancient man were eliminated. The story goes somewhat like this.[27]

The main idea of this paragraph is:

  a. Ancient man made discoveries through trial and error.
  b. Scientists depend more on their knowledge than trial and error to make discoveries and inventions.

---

[26] *Language for Daily Use 6* (Harbrace ed.), p. 67.
[27] *Concepts in Science* (Brown), p. 84.

By examining each sentence the children will realize that the first suggested main idea is not stressed in most of the paragraph. The second one is. By presenting paragraphs whose main idea is located in different sections, children will realize that they must think about a paragraph's contents to locate the main idea instead of relying upon rote means.

Children should not expect every paragraph to have its own main idea. Some paragraphs elaborate on a main idea stated in a previous paragraph or serve as introductions to paragraphs with a main idea. They will understand what purposes these paragraphs serve by deciding if each has its own main idea and what the relationship of one paragraph is to another. Questions about the paragraphs might be used to guide their thinking.

Man, too, depends on his environment and on plants and animals. If you visit a supermarket, you will see how dependent you are on plants and animals for food. As a matter of fact, you don't even need to go to the supermarket to find out. Just ask yourself this question: How many different kinds of plants and animals did I eat today? What products did I use that came from plants or animals?

Besides using plants and animals for food, man uses the hides of animals for shoes, the wood from trees to build houses, the fiber from the cotton plants to make his shirts, and the wool from sheep to make his suits and coats. Even the man-made fibers that man uses are made from matter found in the environment.[28]

1. What is the main idea of the first paragraph?
2. How does the first paragraph develop its main idea?
3. How is the information in the second paragraph related to the information in the first paragraph?
4. Does the second paragraph state a new main idea?

---

[28] *Concepts in Science* (Brown), p. 151.

Probability

In the box shown at the right are six balls numbered from 1 to 6. If you are blindfolded and reach in to choose one ball, how likely is it that you would get ball number 3?

There are six balls in the box. Only one ball is number 3. The likelihood that you will choose ball number 3 is 1 out of 6, or $\frac{1}{6}$.

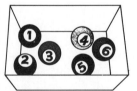

The likelihood that you would choose ball number 3 is called the **probability** of getting ball number 3. Thus the probability of getting ball number 3 is 1 out of 6, or $\frac{1}{6}$. The ratio $\frac{1}{6}$ compares the number of possible events that would be successful with the total number of possible events.

[29] *Source:* From *Elementary Mathematics 6*, Second Edition, by Joseph N. Payne, et al., copyright © 1968, 1966, by Harcourt Brace Jovanovich, Inc. and reprinted with their permission.

1. To what topic do the sentences of the first paragraph refer? Do they tell about the topic?
2. Is the second paragraph different from the first? What information is given about the topic?
3. Does the third paragraph say anything about probability? What is its main idea?

On occasion, main ideas of paragraphs are not stated but have to be inferred from the information they contain. An example of such a paragraph is the one on page 246 about encyclopedias. These paragraphs may be treated in the same way as those whose main idea is clearly stated. Pupils should decide what the topic is. In this case, it is evident that the paragraph discusses *encyclopedias*. The next question they should ask is: *What do the sentences say about encyclopedias?* The main idea may be stated in this way: *There are different types of encyclopedias.*

After children learn how to state the main idea of paragraphs in their own way, they can determine them for paragraphs from which the sentence containing the main idea is removed. Then they can compare their own statements with the one from the paragraph. Such comparisons will help them to develop the ability to think about main ideas as inclusive statements that embrace the major aspects of the paragraph.

Noting Important Details
What details should receive more attention than others depends upon the purpose for reading the content. When children read to answer a specific question such as *Who was the first astronaut to set foot on the moon?* this detail becomes the most important one in information about the moon shot. Ordinarily, this bit of information would not be regarded as one that is necessary to remember. When children are conducting an experiment or following directions, they have to pay close attention to all of the details that are part of the instructions.

Children may benefit from guidance that requires them to pay close attention to details that serve their purposes. This might take the form of establishing a purpose for reading and then seeking to meet it by noting relevant details.

1. Which word in the following problem suggests how to solve it?

Jack weighs 64 pounds and his older brother weighs 98 pounds. What is the difference between their weights?

2. What must you do before you start this experiment? What will tell you how to plant each seed? (See problem on page 250.)

3. How did the Boston Common get its name? (See problem on page 251.)

When children read for main ideas, they have to pay attention to the details for it is through them that they can decide what the important ideas are. Some details give more information about the main idea. Others might explain the main idea or illustrate it. Children should examine the details closely so that they know what function they serve and which ones help them understand the main idea.

Which sentence gives additional information about the main idea?

Sentences such as the following are[30] called **open sentences**.

a. $n + 3 > 6$
b. $\square \times 2 = 18$
c. $4 - x < 2$
d. $7 + \triangle > 7$
e. $m + m > 4$
f. $12 \div p = 2$

An open number sentence has a letter or frame that holds open a place. The letter or frame represents some number from a set of numbers.

How Our Language Grew · · · ●[31]

One thing to keep in mind about our language is that it is continually changing. Words such as *radio, television,* and *movies* are common, everyday words now. One hundred years ago they did not exist.

In this time of jet planes and space vehicles, new words are coming into our language at a faster rate than ever. *Astronaut* is one of these words. It comes from the Greek *astro,* which means "pertaining to the stars," and the Greek word *nautilos,* which means "sailor."

There are other words in our language that come from either *astro* or *nautilos.* See if you can think of some.

[30] *Source:* From *Elementary Mathematics 6*, Second Edition, by Joseph N. Payne, et al., copyright © 1968, 1966, by Harcourt Brace Jovanovich, Inc. and reprinted with their permission.

[31] *Source:* From *Language For Daily Use 6*, Harbrace Edition, by Mildred Dawson, et al., copyright © 1968, 1966, by Harcourt Brace Jovanovich, Inc. and reprinted with their permission.

Which details explain the main idea? Which details illustrate the main idea?

AN INVESTIGATION into Where Green Plants Will Grow [32]

Needed: fifteen or twenty zinnia, or bean, or radish, or squash seeds; eleven paper cups, two saucers, cotton, a little vinegar, soil, sand

First find out which seeds will grow. Soak all the seeds in water overnight. Then place them on wet cotton in a saucer. ■ Cover them with the other saucer. When a root begins to poke out of a seed, you will know that the seed is growing. ●

Number eight of the paper cups, from 1 to 8. Plant one growing seed in each cup, under the different conditions described on the opposite page. Put each seed about one-half inch below the surface of the soil. ▲

Below are the results of one trial. ▲ Under what conditions did the plants grow best? How do you know? Under what conditions was the growth poorest? How do you know?

Additional Investigation: Try planting seeds under still other conditions. Plant one growing seed in cups 9, 10, and 11 under different conditions that you think up. Which plant grows best? How do you explain your result?

[32] *Source:* From *Concepts in Science, Orange,* Second Edition, by Paul F. Brandwein, et al., copyright © 1970, 1969, 1966, by Harcourt Brace Jovanovich, Inc. and reprinted with their permission.

BOSTON [33]

By train, plane, bus, and automobile, summer tourists pour into Boston, Massachusetts. One reason for their coming is that they want to see places they have read about.

A spot to start a history tour is the Boston Common. This grassy piece of land was set aside in the early days for the common use— the use of all. Anyone could graze his cattle on it. Now anyone can park his automobile *under it*—in the huge underground garage.

[33] *Source: In These United States* by Ralph C. Preston and John Tottle, copyright © 1966 by D. C. Heath and Company and reprinted with their permission.

Some passages contain details that are related to the topic but do not expand or illustrate the main idea. If children are reading for main ideas, they should understand that to concentrate on all the details is wasteful of their time and effort. Children should discuss the details in paragraphs and select those details which help them understand the main idea. Have them list these details and discard those which might be interesting but don't focus on the main idea.

Teacher: Some paragraphs contain only details which help you understand the main idea. In addition to these details other paragraphs may contain information which is interesting but does not help you understand the main idea. Let's read these paragraphs to see what type of details they contain. But first decide what the main idea of each paragraph is.

6. The Uses of Oxygen[34]

Think for a moment about how important oxygen is.

Without oxygen, burning could not take place. Matches would not light. The fires that we use for cooking and heating could not burn, whether they were from coal or oil or gas or wood. The gasoline in the car and school bus would not burn, so cars and buses could not run.

Then, too, oxygen is one of the most important "building blocks" in the world. Oxygen combines with many different substances to build many different compounds. When substances burn, oxygen combines with carbon and makes carbon dioxide. Oxygen combines with hydrogen to make water. Oxygen combines with iron to make iron oxide. Oxygen combines with hydrogen to make compounds such as hydrogen peroxide. Oxygen combines with thousands of different substances to build useful compounds.

Child$_1$: These paragraphs tell about the importance of oxygen.

Child$_2$: That's what each paragraph tells.

Teacher: What is the main idea of the first paragraph?

Child$_3$: Oxygen is needed for burning.

Teacher: Do the details of the paragraph explain or give examples of the main idea?

Child$_4$: Yes. Some of the examples are matches for lighting, fires for cooking and heating, gasoline for making cars and buses run.

[34] *Concepts in Science* (Orange), p. 119.

Teacher: Does the paragraph contain any details that don't illustrate or tell about the main idea?

Child₄: No. All the details are about the main idea.

Teacher: What is the main idea of the next paragraph?

Child₂: Oxygen combines with other materials to build compounds.

Teacher: What two sentences give the main idea?

Child₂: The second and the last.

Teacher: What do the details tell about the main idea?

Child₃: They give examples of how oxygen and other materials combine to make compounds.

Teacher: Are there any details in the paragraph that don't tell about the compounds oxygen and other substances make?

Child₃: No.

Teacher: Then we can use all the details to help us understand the main idea.
Now let's read this paragraph and decide what its main idea is.
Cotton makes more money for India than any other product. It is a cash crop of many farmers, especially in the better regions of the plateau. Cotton is the raw material of India's biggest industry, the manufacturing of cotton cloth. Most of the cotton mills are in Bombay. Indian cotton has only short fibers, so it is often spun together with Egyptian cotton as in the picture here.[35]

Child: The first sentence tells the main idea: Cotton makes more money for India than any other product.

Teacher: What sentences in the paragraph expand or tell more about the value of cotton to India?

Child: The second and third.

Teacher: What do the other sentences tell about?

Child: Where the cotton mills are and what happens to the cotton?

Teacher: Do these details give more information about the main idea or illustrate it.

Child: No, they just give other information about cotton.

Teacher: Is it necessary to think about where the cotton mills are or that Indian cotton is spun with Egyptian cotton to understand the main idea?

Child: No, you don't need these details.

Teacher: Which details are important?

Child: Cotton is a cash crop for many farmers and is used in the manufacture of cotton cloth, which is the biggest industry in India.

Teacher: Is it important to know that cotton is a cash crop *in the better regions of the plateau*?

Child: No. It doesn't help us understand the main idea.

---

[35] *Four Lands, Four Peoples,* p. 254.

Other paragraphs could be examined in the same way. The most important aspect of the lesson is the discussion surrounding decisions about the importance or lack of importance of details. To be able to discriminate between them will make the difference between efficient study and aimless reading.

What details children should concentrate on becomes a matter of concern when they read mathematics problems. Authors of mathematics books often include information that does not have great relevance insofar as the solution of the problems is concerned in order to relate the problems to the experiences of the pupils. On occasion, numerical data are given that are not needed to solve the problem; but the recognition that these are unrelated details is dependent on understanding of the processes involved in solving the problem.

Teachers may refer to the problems on which their pupils are working to help them understand what kinds of information are irrelevant to a problem's solution. Questions may be used to guide the children's analysis of the problem's parts.

Mary usually practices her flute lesson 1½ hours each day. Friday she practiced only ¾ hour. How much less time than usual did she practice on Friday?[36]

1. How important is the person's name for solving the problem?
2. Which word in the first statement might be omitted?
3. What word or words could replace *Friday*?

In January, Marjorie saved $2.10, in February $1.65, in March $2.35, and in April $1.93. How much did she save altogether during the four months?[37]

1. How might the first sentence be changed so that the names of the months are unnecessary?
2. What part of the question might be omitted?

Pupils may compare problems as they appear in their books with revised versions that omit or change parts of the problem. This will help clarify their thinking about what details they could ignore as they try to solve them.

Thirty-two children in a sixth-grade class went on an outing. Each child could choose swimming, boating or hiking for the morning activity. Sixteen children chose swimming, twelve chose boating, and four chose hiking.

1. What part of the class chose swimming for the morning activity?
2. What part chose boating?
3. What part chose hiking?[38]

Of thirty-two children sixteen chose to go swimming, twelve boating, and four hiking.

1. What part of the group chose swimming?
2. What part chose boating?
3. What part chose hiking?

---

[36] *Elementary Mathematics 6*, p. 74.
[37] *Elementary Mathematics 6*, p. 64.
[38] *Ibid.*

It might be useful to reaffirm the principles on which the lessons about locating and selecting information are based and which serve as guidelines for developing teaching strategies for the remainder of the study skills in this chapter.

One of the major features that should be apparent is the provision for helping children to learn through their own efforts. The teacher is intimately involved in the learning process but his role is that of a catalyst who suggests and prods rather than tells and does. It is the children who think and react so that they might develop insights into the processes which govern their performances. They are constantly testing hypotheses and exploring and confirming responses in order to identify underlying principles that affect them. More dependence upon searching and less upon receiving is characteristic of the learning climate.

The materials used to help children build patterns of behavior that will facilitate their own learning are the very ones they work with daily. They have been drawn from social studies, science, mathematics, and language books because it is to these content sources that reading-study skills must be applied. One aspect of instruction with which teachers must be concerned is the degree to which pupils can use what they have learned in different settings. This problem of transfer is minimal where learning conditions duplicate performance requirements.

A third characteristic which is common to all of these lessons is the division of skills areas into defined components and their presentation in hierarchical order. If programmed instruction serves a greater purpose than typical teaching practices, it is these features that probably account for the difference. Global and indiscriminate treatments are replaced by limited and precise presentations whose purposes are clear. The answer to this question—*what do learners have to know in order to perform a task?*—provides the design for the instructional program. The ordering of priorities, i.e., to establish what children must know before they can cope with new problems and to provide for their sequential introduction, produces conditions that promote growth and reduces interference with learning.

Organization of Information

Children who engage in independent study must not only understand what they read but also remember important information. The ability to see relationships among ideas and think about them in an organized way furthers this understanding and facilitates recall. Pupils who have learned to follow the author's ideas by noting organizational patterns and recognizing important ideas and details are better able to remember and reproduce information.

Authors of content books adopt different organizational patterns to present information. Depending upon the ideas they seek to emphasize, they typically develop relationship of ideas through enumeration, time order, comparisons and contrasts, and causes and effects. (See Chapter 6, "Reading for Meaning," pages 196–97.) In addition, they generally group information according to topics. Thus children should recognize both the topic and its organization in order to reproduce information for their own purposes.

Preparing Outlines

Children who have studied the organization of their books and learned to preview chapters know that the information in them is organized by topics and subtopics. It might be helpful to examine a chapter or part of one with them and list its topic and subtopics in outline form without formal outline designations. This listing will help them see how each subtopic is related to the topic.

Writing Good Sentences[39] *(topic)*
    Four Kinds of Sentences *(subtopic)*
    The Two Parts of a Sentence *(subtopic)*
    Sentence Patterns: Word Order *(subtopic)*
    The Order of Subject and Predicate *(subtopic)*
    The Subject in Commands and Requests *(subtopic)*
    Writing Sentences Correctly *(subtopic)*

Under what subtopics pupils could expect to find different kinds of information would be explored next. Pupils might examine a subtopic to see what information the author includes under it. In the section about *Four Kinds of Sentences* they find explanations of different types of sentences. These types are then listed under the subtopic so that their relationship to the topic and subtopic can be noted. Designations can be introduced to show the differences between each level of information.

I. Writing Good Sentences   *(topic)*
  A. Four Kinds of Sentences   *(subtopic)*
    1. Declarative Sentence   *(detail)*
    2. Interrogative Sentence *(detail)*
    3. Imperative Sentence   *(detail)*
    4. Exclamatory Sentence *(detail)*

In the same way, they could list the information under the second subtopic. Now the outline begins to take shape.

Writing Good Sentences
  A. Four Kinds of Sentences
    1. Declarative Sentence
    2. Interrogative Sentence
    3. Imperative Sentence
    4. Exclamatory Sentence
  B. The Two Parts of a Sentence
    1. Subject
    2. Predicate

The other subtopics can be treated in similar fashion. To complete some portions of the outline, the details might be given and the children asked to decide under what subtopics each should go. Then they would verify the results by checking them with the book's treatment of the information.

---

[39] *Language for Daily Use 6* (Harbrace ed.), Chap. 2.

For example, details might include:

avoiding sentence fragments; natural order of subjects; inverted order of predicates; avoiding run-on sentences

The children will learn a great deal about preparing outlines and what to include in them by studying the parts of a chapter and seeing how each part is related to the whole and to each other. Since they already know the difference between main ideas and details, they should be able with teacher guidance to prepare a simple outline of material they are reading about. The topic is often provided by chapter headings; they have to decide what the main idea and important details are. Thus, in reading about the importance of oxygen and its production the children find two headings: *The Uses of Oxygen* and *The Return of Oxygen*.[40] These are the big topics and are indicated in the same way as *Writing Good Sentences* was. (The children should discuss how to label them.)

I. The Uses of Oxygen
II. The Return of Oxygen

Three main ideas about the uses of oxygen are discussed in the text: oxygen is needed for burning; oxygen combines with other substances to form compounds; and oxygen is needed for breathing. Details are given about each use. So the partial outline takes shape by listing these main ideas as subtopics under their appropriate topic. The children could decide whether to include any details they thought were necessary. (It is not essential that important details be added to the outline if they can be remembered.) While the structure of outlines based upon this information will be similar, their contents may vary. Some children will want to include information that others do not consider necessary.

I. The Uses of Oxygen
  A. Burning
  B. Building Compounds
    1. Carbon + oxygen = carbon dioxide
    2. Hydrogen + oxygen = water
  C. Breathing

The rest of the outline might be completed by the children with a minimum of guidance. The teacher could indicate how many subtopics there were by writing them in skeleton form.

II. The Return of Oxygen
  A. _____
  B. _____

Headings in textbooks can suggest topics for outlines. However, the children read materials which do not divide information into logical units

---

[40] *Concepts in Science* (Orange), pp. 119, 123. A portion of this text appears on page 25.

and they must seek out the topics and subtopics themselves. Even where headings are given it might be necessary to formulate their own. For example, this heading appears at the top of a page: "Summing Up New England." The text which follows describes New Engand's landforms and then discusses the ways in which its people earn a living. It concludes with a brief section about the area's natural beauty and recreation facilities.

Children who can recognize the different topics and main ideas will be able to outline this information. As an aid to them the teacher should ask such questions as:

What is all this information about?
What is the first large subject the information covers?
What important information is included under this subject?
What is the next large subject?

As they find the answers to these questions, the children should jot each down in their appropriate places. Some groups will find a partial skeleton outline very helpful, particularly when they first undertake to make an outline from materials of this kind.

New England

I. Surface Features
 B. _____
II. _____
 A. Manufacturing
  1. _____
 B. Farming
  1. Potatoes
  2. _____
 C. _____
  1. _____
 D. _____
 E. _____

If children understand what purpose an outline serves and can differentiate between topics, subtopics, and details, they won't have great difficulty in making simple outlines after they have prepared some under the teacher's direction. The point that outlines are intended to help clarify ideas and facilitate their recall by establishing relationships among them must be clear if children are to learn how to make and use outlines to serve their own purposes.

Preparing Summaries

Actually, an outline is one form that a summary might take. It could be a condensed version of information stated in one's own words that contains the main ideas and possibly the important details. It might even consist of a listing, as in recording a series of events or steps in an activity. The form a summary takes will depend upon the purpose for which it is being prepared and the nature of the information.

Since pupils are already familiar with outlines that contain main ideas and details, it will not be difficult for them to understand that only this kind of information should be included in other summary forms. A practical way of clarifying how other kinds of summaries are prepared is to present material that is followed by a summary and compare them for their contents.

Nuclear Energy Against Disease [41]

The work of Marie and Pierre Curie has had great benefits. It has led, for example, to the control of radium and other radioactive substances, which have since been used in the treatment of cancer.

A cancer is a growth of diseased cells in the body. A cancer gets in the way of the normal functioning of the healthy organs in the body.

Because the radium nucleus is radioactive (unstable), it breaks down. As it does so, it gives off radiations that can destroy some cancers. Nowadays, radium and other radioactive substances are used in such a way that their radioactivity can be directed at any spot in the body.

For instance, the patient shown in the picture is being treated in a hospital. The big machine uses a piece of radioactive substance; but in this case, the substance is not radium, but radioactive cobalt. The nuclei of the radioactive substance send out atomic radiations. In other words, the machine is a kind of radioactive gun. When the radiation from this radioactive gun is aimed at a cancer, the radiation can be made strong enough to destroy cancer cells without causing great harm to healthy cells nearby.

Radioactive substances are now be-

ing used not only to treat disease but also for many kinds of medical tests. The advantage of using radioactive atoms in testing is that the path of these atoms through the body can easily be traced with the use of a Geiger counter.

Here is how one such test works. Your thyroid gland absorbs iodine from your blood. If this gland becomes diseased it may absorb iodine too slowly or too quickly. To test whether this is so, a person is given a tiny, harmless amount of radioactive iodine. How long it takes for the thyroid gland to absorb the radioactive atoms is determined with a Geiger counter.

Summary

Radioactive substances are used to treat disease such as cancer. The radiation that radium and other substances give off destroys the cancer cells. Radioactive substances are used also to determine if people have certain diseases. How these substances behave in the body can be determined with a Geiger counter, which measures their radioactivity.

---

[41] *Source:* From *Concepts in Science, Brown*, Second Edition, by Paul F. Brandwein, et al., copyright © 1970, 1969, 1966, by Harcourt Brace Jovanovich, Inc., and reprinted with their permission. Photograph reprinted with the permission of Atomic Energy of Canada Ltd.

Pupils should examine the text and list its main ideas and important details to determine if these have been included in the summary. They should discuss why some information is of less importance to them than others and what would happen to the summary if all of it were included. In addition, they should compare the way the ideas in the summary are stated with those in the text. It is desirable that when they prepare summaries they use their own words for stating ideas wherever possible. In the case of technical information it will be necessary to use the same terms as those in the text.

Pupils should discuss what kinds of summaries they ought to prepare for different types of information. To do this, have the children read short passages from different sources and discuss how they might record their information. If they read about an experiment and wish to take notes on how to perform it, they should understand why a simple enumeration of steps will be more useful to them than a topical outline or a summary in the form of a paragraph. They could prepare more than one kind of summary for the same information and compare their usefulness.

Graphic Aids

The problems associated with the reading of graphic illustrations appearing in content materials are twofold: developing the attitude in pupils that they should pay at least as much attention to them as they do to the printed text and teaching pupils to read them with understanding. The first problem arises from the fact that many books include all sorts of illustrations within the text but either fail to call the children's attention to them or don't require pupils to use them. Children develop the habit of ignoring graphic aids unless they understand that authors include them to make their ideas more clear (illustrations help make abstract ideas concrete) and that to study them will increase their understanding of what they read and possibly provide them with information that doesn't appear in the text.

Science, social studies, and other books contain all sorts of graphic aids —tables, graphs, charts, maps, photographs, etc.—to which no specific reference is made. Some books occasionally suggest that the reader refer to them by such statements as *See Table 1,* but many are just there. Even in books where the same coded symbol appears in the text and on an illustration, the children could ignore the illustration unless they understood its importance and had developed the habit of reading both text and graphic materials.

The following mathematics problems on pages 260 and 261 are ones that some pupils might be able to follow without the illustration that accompanies them. How much more meaningful does a problem become if children refer to the diagram as they read each part? Notice that no reference to the illustration is made until the end of problem 4.

7. The Main Concept: Energy, Machines, and Work[42]

Most of you can lift 50 pounds but with a great deal of effort. With the help of a simple machine you can lift much more. Apply a force of 50 pounds to a block and tackle with four ropes between the pulleys, and what weight can you lift? Each rope supports 50 pounds, making a total lifting force of 200 pounds—enough to lift a small piano! The block and tackle helps you multiply the force of your muscles; but have you done more work? No. Although you have used a machine to multiply the force of your muscles, the force must be applied through a longer distance. The distance is four times as far.

We must put just as much work into a simple machine as we get out of it. Machines may multiply force, but they do not increase the total amount of work done.

In order to do work, we must have a source of energy. Our energy comes from the food we eat. The energy in food supplies our muscles with the force to push against an object. No matter what kind of work is being done, energy is needed. Using a machine does not eliminate the need for energy. A machine only transfers the energy from one place to another.

In any study of science much time is given over to the study of energy. Energy can be changed from one form to another. Steam from boiling water can turn a turbine. The heat energy changes the water into steam, and the energy in steam becomes mechanical energy in a turbine. Mechanical energy can be transformed into electric energy by a generator and used for many purposes.

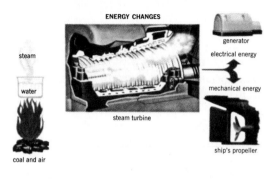

ENERGY CHANGES

steam

water

coal and air

steam turbine

generator

electrical energy

mechanical energy

ship's propeller

[42] *Source:* From *Concepts in Science, Brown,* by Paul F. Brandwein, et al., copyright © 1970, 1969, 1966, by Harcourt Brace Jovanovich, Inc. and reprinted with their permission.

One way to help children develop the habit of using graphic aids is to read such abstract materials with them and ask that they explain or demonstrate the ideas. When pupils experience difficulty in understanding what they read, have them reread the text but stop to study the illustration as they are reading. Thus, their reading will be interrupted by referring to the illustration to see if it helps to clarify the meaning of what they have just read. This procedure should be followed as many times as needed to understand the printed text. Pupils will then appreciate the value of illustrations and understand what they must do when they are engaged in independent study.

Teachers can focus pupils' attention on graphic aids by referring to them continually in their discussions with the group. In addition to raising

Locating points in a plane [43]

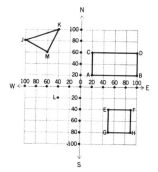

Mel is making a map of the school and of the playground, which is flat.

1. Mel drew two perpendicular lines and marked points on each to represent numbers of yards. On the east-west line, how can he locate the point for 20 yards east? 80 yards east? 100 yards west? 0 yards?

2. On the north-south line, how can he locate the point for 60 yards north? 80 yards south? 0 yards?

3. On a map such as Mel's, 0° is called the **point of origin.** Can you tell why?

4. Mel located 4 points to represent the corners of the school and named the points A, B, C, and D. Point A is 20 yards east and 20 yards north.

Point B is 100 yards east and $\underline{?}$ yards north; C is $\underline{?}$ yards east and $\underline{?}$ yards north; D is $\underline{?}$ yards east and $\underline{?}$ north.

Use the map to find the dimensions of the school building.

5. The four bases for the ball field are labeled E, F, G, and H. Use a pair of numbers with directions to tell the location of each base.

6. Point L shows the climbing rope. What numbers and directions tell its location?

7. Tell the location of each corner of the playing field represented by points J, K, and M.

[43] *Source:* **From** *Elementary Mathematics 6*, Second Edition, by Joseph N. Payne, et al., copyright © 1968, 1966, by Harcourt Brace Jovanovich, Inc. and reprinted with their permission.

questions about the printed text, they could ask how the text and illustrations are related and what purposes the latter serve (whether the illustrations clarify or provide new information). Pupils would read the graphic materials for literal and inferred ideas and evaluate them as well as seek answers to questions which the materials might suggest. But all these activities would be related to the printed text that accompanies the illustrations.

It is necessary to teach children how to read some of the graphic aids which appear in their books. Just as questions are raised about printed text, so can they be asked to bring out the nature of the illustrations and their contents. Maps, diagrams, and pictures are representative of them, and suggestions for treating them will be considered.

Map Reading

Most maps are associated with social studies content, although some, such as weather maps, might appear in science books. In order to read maps children must be able to associate their representations with scales and symbols and be able to "read" these symbols in order to extract information and draw inferences.

Attention should be drawn to the *title* of the map, which might be compared to a topic in a chapter. Just as children determine purposes for reading from a heading, they can speculate about what kind of information a specific map might yield. How to read the *scale* is another of their concerns. Children should realize that a map compresses distances and size (the map is *not* the territory) and the scale makes it possible to determine what the approximate real measures are. Many maps contain *legends* that classify information much in the same way that tables of contents or indexes do. Specific information about the topic the map treats can be

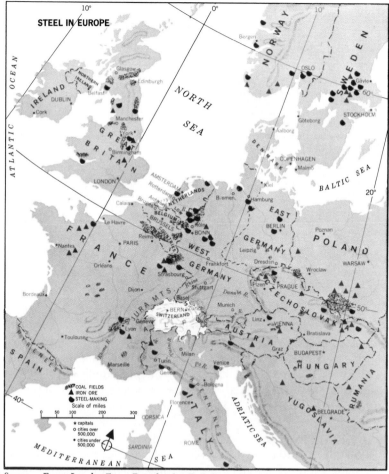

[44] *Source: Four Lands, Four Peoples* by Ralph C. Preston, et al., copyright © 1966 by D. C. Heath and Company and reprinted with their permission

obtained from the legend. While some flat maps do indicate *direction*, pupils must use the grids to pinpoint *location*.

Based upon the map on page 262, the following questions, problems, and activities will aid in teaching children to understand its features and use them to obtain information.

Understanding Its Features

1. What kind of information does the map show?
2. Why is a map a good device for giving this information?
3. Why are there lines that run across and down the map? What are these lines for? Why are distances between the lines that run down the map less at the top than at the bottom? Why are the lines that run across the map curved?
4. How does a map such as this one make it possible to locate places on it? How could you give the location of Warsaw without saying it is in Poland? What is its location?
5. Compare the distances on the scale to inches on a ruler. How may the approximate distance between London and Paris be obtained?
6. The dark arrow at the bottom of 'the map shows which direction is north. Why does the arrow point at an angle? How close to London would you be if you flew directly north from Paris?
7. What symbol is used to show where the coal fields in Europe are located? Where iron ore is mined? Where steel is made?

Obtaining Information

1. What European countries mine a lot of coal?
2. What European countries have iron-ore mines?
3. Why does a map about steel production show coal and iron mines?
4. Which countries have iron-ore or coal but do not make steel?
5. What generalization may be made about the relative location of coal and iron mines and steel mills?
6. Which countries are poor in coal and iron?
7. Why don't all countries that have coal and iron produce steel?
8. Which part of Europe produces most of its steel?
9. How might the raw materials and finished steel reach seaports?

The learning activities in which children engage depend on the nature of the maps they read. But many of the insights they gain from understanding one map will be applied to another. A basic understanding of the nature and purposes of maps and how they may be used for information gathering will reduce the need for spending large blocks of time on maps each time a different type appears.

Diagrams, Charts, and Pictures

As has been noted earlier, pictorial aids are intended by the author to supplement the printed text so that pupils' understanding of verbal materials is increased. Teachers have to concentrate on having pupils refer to them as they read instead of ignoring them. These aids are read for specific information; in addition, the information they illustrate might be used to make generalizations and comparisons, draw conclusions, and infer trends and effects which the verbal materials do not cover.

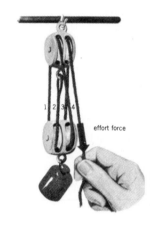
45 *Source:* From *Concepts in Science, Brown*, by Paul F. Brandwein, et al., copyright © 1970, 1969, 1966 by Harcourt Brace Jovanovich, Inc. and reprinted with their permission.

Very often, without the illustrative aids, the meanings carried by the verbal text are quite vague. Note how much clarification the two illustrations of how pulleys work give to the printed text. In fact, the printed text becomes quite involved with arithmetical explanation while the illustrations carry few words but much information. In cases such as this one, some groups might gain their information by studying the diagrams more closely than the text. Questions based upon the diagrams could elicit the factual information from which inferences would be drawn.

1. How many pulleys are there in the top illustration?
2. Which of the two pulleys can move? How many ropes support the movable pulley?
3. On what rope would you pull to lift the load?
4. According to the diagram, how much force would you have to use to lift the load?

5. How much force would you need to lift the load without pulleys?
6. Why don't you need as much force as the load weighs to lift it?
7. What generalization can be made about the number of ropes that support the movable pulley and the effort needed to lift the weight?
8. How much effort would be needed to lift a load of 400 grams? 50 grams?
9. How many ropes support the movable pulleys in the lower diagram?
10. What happens to the effort needed to lift the original load of 200 grams? What is the relationship between effort and number of ropes?
11. How much would 75 grams of effort lift?
12. If there were 8 ropes, how much effort would be needed to lift a load of 800 grams?
13. What kind of pulley arrangement would be needed to lift a piano that weighs 1500 pounds? Could two men lift the piano with the 4-rope pulley?

The first set of questions (1–4) can be answered from the information in the illustration. The answers to question 5–7 are based upon this information and go beyond it. Question 8 calls for the application of a generalization, while question 9 requires careful scrutiny of the illustration. Questions 10–12 call for inferential thinking, and the last question requires the pupils to use the information they have learned and extend it to a new situation.

In reading any graphic illustration pupils must first know what purpose it serves. They may learn this from its title or accompanying text or from its elements. They must be able to interpret symbols and understand the significance of artistic devices that convey meanings, as in the following representation of how precipitation occurs in the western United States.

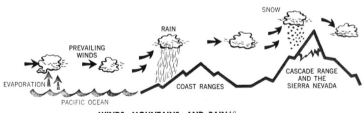

WINDS, MOUNTAINS, AND RAIN[46]

Finally, pupils must draw from it what the author intended to convey. How children think about the information should be related to the purpose for which the graphic material was prepared. In many instances they will be able to establish relationships—time order or sequence, contrast, cause and effect—which the printed text might confirm or which could be the results of their own insights.

Following Directions

How many adults fail to follow printed directions? Is their failure due to inability to understand them or to other factors? Undoubtedly, some of the problems can be explained by weaknesses in vocabulary and sentence

---

[46] *Source: In These United States* by Ralph C. Preston and John Tottle, copyright © 1966 by D. C. Heath and Company and reprinted with their permission.

AN INVESTIGATION
into a Piece of Bread[47]

Needed: a piece of stale bread, a jar with a cover, a magnifying glass

Place the piece of bread in the jar. Add 5 drops of water to the bread. Then cover the jar, and put it in a warm place —but not in sunlight. ■

Observe the bread every day. Here is what happened in one trial. ● A growth has formed on the bread. It is a mold, living and growing on the stale bread. Use the magnifying glass to examine the mold. ▲ The tiny black balls are called spore cases. Each spore case is full of **spores**. A spore is a living cell that can grow into a mold plant.

What is happening to the bread? It is being eaten by the mold and by other growths that appear on it. In time the bread will disappear. It will be consumed by living things.

Additional Investigation: Where did the mold come from?

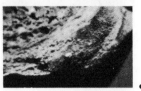

[47] *Source:* From *Concepts in Science, Orange,* Second Edition, by Paul F. Brandwein et al., copyright © 1970, 1969, 1966, by Harcourt Brace Jovanovich, Inc. and reprinted with their permission.

structure. Many are the result of failure to establish a proper set for engaging in this kind of reading and failure to note all the details in the directions.

When a reader has to follow instructions to solve a problem, he must realize that any deviation from them could interfere with his success. Each step is likely to be as important as the next, and failure to follow one will have an impact upon the others. Teachers can help children develop the proper attitude by discussing with them how reading instructions is different from reading other types of information and why the details in instructions acquire significance that they might not have under other conditions. One way to emphasize this point is to remove a few details from a set of instructions and have the pupils try to carry out the directions properly without them. Then have the pupils compare their set of instructions with the original set to see how the added details might make a difference and could influence the results.

If pupils do not follow instructions as they should, be sure to find out if they understand what is required of them. For example, if they are told to cut an *inclined plane* out of paper and don't know what an inclined plane looks like, they will not be able to fulfill the instructions. Present a set of instructions whose steps are few in number and which pupils can understand. Have them read the set of instructions to *determine what its purpose is*. Then have the pupils *list in order the steps* in the set of directions. Finally, have them perform each step in turn.

Don't lift your pencil! [48]

On your paper, copy the paths shown below. Now see if you can start at some point on a path and trace all of the path without going over any segment twice. In other words, don't lift your pencil.

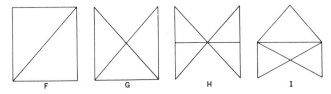

F   G   H   I

[48] *Source:* From *Elementary Mathematics 4*, Second Edition, by Joseph N. Payne, et al., copyright © 1968, 1966, by Harcourt Brace Jovanovich, Inc. and reprinted with their permission.

Some sets of directions in science and mathematics are numbered and listed in order, but these can be as complicated as those which pupils must extract from the regular text. Note that in the set of instructions that appears on page 268 the steps contain more than one direction. It might be helpful to have the children first establish why they are listing the instructions, then have them list the different directions in each step and go through them in sequence before undertaking the project. They would not be required to carry out such a complex set of instructions unless they demonstrated their ability to perform successfully more simple ones. And any complicated instructions would be followed under the guidance of the teacher, who could help them to establish purposes and underscore the details which must be adhered to.

By these means and over periods of time pupils will build attitudes which will affect the ways in which they follow directions. They will not proceed unless they understand them. Moreover, they will approach a set of directions with an inquiring mind, looking for all the information they need to complete the task. They will approach materials that involve instructions differently from those which do not focus on details. In short, they will be able to engage in independent learning successfully, which is a major objective of the reading curriculum.

Making a model of a pyramid [49]

▷ Take a sealed envelope. Make dots at the middle points of the edges at the two narrow ends. Connect your dots as shown. This will serve as a guide line.

▷ Find the measure of the edge of the narrow end. Using this measure, draw line segments from two corners to a point on your guide line as shown.
   Have you formed a triangle with 3 sides of equal measure?

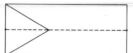

▷ Draw a line segment through the top of the triangle parallel to the end of the envelope. Label the endpoints *A* and *B*. Cut along this line segment.

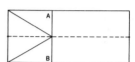

▷ Fold back and forth along the line segments you drew in step 2. Then lay your paper flat again. Open along the cut end. Bring the two open edges together so that *A* and *B* meet. Tape these edges together.

1. How many faces does the pyramid have? Do these faces have the same size and shape?

2. How many edges are there? Are they all the same length?

3. How many corners are there?

---

[49] *Source:* From *Elementary Mathematics 4*, Second Edition, by Joseph N. Payne, et al., copyright © 1968, 1966, by Harcourt Brace Jovanovich, Inc. and reprinted with their permission.

Flexibility and Speed in Reading

How rapidly do and should children read is a question of comparatively recent origin that can be traced to the interest in "speed" reading on the college and adult levels. Offers to increase one's reading rate many times over are made by commercial organizations through advertisements in newspapers which cite testimonials to substantiate their claims. Many colleges offer reading improvement programs of a more comprehensive nature but some do stress increases in rate as their major goal. In the past, few elementary schools have shown much interest in reading rate, but the affects of reports that have appeared in the press and periodicals are filtering down to some schools.[50]

---

[50] "90 in Ocean Hill Schools Reading 33 Times Faster." *The New York Times*, Feb. 27, 1970. This is a report about ninety fifth-graders who are purported to have increased

* *Source: New York Post*, April 14, 1970. Pogo © 1970, Walt Kelly. Courtesy of Publishers-Hall Syndicate.

Before considering the real issues with which elementary schools should be concerned, it might be helpful to analyze reports that contain claims about increasing reading rates. Most are quite similar in character in that they offer data to show that students read much faster than originally after brief periods of instruction with either no loss or some improvement in comprehension. Some of the reading rates cited are more modest than others, but it is not unusual to read about rates of 1500 to 10,000 words per minute and more.

Can students increase their rates of reading? Without raising some pertinent questions about the relationships between the nature of materials

their reading rate thirty-three times and comprehension almost 10 per cent. One child is reported to have had a beginning rate of 309 words a minute and a final rate of 20,250 words a minute "in spurts."

For a summary and critique of speed reading practices and research see Allen Berger, "Speed Reading: Is the Present Emphasis Desirable?" (Pro-Challenger: Vearl G. McBride; Con-Challenger: M. Agnella Gunn). *Current Issues in Reading, 13*, Part 2 (Proceedings of the Thirteenth Annual Convention). Newark, Del., International Reading Association, 1969, pp. 45–84.

and the purposes they have for reading them as well as other factors that influence their behavior, the answer is a qualified yes. Many achieving students are capable of reading some materials faster than they ordinarily do. By making deliberate efforts they can realize improvement. Inherent in this statement is the assumption that meaning is not a problem for them.

How rapidly can mature persons read materials that are not difficult for them? According to estimates, the outer limits for reading continuous text line by line is in the range of 900–1000 words per minute. These estimates have been obtained by photographing eye movements during reading and measuring eye span (how much the eyes take in when they stop or make a fixation), the duration of fixations (stops), and time intervals between fixations and return sweeps (movement from the end of one line to the beginning of the next line).

If these estimates are fairly accurate (there doesn't seem to be any reason to doubt them), how can speeds in excess of them be explained? By understanding how the latter are calculated. If an individual looks at ten printed pages of 400 words each in one minute and can either relate what the contents are about or answer some questions based upon the contents, he has "read" 4000 words per minute. Most observers agree that this kind of "reading" is a form of scanning or skimming and is not to be equated with continuous reading. No one questions the validity of reading some materials for certain purposes this way. What is rejected are the claims of some who say whole sections and pages are absorbed in ways that present instruments cannot measure. In a few cases where students who purportedly achieved unusually high reading rates and good comprehension scores were tested, it was found that they failed to duplicate these performances when expected to respond to typical reading requirements. Insofar as elementary children are concerned, estimates of how rapidly they read silently with comprehension range from 60–80 words per minute for the first grade, 120–140 words per minute for the third grade, and 185–245 words per minute for the sixth grade.[51] These are average rates for reading continuous text line by line; rates for oral reading are not quite as high. Few elementary school reading programs make extensive provisions for rapid reading so it might be assumed that the reading rates that children achieve are the results of typical reading instruction and not special training.

The main skills focus of elementary school reading programs has been on building and strengthening word recognition and comprehension and not on increasing reading rate. Most reading educators would agree that it is to the former that teachers' attention should be given. However, children engage in different reading tasks whose requirements can be met more

---

[51] Stanford Taylor, Helen Frackenpohl, and James Pettee, "Grade Level Norms for the Components of the Fundamental Reading Skill," *Research and Information Bulletin No. 3*, Huntington, N. Y.: Educational Developmental Laboratories, 1960; Robert A. McCracken, "The Informal Reading Inventory as a Means of Improving Instruction," in Thomas C. Barrett, ed., *The Evaluation of Children's Reading Achievement*, Newark, Del.: International Reading Association, 1967, p. 85.

readily in one way than another, and it is to these needs that few reading programs have addressed themselves. Much more attention must be given to teaching children to become flexible readers—readers who know when to read slowly and carefully and when to read more quickly and how to vary their reading styles in accordance with their purposes and the nature of the materials.

Adjusting Rate to Purpose and Materials

When children read to study, they should not read in the same way as they read for pleasure. Study-type reading requires pupils to seek answers to specific questions, to gain general impressions, to separate important ideas from details, to remember and reproduce information. When they read for enjoyment, most, if not all, of these requirements do not have to be met. In fact, to expect children to deal with materials that they read for enjoyment in the same way as they read materials to learn would hardly be making it possible for them to attain any real satisfactions from the experience.

When pupils engage in study activities, the rate at which they read should be governed by the nature of their purposes and the materials. If they are reading for main ideas, it is not necessary for them to read as slowly as when they concentrate upon many details. They might read introductory paragraphs quickly and then read more slowly as they recognize the passages that are important. Very often it will be necessary to stop and think about a passage or reread a paragraph or line that isn't very clear to them. Information that is somewhat familiar will be read more rapidly than less-familiar information. Materials that are packed with details require more careful reading than materials which contain general statements.

Pupils need to know when it is important for them to read carefully and when they may read rapidly. They should discuss under what circumstances it is desirable to reduce and increase their reading rates and engage under the teacher's direction in the kind of reading which their purposes and materials dictate. By contrasting purposes and materials the children will be able to understand more clearly why they should make efforts to vary their reading styles.

Teachers might select appropriate passages and have the pupils read them. Then they could discuss how they read them and why. For example, the excerpts on pages 272–73 are not equally difficult to read and could be used to establish the reasons why one might be read faster than the other.

Children could practice reading passages of varying difficulty and comparable length under timed conditions after they have learned to distinguish between them. Of course, after they read each selection they should be required to answer questions or tell about the content. Some children might discover that they read certain materials much more rapidly than other children because they have knowledge of their contents, but that on other occasions they read more slowly than some because they don't know

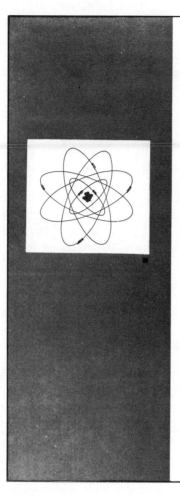

A New View of
Matter and Energy[52]

We are rained on, snowed on, hailed on. We swim in streams, ponds, lakes, oceans. We walk on roads and meadows, we climb hills and mountains, we ride about in all kinds of vehicles. We see, hear, feel, taste, smell thousands of different things. We study the Earth and its neighboring planets, the Sun and other stars, solid rock, and open space. Yet we find that all these thousands of different things are in some ways alike. Let's remind ourselves of these important likenesses— the likenesses we found in our study of matter and energy.

We see, for instance, that all the substances we know have likenesses. All substances can be classified into just three groups. Substances may be solids, or liquids, or gases, according to their structure. Rivers can be classified as young or old, according to their structure. Mountains can be grouped as young mountains or old mountains. Rocks can be classified as igneous, sedimentary, or metamorphic. This is one way we put things in order around us. *Things can be grouped or classified by their structure.*

[52] *Source:* From *Concepts in Science 5* by Paul F. Brandwein, et al., copyright © 1970, 1966, by Harcourt Brace Jovanovich, Inc. and reprinted with their permission.

much about the contents. Or they might discover that they read too rapidly for the type of material they are responsible for.

Opportunities to adjust reading rate to reading purposes could be treated in a similar way. Pupils would know what their purpose for reading was and then read to satisfy it. Upon completion they would explain how they read the material. In the case of the content about India on the opposite page, the children should be alerted by the heading, which tells them that there are three important facts to know. Since they are reading for main ideas, they should concentrate upon them. This means that they would read carefully to find the first one, move along more rapidly until they reached the next important idea, reduce their rate to note what it was and then increase their rate once again until they met the last important idea. The adjustments pupils made in their reading were dictated by their purpose and were indications of reading flexibility. To have read the entire content in the same way would have been a sign of inability to adjust to different reading requirements.

Pupils should practice reading for different purposes and compare notes about the ways in which they cover the content. A reading guide might be used to assist pupils to adjust their rates in accordance with the reading requirements. It would be similar to those which called the children's attention to meaning clues; in this instance the guide would indicate through comments or questions how in view of their purposes they ought to vary reading styles as the nature of the materials changes. Children will not develop automatic responses in making reading adjustments unless they fully understand what kinds of behavior are dictated by different conditions and have opportunities to read under the same restraints they will be facing when engaging in independent learning activities.

[53] **Three Things to Know.** The first thing to know about the Indian people today is that there are many of them—around 500 million. There are more people in India than in any other country of the world except China. If you counted together all the people living on the two big continents of South America and Africa, you would find about the same number of people as live in India.

The second thing to know about Indians today is that most of them are farmers. Seven out of ten Indians make their living by farming the soil, just as their ancestors did. Their ancestors could produce enough food for India because there were fewer people. But now that India is so crowded, the land can barely feed all the people.

Crowding on the land means there is a third important thing to know about the Indian people. Millions are always poor and always hungry. Of course some Indians live comfortably. But the Indians have almost the lowest average standard of living in the world.

[53] *Source: Four Lands, Four Peoples* by Ralph C. Preston and John Tottle, copyright © 1966 by D. C. Heath and Company and reprinted with their permission.

Scanning for Information

When it is the reader's purpose to find the answers to specific questions, there isn't much justification for him to read every word with the same care that he would if he were interested in all the information about a topic. For example, he might wish to know what function white blood cells have or when the first nuclear device was tested successfully. To read all about the blood and nuclear developments could be time-consuming and not very productive in meeting his purposes. Pupils can be taught to find answers to specific questions such as those about the blood and nuclear fission in a quick and efficient way. The technique to use is scanning. Scanning is often used in conjunction with locating information through the index since pupils know only on what page or pages information about a topic is located and have to seek out what they are interested in.

STEP 1.   In order to teach children how to scan for specific information, select some questions on which they might be working and write these on the chalkboard:

1. How large is a *Kodiak bear*?
2. When were the *cave paintings* of *Lascaux* discovered?
3. Is a *frog* classified as a *fish* or *amphibian*?
4. What kind of *government* does *Nepal* have?

Question: When did Isaac Newton make his contributions to science? (Isaac Newton is the key word which will be capitalized, and the answer should be expressed in years.)

Energy and Motion

This earth, this collection of atoms,

is a planet. It is one of nine planets in

our solar system. Like all matter, the

Earth doesn't remain unchanged. As

you have learned, for instance, it is

constantly changing its position. Like

the other planets, the Earth is in

motion around its star, the Sun.

How is it the Earth moves

around the Sun? How is it that the

Moon moves around the Earth?

(Stop! Read the line.)

Isaac Newton must have asked himself these

questions, almost 300 years ago. His answers

gave us two very important concepts.

[54] *Source:* From *Concepts in Science 5* by Paul F. Brandwein, et al., copyright © 1970, 1966, by Harcourt Brace Jovanovich, Inc. and reprinted with their permission.

They should be able to select the key word or words in each question just as they would in deciding what word to look for in an index. Then have them decide what kind of answer they could expect to each of the questions. Both questions are kept in mind as they seek the answer:

1. *Kodiak bear*: size expressed in feet, pounds
2. *cave paintings, Lascaux*: time given by month and/or year (numbers)
3. *frog, fish, amphibian*: classification
4. *government, Nepal*: king (dom), president, legislature

In cases where it is difficult to decide what form an answer to a question will take (as in questions 3 and 4) the children should rely upon the key words to guide their search.

STEP 2.   Present a passage, like the one on page 274, which contains the answer to a specific question. Be certain that the children understand what their purpose for reading is. Explain and demonstrate how they are to read: they are to start at the beginning of the passage and run their eyes over the lines until they come to a key word or the kind of answer that is expected; then they should read the sentence in which these are found to verify if the answer to the question is there; if it isn't, they are to continue from that point and repeat the process until they do locate the answer.

The children move their eyes from line to line just as they would when reading continuously, but they are only interested in spotting the key word(s) and possible answer. They should be encouraged to run their eyes over the lines as rapidly as they can without missing what they are searching for and stop to read when they have found it. If they are able to tell what other information is in the passage, they are moving their eyes across the lines too slowly and should be urged to move them more quickly.

As children develop proficiency in scanning short passages for information, longer ones can be introduced. Questions which contain multiple key words and no real clues to the answers may be used after they have learned to find those which are more obvious. Pupils will also have to read some sentences preceding or following the one in which they think the answer might be located in order to obtain it.

Skimming for Ideas

Another form of rapid reading is skimming. Skimming is used to find what something is about or to obtain some general impressions. When children survey a table of contents or a chapter, they focus their attention on titles and headings. They may look over a section they have already read carefully and pay attention only to those parts which concern them. Skimming refers to "taking off the top" and not concentrating upon all the contents.

Pupils who have learned the basic and specialized reading skills that have been stressed in this and other chapters should be able to apply them efficiently. If they merely wish, for example, to find out what a selection is about, they will use their skills to locate and verify the topic and not read anything more. The selection may have some paragraphs which lead into the topic but the children will not concentrate upon them because they recognize what purpose the paragraphs serve. Should they desire to learn what the author says about the topic, they will read on for any main ideas and skip some or all of the details. In this way they would be able to cover the content much more quickly than if they were to read everything in the selection.

The best way to make it possible for children to skim content for specific purposes is to help them develop and refine their word, comprehension, and study skills—for it is these that they must use well. When children skim, they read selectively. But in order to read in this way they must have good control over the skills. Through their repeated application in solving real problems, pupils will grow in their ability to use and adapt them as their purposes require.

Specific practice in skimming different types of materials for varied purposes can be offered after the aforementioned skills have been taught and learned. Children may examine a table of contents to learn what a book is about or a chapter to determine what concepts it stresses. They might look over an article in a magazine or a newspaper editorial to learn what point of view the author expresses. But in whatever activities they engage, pupils must realize what it is they wish to accomplish and how they must read in order to achieve their purposes.

SUMMARY

1. In addition to refining and extending the skills they have learned in the primary grades, children need to develop ability to read all kinds of materials, particularly those in the content fields. The nature of content materials and the purposes for which they are read vary significantly from those associated with the reading of story or narrative-type materials. The former contain large numbers of concepts and specialized vocabulary and small amounts of descriptive matter. The writing is terse and packed tightly with information. Moreover, not only are pupils required to understand the ideas these materials cover but also to retain them and related information. No similar demands are made when they read stories, whose language and ideas are much easier to cope with.

2. Associated with the reading of content materials is the skills development which will enable pupils to engage in independent learning. All the skills of word recognition and comprehension are required to read content, but pupils must have a good command of them if they are to solve the word and meaning difficulties that are characteristic of the materials. Mastery of the study skills which are applicable to most subject areas is a requisite for learning how to learn.

3. There are two related measures teachers can adopt to help children read difficult content materials with greater ease and more understanding. One is to teach pupils how to survey the books they use to understand their structure and features. Knowledge of a book's organization will facilitate its use. Another is to teach them how to survey content so that they will have some idea of what the information is about as well as develop purposes for reading it. Set for reading may be established through such a device.

4. The directed reading lesson is a means by which children who are likely to find content materials difficult can be aided in reading them. The directed reading lesson consists of preparation for reading, which

includes provisions for relating pupils' experiences to the purposes for reading the content, introducing difficult words, clarifying concepts, and establishing purposes for reading. This preparation is followed by silent and oral reading, discussion and application of ideas gained through reading. The same materials may be used to develop reading skills that will help pupils understand and learn the content.

5. Teachers may develop study guides for pupils to use as they read informational materials. A process guide calls their attention to the ways in which they should apply the reading skills they know to the content. A content guide focuses the children's attention on the information and provides them with purposes for reading. Both types in effect are substitutes for the guidance that teachers might give if they were able to be with each pupil as he read the content.

6. The reading-study skills are tools needed to read informational materials. In terms of behavioral objectives, children locate information through book parts and other sources; select information by recognizing its significance; organize and remember information and ideas by notetaking, outlining and summarizing; determine the significance of graphic illustrations; follow directions; and vary their reading styles in accordance with their purposes and the nature of the materials. To help children achieve these objectives, teachers should identify the skills needed to solve current problems, develop a hierarchy of skills and present them in sequence, and use the materials pupils read for teaching and practicing the skills.

STUDY QUESTIONS AND EXERCISES

1. ". . . the greatest opportunity for progress in teaching reading during the next decade lies in an intelligent attack on reading problems that arise in the content fields." Why is this statement possibly more valid now than when it was issued?

2. What problems are associated with reading content that are not ordinarily met in reading story-type materials? How should reading styles vary for each type of material?

3. Prepare a series of questions which might be used to guide pupils in surveying the contents of a social studies or science book. Do the same for a specific chapter.

4. Prepare a directed reading lesson for selected content. Show how such a lesson might help pupils master the ideas the content contains.

5. Of what value is a process guide? Assume that some pupils need help in "reading between the lines." Select an excerpt from a textbook, reference, or other source and prepare a process guide which will aid such pupils to read the material for deeper meanings.

6. Why should teachers be concerned about hierarchies of reading skills? How might a sequence of subskills for a study skill area be developed?

7. Select one subskill for each of two study skills areas. Design a lesson for each of the subskills, indicating the content and ways in which the subskill is treated.
8. Why is flexibility in reading considered a more meaningful concept than speed of reading?

SUGGESTIONS FOR FURTHER READING

Some publications which elementary school teachers will find helpful for gaining insights about reading in the content fields are:

William S. Gray, ed., *Improving Reading in All Curriculum Areas* (Supplementary Educational Monographs, No. 76). Chicago: University of Chicago Press, 1952.

Harold L. Herber, *Teaching Reading in Content Areas*. Englewood Cliffs, N. J.: Prentice-Hall, Inc., 1970.

H. Alan Robinson and Ellen Lamar Thomas, eds., *Fusing Reading Skills and Content*. Newark, Del.: International Reading Association, 1969.

Information about the study skills will be found in publications that are intended for high school teachers but which contain information that all teachers might apply:

Harold L. Herber, ed., *Developing Study Skills in Secondary Schools*. Newark, Del.; The International Reading Association, 1964.

Ruth G. Viox, *Evaluating Reading and Study Skills in the Secondary Classroom*. Newark, Del.; International Reading Association, 1968.

8

Reading for Appreciation and Enjoyment

■ *He ate and drank the precious words,*
His spirit grew robust;
He knew no more that he was poor,
Nor that his frame was dust.
He danced along the dingy days,
And this bequest of wings
Was but a book. What liberty
A loosened spirit brings!

—EMILY DICKINSON[1]

The promotion of recreational reading is one of the objectives of the reading curriculum. Expressed in behavioral terms a successful reading program leads children to *want* to read so that they seek out books and other materials and engage in personal reading. The cultivation of permanent reading interests should be regarded as highly as the development of reading ability, for to learn how to read and then not do so will serve no great purpose.

Children will reject reading if they do not derive satisfaction from it just as they refuse to participate in any activity that is distasteful to them. The sense of accomplishment that the possession of reading ability assures is a real satisfaction to pupils. Children are more likely to choose activities in which they excel than those that create insurmountable problems for them. But there is another satisfaction that children, like adults, seek and need. Reading must provide the means through which they can experience enjoyment; otherwise, they will not include reading among their preferred leisure-time activities. Reading can be fun for there is joy in children's literature. The teacher's responsibility is to guide children through the world of books so that they can discover their treasures.

---

[1] Emily Dickinson, *Poems for Youth*, A. L. Hampton, ed. Boston: Little, Brown and Company, 1942, p. 70.

The Literature Program

It is possible to enjoy music without knowing much about musical notation or form but the pleasure that is derived from listening to it is immeasurably increased as one's understanding of them grows. In like manner the satisfaction that children experience from reading literature is enhanced as they learn how to understand it better.

Most of the reading instruction in the primary grades has as its target the development of skills which will enable children to engage in independent reading. Although the types of materials that are used as vehicles for developing the basic skills include imaginative writing, little attention to reading them as literature is given. Young readers are involved more with the mechanics of reading than they are with its artistry. Nevertheless, their exposure to such prose through listening to stories read to them by their parents and their teachers and reading some of them for themselves leaves its imprint. They know how delightful some books can be, that others are less so, and that they prefer certain kinds of stories to others. Children who have been read to and surrounded by books, some of which they could read and others which they merely could handle and enjoy looking at know that stories are about real and make-believe people and events, that inanimate objects and living things are treated as though they were humans, that some are humorous, exciting, sad. They may have noticed that the structure of poetry is different from that of prose and that the latter's language creates imagery and sounds different from prose.

Of course, the extent to which any of these understandings are acquired will depend upon the opportunities children have had to become familiar with books and stories. Those who advocate a completely individualized reading program believe that it is the only way to foster an appreciation of and interest in books. But it should be clear that there is nothing inherent in any kind of reading program that prevents teachers from using it and their own resources to give children the experiences they should have. No matter what personal preferences teachers may have for one instructional program over another, all can find time in the school day to read to children, to provide opportunities for children to examine and read books, and to encourage them to talk about and share the moments they have enjoyed with others.

In those classes where young children have had wide and varied experiences with books, there usually has been no deliberate attempt by teachers to instruct pupils in the reading of literature. That children have acquired some understandings about imaginative writing is evident from the ways in which they respond to it. This is all to the good. But for them to build deeper understandings about literature requires more than continuing exposures to books. Just as the reading program provides opportunities for children to strengthen and extend the reading skills they need to read various kinds of materials, so should the program build on what children have learned incidentally about imaginative writing and offer guidance in the appreciation of literature. For with greater appreciation will come the increased pleasure that causes children to turn to books instead of away from them.

Goals of Literature

The main purpose of an elementary school literature program is to involve children in literary experiences which will give them the satisfactions they seek and need. In order for them to gain the benefits from reading and listening to literature, they require some guidance in understanding the nature of imaginative writing. Meaningful experiences in literature will help them develop a number of understandings that will enhance their appreciation of it.

1. *Literature is a means through which human motivations and actions may be better understood.* Children (and adults) often fail to realize why others behave as they do and through the author's treatment of characters and events they may be able to understand how circumstances shape behavior. By seeing how others react to specific conditions they may gain some insights into their own behavior.

2. *Literature may provide solutions to problems that have troubled civilization through the ages.* The lessons that have been learned and the wisdom that has been accumulated could be sources upon which man might draw to settle issues and resolve conflicts. Moreover, the circumstances in which children find themselves will be duplicated in the characters and events of literature, and they might look to them for guides against which to draw comparisons and contrasts and possibly model their behavior. The feelings that they sense in the characters they read about might be their own; how real or imaginary children deal with them could be a source of comfort and inspiration.

3. *Literature makes possible participation in experiences that might not otherwise be enjoyed.* Few can take journeys to distant lands and meet their peoples; climb mountains and explore jungles; taste adventure. Literature makes all these real and much more. Children can be carried to other times and places and relive the past through the words and deeds of ordinary folk, heroes, and leaders. And they can be led into the future to share its mysteries and dream its dreams. Books are not the only means through which vicarious experiences may be enjoyed but they are a ready source that can be tapped at will.

4. *Literature covers a wide range of subjects and writing styles.* There is hardly any topic or theme which literature fails to deal with. Of course, those that are known to be favorites of children receive the greatest attention: real boys and girls, animals, humor, courage, heroism, sports, mystery, adventure, biography, fantasy. Within each of these categories are numerous kinds of stories that have both special and wide appeal to children of different ages.

The styles of literature include fiction which is characterized by realism and fantasy, nonfiction that tells of events and people, and poetry that is lyrical or narrative. Fiction may be represented by stories about people of the past or present who are believable; or it may take the form of legends and myths, folk and fairy tales that stretch the imagination. Nonfiction recreates characters and events—past as well as contemporary—and transports the reader to the scene of action where he may participate in it. Poetry may provide an aesthetic experience, or convey feelings, or tell a story. Its themes are boundless and are characterized by the unique way language and form express them.

Drama might be viewed as another literary genre with which children can become familiar. Meaning and feeling are conveyed in part by the lines each player speaks. Plays for children will deal with subjects and themes that other forms of literature treat and by sampling each type readers will be able to contrast the ways in which writers express ideas and depict action.

5. *Authors and illustrators are responsible for making literature as enjoyable as it is.* To know about the creators of particular stories or poems may add greater appreciation for and insights into their works. It is not unusual for authors or illustrators to include something of their own lives or backgrounds in their writings and pictures. To see relationships between who they are and what they write about can increase understanding and pleasure.

A corollary to knowing about authors and their works is the realization that some literature in the form of folk tales, legends, myths, and fairy tales that have survived the ages have unknown or doubtful origins. Nevertheless, they continue to be sought after for they represent imagination and dreams of men of bygone years and contribute to one's understanding of the past.

Literature Skills

There is no question that children must have some control over the basic reading skills in order to appreciate literature. Without the ability to pronounce words easily, understand what is stated directly and infer meanings, and read critically, they cannot meet the requirements for reading literature. Literature is not intended to be used for teaching these skills, although pupils will grow in reading ability as they study imaginative writing. To appreciate literature children must focus their attention more upon the ways in which language is used to convey meaning than upon the mechanics of reading. They will not be able to read for appreciation if they must struggle to read and understand the ideas that an author expresses.

In order to develop an appreciation of literature children have to acquire a knowledge of its forms and uses of language and learn how to assess its worth. The following list of literary skills and understandings[2] is expressed

---

[2] Adapted from Charlotte S. Huck and Doris Young Kuhn, *Children's Literature in the Elementary School,* 2nd ed. New York: Holt, Rinehart and Winston, Inc., 1968, pp. 688–91.

in behavioral terms and may serve as a basis for planning the literature curriculum:

Understands Types of Literature
    Differentiates between prose and poetry
    Differentiates fiction from nonfiction
    Recognizes folk tale, fable, myth
    Identifies realistic fiction
    Identifies historical fiction
    Identifies fantasy

Understands Components of Fiction
    Recognizes structure of plot
    Recognizes climax of story
    Recognizes character delineation and development
    Recognizes theme of story
    Recognizes setting
    Describes author's style or use of words
    Recognizes point of view

Understands Components of Poetry
    Identifies forms of poetry
    Interprets meaning
    Looks for imagery
    Describes choice of words
    Recognizes sound effects

Evaluates Literature
    Understands that authors write to achieve purpose
    Evaluates setting
    Evaluates plot
    Evaluates characterization
    Evaluates style of writing
    Evaluates point of view
    Evaluates theme

Many of the skills that are listed under each broad heading may be regarded as an umbrella for different understandings. For example, in recognizing the climax of a story children identify the details and events that lead toward it and explain how the author creates a mood of suspense and anticipation. In understanding how a poet creates imagery they can point to figures of speech and describe how effective they are in serving their purpose. These skills are not unlike the basic reading skills in that children develop proficiency in them by learning to master skills that are subsumed under them.

Teaching Literature

The purpose of teaching literature to children is to increase their appreciation of it and thereby enable them to enjoy it more. It is not intended to develop the skills they need to read informational materials nor take the place of recreational reading.

Since it is assumed that children can read the stories or poems that will be introduced to develop some literary understandings, it should not be necessary to prepare and guide the reading of them in the same way that teachers might do when they concentrate on basic reading skills. Nor does it mean that children will merely read selections without any teacher direction. What is needed is a proper mix of teacher participation and freedom to read so that children know in what directions they are moving and at the same time are allowed to enjoy selections without too much interference.

Appreciation of literature may be developed through oral and silent reading, listening to and discussing stories and books. Some stories may be read entirely by the teacher, who may wish the children to listen for intonation and stress that emphasize meaning. All children enjoy listening to stories, and the interpretations conveyed by skillful reading add to their appreciation of them. Poetry is intended to be read aloud; teacher and children may share in its oral reading. Other stories may be read silently, while many could be studied through silent and oral reading. In the latter instance the children might read the narrative parts silently and the dialogue orally. If the reading of a selection were shared, the teacher could read the descriptive parts and the children assume the roles of the speakers.

A brief introduction to a story is usually all that is necessary to launch its reading. If there is some background information that the children should have about the author or some aspect of the story, the teacher can supply it quickly. The purpose for reading the particular selection could be tied to a brief recounting of children's experiences that are related to the story. On some occasions it would be helpful if the teacher read the opening paragraphs to set the stage for the rest of the story and whet the children's appetite for more.

The discussion that follows the reading should not attempt to dissect the story or poem in order to learn what it means. Instead, by calling attention to relevant passages and raising pertinent questions about them children will be helped to discover what they need to learn about the form and language of literature.

The study of literature begins early, and teachers may introduce children to imaginative writing before they can read much for themselves. An outline of a possible literature lesson for first-graders follows.

Madeline
by Ludwig Bemelmans

This is a picture storybook about a devilish little girl who remains a distinct personality despite her surroundings. Since the illustrations are an integral part of the text, the teacher refers to both to help the children understand the author's portrayal of the character.

The following questions could lead the children to discover what kind of person Madeline is after the teacher reads the story and shows the pictures to them.

1. With whom did Madeline live?

2. How were all the children expected to behave? What parts and pictures show this?

3. What did Madeline do that shows that she was different from the other girls?

4. Did Madeline change her ways after her appendix operation? How can you tell?

Note that the questions do not require the children to be concerned with the details of the story except as they help them understand what kind of person Madeline was and how the author developed the character. In this picture storybook as in others the illustrations are as important as the text for they not only illustrate events but also are part of the story itself. An example of the latter function is the drawing of the twelve children walking with Miss Clavel. All heads are facing straight ahead, that is, all except Madeline's, whose body is turned around and facing in the opposite direction. This picture is a clue to what children might expect in the story. It is important that the children realize that the author's pictures may tell as much about a character or story as the words he uses.

The next outline is for a lesson on how poetry uses language to create imagery.

"Rain in Summer"
—HENRY WADSWORTH LONGFELLOW

How beautiful is the rain!
After the dust and heat,
In the broad and fiery street,
In the narrow lane,
How beautiful is the rain!

How it clatters along the roofs
Like the tramp of hoofs!
How it gushes and struggles out
From the throat of the overflowing spout!
Across the window-pane
It pours and pours;
And swift and wide,
With a muddy tide,
Like a river down the gutter roars
The rain, the welcome rain!

Children should not have too much difficulty understanding what the poet is saying to them. But the way in which he uses language to create imagery should be discovered by them. This is a poem that should be read aloud so that the sounds and rhythm of words may be heard.

What does the title of the poem suggest *to you*?

The pupils might say that it reminds them of warm summer rains, or the times they played in the rain or the picnic that was spoiled by a sudden shower.

To what is the summer heat compared?

Have the children read the first few lines to look for the word that tells them how hot it was.

Reread the rest of the poem. What kinds of sounds does the rain make? What words help you to hear the rain?

The rain *clatters* and *gushes* and *roars*.

Besides using words which help you hear the rain, how does the poet create a picture of it?

The children may be able to point to the comparison he makes between the sound of horses' hoofs and raindrops.

What words give the impression that the rain and spout are alive?

It may be necessary to reread these lines:

How it gushes and struggles out
From the throat of the overflowing spout!

The teacher would summarize the techniques the poet used to create mind pictures through words: comparisons, appropriate sounds, and personification. Other poems which utilize similar devices might be read and compared with this poem.

Oral Reading

The following may be reminiscent of the experiences some have had in school:

Teacher: Take out your readers (or social studies books) and turn to page 43. Mary, you begin reading at the top of the page until I tell you to stop.

Mary: (Reads two paragraphs before the teacher interrupts.)

Teacher: That was very good. Dick, you continue.

Dick: The—sky was—turning a—light, uh, I mean pink, etc.

Teacher: Class, what did you think of that?

Class: Dick can't read good.

Teacher: You mean well. Harry, begin reading where Dick left off.

Harry: There was hardly any wind on the lake . . .

Teacher: You weren't paying attention! Anne, tell Harry where to begin.

Anne: I don't know . . . .

Teacher: Margaret!

Margaret: The last paragraph on page 43.

Harry: (Begins to read.)

Teacher: Harry, how many times have I told you to read with expression?

Harry: (Silence. He starts to read.)

Teacher: Class, what word did Harry leave out?

and so on . . . .

This sample of what occurred during oral reading is no exaggeration. It fails to reflect the embarrassment of children who were unable to pronounce the words easily and stumbled along as best they could and in some cases the fear of being called upon to read and not knowing the place. What is evident is the utter uselessness of the practice of merely having children take turns reading aloud and requiring others to follow along and sit in judgment on them. Undoubtedly, one of the reasons oral reading fell into disrepute was because of the way in which it was conducted.

The practice of having children take turns reading aloud has been defended on the grounds that it provides opportunities to use reading and speaking skills and gives teachers information about their reading. Teachers also report that children want to read aloud—even those who read poorly. Insofar as providing practice is concerned, oral reading conducted in the manner previously indicated does not accomplish very much except perhaps to reinforce poor reading habits and negative attitudes toward reading. To remind children to "read with expression" does not teach children how to modify their behavior. Although oral reading is recommended as a diagnostic tool, it is not intended to be used in group settings where its purposes are lost and children are humiliated. There is no doubt that some pupils wish to take their turns during oral reading sessions even though they don't read well. Perhaps they prefer some recognition to none at all. But couldn't conditions for oral reading be made more favorable so that children who don't read as well as others might not be penalized and others who must listen made to suffer through the experience?

During the past four or five decades there has been a decline in oral reading instruction on the grounds that most of the reading that children and adults are required to do calls for silent reading. There is no question about the relative efficiency of silent reading over oral reading in accomplishing these tasks. However, the fact that most people engage in silent reading does not preclude the necessity for learning to read orally. It isn't unlikely that more of us would not avoid oral reading were we better prepared for it.

Purposes for Oral Reading

In everyday living there are untold uses for oral reading. Very often one reads an interesting or entertaining item in a newspaper or magazine and wishes others to hear it. Rather than rely upon memory and chance the possibility of leaving out crucial parts, the material is read rather than told. Then there are occasions when important statements or announcements must be made before others. Many people find it easier to read than memorize them or speak extemporaneously. Persons often debate issues and need to turn to authoritative statements for support. "Listen to this" is not uncommonly heard when points are made. Oral reading is used to share information more than to entertain but there is a growing interest in the formation of small groups that meet regularly to read plays and books for enjoyment. Although the old family practice of setting aside time to read a book has not been revived to any great extent, there are occasions when parents do share choice passages with their children and children with their peers. One does not have to look far for any number of situations that favor oral reading.

Teachers do not have to create artificial conditions to justify oral reading in their classrooms. The emphasis that they give to oral reading in the study of literature is not unwarranted, and its benefits might well be carried over to the reading children do. There is no reason why children should not share in the oral reading of a story or poem if they can do it well enough to hold their listeners' interest. They may provide their interpretations of characters by reading the dialogue in the way they believe the persons in the story would sound. When they engage in discussions about the author's views or writing techniques, the children prove their points by reading selected portions that they believe support them. The reading of a play is a natural setting that demands oral interpretation. When pupils discuss and share the books they have read for personal enjoyment, they will want to read parts of them to the others to demonstrate their good or bad features. Creative activities that emerge from literature experiences—the writing of prose and poetry, puppetry, dramatics—involve oral reading. Some schools make it a common practice for older boys and girls to go into the lower grades and read to the younger ones. Aside from the practical needs which oral reading meets, there is the personal satisfaction and pleasure that children will experience from reading aloud passages that are rich in vocabulary. Much is gained from hearing the beauty of words that create the illusion of reality through the images they evoke. These are selections that *should* be read orally; to do otherwise would leave a gap that silent reading could not fill.

IDEAS FOR DISCUSSION

There is one characteristic that is common to most activities which involve oral reading—the presence of an audience. There isn't much justification for anyone to read aloud when others are present if no one is listening to him. If every individual has a copy of the material and is reading silently as another reads it orally, there is no real audience, for it is doubtful that anyone is paying much attention to him.

When children are just beginning to read, it is a common and useful practice to reinforce what they are learning through oral reading. They do follow along in their books as a child reads a sentence in response to a question or other purposes. In addition, these young children derive satisfaction from knowing that they are learning to read as they demonstrate their ability to pronounce the words and understand their meaning.

But while older children have the same compelling needs for success and approval, they can be met in other ways. They also do not require the same oral reinforcement since they are much more secure in their reading abilities. As children develop independence in reading, they should be encouraged to listen to others who are reading orally; otherwise they will fail to receive the messages which the readers are trying to convey. Besides, it is discouraging to know that one's efforts are not appreciated; the quality of the oral reading will suffer if children know that few are paying any attention to them. This is one of the main reasons why it is important to encourage oral reading that is purposeful: the reader has something to say and the audience has reason to listen.

Promoting Oral Reading

Before pupils are able to convey the ideas and feelings of a writer to others through oral reading, they must first secure them themselves. This means that they have to grasp literal and inferred meanings and evaluate them. Of real value is an understanding of the larger work and the background for the selection. In order to more fully appreciate what the author intended, children must be able to visualize through the words and structure the images and attitudes that both carry. In short, effective oral reading has as a prerequisite a degree of understanding which cannot fall far short of the true meaning.

It is hardly realistic to expect children to pick up material with which they are unfamiliar and read it orally in such a way that others will want to listen and will grasp its meaning and implications. For one thing, they aren't likely to establish any real purposes for this oral reading—a condition that is bound to influence their ability to convey what the author intended. Moreover, they will not have the opportunity to unravel any difficulties in reading and understanding the material, the result of which will be quite evident in their rendering of it.

It is essential that pupils have at least the opportunity to read the material to themselves before they offer it to an audience. This preparatory reading will have occurred in situations where they are discussing outcomes of study and seeking to prove or disprove some points by calling attention to selected portions of materials. More careful preparation is likely to be required for the presentation of a story or poem or participation with others in dramatic or choral readings. One of the surest ways to discourage oral reading is to have pupils read materials they haven't seen before. Not only do the results produce negative feelings toward reading within those who perform poorly but also in the audience who are compelled to sit through unproductive periods that are characterized by reading errors, hesitations, poor phrasing and voice quality, and inappropriate timing.

It should be clear that proficiency in oral reading is closely identified with silent reading and speech. Children whose silent reading abilities are inadequately developed will reveal these deficiencies in the way they read orally. Children with poor speech patterns will have difficulty conveying ideas and moods to others. In both situations the teacher's efforts would be directed toward helping children overcome their basic weaknesses rather than concentrating upon the oral reading which reflects their weaknesses. Effective instruction in basic reading skills and appreciation skills should go a long way toward overcoming oral reading weaknesses. Opportunities to participate in activities that motivate pupils to express themselves clearly and forcefully could produce results that will carry over to their oral reading, with teacher guidance.

Teachers need to be alert to the characteristics of good oral reading so that they may be used as criteria for assessing how adequate their own oral reading is and determining the nature of the reading guidance they should offer the children. Included among these characteristics are the following:

1. adequate articulation of words
2. flexibility in rate, pitch, and loudness
3. proper phrasing
4. effective use of pauses.
5. appropriate facial expressions and bodily movements.

All of the characteristics are present in varying degrees in natural speech, but children ordinarily are not aware of some of the speech devices they use to express their ideas nor are they capable of utilizing them to their fullest extent. That oral reading is an art can hardly be doubted when the performances of professionals are compared to those of lesser talent.

Teachers should read to children not only to foster greater appreciation but to serve as a model that they might emulate. They might interrupt their reading by making a pointed remark that alerts the children to listen to the way in which a given word or passage is treated. For example, before coming to a word such as *swish* they could have pupils note the way it will be read to convey its very sound (by slowly drawing out the word and extending the final sound rather than reading it quickly). Children may listen for the modulations in the teacher's voice as he reads passages that convey such feelings as surprise, doubt, anger, or sorrow and identify each. These brief interruptions should not interfere with the story's continuity.

Recordings of familiar children's literature by excellent readers may be introduced to demonstrate how the voice can be used to make the stories more interesting and appealing. After the children have discussed the ways in which the narrator produced special effects, they might record portions of the same story and play it back to determine if they were able to effectively transmit the significance of the author's words and ideas.

In teaching children to read orally the emphasis should be upon improving the reading rather than on the skill in question. If a child were to place the emphasis on one word rather than another (or on none at all) and thereby fail to convey the intended meaning, the teacher could raise a question about the intended meaning and whether it was realized by his oral interpretation. The child might try reading the passage again after deciding where the stress should fall. Other children could be asked to read the same passage to show how they interpret it.

Activities involving oral expression can have carry-over effects on oral reading since both contain common elements. One activity is *creative dramatics*. Children may read a story themselves or listen to it as it is read or told to them. The setting, events, and characters are discussed so that they understand the circumstances in which the characters find themselves and how the characters feel. A scene is selected for playing and the children take on the personalities of the characters involved. They behave as they believe the characters would and say the things they feel are appropriate. On occasion, pantomime is utilized to create the story thread and characterizations. The same "play" can be done by more than one group of actors and their interpretations compared.

Puppetry is an activity related to creative dramatics. A favorite story—one in which action and words convey ideas, tone and mood—can be the subject of a puppet show. Elaborate preparations are avoided: the children make simple puppets out of paper bags or stockings after they have discussed the characters they wish to portray and speak their roles without written scripts. The actions and dialogue are spontaneous and few if any props are used. How effectively the players portray the characters is revealed through the responses the audience makes to the presentation.

Choral reading is another activity that can promote oral interpretation. Children who don't read as well as others or who are shy or timid will be able to participate in a group without fear of embarrassment. Their confidence in their abilities will grow as they experience the pleasures of creating the meaning and mood of literature through oral expression.

Literature that is rhythmic and lyrical in nature is suitable for choral reading. For this reason poetry is favored over most prose. At the primary level nursery rhymes and simple poems that children understand are recited in unison. If there is more than one speaker, the boys may take one part and the girls another. At higher levels poetry that has been read for appreciation can be discussed for the purpose of deciding how certain parts should be read and which groups should be responsible for them. If the meaning and mood are clearly understood, the children will be able to suggest which lines should be read slowly or rapidly, whether soft or loud tones are suitable, if falling or rising inflections are preferred, where emphasis is given. These same considerations will pertain to individual interpretation, and pupils should be able to transfer the qualities they have learned from group performances to their personal oral reading efforts.

Independent Reading

An important objective of the reading curriculum is to promote permanent interests in reading. It is also the long-range goal of the literature program. There is no reason to repeat what reading can do for individuals except to say that it possesses the seeds of personal and social development and the potential for inspiration and pleasure.

A well-structured and comprehensive reading program will contain the elements which contribute to the development of leisure-time reading habits. Children who are successful in mastering the skills of reading and appreciation are more likely to acquire favorable attitudes toward reading activities than those who fail to do so. The nature of the instruction children receive is bound to be a powerful determinant of their progress in and feelings toward reading. But mere mastery of these skills is no guarantee that children will turn to books and other printed materials as they do to television, films, games, and other leisure-time pursuits. Reading must be as satisfying to them as these other attractions; otherwise it cannot compete with them for children's free time. What teachers can do to create favorable reading climates that promote satisfying experiences is the subject of this section.

Reading Interests

Recognition of the importance of bringing children and books together has led to a continuing study of their reading interests. It is believed that more reading will occur if children are given the opportunity to read what they are interested in. This belief has its origins in the psychology of learning which views interest as a stimulator of behavior that increases as well as reduces drives. An awareness of the importance of interests can be seen in the changing nature of children's materials that are used for reading instruction. Their present contents reflect more of what research reveals about children's reading interests than they have in the past.

Huus[3] has summarized the conclusions from early studies about the general nature of children's reading interests. They are: (1) interests of children vary with age and grade level; (2) few differences between the interests of boys and girls are apparent before age nine; (3) notable differences in the interests of boys and girls appear between ages ten and thirteen, especially at age twelve; (4) girls read more than boys, but boys have a wider interest range and read a greater variety of materials; (5) adult fiction of a romantic type has an earlier interest for girls than for boys; (6) boys like chiefly adventure and girls like fiction, but mystery stories appeal to both; (7) boys seldom show preference for a "girl's" book, but girls will read boys' books to a greater degree.

A number of more recent studies[4] reveal more specific information about the nature of children's reading interests and the factors that influence them. Although the methods that investigators have used to identify reading interests varied significantly—some had children respond to questionnaires or pictures, others read different stories to children, and still others observed their reading and library habits—the results seemed to point to similar conclusions:

1. Intelligence, reading ability, and socioeconomic factors do not seem to influence reading choices significantly but sex and age do.

---

[3] Helen Huus, "Interpreting Research in Children's Literature," *Children, Books and Reading* (Perspectives in Reading No. 3). Newark, Del.: International Reading Association, 1964, p. 125.

[4] Robert Emans, "What Do Children in the Inner City Like to Read?" *The Elementary School Journal, 69* (December, 1968), pp. 119–22; Robin C. Ford and James Koplyay, "Children's Story Preferences," *The Reading Teacher, 22* (December, 1968), pp. 233–37; George Norvell, *What Boys and Girls Like to Read.* Morristown, N. J.: Silver Burdett

2. Six- and seven-year-olds of both sexes prefer stories about real animals, fantasy, humor, heroes, adventure.

3. Older boys favor stories that deal with outdoor life, courage, adventure, animals, sports, science fiction, humor.

4. Older girls prefer reading stories involving mystery, home and school, romantic love, heroines, the supernatural.

It is clear that the reading interests of children at any age level are varied and that the only way to meet those of a particular group is to find out what they are. Perhaps a better way to do this is to observe how children respond to different stories that are read to them and what books they select for their personal reading. Naturally, their responses are limited to the kinds of selections read to them and the availability of books that they are able to read for themselves. The wider the assortment, the more valid will be the assessment of their reading interests. Responses to questionnaires which require children to tell what kinds of activities or stories they prefer or select them from a long list of possible choices will not yield the same results as the former. There is enough evidence to know that expressed reading preferences are not synonymous with actual reading choices.

There are other cautions that ought to be considered. It would be incorrect to assume that because children enjoy animal stories they will want to hear and read stories about all kinds of animals. Some may have a special interest in dogs or horses and are not at all concerned about cats or other pets. Moreover, they may prefer one kind of animal story to another. For example, children might not have the slightest interest in a story that stresses their care and training but will be "turned on" by one in which there is a relationship between animals and people. Story content appropriate for a group cannot be selected solely on the basis of a preferred category.

It is important that teachers start with children's present interests to promote independent reading. However, the assumption that their reading interests are static and cannot be broadened is unwarranted. Children know only that which they have experienced and new exposures to all kinds of writing can foster new reading interests. Moreover, television, radio, movies, and other influences are known to have affected children's interests so that younger boys and girls now show a preference for stories that formerly were the choice of older ones. It is often impossible to know what stories will capture children's fancy and they may be enticed to try new reading diets if good samples of different kinds are readily available. At the same time children's reading tastes are likely to improve with broadened reading interests.

Company, 1958; Helen Rogers and H. Alan Robinson, "Reading Interests of First Graders," *Elementary English, 40* (November, 1963), pp. 707–11; Jo M. Stanchfield, *A Study of Boys' Reading Interests in Relation to Reading Achievement.* Unpublished Doctoral Dissertation, University of Southern California, 1960; Paul A. Witty, "Pupil Interests in the Elementary Grades," *Education, 83* (April, 1963), pp. 451–62.

Selecting Books for Children

Children do reflect reading preferences and these should be honored when considering literature that will be read to or by them. Teachers have the added responsibility of extending children's horizons, for to do less will only reinforce what they already know and as some writers believe, cause them to lose interest in reading. It is comforting to be surrounded by and repeat what is familiar but children do have the capacity and need for new experiences, for this is the way that they grow. No damage is done to the developmental view which suggests that children have needs which must be met in accordance with nature's scheme. Different experiences facilitate children's progress from one stage to the next.

Closely associated with children's reading interests is the question of reading tastes. As children extend their reading interests, so should they be developing an appreciation for good literature. Discriminating readers are not born but made. Only by repeated exposures to finer writing as children grow in their ability to read and appreciate it do they develop some yardsticks of quality. The movement away from comic or series books can be realized if the reader is surrounded by other literature that is as enjoyable and satisfying. "Unless he is exposed to the best during this process, he will not know how exciting a plot can be, how clear a picture words can paint, how cleverly solutions can be devised, what real people he can meet, and how wonderfully the words roll along. . . ."[5] After having experienced the artistry found in quality literature, he is ready to compare it to what he finds in other materials. He will know the difference between the adventure portrayed in comic books and that found in such books as *Treasure Island* and *Bushbabies*.

Evaluating Literature

In order for children to develop an appreciation for good literature, they should experience it. This implies that teachers and others who are responsible for bringing books and children together need to know which ones "can do something" for their readers or listeners in addition to possessing a literary quality that distinguishes them from the ordinary. Children can learn to evaluate literature, too, by contrasting stories that arouse their spirits with others that fail to touch them. Teachers can help children identify the elements which make a difference if they are aware of them.

Children should read stories that "talk" to them. This means that be it realistic fiction, fantasy, biography or other nonfiction, it should have something worthwhile to say to them. Otherwise, children will learn to be satisfied with superficial ideas and surface meanings and will fail to appreciate literature that comes to grips with the real issues of living and the

---

[5] Helen Huus, "Books, Children and Reading," in Marjorie S. Johnson and Roy Kress, eds., *Developmental Reading: Diagnostic Teaching* (Proceedings of the 1967 Annual Reading Institute, Temple University). Philadelphia: Temple University, 1968, p. 91.

motivations of human behavior. It is not enough that children read but that they grow through as well as in reading. For unless they are unwilling to settle for easy and pat solutions to man's problems, they will become adults whose vision is short and narrow and who won't understand what living and people are about. Children can read for enjoyment and at the same time profit from the experiences of others who are willing to share their observations and wisdom.

Insofar as the content is concerned, there are some considerations which distinguish worthy from questionable literature. These have been stated in the form of questions which teachers and children may apply to different forms of literature.[6]

1. Does the reading of the story (whatever is genre) offer a wholesome experience?

2. Does the story leave the reader with positive feelings?

3. Is it possible that some developmental needs will be met by reading the story?

4. Will the story help the reader deal realistically with some of his problems?

5. Does the story help the reader develop worthwhile attitudes and values?

6. Does the story have worthy characters with whom the reader might identify?

Positive responses to these kinds of questions will give some indications of a story's merits and how suitable it is for meeting the objectives of a literature program. Lest there be some apprehensions about the nature of literature that would fulfill these requirements, it should be clear that there is no intention to shelter children from truths and realities and leave the impression that all and everyone are sweet and good. Unfortunate and undeserved treatment and scheming people are part of life and things do not always turn out for the best. At the same time unhappiness is balanced by joy and evil by good. Without attempting to sugarcoat reality, stories can stress the positive aspects of man's relationships and demonstrate that some behaviors are worthy of emulation while others are not to be condoned.

In addition to evaluating the excellence of content the reader should be concerned about the way in which the writer uses his craft to make the reading of the story a meaningful experience. The story unfolds through events and characters which the author may treat in an interesting and entertaining way. Its literary quality will be revealed through the artistry with which the author is able to create characters, plot, theme, and style. The following criteria may be used to judge the literary quality of literature for children.

---

[6] Adapted from Laurel B. Boetto, "From Analysis to Reaction," in Helen Huus, ed., *Evaluating Books For Children and Young People* (Perspectives in Reading, No. 10). Newark, Del.: International Reading Association, 1968, pp. 31, 32.

Characters

1. They behave like real people in situations that confront them.
2. They reflect the actions of those they are supposed to represent by their manner, attitudes, speech, and behavior.
3. They show evidence of change as a result of events and the effects of others upon them.
4. They have identifiable personalities from which the action flows.
5. They demonstrate behaviors with which children can identify.

Plot

1. The action is not contrived but develops naturally from the personality and behavior of the characters.
2. There is a smooth flow from one event to the next and each is tied in some way to the other.
3. Children can relate their experiences to what is happening in the story.
4. There is enough action and suspense to sustain interest.

Theme

1. The idea of the story should emerge from the portrayal of characters, events, and setting.
2. What the story is really about should be revealed through surface events and the actions of the characters.
3. Commonplace ideas should be treated with originality.
4. The story should present worthwhile ideas for children to consider.

Style

1. How the author uses language is influenced by the nature of the characters and events.
2. The language flow is smooth and natural so that it reads easily.
3. Lengthy descriptions and frequent repetitions are avoided.
4. The manner of writing is imaginative, vivid, moving, original, stirring.

Aids for Book Selection

Each year over the past five years well over 2000 new juvenile books have been published in the United States. Add to this amount the number of titles imported from other countries and new editions of older books and the total production is impressive. The problem of trying to keep up with these books is a staggering one even for those who do nothing else but read them for professional reasons. Certainly teachers do not have the time to become familiar with all the titles nor do they have access to most of them. One ready source of information is the reviews of children's literature which appear in a number of different periodicals. It is estimated that close to three-fourths of all titles published annually are reviewed by them. Although all reviewers do not follow the same criteria in evaluating books, teachers may have confidence that their comments represent a fair assessment of them.

The first group of periodicals listed below are the most widely used by librarians and teachers for securing information about the content and quality of children's books. The other listed sources review specialized books or are features in other publications.

Booklist (formerly *The Booklist and Subscription Books Bulletin*). American Library Association. Issued semimonthly.
This publication reviews books for readers of all ages that are recommended for purchase. Included are reviews of reference and audiovisual materials.

Bulletin of the Center for Children's Books. University of Chicago Press. Published monthly.
This *Bulletin* publishes reviews of not recommended and recommended books. Included are lists of bibliographies and professional books.

The Horn Book Magazine. Horn Book, Inc. Published bimonthly.
This magazine presents critical reviews of current children's books with a special section on science. Articles by and about authors and illustrators of outstanding books are featured regularly.

The School Library Journal. R. R. Bowker Company. Published monthly, September-May.
This journal reviews a large number of current books and audiovisual materials. Included are reviews of not recommended books. Featured are lists of paperbacks and other materials and professional reading as well as articles for librarians and teachers.

Appraisal: Children's Science Books. Children's Science Book Review Committee, Harvard Graduate School of Education. Issued three times a year.

Bookbird. International Board on Books for Young People. Available from the Package Library of Foreign Children's Books. Published quarterly.

Book Review Digest. H. W. Wilson Company. Issued annually.

Childhood Education. Association for Childhood Education International. Published monthly, September-May.

Choice: Books for College Libraries. Association of College and Research Libraries. Issued monthly.

Elementary English. National Council of Teachers of English. Published monthly, October-May.

The Grade Teacher. Teachers Publishing Corporation. Published monthly.

The Instructor. Instructor Publications, Inc. Published monthly.

The New York Times Book Review. New York Times Publishing Company. Published weekly.

The Reading Teacher. International Reading Association. Published monthly, September-May.

Saturday Review. Saturday Review, Inc. Published weekly.

Science Books: A Quarterly Review. American Association for the Advancement of Science. Published quarterly.

Virginia Kirkus Service Bulletin. Kirkus Service, Inc. Issued bimonthly.

There are a large number of annotated lists which classify children's books by topics and suggested age levels. Included among them are lists of books of special interest. While many do not evaluate the books they list, some do limit those they include and these may be ascertained from their titles. A number of these lists are revised periodically.

AAAS Science Booklist for Children. Compiled by H. J. Deason. American Association for the Advancement of Science, 1963.

Adventuring with Books: A Reading List for Elementary Grades. National Council of Teachers of English, 1966.

Africa: An Annotated List of Printed Materials Suitable for Children. Information Center on Children's Cultures, U. S. Committee for UNICEF, 1968.

Asia: A Guide to Books for Children. Compiled by M. B. Wiese and others. Asia Society, 1966.

Basic Book Collection for Elementary Grades. Compiled by Miriam S. Mathes and others. American Library Association, 1960.

Best Books for Children. R. R. Bowker Company, 1969.

Bibliography of Books for Children. Association for Childhood Education International, 1969.

Books about Negro Life for Children. Compiled by Augusta Baker. New York Public Library, 1963.

Books for Beginning Readers. Compiled by Elizabeth Guilfoile. National Council of Teachers of English, 1962.

Books for Children. American Library Association, 1960–70.

Books for Elementary School Libraries: An Initial Collection. Compiled by Elizabeth Hodges. American Library Association, 1969.

Children's Books to Enrich the Social Studies. Compiled by Helen Huus. National Council for the Social Studies, 1966.

Children's Books Too Good To Miss. Compiled by May H. Arbuthnot. Case Western Reserve University Press, 1966.

Children's Bookshelf: A Parents Guide to Good Books for Boys and Girls. Child Study Association of America, 1962.

Children's Catalog. H. W. Wilson Company. Annual.

Elementary School Library Collection. Edited by Mary V. Gaver. Bro-Dart Foundation, 1967.

Good Books for Children by Mary K. Eakin. University of Chicago Press, 1966.

Good Reading for Poor Readers. Compiled by George Spache. University of Florida Reading Clinic, 1964.

Growing Up with Paperbacks. R. R. Bowker Company, 1969.

A Guide to Science Reading. Compiled by Hilary J. Deason. New American Library, 1963.

I Can Read It Myself. Compiled by Frieda M. Heller. Ohio State University, 1965.

The Negro in Schoolroom Literature. Edited by M. W. Koblitz. Center for Urban Education, 1967.

Notable Children's Books, 1940–1959. American Library Association, 1966.

A Parents' Guide to Children's Reading by Nancy Larrick. Doubleday and Company, 1969.

Reading Ladders for Human Relations. Edited by Muriel Crosby and others. American Council on Education, 1964.

Subject Index to Books for Intermediate Grades. Compiled by Mary K. Eakin. American Library Association, 1963.

Subject Index to Books for Primary Grades. Compiled by Mary K. Eakin. American Library Association, 1967.

We Build Together. Edited by Charlemae Rollins. National Council of Teachers of English, 1967.

Promoting Reading Habits

Children who participate in a literature program that makes them keenly aware of the joys they can find in books will seek them out as surely as they pursue other experiences which give them pleasure. Children engage in a variety of preferred recreational and leisure-time activities and each competes for their time. Reading will be able to withstand the attractions that other activities have for them if it yields comparable results. Teachers can promote reading through a series of measures that are designed to encourage and stimulate children to explore books on their own.

Classroom Climate

If children are to realize that reading for pleasure is as much a natural part of their daily lives as reading to learn, teachers must demonstrate their feelings and commitment to it. One of the ways they can show how much they value recreational reading is to provide the surroundings and atmosphere that are conducive to the activity.

Classroom Libraries. Each classroom should have its own library of books. Books should be where children spend most of their school day, which typically is the self-contained classroom. The fact that classrooms have their own collection of books does not preclude the need for a central school library; in fact, it provides another reason for its being. The school librarian in partnership with the classroom teacher can arrange for books to be shipped on a regular schedule from and to the library so that classroom collections are changed periodically. Books may be borrowed from the public library and children might also be willing to bring in some of their own books to supplement the collection.

Some part of the classroom should be set aside where children might browse among the bookshelves and be able to read without too much interference and in comfort. They should be able to go to this area whenever they have free time such as before the start of school or after lunch or when they have completed their assignments. It would be desirable to provide tables and comfortable chairs for children's use. Some children might prefer sitting or stretching out on the floor, which could be covered with a colorful rug or mat.

The children will be more eager to use such facilities if they have a share in their planning and operation. They can help decide what books their library should contain and the way in which it might be organized. Some classes are known to establish a simple system for checking books in and out and keeping their libraries in order. Pupils might prefer to select children to act as classroom librarians with specific responsibilities for their care. Others could decide how their libraries should operate and expect everyone to assume a personal responsibility for them.

Book Displays. Room book displays create interest in reading. These may take the form of bulletin boards on which colorful pictures and comments and questions attract children's attention. A sign such as "Have you read this book?" or "Which book do you recommend?" or "What book has more pictures like this one?" or "Who knows who this character is?" or "What book did this author write?" will stimulate children to start thinking about and looking for certain books. These bulletin boards might contain colorful book jackets of books by one author or on a special theme or pictures about stories and characters that children have made. The purpose of the bulletin board is to keep children informed about books they might want to read and excite their interest in them.

Books might be displayed along with illustrated posters and models. Posters might announce the publication of new books which the school has obtained or a coming event such as a book fair or celebration or book awards. Teachers report the effectiveness of using models of characters to entice children to examine books. Who, for example, could resist finding out about the adventures of *Pinocchio* if he were standing alongside the book with a sign that said, "I was swallowed by a whale! Join me!" Dioramas and shadow boxes which depict scenes from books form attractive displays that teachers or pupils might prepare to introduce children to books and authors.

Sharing Literature

There is not a more effective way of bringing children and books together than the teacher's showing enthusiasm for them. This enthusiasm will be reflected in her knowledge of children's books and her ability to share the best of them with her pupils.

Reading to Children. It is a common practice for teachers of young children to read stories to them. There is no reason why teachers of older children should not continue this same practice. Both good and poor readers will delight in hearing a story that is well read and often will then avidly read it for themselves. Oral reading by the teacher is a way to introduce children to books that they might otherwise not know about and to whet their appetites for them. The author recalls the satisfaction of listening to entire shorter stories and parts of longer ones written for children and read by an adult who was enthralled by them and who conveyed these feelings to his audience. He also remembers reading these same stories to fifth-graders who would clamor for books from which he read a few tasty morsels.

It is surprising how much some books written for children will be enjoyed by adults. These books are the ones that teachers should select for oral reading, for it is their enjoyment which they convey that will leave children with a positive feeling for them. Teachers have been known to spoil a book for children that they personally did not care for but read orally because of the recognition others gave it. Other means should be used to introduce children to such books.

Children should be as close to the teacher as possible without crowding. This makes for an intimate atmosphere and enables the children to see the reader's facial expressions as well as any pictures in the book. Some teachers have used an opaque projector to show pictures that are too small to be enjoyed by a large group. The teacher, before reading, might introduce the story by telling some interesting facts about the author and by displaying the book jacket. From the information and illustrations the children could speculate what the story is about. The introduction should be brief but help to establish the mood for listening to the story. Stories for younger children should be completed in one sitting; older children can sustain sufficient interest from one session to the next and wait for the story to be continued.

There is no requirement that stories have to be read from the beginning. The teacher could introduce the children to the story by telling them about the setting and characters and some of the plot. Then she might take up the story from that point. Moreover, the teacher might prefer that children finish the story for themselves after she has led them to the place where they have become too involved not to go on. Other stories might be enjoyed more thoroughly when heard, and these could be read by the teacher in their entirety.

Storytelling. Storytelling and book talks are related to reading to children. In storytelling the children gather around the teacher, who has prepared a story with which she is familiar. It is a good idea to have an outline of the main characters and the sequence of events leading to their conclusion so that the most interesting and crucial parts of the story will not be forgotten. The storyteller uses her voice, body and personality to convey the setting and mood of the story and express the feelings of the characters as well as to create images that help make the listeners know exactly what is occurring and transport them into the world that surrounds them.

Chalktalks are an effective means of interesting children in a particular book. As the tale unfolds, the storyteller makes quick sketches on the chalkboard or uses charcoal or a sketching pencil on paper fixed to an easel. The main character is drawn quickly as he is introduced so that the children have a picture of what he looks like. The setting and special events may be shown to make the story more vivid and real. In order to give an effective chalktalk the storyteller must be able to sketch the pictures as he tells the story. Teachers who do not feel capable of conducting such story sessions might use flannel or felt cutouts which they have prepared in advance and place them on a board covered with similar material as they tell the story. Simple stories with few characters are more appropriate to this form of presentation than long and complex tales.

A *booktalk* is a simple device that teachers might use to introduce children to and interest them in many books. A booktalk is intended to acquaint them with books by telling them in summary form what they are about without giving away the more interesting and crucial parts. Enough about the story is revealed so that the children can decide if they wish to read the book for themselves.

Teachers must be familiar with children's books in order to share their joys and beauty with pupils. They must read the books themselves if they are to present them effectively. All stories do not lend themselves equally well to storytelling or booktalks. Some whose language needs to be heard for its rhythm and character should be read orally rather be told. Stories with long descriptive passages and less action might better be subjects for storytelling than oral reading. However teachers introduce children to books, they must know them. To give superficial treatments of stories defeats their very purpose.

Reading and Discussing Books

In addition to sessions at which children read and discuss literature in order to learn how to appreciate it, there should be time in the school day for reading books of their choice and discussing them informally. One way that teachers can impress children with the importance of recreational reading is to give them opportunities to read whatever they prefer. Another is to read books at the same time as the children. Children are quick to learn what activities adults consider valuable by the time they devote to them. If as much time were spent in reading as in doing arithmetic computations, there would not be nearly the same need for trying to entice children to sample books.

Book Reports. One of the real benefits of the individualized reading program is the amount of reading children are able to do in the classroom. Is there any reason why children who participate in other reading programs should be denied the same benefits? Independent reading can be an outgrowth of learning activities or be separate from them. Whenever children complete reading a selection that has been used to develop or strengthen skills, they should be able to read related stories if they wish to do so. Teachers who conduct group reading activities can encourage those with whom they are not working to read for recreational purposes or set aside time when everyone is free to select books of their own choice.

Children who have enjoyed reading a good story should be encouraged to share their experience with others with the expectation that they might be encouraged to read it also. One way that they can share books is to give oral reports or reviews of them. These oral reports should be informal and not follow an established format. Who cannot remember one child after another standing before the class and reciting as if by rote the title and name of the author, the characters in the story, what happened, and why they liked the story? (Were there any children who dared to say that they didn't like the story or found it dull?) It might be useful for the teacher to discuss several books with them so that the children gain some notions about what they could include in their presentations. One of the purposes of a report is to entice the audience to read the story too (or to convince them that it isn't worthwhile bothering with). Therefore, the report should cover those aspects of the book which will help children make up their minds about it: how appealing the story and way of telling it are, what experiences the story discusses that children might know and enjoy, how this book compares with others they have read. To enliven the report children could read selected passages or show pictures that illustrate one or more of these points. Information about the author that is of interest to children and about other books he has written might add flavor and interest to the reports.

Small group reports can be arranged so that children who have read similar types of stories can exchange views about them. One group might consist of children who read informational books about nature, another of those who read biographies, and so on. Other children who might be interested in hearing about certain kinds of books should have the option of joining one of the groups. Another way to form informal sharing groups is to have children who are ready to give an oral report announce which book they will discuss and allow pupils to decide for themselves which one they prefer to listen to. These reports could go on simultaneously in different parts of the room or in separate areas (out in the corridor, for example) if some were available.

7 Source: Newsday, January 26, 1970. Peanuts © 1970 United Feature Syndicate.

The audience should be encouraged not only to listen attentively but to participate in the discussion that follows the reports. Some children may have read the same book and reacted differently to it than the reporter did. Opportunities to present different viewpoints about characters and story might cause some children to seek confirmation for themselves by reading it. Some children might be able to recommend similar books on the same topic or suggest even better ones. The children may pose questions for the reporter that will clarify some issues and aid them in deciding whether or not to read the book too. Teachers should take part in the discussion and guide it if it seems to lack direction or fails to enlighten.

IDEAS FOR DISCUSSION

Whether or not children should prepare written book reports is a debatable question. Some literature specialists take the position that there is nothing wrong in encouraging written book reports if children have the ability to prepare them. Others feel that nothing will dampen reading interests more than requiring them. Undoubtedly there is some middle course that teachers might take. They could give children the option of writing reports or presenting oral ones. Some children might prefer to give a report in the form of a series of pictures or mural or a dramatic presentation. But to compel children to give book reports, whether written or oral, is hardly a way to foster interest in reading.

Younger children might write a few sentences about a book and illustrate them with pictures drawn by them or cut out of magazines.

The Blue-Eyed Pussy

Did you ever see a blue-eyed pussy?
He looked for the land of many mice.
Can you guess what happened to him?

Or they might merely list the books they would recommend to others without writing any comments about them. These lists could be accompanied by pictures illustrating each of the stories.

Older children who prefer not to tell or write about the books they have read might just react to them with a comment or two which they could record in their notebooks or on cards. These comments might be used by the teacher in individual conferences with children as a basis for discussion and might give the teacher some indication of what directions his guidance of their independent reading should take. Those who are willing could prepare written reports for the class or school newspaper or comment on a professional review of a book which they have read but perhaps with which they differ.

Reading and the Communication Arts

Films and television may be used as springboards to reading. Librarians report that there is a run on books which are featured in dramatic presentations. Naturally there is no guarantee that children who see a film about

Heidi or a television program of *Hans Brinker* will rush out at the end of the programs to secure the books. But some children will be motivated to do just that, particularly if teachers call these special programs to their attention in advance of their showings and suggest the possibility of comparing the filmed or televised version with the book.

There is some debate about the nature of the influences the mass media have upon the behaviors and attitudes of children and adults. Some people claim that they have a great impact on their motivations and feelings. However, it appears that the mass media reinforce existing conditions rather than modify them. It is equally apparent that film and television can exert strong influences where information is lacking or no real commitment has been made. So it is entirely possible that both media can be used as springboards to certain types of literary materials. They might also help shape children's attitudes toward and appreciation for good literature and develop tastes in reading.

Films and filmstrips of children's literature are available from a number of distributors.[8] Filmstrips contain captions and texts and many have recordings to accompany the pictures. Filmstrips have an advantage over films in that they are more adaptable to individual requirements since children can easily operate the machines and view them without interfering with the rest of the class's activities. Films that are specially prepared for the enjoyment of literature and some produced for commercial showings may be rented or purchased. These may be used to introduce children to books or serve as a follow-up activity after reading them.

Some of the best literature for children is available on recordings.[9] Classics such as *Peter and the Wolf, Tubby the Tuba,* and *Peter Pan* have been recorded by well-known artists with musical accompaniment that can delight young and old. Such accomplished storytellers as Ruth Sawyer and such poets as Robert Frost and Carl Sandburg are featured on other recordings. Teachers might use these records to stimulate interest or provide enjoyable listening experiences.

SUMMARY

1. The study of children's literature has as its objectives the development of an appreciation of good writing and the promotion of permanent interests in reading. The enjoyment of literature is a long-range

---

[8] *American Library Association* (Chicago, Illinois 60611); *Coronet Films* (Chicago, Illinois 60611); *Encyclopaedia Britannica* (Chicago, Ilinois 60611); *National Education Television* (Bloomington, Indiana 47401); *Society for Visual Education* (Chicago, Illinois 60614); *Weston Woods* (Weston, Connecticut 06880); *Guidance Associates* (Pleasantville, N. Y. 10570).

[9] *American Library Association* (Chicago, Illinois 60611); *Caedmon Records* (New York, N. Y. 10001); *Folkway Records* (New York, N. Y. 10019); *Pathways of Sound* (Cambridge, Massachusetts 02188); *Spoken Arts* (New Rochelle, N. Y. 10804).

goal of the reading program; reading which successfully satisfies children's need for pleasure is apt to become one of the activities they turn to when they seek relief from the routines of home and school. Reading can be fun as well as enlightening for children who experience the treasures and delights that books hold. The study of literature gives promise of enhancing these satisfactions.

2. Children should learn how language is used to convey meaning, the differences between literary forms, and ways to assess their quality. The study of literature will enable them to differentiate between prose and poetry, fiction and nonfiction. It will help them to understand how authors develop characters, plot, theme, and setting, how words are used to create imagery and effects, how the imaginative is identified from the trite. These outcomes are the ingredients of appreciation and the means to increased enjoyment of literature.

3. The teaching of literature is intended to increase children's appreciation of it and not to develop their basic reading skills. It is assumed that children possess the skills to read stories and poetry but require instruction in order to develop literary understanding. Therefore, there is no need for the same kind of preparation and study that teachers might provide in reading selections that build word and comprehension skills. What will be stressed are the form and language of literature and how the author uses them to convey meaning and feeling.

4. Much prose, and all poetry, is written to be read orally. Children derive pleasure and understand more from hearing or reading aloud selections that are rich in vocabulary. Oral reading requires an audience, whether the teacher or children assume the main responsibility for interpreting selections. This implies that there are others who are as interested in listening to what is read as there are ones who are interested in doing the reading. On occasion, the teacher will carry the entire responsibility for oral reading; at other times he will share it with children, who have had ample time to study the material so that they can convey the author's meaning through variations in rate, inflection and loudness, proper phrasing, and the effective use of pauses, facial expression, and body movements.

5. One of the ways children can learn to improve their oral reading is by using the teacher as a model. He can alert children to listen to the use of his voice as he conveys different meanings and feelings in selected passages. Listening to recordings of children's literature by professionals and comparing their own interpretations will aid children in gaining insights into oral reading techniques. Participation in creative activities such as dramatics and puppetry and group choral reading will promote oral interpretation of literature.

6. The long-range objective of teaching literature is to promote permanent interests in reading. It is also a major objective of the reading program. Children who master the basic reading skills and skills of

appreciation are more likely to turn to reading as one leisure-time activity than others who fail to do so. Other pursuits are at least equally satisfying and teachers can create reading climates that promote independent recreational reading.

7. The reading interests of children seem to be influenced by factors of age and sex. Intelligence, reading ability, and socioeconomic factors do not appear to affect children's reading choices significantly. Six- and seven-year-olds of both sexes prefer humorous stories as well as stories about adventure, heroes, familiar animals, and fantasy. Older boys prefer stories of adventure, sports, science fiction, humor, courage, and animals while older girls choose stories that deal with romantic love, home and school, mystery, heroines, and the supernatural. Even though groups of children appear to prefer the same types of stories, individuals within the group will favor one kind over another. Teachers have been able to broaden the reading interests of children by exposing them to a variety of reading experiences.

8. Children can be taught to evaluate literature and thereby improve their reading tastes and broaden their reading interests. Teachers and children should consider the degree to which the content has something important to say to the reader and stresses positive attitudes about life and people. In addition, the quality of writing as measured by the way in which the author develops his characters, plot, theme, and style can be studied and compared with other literature. The realism of the characters and the plausibility of the plot are some indicators of literary quality that should be explored.

9. Teachers have a formidable task in trying to keep abreast of the quantity of books that are published each year. To aid them in selecting books that are appropriate for their pupils are professional publications that periodically review children's literature. Among these are *The Horn Book Magazine, Booklist, Bulletin of the Center for Children's Books,* and *The School Library Journal.* Annotated book lists of older and current books are published periodically and these are useful sources of information for becoming acquainted with all types of children's literature.

10. Teachers can stimulate interest in reading by making the classroom an attractive place where reading is enjoyed. Each classroom should have its own library of books and a comfortable corner where children may select and read the books they might want to read.

One of the best ways of bringing children and books together is to read books orally to them. Children experience real satisfaction from listening to a good story that an adult reads well. Teachers should read regularly to children of all ages. Some books could be read in their entirety while others would be read to tempt children to finish them on their own. Storytelling and book talks are other means that teachers may adopt to acquaint children with books that they will want to read.

Time within the school day should be set aside for reading and discussing books. If teachers truly believe that independent reading is an activity that schools should promote, they will consider the time spent reading and sharing books as productive as any. Children can be encouraged to share their reading experiences with others through oral book reports and reviews. Some children might prefer to use pictures or creative dramatics to convey their impressions of books. Whatever form the report takes, it becomes the basis for further discussion and evaluation.

STUDY QUESTIONS AND EXERCISES

1. In what ways are reading for appreciation and reading for enjoyment related?
2. "The skills and understandings children need for appreciating literature are not identical to those required to read other types of materials." How are they different?
3. In what ways is a lesson in appreciating literature different from a lesson in reading other kinds of writing?
4. Choose one skill from the outline of literary skills and understandings on page 285. For a selected piece of imaginative writing prepare a lesson that focuses its attention on that skill. Show how the material is used to achieve greater appreciation of it.
5. What can a classroom teacher do to promote life-long interest in reading? What aids can she utilize to increase her knowledge of books and stimulate children's interest in reading them?

SUGGESTIONS FOR FURTHER READING

See the following publications for a comprehensive treatment of children's literature:

May Hill Arbuthnot, *Children and Books* (3rd ed.). Glenview, Ill.: Scott, Foresman and Co., 1964.

Charlotte S. Huck and Doris Young Kuhn, *Children's Literature in the Elementary School* (2nd ed.). New York: Holt, Rinehart and Winston, Inc., 1968.

Lillian Smith, *The Unreluctant Years: A Critical Approach to Children's Literature.* Chicago: American Library Association, 1953.

Among the publications of the *International Reading Association* are several that are of special interest to students of children's literature and reading interests:

Mildred Dawson, ed., *Children, Books and Reading* (Perspectives in Reading No. 3). Newark, Del.: International Reading Association, 1964.

Dorothy Dietrich and Virginia H. Mathews, eds., *Development of Lifetime Reading Habits.* Newark, Del.: International Reading Association, 1968.

Helen Huus, ed., *Evaluating Books for Children and Young People* (Perspectives in Reading No. 10). Newark, Del.: International Reading Association, 1968.

Sam Leaton Sebesta, ed., *Ivory, Apes and Peacocks: The Literature Point of View*. (Proceedings of the Twelfth Annual Convention, Vol. 12, Part 2). Newark, Del.: International Reading Association, 1968.

See also these publications on reading interests:

Geneva H. Pilgrim and Mariana K. McAllister, *Books, Young People and Reading Guidance* (2nd ed.) . New York: Harper & Row, Publishers, 1968.

Helen M. Robinson, ed., *Developing Permanent Interest in Reading* (Supplementary Educational Monographs, No. 84). Chicago: University of Chicago Press, 1956.

9

Meeting Individual Differences

■ *No matter what difficulties they make for schoolmen, individual differences are real, inevitable, ineradicable, desirable, and, indeed, essential.*[1]

It is a well-established fact that children of any given grade differ in reading ability. As they progress from grade to grade the differences become even greater. By the time they reach the sixth grade a range of as much as eight years between the achievement levels of the poorest and best readers is not unusual. In some schools these differences are more marked than in others, but regardless of their general levels of reading achievement children in all schools show variation within a grade.

The normal probability curve represents the distribution of reading measures for a heterogeneous group of children. Scores will fall along the continuum in expected fashion so that the smallest numbers will be at the lower and upper ends of the scale, with the greatest concentration in the middle and fewer numbers on either side. The distribution would be skewed in one direction or another if the group were less than heterogeneous. Whether normal or skewed, the distribution represents variability in performance for which provisions in instruction have to be made.

Personal and environmental factors account for differences in reading achievement. Whatever their etiology, the fact remains that children progress in different ways and at different rates and efforts must be made to accommodate these differences. It is not possible to ignore them since the levels of children's performances vary so much. To do so would be wasteful of teaching efforts and damaging to learners.

---

[1] Fred T. Tyler and William A. Brownell, "Facts and Issues: A Concluding Statement," in Nelson B. Henry, ed., *Individualizing Instruction* (Sixty-First Yearbook of the National Society for the Study of Education, Part 1). Chicago: University of Chicago Press, 1962, p. 316.

How to provide for individual differences in reading ability is one of the most difficult problems which teachers face, and there do not seem to be perfect solutions. Undoubtedly, it is as unrealistic to expect all teachers to function equally well as it is to expect children to do so.[2] The problem is confounded by the variability that exists at any reading achievement level. Children who are reading at approximately the same level vary in specific skills development. One child whose instructional level is third grade may require some intensive help in word attack that another on the same instructional level doesn't need. The latter could benefit, perhaps, from some work in literal comprehension which the former manages quite well. Multiply these differences—levels and specific requirements—and it becomes apparent why the learning needs of all children might not be met by even the most conscientious teacher.

In spite of the difficulties that individualizing reading instruction implies, teachers are making some progress in overcoming them. They are receiving help from publishers in the form of multilevel and programed materials and through products of the new technology. There may come a time when children's reading needs will be analyzed by a computer which then presents to each one whatever instruction he requires in order to move along the reading continuum. But until that day arrives the teacher will have to make the proper adjustments to his children and utilize as aids whatever outside resources are available to him.

Adjustments to individual needs may be *organizational* and *instructional*. Organizational adjustments refer to provisions that teachers make in the way they work with a view to increasing their contacts with individuals. Instructional adjustments are those that affect their teaching styles so that all children do not read the same selections, learn the same skills, do the same practice exercises. Organizational changes do facilitate instructional adjustments but there is nothing inherent in organization that insures adequate instruction. A classic example of failure to take advantage of conditions that organization makes possible is the one in which a teacher grouped children for reading instruction and then proceeded to conduct identical lessons with each group at different time intervals. Children had on Tuesday what others had on Monday. Here was a case where the teacher just did not understand the rationale for individualizing instruction.

Organizational Plans

To individualize instruction does not necessarily mean that the teacher works with each child on an individual basis at all times. The purpose of various organizational plans is to enable the teacher to differentiate instruction to meet the needs of individual children. By meeting with fewer chil-

---

[2] Variability in teacher performance is one of the factors believed to have influenced the results of some First Grade Studies. See the reference to Chall and Feldmann in Chapter 1, page 10.

dren in smaller groups he is able to give each one more of his attention and offer more individual help to those who need it. At the time he sees children individually he can learn more about their reading strengths and weaknesses and provide individualized guidance in accordance with each one's requirements. Individualized plans permit closer contacts with children with the expectation that their needs will be more precisely met.

Individual Instruction

Theoretically, at least, individual instruction is a preferred means of providing for differences in learning ability and achievement. The present interest in programed materials, computer-assisted instruction, and individually prescribed instruction is an expression of confidence in this belief. There are those who are convinced that these are practical and excellent means of individualizing reading instruction. (Each of these methods will be considered in the section, "Instructional Adjustments," pages 327–33.)

Individualized Reading

In the words of one of its strongest advocates, individualized reading "is not a single method or technique but a broader way of thinking about reading which involves newer concepts with class organization, materials and the approach to the individual child."[3, 4] Like most organizational plans for individualizing reading instruction, there are variations in how teachers conduct individualized reading, but the one feature which seems to be present in almost all classrooms where the program operates is the periodic conference period between teacher and child.

Individual teacher conferences are held with each child about twice a week (some are scheduled more or less frequently depending upon class size and length of reading periods) for approximately ten minutes each. When children complete a selection or indicate a need, they sit down with the teacher to discuss their reading. Naturally, all teachers do not conduct the conference in the same way but advocates of the program suggest that they keep careful records of what each child reads and how well his reading development is progressing so that this information may be used in planning subsequent conference sessions.

A knowledgeable and skillful teacher can use these conference periods to analyze a child's vocabulary and comprehension skills and provide instruction to extend their scope or overcome any deficiencies that might exist. Information about a child's reading could come from listening to him read passages of a selection he has completed and discussing his reactions to the

---

[3] May Lazar, "Individualized Reading: A Dynamic Approach," *The Reading Teacher*, 11 (December, 1957), pp. 75–83.

[4] See Chapter 4, "Developmental Reading," pages 125–29, for a review of the program, and Chapter 1, "Emerging Concepts in Teaching Reading," pages 11–12, for a summary of research on individualized reading. See also the sections on children's reading interests, selecting books for children, and aids for book selection in Chapter 8, pages 294–301.

content. If he had any questions about the selection or indicated he had difficulty in pronouncing words or following the author's ideas, on-the-spot help might be offered and instruction planned for the next conference or time when he and others with similar needs could meet for a group lesson.

The results of individualized reading programs show that some are highly effective in promoting specified aspects of reading development[5] while others are less so. How well children progress in individualized reading programs seems to depend upon the ability of the teacher to utilize the conference periods, which are admittedly brief in duration and relatively few in number. With a normal complement of typical children teachers must limit their individual contacts if they wish to meet with each one and not create difficulties that arise from extended periods when children are expected to engage in independent reading with little or no teacher direction. Superior readers appear to do better in these programs than poorer readers, perhaps because they do not require as much attention and can read without interruption for longer periods of time than the latter.

Perhaps a more practical plan for many teachers is one which combines group instruction with the individual conference. In this way they may provide for general and specific reading needs with the greater assurance that children will not be overlooked and those who require more help will obtain it. The individual conference is an asset to any reading program for it not only provides an opportunity for the teacher to become familiar with a child's reading but also serves to motivate the child who lacks confidence in his reading ability and needs teacher support. Reading instruction can be scheduled so that group activities might occur during one part of the day and some individual conferences during another. An alternate plan is to conduct group sessions on some days of the week and conferences on the remaining days. A third possibility is to schedule longer periods of time when children work in groups and follow these periods with comparable sessions when the major portion of reading instruction is conducted on an individual basis.

The availability of large amounts and different types of reading materials is a requirement that many individualized reading programs fail to meet. There isn't much point to conducting such programs unless the reading materials available to children represent a cross section of fiction and nonfiction that appeals to them, as well as levels of difficulty that match their reading abilities. Multiple copies of the same materials are necessary since the desires of children to read a given selection will be thwarted unless it is available when they want it.

Individualized reading has the potential for creating favorable attitudes toward reading through its application of the principles of interest, self-selection and pacing. In view of the problems it fails to resolve, wisdom suggests its rejection as a panacea for curing all reading ills, but the adop-

---

[5] Some observers have pointed out that in most individualized reading programs effective study skills instruction is lacking due to the fact that most of the reading children do is in books that feature narrative and imaginative writing.

tion of its strongest features for fostering reading development—opportunities for reading extensively and working on individual requirements. Individualized reading has no monopoly on providing children with the personalized attention they deserve. But there is no doubt that it has thrown the spotlight on indiscriminate reading practices and sparked efforts to do more than pay lip service to the concept of individual differences.

Group Instruction

Grouping children for reading instruction is not a perfect means of dealing with differences in reading achievement. It is an administrative device which permits the teacher to provide for these differences in ways that he could not do if all the pupils in the class were taught by him as a single group. In other words, grouping of children into smaller teaching units approaches individualization since the needs of the group are narrowed and the teacher has fewer children with whom to deal at any one time. Some grouping plans make possible greater individualization than others, but the actual attention that is paid to individual needs is dependent upon the degree to which the teacher is able to plan for and work with different groups of children.

Criteria of Instruction

Regardless of the form that group instruction takes, there are several criteria in the form of questions that teachers might raise in order to evaluate the effectiveness of their efforts to individualize teaching. There isn't much justification for grouping pupils in reading if they are going to be treated in the same way as they would if they were all together. Pupils who participate in unproductive learning activities or learn poor work habits under the guise of group instruction probably would be better off if they were kept together as a unit and taught as usual. Answers to the following questions might give some indication about the effectiveness of group instruction:

1. How are the individual and common needs of pupils determined?
2. Do the reading activities actually fit individual and group needs?
3. Does each group engage in the same kind of activities day after day?
4. Does the independent work of groups have any relation to teacher-directed activities?
5. Are the independent activities in which pupils engage worthwhile?
6. Do all the pupils participate in common learning experiences?
7. How are the results of group instruction evaluated?

There is no doubt that grouping can facilitate a teacher's efforts to offer instruction that benefits more children than would occur otherwise. But the mere fact that children are taught in groups does not of itself insure any changes in the teacher's or children's behavior. Too many pupils have not engaged in purposeful learning and have wasted their efforts in classrooms where the purposes of group instruction were lost. But grouping does become a valuable tool in the hands of the teacher who understands its advantages and limitations and ways to use it productively.

Types of Groups

The most obvious condition which calls for some form of grouping is one in which there are children whose reading achievement levels vary significantly. As has been noted earlier, the range of reading achievement increases as children move through the grades. In a typical second grade there will be a few children who are reading at the primer level, a larger group of children who are ready to read more difficult materials, and another consisting of some children who can receive instruction in materials intended for third- and fourth-grade levels. In a fifth- or sixth-grade class the spread between the poorest and most able readers will be even greater.

Another condition that is common to all classrooms at any level is the diversity in skill development among pupils. One group of children might require intensive help in word recognition; a second group will need to spend more time on comprehension; another has a good command of the basic reading skills but is weak in the study skills; and some pupils from each of these groups possibly need work on appreciation skills. As every teacher knows, within each of these different groups will be children whose learning needs are not identical. In the word recognition group there might be a few children who should work on phonics and structural analysis and a couple who need practice with the dictionary; in the comprehension group there may be some who are confused by complex sentences and others who fail to assess context clues for word meaning; the study skills group might consist of some pupils who have to learn how to discriminate between important and irrelevant details and others who need to know how to locate an entry in an index. It would be just as wasteful of their time for the teacher to offer the same instruction to all members of each group as it would to expect children whose achievement levels varied to read the same books.

Children engage in different reading activities which might require still other groupings. One group could be formed for the purpose of dramatizing a story or participating in other creative activities. Another might come together for the purpose of sharing independent reading or preparing a choral reading. Whatever activities grew out of their reading experiences might dictate the formation of new groups.

It should be apparent that a workable grouping system is sufficiently flexible to allow children to move into different groups as their learning requirements change. It is possible that some groups, particularly those involving achievement levels, will be more stable than others. But even in such groupings the teacher should be alert to opportunities that make movement desirable. There is hardly any justification for assuming that all children will grow in the same way and at the same rate. A child should be in a group where he is most likely to progress in reading. Under a flexible arrangement children will be regrouped from time to time and will participate in more than one group for different reading activities.

Intraclass Grouping

Children are grouped on the basis of achievement levels, special skills requirements, and special activities. Grouping for the purpose of instructing children at or near their instructional levels creates different kinds of problems from those involving special skills and activities. Since the range of reading levels will vary from class to class, each teacher who seeks to differentiate his instruction will have to form reading groups in accordance with the achievement distribution *and his ability to administer them*. No more groups should be formed than the number he can teach well.

Forming Groups

A teacher who hasn't any experience planning for and teaching multiple reading lessons probably will be wise to start with two reading achievement groups and increase the number as he develops confidence and ability in working with them. Most teachers find that with experience they are able to divide the children into three groups, although some establish four. There may be a few children who don't really fit into any group and they might need to have a group of their own. If a larger number of groups were formed, the time the teacher could spend with each group might not be adequate unless most of the school day were devoted to reading instruction. Multiple groups can be formed if the children engage in more independent than teacher-directed activities as in team learning.

How shall children be grouped for reading on the basis of achievement levels? Assume that a second-grade class has twenty-five children who are distributed in the following way:

Instructional Level	No. of Children
Primer	2
First Reader	3
Second Reader (low)	12
Second Reader (high)	4
Third Reader	3
Fourth Reader	1
	25

It should be obvious that to form two groups would not really provide for this range of achievement levels, but two are better than one. The formation of three groups would be more satisfactory and would come closer to meeting the children's requirements. As the number of groups is increased, the range of achievement within each group becomes less, thereby making it possible for them to work more nearly at their instructional levels. The distributions shown above are not to be considered firm since teachers will

Two-Group Plan	Three-Group Plan	Four-Group Plan
Primer-First Reader (5) *	Primer-First Reader (5)	Primer-First Reader (5)
Second-Fourth Reader (20)	Second Reader (16)	Second Reader: Low (12)
	Third-Fourth Reader (4)	Second Reader: High (4)
		Third-Fourth Reader (4)

* The number in parentheses indicates how many children there might be in each group.

discover after forming the groups that adjustments have to be made. Under the three- or four-group plan some of the children at the first-reader level might be able to function with the second-reader group, while the children at the high second-reader level might be moved into the next higher group. In all likelihood the child whose instructional level is fourth grade will engage in more individualized reading, although he could benefit from working with the other children in his group.

Methods and Materials

When there is an overlapping of achievement levels in any group, the teacher must find out what materials are suitable for the children. The materials should not be so easy or so difficult that some don't gain any benefits from them. The choices become more difficult in two-group plans than they do in three- or four-group plans. It is not possible to know in advance what book, for example, should be used with the children who are in the primer-first reader group. The teacher must try out the books for each level with the children and then decide which one is more suitable. The same is true for a group which consists of children whose reading levels are more sharply defined, as in the second group under the two-group plan. With these children it might be advisable to try out higher-level second-grade materials to see if the poorer readers in the group can manage them. Flexibility in the use of materials, as in the assignment of children to groups, will reduce the distance between the capabilities of the children and the expectations of the teacher.

Skills instruction will be offered children who are grouped on the basis of achievement levels as a part of the regular developmental program. However, as teachers discover that some children in the group need special help with a particular skill, they may establish a small subgroup for just these children. The teacher may find that additional children in other groups require the same kind of instruction. In that case he could invite them to join the subgroup and teach them at one time instead of repeating the same lessons with different groups. In this latter arrangement the teacher will use instructional materials that are not too difficult for any of the children since their instructional reading levels vary. The teacher could provide practice in the skill at the level on which the children are reading.

Teachers will want to group children for skills instruction periodically.

Unlike achievement groups, skills groups will be formed and disbanded as soon as the purpose for forming them has been met. The formation of such temporary groups makes it possible for the teacher to deal with specific learning tasks without requiring children who are proficient in them to engage in them too. Skills grouping is an efficient way of individualizing instruction in reading.

The charts on this page indicate what might occur as children are organized into two or three groups for reading instruction. In the two-group plan the teacher can be with each group every day in the week without extending the reading period for too long a time. With three groups the teacher might not be able to work with each one every day unless he lengthened the reading period or reduced the amount of time he spent with each. There will be times when this is possible; in any case, he can take a few minutes to meet with any group that isn't scheduled for a regular session with him to determine its progress or give it some direction if needed.

TWO-GROUP PLAN

	GROUP I	GROUP II
Monday	Independent Activity→Teaching	Teaching→Independent Activity
Tuesday	Teaching→Independent Activity	Independent Activity→Teaching
Wednesday	Independent Activity→Teaching	Teaching→Independent Activity
Thursday	Teach Class as a Whole	
Friday	Teaching→Independent Activity	Independent Activity→Teaching

THREE-GROUP PLAN

	GROUP I	GROUP II	GROUP III
Monday	Indep. Activity→Teaching	Teaching→Indep. Activity	Indep. Activity
Tuesday	Indep. Activity	Indep. Activity→Teaching	Teaching→Indep. Activity
Wednesday		Teach Class as a Whole	
Thursday	Teaching→Indep. Activity	Indep. Activity	Indep. Activity→Teaching
Friday	Indep. Activity→Teaching	Teaching→Indep. Activity	Indep. Activity

The term *Teaching* refers to the time when the children are under the direction of the teacher. At this time he might introduce a new lesson, discuss the reading the children have been doing, or evaluate the work they have been doing independently. Out of the teaching sessions come some independent reading activities. The teacher might prepare the children for a selection which they then could read while he moves to another group. If he has taught a skill, there will be practice exercises for pupils to do. Perhaps the children will be engaging in some activities that are outcomes of having read a story or will read books for enjoyment. All these activities are referred to in the charts as *Independent Activity*.

Group instruction is alternated with whole class instruction. It is possible that teachers will bring children together for a reading activity more than once a week. There is no set rule for anyone to follow: the nature of the class and reading activity should determine how the children are organized. If the children are benefiting from an activity in which all of them can participate, there is no reason to cut it short merely for the sake of having group instruction. Grouping for reading is not an end in itself; it is the means by which instruction can become more personalized and relevant and should be employed when circumstances indicate that superior results would be obtained than are otherwise possible.

Facilitating Group Instruction

The reading activities in which children engage while in groups are no different from those that are conducted with the entire class: preparing to read a selection, reading silently and orally, discussing a story, learning and practicing skills, listening to and discussing a poem, reading for enjoyment, sharing books, and so on. The children work with and without the teacher in groups as they do in the whole class setting. However, group instruction places greater emphasis upon self and group reliance than does whole class instruction. The teacher cannot be with all the children at the same time. This means that they have to learn to work by themselves after they have been prepared for a given task so that the teacher can give his attention to another group.

Teachers have to plan carefully so that all the children are involved in worthwhile activities. They must be certain that the children know what to do before they leave them for another group: otherwise, there will be many interruptions by children who are bewildered and not ready to read on their own. Children should be encouraged to work together if there is need to do so; this means that a child who isn't sure of what he is doing could consult with another child in his group instead of asking the teacher. Freedom of movement reduces the number of situations with which teachers must deal and allows them to devote more time to instruction than to organizational details.

In addition, the children will be completing their reading tasks at different times and should not have to wait for the others to finish. They can engage in useful reading activities such as working on skills on which they need more practice developing and extending vocabulary, reading related topics for enjoyment, sharing reading experiences, preparing oral or written reports from different materials, and so forth. Teachers should check what each will do (or give each child an activity sheet based upon his own reading requirements) to maximize each one's efforts. Files of appropriate materials will have to be prepared so that the children who need skills practice or vocabulary work can locate what they need. The children will have ready access to whatever books and other reading materials enable them to proceed with their work without interrupting the teacher or interfering with others. There is no reason why some children with similar read-ing requirements cannot work together, e.g., do a word puzzle, check each other's responses to a reading exercise, read orally to each other, and so on. Whatever each child does is intended to increase his reading ability and not merely keep him busy and quiet.

A class in which several reading groups are functioning cannot be one in which absolute silence reigns. Children might be talking to each other in one part of the room while the teacher is working with other children in another corner. On the other hand, unrestrained behavior cannot be tolerated since it is bound to interfere with the work of others. Children can learn to work quietly and productively without constant teacher super-vision, but some groups might need more time than others before they are able to assume this responsibility. A classroom in which learning is occur-ring hums with activity, but learning is unlikely where the din is over-powering.

Pupil Teams

Another form of intraclass grouping is one in which two, three, or four children are organized into pupil teams on the basis of reading ability.[6] After the teacher has taught a lesson, the members of the team work to-gether on materials that have been prepared for them. Although the teacher is available to work with the team or its individual members, pupils are expected to help each other with the assignments.

Advocates of pupil-team learning believe that it is possible to increase the amount and quality of children's learning through this type of organi-zation because children do not have to wait to receive feedback about their responses from the teacher and have more opportunities to recite than would be possible in a typical class. Presumably each team has a leader who can assume some of the responsibilities of the teacher. There is no doubt that some pupils can improve their reading skills with the help of other pupils, but it is questionable whether children can assume a major responsibility such as this unless they work under the close supervision of the teacher. On the other hand, if the materials on which children work are of a self-instructional type, the amount of time the teacher needs to spend with the teams will be reduced. Another possible limitation of this organizational plan is the number of different sets of materials that might have to be prepared for the pupil teams. This problem could be overcome if teachers were given the opportunity to prepare instructional and prac-tice materials or gather them from commercial sources. These could be duplicated so that each teacher who needed materials for the development and practice of reading skills would not have to prepare most of them himself.

---

[6] Donald D. Durrell and Helen A. Murphy, "Reading in Intermediate Grades," *Journal of Education, 146* (December, 1963), pp. 36–53.

Interclass Grouping

In order to facilitate grouping for reading instruction, some schools have been following a type of differentiated instruction in which several teachers participate. Pupils are grouped on the basis of reading achievement and assigned to one class for reading instruction.[7]

Under this arrangement, a school which has one or more classes at different grade levels classifies the children of these grades in reading ability through standardized testing and/or informal means. Reading classes are established in accordance with the number of reading levels found to exist in the different grades and the availability of teachers. Thus, if there were two classes each in grades four, five, and six, six reading classes could be organized for the children in these grades. The more classes there are in each grade, the smaller can be the range of reading levels within any one reading class.

At a given time in the school day, the children go to their assigned reading classes for instruction. They may be taught by their regular teacher or by a different teacher. A teacher of a fourth-grade class might be assigned children whose reading achievement level is fourth grade. This teacher would receive children from his own and other fourth grade classes as well as children from other grades whose reading level was fourth. Teachers might be assigned to teach a fifth- or sixth-grade level reading class even though they have a regular fourth-grade class.

Theoretically, reading instruction is facilitated by this organizational plan since teachers are responsible for dealing with fewer reading levels and can concentrate their efforts. However, it is a well-established fact that unless each teacher grouped children within the originally determined group, he would be failing to offer them the instruction they needed. The skills needs of children on any particular instructional level are not necessarily the same. Nor should the instructional time allotted to high and low groups be equal. Moreover, if most or all the reading instruction were given in the reading classes, children would have to bridge the gap themselves between the reading they did in the special classes and the reading associated with their regular school work. Unless their own classroom teacher made provisions for additional reading instruction, particularly in the content fields, many children would not realize their potential in reading development. So while this form of interclass grouping does narrow the reading range within any one group, assumptions that it obviates the need for further individualization and additional instruction are not warranted.

There have been a number of studies to measure the outcomes of this form of grouping.[8] The results seem to indicate that it is not the plan that

---

[7] This type of organization has come to be known as the Joplin Plan since it was popularized by the Joplin, Missouri, public schools. Other school systems had tried the plan before Joplin instituted it.

[8] Roy Carson and Jack Thompson, "The Joplin Plan and Traditional Reading Groups," *The Elementary School Journal,* 65 (October, 1964), pp. 38–43; Donald C. Cushenbery, "Two Methods of Grouping for Reading Instruction," *The Elementary School Journal,*

accounts for any advantages it *might* have over other organizational patterns but how it is conducted. Many schools discontinued the "Joplin" plan when they found that children were not progressing as they should. It does seem clear that where teachers are not required to spread their efforts too thinly they can be more effective, but no organizational pattern can assure this. What the teachers do within the pattern is what counts. Since it is very difficult to maintain communication between the teacher of the reading class and the grade teachers and impossible to avoid further grouping, schools have accomplished the same objective as the "Joplin" plan by assigning children who fall within a reading range to one class and others within a different range to another. Thus, one second-grade class might consist of children whose reading achievement levels fall between primer- and second-grade levels, while another consists of those whose reading achievement levels are between second and third grades. A reduction in reading range has been achieved by such placement and the difficulties outlined above are avoided.

Team Teaching. Team teaching[9] is a form of interclass grouping designed to narrow the range of achievement levels within working groups of children. "A teaching team is a group of several teachers . . . with joint responsibility for planning, executing and evaluating an educational program. . . . At the elementary level, the team may include pupils of the same age or grade level or of adjoining age or grade levels. In general, each teacher in an elementary team teaches all subjects taught in her grade and works at one time or another with every child in the group. Each teacher might, however, have special competency. . . ."[10]

Two or more teachers combine their classes to form one large group. Thus, two teachers might be responsible for fifty to sixty children who are in the same grade or in adjoining grades, e.g., grades one and two. These teachers share teaching responsibilities throughout the day. This arrangement makes it possible for them to offer differentiated instruction in a way that would be difficult to duplicate were they in separate classrooms. Insofar as reading instruction is concerned, at least six achievement groups might be formed in the dual class. These could be supplemented by skills and activity groups taught by one or both teachers. One teacher might be in charge of the children for a literature lesson in which all could join. Or both teachers might engage the children in simultaneous group and/or

---

66 (February, 1966), pp. 267–71; Wallace Ramsey, "An Evaluation of a Joplin Plan of Grouping for Reading Instruction," *Journal of Educational Research, 55* (August, 1962), pp. 567–72; Dayton G. Rothrock, "Heterogeneous, Homogeneous or Individualized Approach to Reading?" *Elementary English, 38* (April, 1961), pp. 233–35.

9 Robert H. Anderson, Ellis A. Hagstrom, and Wade M. Robinson, "Team Teaching in an Elementary School," *School Review, 68* (Spring, 1960), p. 84; Philip Lambert, "Team Teaching for the Elementary School," *Educational Leadership, 18* (November, 1966), pp. 85–88, 112.

10 Robert H. Anderson, "Organizing Groups for Instruction," in Nelson B. Henry, ed., *Individualizing Instruction* (The Sixty-First Yearbook of the National Society for the Study of Education, Part I). Chicago: University of Chicago Press, 1962, p. 257.

individual activities. Another possibility is one in which a teacher works with the entire group while the other circulates and offers individual guidance where necessary. The advantage of team teaching is a flexibility that is unavailable to a single teacher operating independently.

More than two teachers might combine classes and make further individualization possible. Anderson[11] reported groups ranging in size from fifty to two hundred pupils. Whether or not groups of the latter size are efficient teaching units is a question whose answer depends upon the variability of the group, the teacher's ability to work with a group of this size, and the nature of the learning activity. Certainly a large group could listen to a story that the teacher reads or a recording of it or view a television program, film, or dramatic presentation. But it isn't likely that most teachers will want to teach a reading skill or direct the reading of a selection with groups of one hundred or more children.

It appears that two or three teachers can combine their classes to increase teaching efficiency. If this is done, there has to be enough space to accommodate from fifty to seventy-five children. A large multi-purpose room is needed, preferably one in which all furniture is movable and which contains sliding partitions which could section the large room into smaller units. The availability of such space would make it possible for teachers to conduct simultaneous lessons without interfering with each other and increase available space when larger groups of children were formed.

There isn't much research on the value of team teaching for reading instruction. Lambert[12] compared the effects of a five-member team and a self-contained organization at the primary and intermediate levels. At the end of the first year the self-contained groups scored significantly higher in reading in grades two to six. At the end of the second year the team teaching groups showed greater gains. It is possible that the team teachers needed time to become accustomed to the new organization and to utilize it to fuller advantage.

Team teaching does permit teachers to share their abilities and learn from each other. But like any other organizational plan, there is no guarantee that team teaching will *insure* superior outcomes in reading. The instructional program can be affected by the ways in which teachers are freed to work with children. But studies of individualized reading and different forms of grouping for reading instruction show that the plans do not possess inherent qualities that produce good results. Undoubtedly, the teacher variable accounts in large measure for the mixed results that investigators of organizational patterns for teaching reading have obtained. Teachers cannot expect positive changes in children's reading behaviors to occur unless they are able to convert their knowledge of reading into teaching strategies that meet the needs of different children.

---

[11] Robert Anderson, *op. cit.*, p. 260.

[12] Philip Lambert, William Goodwin, Richard Roberts and William Wiersma, "A Comparison of Pupil Achievement in Team and Self-Contained Organizations," *Journal of Experimental Education, 33* (Spring, 1965), pp. 217–24.

Instructional Adjustments

There isn't a clear dichotomy between organizational plans and instructional adjustments for individualizing the teaching of reading. The purpose of following different organizational forms is to make it possible for teachers to more readily adjust their teaching to varying needs, and this is accomplished through instruction. It would appear that any differences are matters of priority, i.e., whether the organization determines the type of instruction that is offered or the nature of the instruction influences the organization. However, there might be some instructional adjustments which do not affect organizational forms.

Individually Prescribed Instruction

Any efforts which teachers make to meet specific learning needs of individual children may be described as individually prescribed instruction. When a teacher assigns some reading exercises to a child who is weak in a given skill, he is "prescribing" work to help overcome the deficiency. The pupil teams that were described in the previous section worked on assignments of one kind or another that were geared to their peculiar requirements. Moreover, there has been in operation, under laboratory conditions, a plan that attempts to deal with children on an individual basis, and this plan has become known as individually prescribed instruction.[13] In addition, computer-assisted instruction is being tried with limited numbers of children,[14] and this system also qualifies under the same descriptive term. These two latter plans seem to be the direction in which future reading instruction will move, if not in entirety, at least in part.

Individually prescribed instruction was developed by the Learning Research and Development Center of the University of Pittsburgh in cooperation with a public school staff. On the basis of pretest information and teacher observations and evaluations, individual lessons are assigned to each child, who obtains them from files and shelves in accordance with the instructions he has received. The materials on which the pupil works are drawn largely from commercial sources, such as reading textbooks and trade books, workbooks, programed and boxed materials, tapes, etc. The child works through the lesson on his own, but he can obtain the teacher's help if he requires it. Each lesson the child completes is checked by the teacher in order to determine on what lesson he should work next. Continuous evaluation through observation and tests suggests what assignments the children should have.

---

[13] C. M. Lindvall and John O. Bolvin, "Programed Instruction in the Schools: An Application of Programing Principles in Individually Prescribed Instruction," in Phil C. Lang, ed., *Programed Instruction* (Sixty-Sixth Yearbook of the National Society for the Study of Education, Part II). Chicago: University of Chicago Press, 1967.
[14] Richard C. Atkinson and Duncan N. Hansen, "Computer-Assisted Instruction in Initial Reading: The Stanford Project," *Reading Research Quarterly*, 2 (Fall, 1966), pp. 5–25.

On occasion, the children meet in groups to discuss their own work. The teacher uses these sessions to answer questions they may have and instruct them in those aspects of reading which the prepared lessons have failed to accomplish or cannot deal with satisfactorily. One such case might involve inferential reading in which it would be desirable to consider several possible implications that could be drawn from a selection and the justifications for them.

In order for a plan of this type to succeed, there must be available extensive resources in the form of experts, staff, and materials. Few teachers could develop such a program on their own. However, a team of teachers could, for each or some components of the reading curriculum, gather materials and prepare lessons that would be available to individual children. For example, a series of graded lessons on main ideas that are self-explanatory and geared to a particular reading level can be developed, duplicated, and filed so that when one or more children are identified as needing this instruction they can obtain the material and work independently on it. Files of such materials could be developed and stored in a learning materials center where teachers would have access to them.

Computer-Assisted Instruction

Computers have been used to provide practice on reading skills that a teacher has taught and to offer direct instruction in the skills without teacher involvement. In the latter instance all instruction in sequential form is prepared in advance and fed into the data bank so that it becomes available on demand. All computer-assisted instructional systems do not consist of the same components but more advanced systems use audio and visual presentations to which the pupil can respond through a keyboard or marker called a light pen.

Visuals are presented on the cathode ray tube of the computer or screen from a projector. Recorded messages accompany the visual presentations so that the child understands what he is expected to do. He responds to the instructions he receives by pressing the proper keys on the board or touching the computer screen with the light pen. For example, for beginning reading, there might appear on the cathode ray tube three words—*big, boy, cat*—and the child would be told to touch the word which starts with a letter that is different from the first letters of the other words. A recorded voice might also read the words as they appeared on the screen. If he were to touch *boy* with the light pen, the computer would tell him that he hadn't selected the correct word and to look at the words again. A series of instructions and presentations would be given him depending upon the responses he made.

It is conceivable that dialogues between computer and child will become possible so that the latter isn't as far removed from a "live" teacher as is now the case. Most of the experimentation with computer-assisted instruction has involved development of basic reading skills, but it is apparent that other aspects of the reading curriculum could be programed. But even if the sophistication of electronic devices and programer efforts improve, there still is the question about the effects of impersonal treatments and isolated surroundings upon the development of children. Whether all children would prosper in the highly efficient and sterile climate of such individual instruction has yet to be determined.

While teachers might regard these newer developments with some suspicion, they ought to consider the rationale on which they are based and determine to what uses, if any, they can put them. Without question, the concepts of sequential treatments and immediate feedback that computer-assisted instructional systems offer have demonstrated their value. Teachers can apply these same principles as they develop lessons to meet special requirements and organizations to facilitate their individualized efforts.

It is clear that schools of the future will be unable to ignore advancements in the science and art of teaching as some have in the past. Since reading ability is a tool, to the development of which our society assigns a top priority, the thrust to produce more and better readers is bound to grow stronger. Technology is sharing and will share a greater role in this effort. Teachers must be ready to assess developments in light of agreed-upon goals and assume leadership in making decisions about their use. Summary rejection is not a stance that anyone can defend and might produce consequences that are exactly the kinds teachers wish to avoid. Individualization of instruction is necessary and desirable and teachers ought to consider seriously how they can utilize whatever means exist to achieve this end.

Differentiated Reading

One of the main reasons for grouping children for reading instruction or working with them on a one-to-one basis, as in individualized reading, is to facilitate instruction that takes into account differences in ability. Recognition of these differences is shown by teachers who provide materials of varying difficulty for children to read and who differentiate their instruction in accordance with pupil requirements. Thus, if a teacher were to divide his pupils into three instructional groups, each group would read materials that were at or near its instructional level. The group of highest achievement might be reading in books one to three levels above their grade placement, the middle or average group in books intended for the grade and the pupils of lower achievement in books one to three levels below their grade placement. There might be one or more pupils in the class for whom the materials of the lowest group would be too difficult or others who found the books of the highest group insufficiently challenging, and other provisions would have to be made for those at either end of the scale. In an individualized reading program there would have to be books that all children were able to cope with so that each child could select not only the books he would prefer reading but also could read with some success.

Instruction in the skills of reading might vary from group to group or child to child. The poorer readers undoubtedly will have needs that are no different from those of the better readers, but they certainly will have to concentrate on some specified skills that are not as pressing for other pupils. The latter will be at different stages of reading development and further differentiation will be required. At any one time in the reading program children might be engaged in activities that are intended to promote competencies within the same growth area or different ones. One group may have to spend time on phonic analysis involving vowel digraphs; a second group for whom phonics is no real problem should concentrate on analyzing words through root forms and other structural elements; a third group merely needs some additional practice in relating the respellings of words in the dictionary to the key words which govern symbol-sound relationships. All these activities involve word recognition but demand different understandings. If children in the same class were concentrating at a given time on different growth areas, some might be analyzing paragraph patterns to increase their understanding of the material (literal comprehension), others could be learning to differentiate between important and lesser details (selection), while still others who are proficient in both of these aspects of reading would be learning how to skim and scan (flexibility).

IDEAS FOR DISCUSSION

All of the foregoing is based on the assumption that these degrees of differentiation are necessary and desirable and that they are not pursued merely to enable teachers to demonstrate their commitment to the concept of individual differences. The degree to which individualization is practiced should be determined by real and not theoretical needs. It would be as improper to assume that all reading instruction must be individualized in ways that have been suggested as it is to believe that all children can benefit from the same reading treatments and that there is no need to provide for any individual differences.

The task of providing for individual differences in reading is not an easy one, particularly for teachers in a self-contained classroom who are responsible for all curriculum areas and recognize the importance of differentiating their instruction in them. More and better differentiation would occur if teachers could judge with greater precision in what types of activities all children can participate so that there is less need to plan for and conduct multiple lessons. To expect all teachers to be able to individualize instruction equally well when they have so much to do is not helping them to cope with the problem. A reasonable *modus operandi* would be one that encourages teachers to learn as much about their pupils as they can so that they are in a better position to decide which children do require special treatments and offer them in the best way they know how.

Teachers will be in a better position to work with individuals and groups if they have at their disposal the resources they require. This means that they should not have to seek out or prepare all of the materials they might need. As has been suggested earlier, the establishment of a learning materials center which contains printed and other kinds of materials that teachers may use to develop reading skills would go a long way toward reducing the frustrations that accompany efforts to individualize instruction. In addition, assistance in the form of teacher aides would free teachers to devote more of their energies to working with the children who need specialized help and make possible more frequent contacts with individuals. The one advantage that team teaching has over the typical self-contained classroom is the opportunity it gives teachers to be released from some responsibilities so that they can assume others. The teacher who is by himself must learn to pace instruction so that his efforts don't become so thin that learning suffers. This is why he must find the proper mix of group and individual instruction.

Varying Purposes for Reading

It is possible to differentiate some reading instruction without separating children into groups. The differentiation of reading tasks is a means of meeting individual differences in situations where the instructional level of the pupils is not so far below the level required to read the material that it will be a frustrating experience regardless of what measures the teacher takes. One way to do this is to vary the purposes for which different children will read the same material. Poorer readers might focus their attention upon problems whose solutions do not require much more than grasping literal meanings. Better readers could devote their attention to reading for deeper meanings, or some children might read for details while others concentrate on main ideas. In this way all children could participate in the same learning experience and contribute to the extent they are capable of.

If children were to read for different purposes, it would be necessary to prepare in advance questions to which each should address himself. These might take the form of reading guides (see page 232) in which some differentiation in reading requirements is noted by scaling items on different difficulty levels. The teacher could prepare one set of items and indicate by a numbering system which ones each group of children should be concerned with. While all children would not be reading in the same way, everyone could participate in the activities that followed and benefit to the extent he was able.

Another way to differentiate a reading assignment is not to require all pupils to read the entire material. Those who read slowly need more time to complete a task and hold back the rest of the group. Even though some pupils do not read an entire story, they will be able to participate in the ensuing discussion and engage in related activities. By guiding any discussion the teacher can make certain that those parts some have omitted are covered sufficiently so that closure is effected.

Using a Process Guide

The process guide (see page 231) is another device teachers may use to help pupils who require special guidance. More than one guide can be designed for the same material by directing the pupils' attention to the reading processes he should be aware of as he reads. One guide might stress vocabulary by noting words whose meanings could be determined from context clues and other words that are used in a special way. By indicating that there are aids that they should use for determining word meanings, the children who need this type of direction would be receiving assistance that the teacher couldn't provide for all of them. Another group of children might require more assistance in recognizing paragraph patterns; the process guide would call them to their attention by noting or raising questions about paragraph structure so that they could recognize them more readily. Process guides focus attention on elements in materials that facilitate understanding and can be of real benefit to children whose special needs the teacher cannot personally meet all the time.

Multilevel Materials

Some schools have been depending upon commerical programs to provide differentiated instruction in reading. These programs take the form of workbook-type materials[15] which are graded in difficulty and designed to allow pupils to work independently at their own reading level and rate. The teacher is free to work with individual pupils who need his help.

Many of the materials contain short selections that are either of a narrative or expository type. Some offer timed reading exercises and most contain exercises that are supposed to develop word recognition and vocabulary and skill in reading for details, finding main ideas, drawing inferences, locating and organizing information, etc. Pupils begin working with materials at their instructional level and move to the next higher level as they complete the exercises. Several provide pupils with answers so that they can check their own work and chart their progress.

Several of the programs are designed to be used with a minimum of teacher involvement. However, since these materials offer little or no instruction in any of the areas covered by them, it is apparent that they will benefit only those children who already have the ability to perform the reading tasks covered in the materials. These materials in their present form can be used more effectively as practice exercises after the teacher has taught the skills than as instructional lessons to develop them. Through judicious evaluation teachers can identify some of the selections for teaching skills and utilize appropriate exercises for developing understandings. Children do need practice to strengthen and refine their reading performances, and materials of this kind have served teachers well. But no amount of practice in reading situations where children are unable to cope with difficulties can take the place of teacher assistance in overcoming them.

Programed materials[16] are multilevel in the sense that they take the

---

[15] Included among these materials are *It's Your World* (Continental Press); *Study Skills Library* (Educational Developmental Laboratories); *Reading Skills Lab* (Houghton Mifflin); *Be a Better Reader Series* (Prentice-Hall); *Reading Laboratory* (Science Research Associates); *Reading for Understanding* (Science Research Associates).

[16] *Lessons in Self-Instruction in the Basic Skills* (California Test Bureau); *Programed Reading* (Globe); *Programed Reading* (McGraw-Hill).

learner through a series of steps that become progressively difficult with the expectation that when the program is completed, the learner will have mastered whatever has been covered by it. There is a major difference between truly programed and other materials: programed materials have built into them instructional and not merely practice units. In theory at least, the program is supposed to provide the instruction necessary to master whatever is to be learned so that little or no teacher direction is required.

There is a real problem associated with programed materials that few of them overcome. Most lack branching, i.e., when a child makes an error, he is not referred to another section which helps him discover the error and correct it, but instead he is required to do the same exercise again with the hope that he will understand it the second or third time. Of course, there is no assurance that he will. This weakness is one of the chief reasons that most programed materials for reading are inadequate and certainly not self-teaching.

Relatively few programed materials in reading are available and the ones which have evoked the greatest interest are those that are intended to develop beginning reading skills. Such materials were used in a First Grade Study, and the investigator reported that children who were taught through them did as well as other children who received instruction with typical reading materials.[17]

As in the case of other instructional devices and materials there is nothing absolute about programed materials. The rationale on which they are supposed to be based—graded instruction and immediate reinforcement—has been found to have merit. But each program must be judged solely on its own, for programed materials can be as poorly designed as any other type. Their effectiveness depends upon how well they have been constructed and upon other factors such as the nature of the learning and the learners. Some understandings require more "give and take" than programed materials seem able to provide. It appears also that not all learners are able to profit equally from them. Reports suggest that slower learners respond better to them than more able learners. It is possible that some programed materials offer the fine gradations in lessons that teachers don't provide and this kind of treatment is what these children require.

There is no question that programed materials of high quality can be useful as aids to teachers who seek different means of differentiating instruction. But as one observer has noted, "Information is needed regarding the optimum gradation of steps for slow and fast learners, the proper balance between right and wrong answers, the transfer of learning to other subjects, and the best ways to incorporate programed learning into the total curriculum. . . ."[18]

---

[17] Robert Ruddell, "Reading Instruction in First Grade With Varying Emphasis on the Regularity of Grapheme-Phoneme Correspondences and the Relation of Language Structure to Meaning," *The Reading Teacher,* 19 (May, 1966), pp. 653–60.

[18] Helen Huus, "Innovations in Reading Instruction: At Later Levels," in Robinson, ed., *Innovation and Change in Reading Instruction* (The Six Yearbook of the National Society for the Study of Education, Part II) University of Chicago Press, 1968, p. 156.

SUMMARY

1. Variability in reading achievement is an expected outcome of the influences that personal and environmental conditions have upon individual growth. As children progress through the grades, differences in reading ability become more marked. The tendency in the past to regard variability in achievement as abnormal could account for the ways in which schools organized for instruction and the common standards they established for children. Today schools operate on the assumption that children are alike in some respects and different in others and that they must seek better ways to meet individual and group needs.

2. There is a close relationship between the administrative devices and instructional plans teachers adopt to personalize the teaching of reading. Teachers recognize that changing forms of organization are not ends in themselves but the means through which their behaviors may be modified to accommodate the learning requirements of children. The relevance of reading instruction is measured not by how the teacher arranges contacts with pupils but by what occurs during his association with them.

3. The individualized reading program is a means by which the reading requirements of children might be met. The program rests on the principles of self-interest, self-selection, and pacing that are realized through individual reading and conferences. Teachers have found that they can combine the best features of this individualization with group practices to provide for general and specific reading needs.

4. Children may be grouped for reading instruction on the basis of their reading achievement levels. This grouping plan is designed to meet the developmental reading requirements of all children through the adoption of materials of varying difficulty and provisions for different learning sequences. A second grouping takes into account the diversity in skill development among pupils. Proficiency in reading skills might vary as much within achievement levels as it does between achievement levels. Children come together because they have common requirements. A third grouping is based upon the nature of reading activities which cross achievement and skills lines. Children participate because of special interest or ability in them.

5. Intraclass grouping is the most common way of individualizing reading instruction. Two to four reading groups might be formed with the knowledge that further individualization probably will be required. The teacher divides his time among the groups so that during any one day he meets with as many as he can without creating conditions which interfere with the quality of instruction and the ability of children to profit from it. The formation of smaller groups through pupil teams requires greater dependence upon individual pupil initiative, advance planning, and the availability of appropriate materials.

6. Interclass grouping is a procedure intended to narrow the range of reading achievement levels among pupils. Children are assigned to reading classes which might be taught by teachers other than their own. The greater the number of available teachers who can participate in the plan, the narrower can the range of achievement levels of each class become. This possible advantage could be lost by the failure to differentiate instruction within each reading class and relate the instruction to the reading children have to do in their regular classes. Team teaching, a system whereby two or more teachers join to plan and execute the instruction program, is an alternate plan that might offer equal possibilities for differentiating reading instruction and avoid the disadvantages of separateness that other interclass groupings foster.

7. Individually prescribed instruction and computer-assisted instruction are efforts to narrow the gap between what children have to learn and what they are taught. Individually prescribed instruction involves continuous evaluation of each child's reading and the preparation of separate assignments based upon his reading performance. Computer-assisted instruction offers guidance in the development of reading skills through predetermined lessons fed into and stored in a data bank that is activated by the nature of children's responses to instruction. Both systems might be utilized to supplement a teacher's efforts to individualize the teaching of reading.

8. Instruction in reading may be differentiated by varying the materials children read, providing different learning experiences, and adjusting reading requirements. Books for different instructional levels and multilevel and programed materials are the vehicles through which differentiation becomes possible. The introduction of reading guides enables the teacher to offer special help to many children and makes possible some differentiation without class sectioning. Variations in the amount of reading children do and the kinds of responses they are expected to make are other ways of providing for individual differences and allowing children to participate in common reading experiences.

STUDY QUESTIONS AND EXERCISES

1. What is the difference between organizational and instructional adjustments to individual reading needs?
2. "Individualized reading, individual reading instruction, and individualization of reading instruction are not necessarily synonymous terms." Explain.
3. What administrative devices might schools and teachers adopt as aids in individualizing reading instruction? What criteria could be used to judge the effectiveness of such measures?

4. What are some problems associated with individualized reading that teachers should be aware of? With grouping plans?
5. "Hardware" is not nearly as important as "software" in efforts to individualize reading instruction. Explain.

SUGGESTIONS FOR FURTHER READING

There are a number of publications that deal specifically with problems and methods of differentiating instruction in reading:

Donald C. Cleland and Elaine C. Vilscek, eds., *Individualizing Reading Instruction* (Report of the Twentieth Annual Conference on Reading). Pittsburgh: University of Pittsburgh Press, 1964.

Alice Miel, ed., *Individualizing Reading Practices*. New York: Teachers College, Columbia University, 1958.

Wallace Z. Ramsey, *Organizing for Individual Differences* (Perspectives in Reading No. 9). Newark, Del.: International Reading Association, 1967.

H. Alan Robinson, ed., *Meeting Individual Differences in Reading* (Supplementary Educational Monographs, No. 94). Chicago: University of Chicago Press, December, 1964.

Helen R. Robinson, ed., *Reading Instruction in Various Patterns of Grouping* (Supplementary Educational Monographs, No. 89). Chicago: University of Chicago Press, December, 1959.

In addition to the aforementioned publications are others that consider various aspects of individualization in different curriculum areas including reading:

Nelson B. Henry, ed., *Individualizing Instruction* (The Sixty-First Yearbook of the National Society for the Study of Education, Part I). Chicago: University of Chicago Press, 1962.

Phil C. Lange, ed., *Programed Instruction* (The Sixty-Sixth Yearbook of the National Society for the Study of Education, Part II). Chicago: University of Chicago Press, 1967.

Judson T. Shaplin and Henry F. Olds, Jr., eds., *Team Teaching*. New York: Harper & Row, Publishers, 1964.

10

Overcoming Reading Difficulties

■ *It is a strange paradox that, in a country whose world reputation is one of leadership and industry, we should be concerning ourselves with the topic of underachievement. But the underachiever is with us, and we know that . . . we can ill afford the luxury of his presence.*

The school concern for the underachiever in reading is society's concern. . . .[1]

Teachers, reading specialists, parents and representatives from a variety of disciplines have been wondering for some time why so many of our pupils fail to develop skill in reading. A variety of reasons have been suggested for reading weaknesses but the validity of each explanation has been questioned by those who are close to children with reading problems. There has been a tendency to regard all reading failures as the products of single causes, but the results of research suggest that most cannot be explained simply. In fact, many reading disability cases defy differential diagnoses because examinations reveal the presence of multiple conditions, some or all of which *might* be contributing to the reading failures.

Problem Readers

Children with serious reading difficulties have been described in many ways. Sometimes they are called "retarded readers" and at other times

---

[1] Constance M. McCullough, "The School's Concern With the Underachiever," in H. Alan Robinson, ed., *The Underachiever in Reading* (Supplementary Educational Monographs, No. 92). Chicago: University of Chicago Press, 1962, p. 4.

"disabled readers."[2] Whatever name is given to them, we know that their reading is poor when compared with that of children of similar age and grade and that they often fail to achieve to the extent that their potential ability suggests.

Problem readers are found among several groups of children. The first group consists of those who are of normal or superior intelligence but whose reading ability is significantly below average for their age and grade and who have the capacity for better performance. Approximately four out of every five poor readers fall into this category.

Slow learners are children whose intelligence quotient is between eighty and ninety-five. They form the 15 per cent of the school population who cannot quite "keep up" and are usually doing the poorest work in the classroom. Many of these children are poor readers but are achieving as well as can be expected. Among these slow learners, however, are many who are capable of improvement in reading achievement, and they are problem readers too.

The third group consists of children whose intellectual development is significantly retarded and who, as a group, are not able to do much academic work. Some mentally-deficient children have been known to achieve second- and third-grade levels in reading. Mentally handicapped children make up from 2 to 3 per cent of the school population, and special provisions are usually made for them.

Another group of children may be considered problem readers. They possess superior intellectual capacity but are reading only as well as the average children of their age or grade. These bright children are often overlooked because their reading peformances are satisfactory and they do not create difficulties for teachers. Schools ought to be as concerned about them as they are about others who are reading poorly.

Results of Poor Reading

The child who comes to school without the capacity to read for information or enjoyment lacks skills which are essential for his personal efficiency and satisfaction. There is hardly an hour during the school week when his lack of reading ability does not produce and reinforce his feelings of inadequacy and frustration. Because reading ability is so highly valued in our culture, continued failure to read often results in social disapproval, not only by parents and teachers but also by age peers. This social disapproval can prove so damaging as to leave permanent scars on the child's growth.

Frequently the problem reader is thought to be a dull child. Not only is he deficient in reading but also in other areas. He lacks many skills that

---

[2] Various terminology is applied to children whose poor reading stems from their inability to recognize words readily: *dyslexia, specific language disability, maturational lag, primary and secondary retardation*. All except secondary retardation are said to be tied to constitutional deficits of the brain and/or nervous system.

he needs for success in school and undoubtedly realizes his shortcomings. Since he is unwilling to draw attention to himself, he tends to make only minimal efforts. Often he prefers to remain unnoticed.

Some problem readers resort to aggressive behavior toward their teachers, parents, and other children. They do so perhaps because they fail to understand the situation in which they find themselves and react in the only way they know. The disturbed problem reader has had few legitimate experiences of success and though the recognition which hostile behavior brings is brief and comes to nothing in the end, there is some temporary inflation of the self-feelings in the attention he receives. The aggressive behavior also brings for the moment some relief from tensions.

A high incidence of reading failures is found among truants and delinquents. It is natural for children to want to escape from an unpleasant environment where so much emphasis is placed upon reading. While there is no evidence to support the conclusion that reading disabilities lead to delinquent behavior, there is no doubt that attitudes toward self and others are influenced by failures of any kind. Poor reading ability is one of the major reasons given by children for wanting to drop out of school. Some are bound to engage in asocial behavior when they fail to satisfy their needs for self-esteem and recognition through other channels.

A study of the problem reader reveals a complex of conditions that may contain traumatic elements. Not all problem readers are so affected. But it is obvious that those who are suffer from untold anxieties. Anything that can be done to relieve these tensions is welcomed by these children. Children with severe reading difficulties are not very numerous in comparison with the numbers of good readers but their presence is felt because nowhere do they fit smoothly into the school organization. Unless the school provides a program to deal with their requirements, it will create problems for itself and the children. Before any needs may be met, the reasons for their weaknesses must be understood.

Causes of Reading Failure

Why do some children fail to learn to read as well as others? The results of research show that reading failures cannot be explained by single causes and that multiple factors account for most of the cases.[3] Since several conditions that might affect reading behavior are usually present in disabled readers, it is often impossible to determine which ones are actually respon-

---

[3] Students are referred to the following sources for summaries of research on the causes of reading failure: Guy L. Bond and Miles A. Tinker, *Reading Difficultes: Their Diagnosis and Correction* (2nd ed.). New York: Appleton-Century-Crofts, 1967, Chap. 5–6; Albert J. Harris, *How To Increase Reading Ability* (5th ed.). New York: David McKay Co., Inc., 1970, Chap. 9–11; Marjorie S. Johnson, "Factors Related to Disability in Reading," *Journal of Experimental Education, 26* (September, 1957), pp. 1–26; John Money, ed., *Progress and Research Needs in Dyslexia.* Baltimore: Johns Hopkins Press, 1962; Helen M. Robinson, *Why Pupils Fail in Reading.* Chicago: University of Chicago Press, 1947; M. D. Vernon, *Backwardness in Reading.* Cambridge: Cambridge University Press, 1958.

sible for their failures. This situation is complicated further by the fact that one or more conditions might have produced the others or that a problem not readily recognized might be responsible for behavior one can observe.

Physical Factors

There has been a growing tendency to explain reading disabilities in biological terms. Because there are children who have failed to respond to remediation (the nature of which is not clear), some specialists—particularly in the medical profession—believe that their failures may be traced to organic conditions. Critchley[4] uses the term *developmental dyslexia* to refer to a constitutional disorder of the nervous system which produces reading disability. Rabinovitch[5] speaks of *primary reading disability* "to reflect a basic disturbed pattern of neurological organization" that interferes with one's ability to deal with letters and words. He also attributes some reading failures to brain damage. Followers of Orton[6] suggest that *minimal brain damage* accounts for serious reading difficulties while Clements[7] prefers to explain them as products of "minimal brain dysfunction." Related to the aforementioned theories is Delacato's,[8] who attributes reading difficulties to neurological immaturity and failure to establish cerebral dominance. In addition, there is the view held by Smith and Carrigan[9] who believe that a chemical imbalance in the body accounts for reading disability.

There isn't much hard evidence to support any of these explanations. Proponents of the *developmental dyslexia, primary reading disability,* and *minimal brain damage* schools of thought rely upon the presence of some "subtle" symptoms of neurological dysfunction and inability to link reading failures to other conditions as evidence for their beliefs. Some also point to the fact that a tendency toward severe reading problems seems to run in families, which could suggest genetic factors. These findings are more negative than positive and are used in the absence of real data to infer causality. The notions about neurological immaturity and incomplete dominance have been challenged[10] and substantive questions have been raised about the relation of body chemistry to reading failure.[11]

---

4 Macdonald Critchley, *Developmental Dyslexia*. Springfield, Illinois: Charles C. Thomas, 1964.

5 Ralph D. Rabinovitch, "Dyslexia: Psychiatric Considerations," in John Money, ed., *Progress and Research Needs in Dyslexia*. Baltimore: Johns Hopkins Press, 1962, pp. 73–79.

6 Samuel T. Orton, *Reading, Writing and Speech Problems in Children*. New York: W. W. Norton, 1937.

7 Sam D. Clements, *Minimal Brain Dysfunction in Children: Terminology and Identification* (Public Health Service Publication, No. 1415). Washington: Government Printing Office, 1966.

8 Carl H. Delacato, *The Diagnosis and Treatment of Speech and Reading Problems*. Springfield, Illinois: Charles C. Thomas, 1963.

9 Donald E. P. Smith and Patricia Carrigan, *The Nature of Reading Disability*. New York: Harcourt Brace Jovanovich, Inc., 1959.

10 Melvyn P. Robbins, "Delacato Interpretation of Neurological Organization," *Reading Research Quarterly, 1* (Spring, 1966), pp. 57–78.

11 Albert J. Harris, "A Critical Reaction to 'The Nature of Reading Disability,'" *Journal of Developmental Reading, 3* (Summer, 1960), pp. 238–49.

There is no question that some reading disability cases seem to make little progress although intensive instruction is provided them. In these instances it would appear that some constitutional conditions could be the cause of intereference. However, it is this writer's view that until more data become available, such explanations be considered highly hypothetical and that efforts to improve these children's reading be sought in improved teaching procedures. Even if data were to confirm the presence of biological deficits, it would still be necessary to deal with the problem on an educational basis.

Visual and Auditory Factors. Insofar as vision and hearing are concerned, it appears that specific defects may be contributing factors in reading disability. Immaturity of vision, especially in the younger child who is entering school, near-sightedness, and eye imbalances might interfere with a child's ability to read. Defects in hearing acuity may lead to improper associations between spoken words and the symbols they represent. However, unless children were suffering from severe vision and hearing losses, it would seem that these are not significant factors in reading failures. Nevertheless, it would be desirable to remove any conditions that might stand in the way of their progress. Corrective measures should be taken with children who do not see or hear as well as they might. Glasses or hearing devices could make a difference in their attitudes toward school and achievement.

Auditory and visual discrimination seem to be related to reading success. As has already been indicated in the chapter on reading readiness (see pages 81–83), there appears to be a significant relationship between the ability to distinguish between spoken sounds and learning to recognize words. Children who can recognize initial and final consonants in words, rhyming words, and separate sounds in spoken words have less trouble learning to identify words than those who are weak in these abilities. Efforts to produce changes in the way children respond to word recognition tasks through auditory discrimination training have proved successful. Therefore, it is reasonable to conclude that auditory discrimination is a factor in learning to read.

Visual discrimination (see pages 79–81) involving letter recognition and ability to discern likenesses and differences in words has been shown to be a factor in reading achievement. As with auditory discrimination, changes in visual discrimination performances have had a positive effect upon the ability of children to recognize words. It would appear from such results that discrimination skills are learned and therefore subject to training. If weaknesses in perception are caused by neurological aberrations, these might not respond to treatment in the same way as those which result from the lack of appropriate experiences.

Health. While no direct relationship may be said to exist between reading disabilities and physical status, it is apparent that poor health can and does interfere with learning. Since learning to read is for many children a difficult undertaking, any condition which adds to the difficulty should be scrutinized. Children who suffer from malnutrition, frequent colds, and other serious conditions are not free to give to reading the attention it requires. Inattention and restlessness in class combined with frequent absences due to illness are known to create hardships that can have a direct bearing upon the progress children make in reading.

Handedness.   Laterality as a possible factor in learning to read has been the subject of extensive study. While surveys of populations with reading disabilities show that some poor readers have failed to establish a preference for using one side of the body to the other, i.e., the right eye, right hand and right foot, there is no proof that confused or mixed dominance is responsible for or related to reading failure. Almost as many good as poor readers do not consistently use the same side of the body to sight a gun, point a finger or kick a football. Orton, Delacato, and others have explained mixed or confused dominance in neurological terms but present evidence lends little support to their beliefs.

Brain Damage.   Children who have suffered actual brain damage at birth, or from diseases, or in subsequent accidents often manifest an inability to perceive word symbols. In these cases there is a confusion of figure and ground that affects their perception of letters and results in interference with word recognition. In addition, they are easily distracted, are hyperactive, and tend to perseverate. Some successes in teaching such children to read have been realized by highly skilled teachers.

Intellectual Factors

In spite of efforts to assemble several measures that identify children who are likely to have difficulty in learning to read, one of the best predictors of reading success is intelligence as measured by individual mental and valid group tests. The correlations between intelligence test scores and reading ability range from .40 to about .65. The addition of other measures haven't accounted for variability in reading performances to any appreciable extent.

How shall the correlation between intelligence and reading ability be interpreted? Simply stated, children who do well on intelligence tests could be expected to be better readers than those who appear to be less gifted. This interpretation refers to groups of children and not to individuals. If a group of one hundred brighter children were to be compared in reading ability to one hundred children of average or less than average ability, one could expect more children of the former group to be the superior achievers in reading. Because of the size of the correlation, it would be impossible to identify the better readers from a knowledge of their intelligence test scores.

Intelligence tests, particulary group tests, appear to be less valid instruments for measuring the mental ability of severely disabled readers than they are for average and good readers. Even individual mental tests are not completely free of verbal influences. Teachers have noted that many poor readers are alert and do well in tasks that do not require reading. It is well to repeat that four out of five children with severe reading handicaps are of normal or superior intelligence. They simply are not keeping pace with their intellectual development and reasons for reading failure must be sought elsewhere.

The ability to remember sequences of letters and words could be a factor in learning to read. Such weaknesses might be tied to inability to perceive details for reasons that are possibly innate or external. Present practices seem to indicate unwarranted confidence in the belief that all children with poor memory for visual symbols suffer from constitutional defects. Changes in learning climate often improve these children's ability to manage visual symbols.

Emotional Factors

Most studies of poor readers with emotional problems might be described as *ex post facto*. Little information about the behavior of such children before they entered school is known. It is difficult to determine whether they brought their problems with them or developed them after they experienced school failure. It is clear that *some* children have not been able to achieve in reading to the extent they are capable of because of interference resulting from emotional upset. How many children are so affected is not known but more recent estimates tend to scale down the number of reading disability cases that are due to personality factors.

Psychologists who have studied disturbed children have explained that feelings of hostility, dependency, and insecurity can produce an intense dislike and rejection of reading. If such were the case, it would appear that placement in a therapeutic relationship might relieve these pressures and free such children for learning. There have been reports of success in treating these children, who showed subsequent improvement in reading. Other studies indicate that appropriate reading help not only produces reading gains but also affects personal adjustment. In these instances it is possible that the relationship established between the teacher and pupil is as important as the instruction.

Sociocultural Factors

There is ample evidence that home and family influences do affect success in school. Children who come from higher socioeconomic classes as a group are far better readers than comparable children who do not have the same backgrounds. There are proportionally many more reading failures among children who come from poor homes than there are among their more affluent age peers. Studies of culturally different children show that they do not enter school with the background of experiences that successful readers possess. They are generally weak in the use of standard spoken English and exhibit a low level of self-esteem and aspiration.

Efforts to overcome some of the deficiencies that appear to handicap the progress of the poorest black and white children have been partially successful. Federally sponsored Head Start programs have not always paid dividends but some of their failures have been explained in terms of program weaknesses and lack of primary grade follow-up. Encouraging preliminary results have been obtained from television programing such as "Sesame Street," which capitalizes on mass-appeal devices, but long-term outcomes have as yet to be determined. There are isolated cases of successful reading programs which seem to be characterized by emphasis upon language development, continuous evaluation, and individual needs.

School Factors

As more information about the adequacy of reading programs becomes available, it seems increasingly clear that many reading failures might have been prevented. As has been noted in the discussion on the First Grade Studies (Chapter 1, pages 7–9), there appeared to be as much variability in the results obtained from the conduct of similar programs as from different programs. Such results would suggest significant differences in teacher ability.

There is no question that some teachers know more about reading than others. The preservice education of prospective elementary teachers varies significantly. Some students receive excellent training in how to teach reading; many have so few meaningful exposures to reading theory and practice that they feel and are woefully weak.[12] Most children who are taught by the latter do achieve in reading. But those who for whatever reason experience difficulty in learning to read do not receive the instruction they require. All too often their problems are not even recognized until they have become severely retarded in reading.

Some school administrations have contributed to the reading problem by failing to give teachers the support they need. They burden teachers with duties that have no relationship to instructional tasks. They allow classes to become unreasonably large so that teachers lose confidence in their ability to provide for individual differences. They fail to provide teaching resources, in-service assistance and leadership. Even if college preparatory programs for teaching reading improve, schools will have to assume a major responsibility for the continuing development of reading teachers and the improvement of reading programs.

Identifying Problem Readers

A rule-of-thumb guide that some reading specialists suggest schools should follow places children who are about two or more years below their reading potential in the disabled reader category. This means that if their reading ages (the grade placement score plus five years) are two or more

---

12 Mary C. Austin and others, *The Torch Lighters: Tomorrow's Teachers of Reading.* Cambridge: Graduate School of Education, Harvard University, 1961; Mary C. Austin and Coleman Morrison, *The First R: The Harvard Report on Reading in Elementary Schools.* New York: The Macmillan Company, 1963.

years below their mental ages, they are so considered. Thus, if a pupil attained a reading grade placement score of 3.1 on a standardized test and his mental age as determined by an intelligence test was 11 years, he would be retarded more than 2 years:

Mental age = 11 years
Reading age = 3.1 +5 = 8.1 years

There are alternate arithmetical ways to calculate the discrepancy between reading achievement and reading potential but most rely upon the results of intelligence tests to determine reading expectancy. Such procedures are formulated on the assumption that there is a perfect correlation between intelligence and reading achievement when in fact this is not the case. Other factors might be contributing to a child's reading failure. However, teachers may compare a pupil's achievement with his potential to achieve in order to obtain a gross indication of his present status.

One caution should be noted by teachers who seek to determine how severe a child's reading problem is. The method cited above is less valid for children in the early grades than it is in the higher grades. A child who enters second grade with a reading grade placement of 1.2, and a mental age of 7 years would not be considered a disabled reader:

Mental age = 7 years
Reading age = 1.2 +5 = 6.2 years

In reality, such a child will have real difficulty in trying to cope with reading materials that are intended for second grade. The reading score of 1.2 suggests little reading ability since the floor of the test is 1.0 or 1.1. He may have made four or five correct responses to achieve the reading score and some of these could have been the result of guessing. This child should be identified as one who requires immediate help. The administration of an informal reading inventory which assesses the child's ability to recognize and attack words and understand what he reads will reveal just what kinds of help he requires.

Reading potential may be determined by having children respond to materials that are read to them orally. This procedure is particularly useful for assessing the reading potential of children who have severe word recognition weaknesses. The responses they make to literal and inferential questions and vocabulary items will indicate what level materials they could read if there were no interference from their inability to recognize what the words said. The same procedures are followed as outlined in Chapter 2, pages 53–60, for preparing and administering informal reading inventories to determine reading levels, except that the text is read to the child by the teacher instead of having him read it orally or silently. A child who failed to understand material that he read himself might have no trouble when he listened to the same material. Not only would his responses indicate his level of understanding but also underscore his ability to remember.

Diagnosing Problem Readers

How intensive an analysis of the problem reader should be made depends upon the resources that are available and the uses to which any information is put. There has been a tendency to spend hours in gathering vast amounts of information about children with reading difficulties and then structuring programs that bear no relationship to the data that have been accumulated. A reasonable course that schools might follow is to explore some of the more obvious problem areas and then seek to deal with them if necessary. If progress were not noted, deeper study could be undertaken.

Some basic procedures might be followed with all problem readers. Examination of school records might yield information about their physical status, health, and school progress. All children, not just problem readers, should have their vision and hearing checked periodically for possible weaknesses with instruments that measure more than the ability to see at distances and hear whispered sounds.[13] Teachers might look for such symptoms as squinting, itching, watery eyes, and redness that could be indicators of eye problems, and poor speech, straining to hear, and requests for repetition that may signal auditory weaknesses. Referrals to appropriate professionals should be made if there were indications that children might have visual and/or hearing difficulties that could interfere with learning.

In their daily contacts with problem readers, teachers should reach some decision about their intellectual ability and personality development. How well a child functions when faced with learning tasks other than reading should be some indication of his ability to profit from instruction. His attitudes toward school, teacher, and other children will be revealed through his behavior in different situations. In many cases teachers need not be overly concerned with such factors but if they have reason to believe that children could be handicapped because of them, they should consult with qualified school personnel, who might recommend further study of individual cases by psychologists and other professionals.

Teachers should consult with parents to obtain information that might not be recorded on school records. This information about children's past and present physical condition, behavior in the home, attitudes and interests will supplement what they know about them and possibly be of use in working out a plan for overcoming the reading difficulties.

The identification of specific reading weaknesses is essential if any remediation program is to have an impact upon the problem reader's progress. The evaluation procedures as described in Chapter 2 should be followed to assess reading levels and pinpoint strengths and weaknesses. In fact, it might be necessary to be even more precise in measuring and evaluating reading performance than this section suggests. Responses to items on standardized survey and diagnostic tests should be studied carefully, prefer-

---

[13] Many schools use the *Telebinocular* or *Vision Tester* to check near- and far-point vision. The *pure-tone audiometer* is recommended for auditory screening.

ably with the children, so that the nature of and reasoning behind their responses are understood. Teacher-made tests could focus on specific aspects of general areas identified by standardized tests as those in which the children are weak. The more exact information teachers have about the reading performance of problem readers, the better able are they to plan lessons for overcoming weaknesses. If the classroom teacher is unable to interpret the results of standardized tests and prepare others which are more specific in measuring subskills the former do not cover, he might seek help from the reading specialist, who should have the professional preparation and experience to complete a thorough reading evaluation. In any case, informal reading inventories would be used in conjunction with standardized instruments to assess reading levels and skills performance.

Guidelines for Treating Problem Readers

Weaknesses in word recognition interfere with the progress of many elementary school children. Seriously disabled readers who fall in this category cannot recognize a large stock of words at sight nor are they able to analyze words easily. Their inability to recognize most common words and unlock less familiar ones prevents them from obtaining meaning from what they read.

Problem readers often suffer from subsidiary or other weaknesses. For pupils in the earlier stages of reading, vocabulary difficulties are less obvious because of the familiar subject matter, illustrations, and simple vocabulary of the reading materials. At higher levels and in more unfamiliar materials the vocabulary difficulties become greater. Since meager vocabularies are strikingly common among some poor readers, it is important to help them expand their supply of word meanings and teach them how to cope with new words.

There is another group of children who have little difficulty in pronouncing words but are weak in reading for literal and/or inferential meanings. They become lost in a jumble of words and fail to see relationships among ideas. They do not distinguish between major ideas and lesser ones and regard all details as of equal value. As a result the most they can do is parrot some sentences; they do not get the message. These same children are deficient in those study skills whose mastery depends upon substantial understanding.

Developmental and Remedial Instruction[14]

What is remedial reading instruction? One might think of it as instruction designed to overcome weaknesses which are present because initial or subsequent teaching was not successful. In any discussion of remediation

---

[14] This section is adapted from a paper presented by the author at the International Reading Association Annual Convention in Detroit, 1965.

efforts by schools there is the assumption that whatever the reason for the difficulties, pupils can profit from instruction.

Most school personnel believe that there are two main types of reading instruction. One they call *developmental* and the other *remedial.* (A third type, *corrective,* is sometimes used to refer to efforts by the classroom teacher to overcome mild weaknesses.) Developmental reading, they say, is for pupils who are progressing satisfactorily. It is begun in the primary grades, pursued through the years as the needs of learners dictate, and treated as a continuous process. Instruction is based upon the concept of readiness for learning and the sequential development of reading skills. On the other hand, remedial reading is reserved for seriously disabled readers who are on levels two or more years below their capabilities. Special teachers are assigned pupils either on an individual, small group, or class basis. Methods of instruction vary but whatever their nature, remedial reading is different from developmental reading in methods and materials.

IDEAS FOR DISCUSSION

What is this author's view about developmental and remedial instruction? Insofar as methodology is concerned, there are no real basic differences between them. Programs that are suitable for pupils who are progressing satisfactorily are equally suitable for those who are not achieving to the extent of which they are capable. The contention that "good" instruction has failed pupils with severe reading problems and that other means to overcome them must be sought cannot be supported by research. The experiences of teachers in schools and clinics do show that most poor readers respond to proper instruction.

Poor readers require the most highly skilled help teachers can provide. This means that developmental reading procedures probably have to be refined if they are to be successful with poor readers. For example, in a good learning climate some measurement and evaluation occur before instruction begins. Ordinarily they are not extensive, without any apparent losses to pupils. However, more detailed and specific information about the status of pupils with reading problems must be known if instruction to overcome them is to be truly effective. Good readers do not seem to be affected adversely by teaching procedures that fall somewhat short of the mark; poor readers are unable to compensate for any such deficiencies.

To repeat, there are no basic differences between developmental and remedial reading. If any differences do exist, they are not of kind but degree. Children with reading problems due to some organic problem may require different treatments than those followed with children whose difficulties originate in other factors. But even in such cases there is little evidence of their validity.[15] It seems to many reading specialists that poor reading practices have been substituted for sounder ones. Although experiments with and inquiries into different kinds of teaching methods are vital, objections can be raised when fancy is substituted for fact and limited findings for demonstrated realities. Programs with less than solid foundations cannot be expected to meet the challenge poor readers offer.

---

[15] William M. Cruikshank et al., *A Teaching Method for Brain-Injured and Hyperactive Children.* Syracuse: Syracuse University Press, 1961.

Principles of Remediation

Just as no one can guarantee that any method or procedure will lead to reading success, so are there no surefire techniques for overcoming reading deficiencies. Nevertheless, experiences with disabled readers demonstrate that some practices produce better results than others. It is with these practices that teachers should become familiar if they would increase their pupils' chances of overcoming reading difficulties.

Early Identification

Common practice is to not offer special reading help to children until they have demonstrated that maturational factors are not responsible for their failure. Therefore, many children who are failing in reading are not treated any differently from others until they reach the third or fourth grade, at which time some efforts to correct their weaknesses are made. All too often these children have fallen so far behind that typical measures fail to work. In addition, these children often have developed negative attitudes toward themselves and school because their reading failures have affected their general progress.

Teachers should be alert to identify the children who are experiencing reading difficulties in the first grade. If by the end of the year there are some who have made small progress, closer examination of these children should ensue. The teacher who receives them the following year should be informed of their problems so that she can make whatever adjustments are necessary to accommodate them. If pupils fail to progress after two or three months of the second year, assistance from a reading specialist should be sought and possibly out-of-class help provided.

Assurance of Success

Pupils with reading difficulties have experienced failures in varying degrees and some of them are not likely to be highly motivated. Nevertheless, most problem readers want help desperately, but past failures have conditioned them to expect more of the same.

One of the ways to prevent new failures is to initiate instruction through narrative and expository materials at levels they can manage without great difficulty. Another is to build on what pupils know to teach them new skills in and develop new attitudes toward reading. Insofar as possible this development should occur in sequence. Proper pacing also will help to insure success. Too much too rapidly can overwhelm poor readers. It is better to start slowly and increase the pace as progress occurs.

Teacher Support

Successful teachers of children with reading problems are those who can gain their confidence. Pupils who have experienced failures have to feel that someone is truly interested in them and working in their behalf. Such teachers like children and those who have felt rejection know who their friends are.

Successful teachers are those who seek opportunities to praise their pupils for each forward step no matter how small. They avoid criticism and express positive attitudes toward children and their efforts. They are approving; at the same time they do not adopt laissez-faire attitudes which imply that anything goes. Limits are established with common agreement, and children know the reasons why they must function within this framework.

Understanding teachers are good listeners. Children "talk" to adults in many ways and those who know failure are particularly sensitive to indifference and tend to withdraw when they believe no one pays attention to them. Teachers who show genuine interest in their pupils convey to them feelings of worth and acceptance, without which positive results are not likely to be realized. The teacher is perhaps the most important ingredient in remediation programs; what he is is as important as what he does.

Sound Procedures

How shall problem readers be taught? It is a fact that children learn under all kinds of conditions, but it appears that some of them require more favorable ones if they are to prosper. It is this writer's belief that no method of teaching reading can insure success, but methods that are compatible with established principles of learning are more likely to facilitate growth than those which are not in harmony with them.

Too many remedial programs are not based upon any reasoned rationale. Instead, they exemplify a "shotgun" approach to learning. The indiscriminate use of commercial materials prevails, and sequential instruction is ignored for casual efforts. Total learning is replaced by isolated exercises and drills. Such programs are hardly suitable for children who have no learning problems, let alone for those who do.

The following principles should serve as guides for any reading instruction:

1. An important condition for learning is preparation for undertaking a given task. This preparation involves knowledge and understanding, motivation and goal seeking. New learning is an outgrowth of old learning which is used as a basis for understanding new principles and ideas.

2. Meaningful learning is preferred to rote or isolated learning since it is more lasting and more likely to be applied.

3. Guided learning is preferred to trial-and-error learning, especially during the early stages. Guided learning is more efficient and avoids the reinforcement of improper responses.

4. Avoidance of interference with learning should be sought. The presentation of more material than pupils can manage and activities to which responses different from those anticipated are required can inhibit progress.

5. Learners must achieve legitimate success and recognize growth when it occurs. The ability to withstand failure is best developed through suc-

cessful experiences. Repeated failures merely condition the learner for additional ones.

6. The goals of the learner must be recognized. It is more important to teach what the learner needs to know than what the teacher would have him learn.

These principles have served as the basis for the "how to" recommendations found throughout this textbook. All the suggestions that the author has offered can be applied with confidence to the problems poor readers have. The only additional requirement that could make the difference between success and failure with these children is more precise application of these principles and practices through masterful teaching. This same masterful teaching will go a long way toward preventing many, if not most, reading failures.

SUMMARY

1. Problem readers are found among children of normal and superior intelligence. Their reading ability is significantly below average for their age. Approximately four out of five children with reading difficulties possess the intellectual potential to achieve higher reading levels. Other problem readers are found among slow learners and mentally handicapped children. Many of those in the former group are not achieving to the extent of which they are capable and may also be considered underachievers in reading.

2. Physical, intellectual, emotional, sociocultural, and educational factors may contribute to reading failure. Children with reading problems frequently exhibit multiple conditions which might interfere with their learning ability. In most instances, however, it is difficult to establish causal relationships between one or more of these conditions and failure to achieve in reading.

3. Problem or disabled readers are those children who are approximately two or more years retarded in reading. A significant discrepancy between their learning potential and reading growth exists. This formulation assumes that intelligence as measured by valid tests accounts for all or most of the variation in reading performance. Awareness of this limitation plus the realization that readers in the primary grades may be experiencing real difficulties despite not showing a two-year gap will increase the validity of a teacher's judgment in applying such a guide. The potential for reading achievement may be assessed through responses to materials read orally to children.

4. It is generally not necessary to make a comprehensive case children with reading difficulties. There is no point in gath mation that will not affect the way in which they will be understand individuals better it is desirable to explore w

and others who know the children their past and present performances as well as more obvious problem areas that could affect their behavior. Referrals to appropriate professionals should be made if conditions warrant further study.

5. Some diagnosis to identify reading problems should be undertaken before efforts to overcome them are made. Standardized tests and informal inventories should be employed to establish the level at which the children can be taught with success and identify specific aspects of their reading performances that are shown to be weak. Teachers will supplement this preliminary evaluation with additional information gained from working with the children and make adjustments as required.

6. There is no basic difference between developmental and remedial reading; any differences that do exist are of degree and not kind. Teachers who work with poor readers must apply the same principles they use with other children but with greater precision and intensity. This is their best assurance that the needs of such pupils will be met.

STUDY QUESTIONS AND EXERCISES

1. What conclusions might be drawn from the research on the causes of reading difficulties?

2. Evaluate the following statement: "There are no basic differences between developmental and remedial reading. If any do exist, they are not of kind but degree."

3. How might the author of this textbook react to the suggestion that all methods are appropriate for teaching poor readers and that anything which "works" is good?

4. What measures should the classroom teacher take with children who are experiencing more than average difficulty in learning to read?

SUGGESTIONS FOR FURTHER READING

Two textbooks which cover the causes and treatment of reading difficulties in detail are:

Guy L. Bond and Miles A. Tinker, *Reading Difficulties: Their Diagnosis and Correction* (2nd ed.). New York: Appleton-Century-Crofts, 1967.

Albert J. Harris, *How to Increase Reading Ability* (5th ed.). New York: David McKay Company, Inc., 1970.

Less comprehensive treatments of the same topics will be found in these publications:

Dorothy L. De Boer, ed., *Reading Diagnosis and Evaluation*. Newark, Del.: International Reading Association, 1970.

William K. Durr, ed., *Reading Difficulties: Diagnosis, Correction and Remediation*. Newark, Del.: International Reading Association, 1970.

Leo M. Schell and Paul C. Burns, *Remedial Reading: An Anthology of Sources*. Boston: Allyn and Bacon, Inc., 1968.

George D. Spache, ed., *Reading Disability and Perception*. Newark, Del.: International Reading Association, 1969.

The last group of publications contains treatments of theoretical and practical problems:

Marjorie S. Johnson and Roy Kress, *Corrective Reading in the Elementary School* (Perspectives in Reading No. 7). Newark, Del.: International Reading Association, 1967.

Carl B. Smith, *Correcting Reading Problems in the Classroom* (Target Series, Book 4). Newark, Del.: International Reading Association, 1969.

Carl B. Smith, *Treating Reading Disabilities: The Specialist's Role* (Target Series, Book 3). Newark, Del.: International Reading Association, 1969.

Index

(See also Index of Names.)

Catalogues, library-card, 242–43
Chalktalks, 303–04
Charts
  language-experience use, 113–14, 115–18
  understanding, 263–65
  tests, standardized, 45, 46
Choral reading, 293
Cloze exercises and procedures
  comprehension development and, 15–16
  evaluation tool, 24
  informal test use, 60–61
Cognition
  concept development and, 19
  readiness, reading, 75
  study materials and level of, 20–21
Comprehension (see also specific aspects)
  Cloze exercises and procedures
    as evaluation tool, 24, 60–61
    as stimulant, 15–16
  components of, 182
  cognitive devlopment and, 19, 20–21, 75
  content fields, reading ability and, 14–15
  inferential, informal tests of, 52, 53, 54
  language
    experience and, 118
    tests, 85
  listening
    power of reading and, 18
    skills, 133–35
  literal, informal tests of, 52, 53, 54
  operational model of, intellect and, 18
  paragraph
    details, noting important, 14, 249–53
    main ideas, recognition of, 14, 246–49
    organization, 195–98
  teaching methods, comprehension and, 8, 11
  tests, standardized reading, 48
  topic recognition, 245–46
  program evaluation, 66
  psychology
    concept development and cognition, 19
    theories of reading, 17–18
  skills, classification of, 34
  tests informal (see also Tests, reading), 52–63
    standardized reading, 46–48
  vocabulary and (see also Word meaning), 15–16
Computer-assisted instruction, 28–29, 328–29
Concept development
  cognition and, 19
  language use, 104
  readiness, reading, 75
Conferences, teacher-pupil, 126–29, 315–16
Consonants, blends and digraphs, 153–54, 157–62
Content fields, 217–78
  basal reading, 25, 26
  comprehension, ability and, 14–15
  demands of, 10–11, 14–15, 218–21

discussion ideas, for teachers, 221, 254
guiding reading in, 222
  directed reading, 227–33
  study guides, 231–33
  surveying content materials, 222–27
integration of reading and content, 222
  guided reading, 222–33
  study skills (see also Content fields, skills, reading-study), 218–21, 233–76
rate and flexibility of reading, 16, 268–71
  purpose and materials, 271–73
  scanning for information, 273–74
  skimming for ideas, 274–76
research, 13–15
skills, reading-study, 14–15, 218–21, 233–59
  book parts, 235–41
  details, noting important, 14, 249–53
  diagrams, charts, pictures, 259–61, 263–65
  encyclopedias, 241–42
  following directions, 265–67
  graphic aids, understanding, 259–65
  index, using, 237–41
  library-card catalogue, 242–43
  location of information, 235–44
  main ideas, recognition of, 14, 246–48
  map reading, 263–65
  objectives, 233–34
  organization of information, 254–59
  outline preparation, 255–57
  rate and flexibility of reading, 268–76
  Reader's Guide to Periodical Literature, 243–44
  scanning for information, 273–74
  selection of information, 244–53
  sex preferences, 17, 294–95
  skimming for ideas, 274–76
  summary preparation, 257–59
  table of contents, using, 223–24, 235–38
  teaching guidelines, 234–35
  tests, standardized, 45, 46
  topic recognition, 245–46
  vocabulary development, 15
Content guides, 232–33
Context clues
  word meaning and, 5, 184, 185–86
  word recognition and, 149–52
Corrective instruction, 350
Critical reading, 182, 208–13
  accuracy judgments, 209–10
  facts and opinions, recognition of, 210–12
  persuasive statements, recognition of, 212–13
Curriculum (see also Programs; specific subjects), 32–33
  developmental reading, 103–38
  skills components, 33–35

Decoding (see also Word recognition)
  basal reader use of, 25–28

Index of Names

(Page numbers in *italics* refer to illustrations.)

E 4 5
F 6
G 7
H 8
I 9
J 0